PILGRIMAGE and EXILE

PILGRIMAGE and EXILE

Mother Marianne
of Molokai

Sister Mary Laurence Hanley, O.S.F.
O.A. Bushnell

University of Hawaii Press
Honolulu

University of Hawaii Press edition 1991
97 96 95 94 93 91 5 4 3 2 1
© 1980 by Sisters of the Third Franciscan Order Minor
Conventual, Syracuse, N.Y.
Printed in the United States of America

Library of Congress Cataloging-in-Publication Data

Hanley, Mary Laurence.
    [Song of pilgrimage and exile]
    Pilgrimage and exile: Mother Marianne of Molokai/Mary
        Laurence Hanley and O.A. Bushnell. —University of
        Hawaii Press ed. p.   cm.
    Originally published: A song of pilgrimage and exile.
        Chicago, Ill.; Franciscan Herald Press, c1980.
    Includes bibliographical references (p.   ) and index.
    ISBN 0–8248–1387–1 (acid–free paper)
    1.   Marianne, of Molokai, Mother, 1838–
1918.   2.   Sisters of St. Francis (Syracuse, N.Y.)—
Biography.   3.   Missions to lepers—Hawaii—
Molokai.   I.   Bushnell, O.A. (Oswald A.),   1913–
II.   Title. [BX4705.M346H36   1991]
266'.2'092—dc20
[B]   91-34539
                                                            CIP

University of Hawaii Press books are printed
on acid-free paper and meet the guidelines
for permanence and durability of the Council
on Library Resources

Photographs follow page 144

Nihil Obstat: (Rev.) J. Robert Yeazel

                                        Chancellor, Diocese of Syracuse

Imprimatur: Most Rev. Frank J. Harrison, D.D.

                                              Bishop of Syracuse

March 29, 1979

THAT MAN (St. Francis) not only hated pride in regard to homes; he even shrank from the numerous and exquisite furnishings of homes. He wished for nothing on the tables, nothing in the utensils, by which the world would be remembered so that all things should sing pilgrimage and exile....

—Thomas of Celano

THIS IS HOW GOD inspired me, Brother Francis, to embark upon a life of penance. When I was in sin, the sight of lepers nauseated me beyond measure; but then God himself led me into their company, and I had pity on them. When I had once become acquainted with them, what had previously nauseated me became a source of spiritual and physical consolation for me....

—The Testament of St. Francis

I AM HUNGRY for the work and I wish with all my heart to be one of the chosen Ones, whose privilege it will be, to sacrifice themselves for the salvation of the souls of the poor Islanders.... I am not afraid of any disease, hence it would be my greatest delight even to minister to the abandoned "lepers."... Waking and sleeping, I am on the Islands. Do not laugh at me, for being so wholly absorbed in that one wish, one thought, to be a worker in that large field....

—Letter of Mother Marianne

CONTENTS

PREFACE

I AM delighted to introduce to a wide reading public this fine biography of Mother Marianne, the second Superior General of the Franciscan Sisters of Syracuse, New York. I do this with full heart, since Syracuse, New York, is my home town. I did not know Mother Marianne, since she died the year after I was born. However, I have seen her works on the Island of Molokai and know of her good works there for so many years among the lepers.

In a day when so many Christians are inspired to work for the poorest of the poor and the most rejected of all, her work among the lepers stands as an inspiration to all. Especially, one can be inspired by her following of the will of God, even though this meant great personal danger to herself and the ultimate in personal sacrifice.

I shall not recall all of the good works she performed in Hawaii, which is now one of the United States, but her work there lives on after her and continues to inspire not only the people there, but religious Sisters throughout the world and good Christians everywhere who need her example to go and do likewise. One is especially touched that her work should have been among the lepers to whom Our Lord showed such special care and curing.

I am very happy to recommend this critical biography most enthusiastically. It should be an inspiration to all of us. May her spirit inspire us all.

(Rev.) Theodore M. Hesburgh, C.S.C.
President, University of Notre Dame

FOREWORD

IN PREPARING this biography, we have drawn upon a large collection of documents that have been gathered in many places, from Rome to Honolulu. Only a few of these documents were available to L. V. Jacks when, in the early 1930s, he wrote the first extensive account of Mother Marianne. Accordingly, most of the excerpts from letters, diaries, and chronicles that are presented in our study are being published for the first time. Together with quotations from government reports and newspaper articles, they tell the story of Mother Marianne in the context of the social, political, religious, and scientific setting of her time, especially as those ideas affected the attitudes and actions of people living in the Kingdom of Hawaii.

These quotations are taken from the writings of many observers, who expressed themselves in several different languages. In borrowing their words, we have tried to retain the characteristics of each writer's personal style. Naturally, this has been easier to do with the works of people who wrote in English. In some cases, however, their vagaries occasionally make for difficult reading or lead to obscurities.

Our prime and wonderful example of such an unschooled writer is Sister M. Leopoldina Burns. Even so, we have resisted all advice to edit her contributions. Spelling, grammar, style, sentimentality, philosophy, religious fervor, naivete: all these of Sister Leopoldina's attributes, and more, are preserved just as she set them down in her schoolgirl's hand in scores of children's composition books. Before you sneer at her quaint spelling and errant syntax, we ask you to remember that she composed her long chronicle during the late 1920s, when she was more than sixty-five years old. By then she had been a nurse to Hawaii's lepers since 1885. She was weary, aging, ailing; and she wrote late at night, after having worked hard all day among the patients to whom she ministered so faithfully. During all those years of service—in which she could have heard and spoken little else than pidgin English, and rarely found time to read anything other than her prayerbooks—Sister Leopoldina had every reason to forget how to spell correctly and how to join words together in sentences of which teachers might approve. Despite this lack of polish, her journal is as full of life as she must have been. And it reveals as nothing else does a companion's joy in her association with Mother Marianne, and her enduring love for that holy woman.

We have treated with the same regard the letters and accounts written by other contemporaries of Mother Marianne. Their idiosyncrasies have been kept, not only because honest reporting demands this respect for documents but also because we believe that these variations reveal the personalities of the writers and—almost as important—emphasize the diversity of the cultural influences that were helping to shape America and Hawaii during the late nineteenth century.

We have chosen, also, to use the word "leper." Our justification for doing so is clear: it was the only name, whether in English or French or Hawaiian, that people applied to the unfortunate victims of leprosy in Mother Marianne's time. It appears in all contemporary documents, as ineradicable as was the disease itself, as accepted as any other forthright term describing any other hard fact of life. The euphemisms that are recommended today—such as "a leprosy patient" or "a person affected by Hansen's disease"—were devised only during the 1950s, in response to patients' sensitivity to the fear and horror that the word "leper" evokes in uninstructed members of a population. We believe that leprosy patients of today will not object to our using this grim epithet from an earlier age in our endeavor to remind readers of this book about Mother Marianne and her companion-sisters how ghastly was the vocation they embraced, and how great was their sacrifice.

This biography itself will serve as yet another document among the many that will be submitted to Rome in support of the Cause for the Beatification and Canonization of Mother Marianne. Belief in her sanctity has increased, rather than waned, since she died on August 9, 1918. Responding to this growth in faith, in the 1970s Mother M. Viola Kiernan, Superior General of the Sisters of the Third Franciscan Order in Syracuse, New York, applied for permission to initiate proceedings that would lead to the establishing of an official Cause. By 1976 most of the preliminaries had been finished, and arrangements were concluded in Rome in preparation for the formal introduction of the Cause. Rev. Father Ernesto Piacentini. O.F.M. Conv., was named Postulator, to represent the Franciscan Community in subsequent stages of the process.

After the historical commission set up in 1980 finished its task of collecting all available documents concerning Mother Marianne, a Tribunal was appointed by the Most Rev. Joseph A. Ferrario, Bishop of Honolulu, to finish the inquiry. When its investigation was completed in November 1988, the first stage of the cause was officially concluded, and the documentation submitted to the Congregation of Saints in Rome. In 1989, the discussional stage of the Cause commenced. Meanwhile, strong support for the Cause has been given by both religious and laity in all levels of society and in many parts of the world, from Germany, where Mother Marianne was born in 1838, to Hawaii, where she ended her life of service in 1918.

ACKNOWLEDGMENTS: Inasmuch as the collecting of documentary evidence required visiting a number of institutions, our list of people to be thanked is long. To all of them we express our gratitude for generously sharing thoughts, time, and materials.

For allowing us to make copies of the many pertinent documents preserved in their several institutions:

In Honolulu: Ms. Agnes Conrad, Archivist of the State of Hawaii; Rev. Raymond J. Nishigaya, Chancellor of the Diocese of Honolulu; Rev. Louis Yim, Pastor of Our Lady of Peace Cathedral; and Rev. Albert Leunens, former Provincial of the Sacred Hearts Community in Hawaii.

In Louvain: Rev. Télesphore Bosquet, Archivist for the Congregation of the Sacred Hearts of Jesus and Mary, and Rev. Odilon Van Gestel.

In Madison, Wisconsin: Dr. Josephine Harper, Reference Archivist of the State Historical Society of Wisconsin.

In Rensselaer, New York: Rev. Andrew Ehlinger, Archivist of the Order of Friars Minor Conventual of the Immaculate Conception Province in America.

In Rome, Italy: Rev. Amerigo Cools, Archivist for the Congregation of the Sacred Hearts of Jesus and Mary, and Rev. Jan Scheepens, Superior General.

In South Bend, Indiana: Rev. Thomas Blantz, C.S.C., Archivist of the University of Notre Dame.

For the collection of invaluable microfilmed copies of documents concerning Father Damien de Veuster: Dr. A. Gavan Daws, formerly Professoɪ of History at the University of Hawaii in Honolulu, now Professor of Pacific History at Australian National University in Canberra. Dr. Daws himself made these microfilm copies at Sacred Hearts Archives in Rome, in preparation for his biography of Father Damien, entitled *Holy Man.* He deposited his research collection in the Hamilton Library at the University of Hawaii. Generous with advice, Dr. Daws suggested that further information about Mother Marianne and her Franciscan mission in Hawaii might be found at Sacred Heart Archives in Rome, in *Le Père Damien—Vie et Documents*, a three-volume collection in typescript of authenticated copies of papers assembled in 1935 by Rev. Odilon Van Gestel, SS.CC., Vice-Postulator of the Cause of Father Damien de Veuster at Louvain, at the time of the informative process.

For critical reading of our work in progress and welcome suggestions for improving it:

In Syracuse: Sister M. Aileen Griffin; Rev. Patrick Gallagher, O.F.M. Conv.; Dr. M. Catherine Kenna; Sister M. Davilyn Ah Chick; Sister M. Robertine Palladino; Sister M. Tarcisia Ball; Sister Mary Jacob Schmidbauer; Sister Edward Daniel Sheehan; and Sister M. Rosalie Brady.

In Honolulu: Mrs. Aldyth Morris and Mr. Patrick Boland.

For translating letters and diaries written in French or in German: Sister Mary Jacob Schmidbauer; Sister M. Tarcisia Ball; Sister M. Charlotte Miller; Sister M. Pauline Reissfelder; and Mrs. Thomas Braunmueller. These letters and diaries, written by Sacred Hearts priests who were contemporaries of Mother Marianne in Hawaii, presented a formidable challenge. Our translators had to work with passages and whole letters, often in almost illegible reproductions, selected from thousands of pages of manuscript which had been searched through by one of us for direct and indirect references to Mother Marianne and her co-workers. Translating these letters from colloquial French or German—frequently interspersed with words or phrases borrowed from English or Hawaiian—proved to be a monumental task. Also helpful with these and other translation labors were Mrs. R. M. Evan-Iwanowski, Sister M. Ambrosia Rigg, Sister Rose Francis Ottolino; and Sister M. Thaddea Thren.

For her devoted daily assistance with countless small tasks, and for the heroic labor of typing thousands of pages of manuscripts written in English, including making readable transcripts of copy obtained from other sources: Sister Martin de Porres Messier.

For drawing the map of the Hawaiian Islands: Sister Rose Raymond Wagner.

A great number of people cooperated in other ways, with advice, opinions, documents, photographs, information, testimonials. To them, too, we offer our thanks. Foremost among them were Dr. Jacob Adler, Anwei Skinsnes and Sister M. Francine Gries in Honolulu; Sister M. Wilma Halmasy and Sister Richard Marie Toal at Kalaupapa, Molokai; Mrs. Paul Cope in Kansas City, Missouri; Dr. Gwynn Barrett in Boise, Idaho; Mr. Edward Morrissey of Chicago, Illinois; Mr. Clifford W. Wells and Rev. Edward A. Lenk, O.F.M. Conv., of Utica, New York; and Sister M. Rosanne La Manche of Syracuse, New York.

Other helpers, who remain unnamed because of their very positions, provided records and pertinent data:

In Germany: Heppenheim, Darmstadt: St. Peter's Rectory.

In the United States: State Historical Society of Wisconsin; Brigham Young University, Provo, Utah; Dartmouth College Library, Hanover, New Hampshire.

In the State of New York: Oswego: St. Peter's Rectory. Rome: Jervis Public Library Association. Syracuse: Bird Library, Syracuse University; Lemoyne College Library; Maria Regina College Library; Onondaga Historical Association; Onondaga County Medical Society; Roman Catholic Chancery; Generalate Offices of Sisters of Third Franciscan Order Minor Conventual; St. Joseph Hospital Health Center; Onondaga County Public Library; Onondaga County Court House. Utica: Oneida County Office Building; Oneida Historical Society, Munson-Williams-Proctor Building; St. Clare Convent; St. Elizabeth Hospital; St. John's Rectory; St. Joseph-St. Patrick Rectory; Utica Public Library; Utica City Hall.

In Hawaii: Honolulu, Oahu: Hawaii State Library; Our Lady of Peace Rectory; Roman Catholic Chancery; State Archives of Hawaii; St. Francis Convent; University of Hawaii.

Our requests for information addressed to several other institutions were answered cordially, if not always fruitfully.

This by no means concludes the list of persons who have assisted or encouraged research for the Cause of Mother Marianne. Although naming all of them here is not possible, they will know that we are grateful.

Our greatest debt, of course, is owed to the two most recent Superiors General of the Sisters of St. Francis, Mother M. Viola Kiernan and Sister M. Aileen Griffin, and to their companion sisters. Their wholehearted support of the Cause of Mother Marianne has made possible the collecting of all known written materials about her. Without that treasury of documents to tell us about Mother Marianne, we could not have written this biography.

Syracuse, N. Y.   Sister Mary Laurence Hanley
Honolulu, Hawaii   O. A. Bushnell

Chapter I

BEGINNINGS

IN THE Year of Our Lord 1838, at seven o'clock in the morning of the twenty-third day of January, in the town of Heppenheim in the Grand Duchy of Hesse-Darmstadt, a daughter was born to Barbara Witzenbacher Koob, wife to Peter Koob. On the following day, Father Spreng at St. Peter's Church in Heppenheim baptized the infant child, who received the name Barbara. The godmother-by-proxy to the child was her half-sister Barbara, the single surviving daughter of the nine children whom Peter Koob's first wife had given him before she died. This older Barbara stood as godmother in place of Elizabeth Luley, a single daughter of Franz Luley, also a resident of Heppenheim.

The child baptized in St. Peter's Church on that cold winter morning in 1838 grew up to be the remarkable woman who is known today as Mother Marianne Cope of Molokai.

Peter Koob's second wife had borne him four other children before Barbara. The first of those, Eva, was seven years old in 1838. Maria Anna, the second child, lived only a few months and died on July 18, 1834. Two boys—Leonhard, born March 15, 1834, and Mathias, born December 22, 1835—also enlivened the household. None of Peter Koob's nine children by his first wife would have been sharing his home in 1838. Seven had died in infancy, before any reached the age of five. The two who survived—Peter, 25 years old in 1838, and Barbara, 21—would long since have left their father's house.

Records kept at St. Peter's Church indicate that the Koob and Witzenbacher families had dwelled in the district of Heppenheim for at least two generations before 1838. More than likely their ancestors were native to the region, having settled in the lands of Hesse long before records of any kind were made by either church or state. The registers of St. Peter's Church yield no information about Koobs, Witzenbachers, and similar common folk other than the religious events in their histories, the succession of dates marking their progression from birth and baptism through confirmation and marriage to death. They reveal that Peter Koob was born April 1, 1787, and Barbara Witzenbacher on June 24, 1803, and that they were wed on February 14, 1830.

Peter himself was "a Citizen and Farmer of Heppenheim on the Bergstrasse," according to the marriage records of St. Peter's Church. Inasmuch as his parents had two sons before him, he could hardly have been the owner of the family's farm. Moreover, as the father of a rather large and growing brood of children, he could not expect to prosper if he remained in Heppenheim, whether as assistant to an older brother or as a tenant farmer working land belonging to some other proprietor. The primitive agricultural economy of Hesse-Darmstadt added a further hazard: most of the duchy's parishes, including the one of Heppenheim, were so poor that many tillers of farms, artisans in towns and villages, and lesser merchants lived in wretchedness, and were not always able to feed or clothe their families well.

The constant threat of poverty, if not the actual experience of it, forced Peter Koob to join others of Europe's hard-pressed folk in seeking a new start in the land of promise and plenty across the sea. In 1840, when he was 53 years old, and she was 37, Peter and Barbara Koob, with their four small children, emigrated to the United States of America.

Peter chose to go to Utica, a small town in the central part of New York State. A considerable number of immigrants from Germany had already settled in that peaceful, fertile, and seemingly empty country. Some of those German settlers had ventured forth from Hesse-Darmstadt, perhaps even from Heppenheim, and the good tidings in their letters home would have helped to encourage Peter Koob to follow them. Adam Witzenbacher, a younger brother of Peter's wife, who came from the hamlet of Unterhambach, near Heppenheim, also settled in Utica. He may have accompanied the Koobs on the long journey to New York.

In 1835 Catholic Germans in Utica had organized a Bethaus, or house of prayer, for settlers who did not understand English-speaking priests at the older St. John's Church. Later, in 1839, following the example of many immigrants, they founded a benevolent association to care for sick and destitute members who contributed to it in time of health and prosperity. They called this organization St. Joseph's Society, from which group the parish later received its name. When the parish began in 1835 there were only forty families or about 200 persons in a city of ten thousand people. In 1840 a committee of trustees purchased a former Protestant church which would accommodate more parishioners. It was one of the few German Catholic churches in the entire region extending from Albany in the east to Buffalo, 410 kilometers to the west. Soon the existence of so congenial an enclave attracted other German immigrants to Utica and to the countryside nearby. Peter Koob and his family joined St. Joseph's parish soon after they arrived in Utica. At that time the congregation numbered about 400 people, belonging to sixty-five families.

In Utica itself Peter and Barbara Koob found nothing to remind them of Heppenheim. Although it may have been poor in worldly things, Heppenheim was a beautiful and comforting little village, in which they knew each person and every street and house. They felt safe there, sheltered behind the moat and the encircling walls, guarded from above by the towers and ramparts of fortress Starkenburg, atop its steep hill. They felt pride in great St. Peter's Church, soaring up from Heppenheim's very heart. Like the Starkenburg, its body and its tall steeple could be seen for leagues around. The octagonal dome, ribbed and folded, rested upon the high transept of the cathedral as a biretta sits upon the head of a priest. Unexpectedly grand for so small a place, St. Peter's was as venerable as an ancestor: it was so old that already some of the hewn stones in its single bell tower were crumbling. The Koobs, like most Heppenheimers, had prayed in every side chapel within that shining church; and they could recount all the stories told by those tall picture windows of stained glass that pierced the walls of the nave and of the curved apse. Even if he had been struck blind, Peter could have found his way to the baptistry, an alcove at one side of the wide west portal. He had stood in it so many times, as hopeful father and trusted godparent. And how often had he lifted the heavy cover from the baptismal font as a courtesy to the unmuscular priest who administered the sacrament. The font itself was a glittering and heavy eight-sided vessel wrought of gilded copper. Its ornamented cover was like a mirror-image to the basin. And the handle for the lid was an orb representing the world, topped by the cross triumphant. In all of Utica Peter could find nothing like it. Certainly nothing so splendid stood in the plain little unadorned St. Joseph's Church, still almost as stark as it had been when the Methodists built it for their chapel.

Utica was so different from Heppenheim. It was large and very rich, of course, full of wealthy burghers and their grand houses. But it was a dismal city, sprawling over the flat plain made by a lazy winding river. Twelve thousand people lived in this maze of streets. So many people and streets and alleys were found in Utica that a man could not possibly know them all. Houses were crowded close together, amid tall buildings, some as much as four stories high; and great factories with slender chimneys poured black smoke into the sky. Wagons, low drays, carriages, buggies filled the streets, all day long and far into the night. The noise made by all those machines and all those busy people was beyond belief. And the ugliness, the dreariness of Utica, after Heppenheim, was disappointing. Instead of trees, Utica grew chimneys. Instead of one great uplifted House of God, to which everyone went, Utica held at least a score of churches, all small, low, and unpleasing, to which only the devoted few would go. At first the Koobs felt lost in this wilderness of pavements, this clutter of red bricks, yellow stones, and gray concrete. The screeching of factory whistles, morning, noon, and night, woke the babies from sleep. But then, before many weeks had passed, as with all newcomers to the city, the Koobs too became accustomed to everything—to noise, confusion, crowds, soot, and tawdriness—and Utica became home. And the children, when they grew old enough to play with their friends in the streets, could find refuge from wagons and buggies and runaway horses in the spacious grounds of the New York State Lunatic Asylum, only three blocks to the west of 68 Schuyler Street.

Peter Koob did not become a farmer in this new land. Perhaps age and a lifetime of toil made him wary of the eternal demands and unending worries that farming imposes upon a man. Possibly he could not afford the expenses of setting himself up as an independent farmer. Although Utica, in the early 1840s was not expanding as actively as local businessmen wanted, more than likely its need for able-bodied workingmen offered Peter Koob immediate and steady employment at wages that would support his family. Whatever his reasons may have been, he went to work as a laborer, as subsequent census records and city directories indicated. During their first year in Utica the Koobs lived on Varick Street, very close to "the German Church."

Apparently savings from his wages enabled Peter to buy a piece of land sometime during 1841. In January 1842 he and a friend, Baltzer Taub, mortgaged that property for $250 and used the loan as an initial payment for "premises on Schuyler Street." These premises were located in the older and crowded part of Utica, near the south bank of the meandering Mohawk River. The original house on the property, where the Koob family lived for more than thirty years (which, after many changes in number, is identified now as 706 Schuyler Street), has long since been razed.

Being men of probity, Peter Koob and Baltzer Taub paid off the mortgage in five annual instalments of $50 each, the last of which fell due on November 1, 1845. The manner in which Baltzer Taub shared those premises on Schuyler Street is not known. Perhaps he was only the loyal friend whom Peter Koob needed as co-signer of those mortgage papers.

In 1847 the founders of the Utica Steam Woolen Mills constructed an enormous factory directly across the street from the Koobs' home. The big mill house, the dye works, assorted sheds, and out-buildings covered almost the whole large block between Schuyler Street and Nail Creek. All day long, six days a week, the street hummed with the sounds of carding machines, looms, and whirring spindles; of coal furnaces generating the steam to turn those busy machines; and of 175 factory hands, coming to work in the dark mornings and going home in the gray evenings.

Five more children were born to the Koobs in Utica: Elizabeth, in 1841 (in the year before St. Joseph's priests began to keep a baptismal register); Adam, on November 12, 1842; Catharina, on June 6, 1844; a short-lived child of unknown sex sometime between 1845 and 1848; and (something of a surprise to everyone, considering his mother's age), John Peter, on February 25, 1849. Adam, probably named for his mother's brother who was living in Utica by then, died on June 25, 1843, little more than seven months old.

A number of other families named Koob (or Koop, Kob, Kop, Kopp, or any of the several variations that German ears and orthography allow) also lived in Utica. They may have been cousins of Peter, come from the lands of Hesse, or strangers unrelated to him. Census takers and other compilers of records, in true American fashion, complicated matters by introducing spellings of their own invention, or by using a variant of the name for a family which wanted to be known by another. The most popular of those phonetic contrivings turned out to be Cope.

Although many another man tried to apply those variants to Peter Koob, he—more vigilant or more insistent than most—kept his ancient patronym to the end. But his sons Mathias and Peter adopted the Americanized version, Cope. So also did his daughter Barbara, when she became a Franciscan novice.

Despite a modest income, Peter Koob sent all his children to school, instead of putting them out to work. Probably they went to a public school at first, for want of a Catholic one to attend; St. Joseph's parish school did not open until 1851. Thereafter, Barbara at least, and probably Elizabeth, Catharina, and John Peter also, attended that parish school. Barbara spent five years at St. Joseph's, but the year in which she finished her schooling is not known. It is likely that, in common with other girls and most boys of the time, she did not go beyond the eighth grade in grammar school.

As are the offspring of most immigrants to the United States, the Koob children would have been bilingual. They spoke German at home, English in the schoolroom, and a pragmatic mixture of both in Utica's streets. Their parents could have had little opportunity to learn English, although Peter must have acquired a smattering of common expressions from his associates at work. Even as late as 1865 census recorders noted that Mrs. Kobb could read and write German, but not English. On the other hand, her youngest daughter Catharina, then 21 years old, could read and write only English.

Barbara Koob, during her career as a religious, knew German well enough to speak, read, and write it. Sometimes official records of the religious community had to be written in German, in part for the sake of sisters who did not undertand English, in part as a means of preserving the transported German culture in America. Nonetheless, she did not write German in official letters addressed to persons outside the Order. In personal letters she was content to introduce only an occasional German word or phrase into the English she preferred to use. Otherwise, her letters do not reveal the slightest influence of the German language upon word order or idiom. And her spoken English was just as fluently American—when she wanted it to be. Church Latin she learned in school and convent. And later, much later, she heard the soft speech of Hawaiians, and conversed with alien folk in briskest pidgin English.

The younger Koob children, beginning with Barbara, became thoroughly Americanized. Playmates, schoolmates, and teachers helped in that assimilation. Barbara herself remembered nothing about either Heppenheim or the voyage to America. Peter Kobb, too, wanted his children to take their place in the new homeland: census reports indicate that by 1855 he had become a naturalized citizen. Through the existing nationality laws, his German-born children under the age of twenty-one automatically became citizens upon the naturalization of their father. Barbara, therefore, was an American citizen.

Father and Mother Koob did not neglect to provide religious instruction for their children. The family went regularly to Sunday Mass at St. Joseph's Church, only three blocks away from the house on Schuyler Street. In 1848, her tenth year, Barbara received both the Sacrament of Confirmation and Holy Communion for the first time on the same day. As was the custom, the bishop of the diocese came all the way from Albany to administer the Sacrament of Confirmation, not at St. Joseph's but at St. John's, the squat, box-like edifice in the Greek-revival style that was Utica's principal Catholic church. Children would not be confirmed at St. Joseph's until 1862, although infants were being baptized at "the German church" long before that date. Barbara herself stood as godmother to her sister Eva's first two daughters, born in 1851 and 1853.

Barbara went to work immediately after she finished school. Census reports for both 1855 and 1860 identified her occupation with the formula "in factory." She may have worked in the Utica Steam Woolen Mills, the city's largest factory, which stood just across the street from her home on Schuyler Street.

No other facts can be discovered about the childhood of Barbara Koob. In her years as Mother Marianne she was modest at all times about her personal life. She spoke little about herself or her tasks, and wrote even less about those subjects. Although she never failed to show great concern for other people, either in person or in correspondence, she preferred not to waste precious time and energy upon matters relating to herself. Friends, relatives, and associates complied with her wishes until after she died. By then no one knew or could remember the events and influences that shaped her life sixty and seventy years before. Her humility in these matters may frustrate historians, but it achieved the purpose she intended by directing attention upon her work, not upon herself, the silent worker.

Amid all such conjectures about influences affecting her during those early years, we can be sure of one other fact: in common with most Americans, she knew nothing at all about the distant Kingdom of Hawaii.

Even so, the thoughts she did express about her duties as a religious, and most especially the deeds she performed during the years when, as she said, she was "working for God," allow a number of reasonable conclusions about those formative years in Utica. The small fund of information that is known about her brothers and sisters and their children supports these impressions about herself.

For the most part, emotionally and spiritually if not always physically, those must have been healthy, helpful, and happy years. The family gave her both a sense of security and a feeling of responsibility. Her devotion to both parents, even to the point of suppressing her own wishes for many years, and her affection for brothers, sisters, and their offspring, suggest that it was a loving family. She honored her father and mother out of love, rather than because the commandment ordered her to do so.

The Koobs could never have been comfortable financially. But neither were they miserably poor. Peter Koob could afford to buy a house and land on Schuyler Street and to pay off a mortgage in five years. He could afford to send all his children to school, instead of hiring them out for the wages they might bring in. But when schooling ended, the children did go to work and did take their wages home, helping to support the family. In those days, in most households, women were not yet liberated, and neither were sons: the family came first, not the individual. The individual son or daughter recognized the duty owed to parents—at least for the while, until he or she left the parental establishment, to marry and set up a new home, or to take a job in some distant place. In Barbara's case, duty and assistance were given willingly, not grudgingly. Later, in the convents and hospitals to which she was assigned, she gave help "cheerfully." That is the key word in her letters and responses to requests for help of any kind. Cheerful giving usually is learned at home, in childhood, not after one has grown up and gone away from home. And cheerful giving is the sign of a happy person, confident in her strengths. Although St. Francis himself introduced the word—and the concept—into his manner and teachings, cheerfulness is not necessarily a virtue that all his disciples can acquire.

It is safe to assume that even while Barbara at home learned to adapt cheerfully to the claims of others, she was learning also the domestic skills by which she might offer cheer to others. Her ability to cook and to sew and to devise little presents for gladdening the lives of leprous girls and boys in the forlorn Settlement on Molokai was something she learned on Schuyler Street, not in a convent. So, also, was the trick of making a little bit go a long way—to simplify a recipe for a cake, for example, or to adjust a pattern for a dress, to spend pennies rather than to squander dimes. She learned about frugality and austerity long before she became a poor sister of St. Francis.

Not the least of the skills she would have learned at home was the ability to organize things, to set up efficient procedures, and to manage people. Her religious career, first as a sister, later as a mother superior, would show, from beginning to end, that she was an excellent teacher and administrator. She did not command: she led—cheerfully, with tact and humor and grace, by example at all times, and with a most marvelous understanding of the feelings of her associates. After a while, when she grew older and more confident, she led her people with a dignity, a serenity, that subdued the most obstreperous adversary and soothed even the most weary sister.

Shadows darkened the girl's life, of course, sorrows wounded her spirit. Rather early in life, apparently, they taught her to fix her faith upon the hope of heaven, rather than upon the attractions of this world. The death of her little brother Adam, when she was only five years old, must have been a shattering experience. The death of Leonhard, a youth twenty years old, and probably handsome, like all the Koobs, must have been another terrifying proof of mortality to a sixteen-year-old girl already wanting to flee to a convent. Her mother's several pregnancies would have involved Barbara in the inescapable drudgeries of housekeeping as soon as she could be trained to haul water from the pump or carry dishes to the table. In that era of almost incessant epidemics and innumerable chronic diseases, many a mystifying sickness must have afflicted one Koob or another, to fill everyone with dread as well as with pain. But, except for little Adam and another newborn child who did not live long enough to acquire a name, seven of Barbara Witzenbacher Koob's brood survived until they were full grown. And for that dispensation they thanked the good God who gave them so much, and took away from them so little.

Judging by the letters Mother Marianne wrote, in her successive official positions, Barbara Koob must have been an excellent student in Utica's schools. Probably her enjoyment of studies made her want to be a teacher. She had a fine command of English: it is clear, direct, uncomplicated, and yet not without the graces of a woman perfectly at ease in both the language and the social situations in which she is employing it. Spelling, diction, syntax, style are correct without being stiff. Like most Americans, now as then, she did not pay much attention to the rules of punctuation. When circumstances warranted, she used the German and American colloquialisms of her era. And almost always she did not waste much time in hunting for fine words. She was too busy to worry about such niceties of expression, and wrote just as she thought and spoke. She exhibited none of the fantastic aberrations in spelling and grammar achieved by many of her contemporaries, or by many of America's young folk today, for that matter.

Her penmanship was neat, precise, rounded in the fashion of the time, indeed "Spencerian" before that term was applied to handwriting. Certain capital letters resembled those of the Gothic German script of her day, but in general her writing was not bedecked with whorls, loops, and imbrications such as many a time-waster affected.

All these abilities in the use of the language, as well as the ideas she expressed with it, reveal a mind quick to learn and trained to remember everything. Her letters, like her deeds, are expressions of an intelligence that addressed itself to facts and to people. She could manage a convent, supervise a hospital, or dress the stinking sores of lepers as easily as, once upon a time, she scrubbed floors in her mother's house on Schuyler Street. She indited letters to ministers of state and to reverend bishops as easily as she compiled a list of supplies to be ordered through a government clerk.

And, somehow, in all these manifold relationships with people of high state or low, she managed, by means that seem almost magical, to keep almost every one of them content. In the thousands of pages of communications written to her or about her that are preserved in archives from Rome to Honolulu, only a very few utter words of complaint about her decisions or actions. And these few, as statisticians would point out, are not significant in comparison with the total number of comments. The exceptions only emphasize what everyone knows: that in any organization some people can never be pleased by any leader, regardless of his abilities.

Sometimes, as she grew older, she would blame herself for a minor oversight in keeping the accounts on Molokai. But no one else ever did. If a government clerk needed to remind her that she had forgotten to send in a payroll list, or an accounting for postage stamps sold, or something equally trivial, he did so with respect, wanting to help rather than to scold.

For a girl of her intelligence and aspirations, the years she spent as a factory worker must have been all but maddening. And yet she endured the work for nine years, for the sake of the few dollars she earned each month, and because she felt her aging father needed her at home. The servitude in the factory may or may not have been given cheerfully. But most certainly she used the experience to strengthen the virtues of patience, forbearance, tolerance, compassion, and fortitude that sustained her in the years to come. And the exposure—not to the labor but to the harshness of the factory environment—strengthened her wish to leave the world, in order to serve its people more effectively.

She must have been a beautiful maiden, because she was a most handsome woman. Portrait photographs taken of her as Mother Marianne, when she was about forty years old, show little more than the face, framed in the immaculate white coronet and band, the broad dazzling collar, and the flowing black veil lined with white that were worn by a Franciscan sister. The strong well-shaped nose and wide firm mouth, above all the black eyebrows and the dark eyes looking out upon the world with an insuperable dignity, compose a countenance that is noble as well as beautiful. We today, seeing that face in an aged photograph, can understand how, without having to say a word, she could quell rioting lepers, captivate a Hawaiian king and his queen, charm niggardly politicians into fits of generosity, win profligate patients to continence, and even soften the stony hearts of Hawaii's most suspicious Calvinists.

Group photographs taken with companion sisters in Hawaii show that she was not tall, but rather of middle height. The figure under the voluminous habit seems to be slight rather than matronly, as, so often, were sister-companions of comparable age. These pictures, together with descriptions of her features and fair complexion written by Sister Leopoldina and others, show that she kept her beauty even into old age, until near the end of her long life sickness destroyed that comeliness.

Yet always, because she disliked being photographed, to begin with, and because in those days the taking of pictures was considered an official occasion, not to be wasted upon idle chatter and vapid smiles, she looked serious, even somber. The famous wide "Franciscan smile" is missing from the pictures. But it was generously given in life. And several pleasing little anecdotes told about her responses to certain officious people, in and out of convents, or to delicate situations created by such busybodies, prove that she was by no means humorless.

No one knows when she first thought of becoming a sister, or why she should have chosen to take the religious path to service rather than the secular. Somehow, somewhere in Utica, Barbara Koob heard the message from Christ that St. Francis had transmitted to his companions: "I am not here to be served, but to serve." Apparently she decided upon leaving the world when she was about fifteen years of age. She said as much, in a letter written in 1898 to a young nephew, Paul Cope. He was the son of her brother Mathias, who in 1857 had settled in Chicago. In 1898 young Paul wrote to his sympathetic aunt in far-off Molokai, expressing doubts about his choice of a career. His uncertainty drew from her the only statement she ever made in writing about a similar time of trial in her own life: ". . . I am happy to know that you are so resigned to God's holy will regarding your Vocation to the Religious state—When I was your age and younger my desire to retire from the world was very strong—but God did not will it—I was obliged to struggle and wait nine long years before it pleased God to open the convent gates to me.—Now I have been in His service since 1862. 36 years.—Have patience and be faithful to your duty towards your poor Papa, and the good God will reward you a hundred fold for making the sacrifice of your heart's wishes to give the necessary care to your Papa. . . ."

She could send this good counsel to Paul Cope in perfect faith, because she had accepted it for herself about forty years earlier.

Although she may have been "obliged to struggle and wait nine long years," she never regretted having offered that time of faithful duty to her own "poor Papa." After 1855 Barbara was the oldest of Peter Koob's children to live with the family in the house on Schuyler Street. Eva had married Francis Lehrscholl of Utica in 1850; Leonhard had died in 1854; and Mathias seems to have parted from the family, in the course of making his way toward Chicago. Barbara labored as a factory worker by day, helped her mother in the evenings, comforted both parents by her presence, and undoubtedly contributed all her wages to the family's resources. And faith in the future, and in God's will, sustained her.

During those nine years of waiting, two events occurred in Utica that directly affected her future as a religious. In March 1859 Bishop John McClosky in Albany assigned the administration of St. Joseph's parish in Utica to the Franciscan Friars, Minor Conventuals. And on April 10, 1860, four sisters of the Third Order of St. Francis came from Philadelphia to teach the younger boys and girls at St. Joseph's parish school—and, when time permitted, to give care to the sick people of the town. Their leader was Mother M. Bernardina Dorn. Only five years before, "a pious young maiden from Bavaria" newly arrived in Philadelphia, Sister Bernardina had helped to found an American branch of the Sisters of the Third Order.

In Utica the four sisters established a little convent named, appropriately, after St. Clare, the first woman to be a disciple of St. Francis. To sinners in this world who harbor the merest spark of poetry, nothing is more entrancing than the sight of a Franciscan sister, clad in her black and white habit, seeming to float rather than to walk along a city's streets or down a church's aisle. To Barbara Koob, eager to answer the call she had been hearing for five years, the sight of those four Franciscan sisters must have been both a promise and a hurt.

By her very presence, Mother Bernardina—even though she was only four years older than Barbara Koob—would have drawn the younger woman to her side. Even in photographs Mother Bernardina—with her big maternal body, deep-set eyes, serene countenance, and gentle smile—is the personification of mother-love, the very image of the fostering mother. In life she would have been beyond resisting to a girl with Barbara Koob's aspirations.

The consequent important event in her life can be imagined: Barbara Koob went to see Mother Bernardina, to speak of her hope, to ask for counsel. Mother Bernardina, perceiving the valor and the virtue in this serious young aspirant, advised and encouraged. Some of her counsel must have been exactly the same as that which Mother Marianne gave to her nephew Paul Cope thirty-eight years later: she must fulfill her duties to parents, bear with patience the delaying of her wish to retire from the world, and, in the meantime, hope for God's reward when He is ready to grant it.

Thus sustained, Barbara knew what she must do. And Mother Bernardina prepared the way for the convent gates to open to Barbara Koob when the time should come.

In July 1862 Peter Koob died, at the age of 75. Barbara's long testing came to its appointed end.

With her mother's blessing, she applied for admission to the Sisters of the Third Order of St. Francis.

On August 26, 1862, at a chapter held in St. Clare's Convent in Utica, Barbara Koob's application for admission as a postulant was accepted.

NOTES on Chapter I

1. Birth and baptism of Barbara Koob: *Records of Births*, the Catholic Parish of St. Peter at Heppenheim, vol. 1838–1842, p. 6, no. 11.
2. Certification of data about births and deaths of Peter Koob's older children, received from St. Peter's Church, Heppenheim, July 1974.
3. Marriage of Peter Koob and Barbara Witzenbacher: *Marriage Records*, the Catholic Parish of St. Peter at Heppenheim, vol. 1830–1836, p. 517.
4. Birth and baptism of Barbara Koob's full brothers and sisters: (a) those born in Heppenheim: *Records of Births*, the Catholic Parish of St. Peter at Heppenheim, vol. 1831–1837; (b) those born in Utica, N.Y.: census records for 1850 and 1855; and *Baptismal Records*, St. Joseph's Catholic Church, Utica, N.Y.
5. Early history of Catholic Church in Utica, N.Y.: (a) H. Paul Draheim, "St. Joseph's Catholic Church Founded in 1842," in *Utica Observer Dispatch*, n. d. *ca.* 1960; (b) *St. Joseph's Parish Centennial* 1841–1941, Utica, N.Y., 1941.
6. Description of Utica: (a) photographs and maps preserved at Oneida Historical Society and Oneida County Office Building in Utica, N.Y.; (b) Samuel W. Durant, *History of Oneida County, New York. . . .*, p. 306; (c) *Utica City Directories 1840–1900;* (d) Industrial Statistics, *Census Record of Oneida County*, N.Y. June 1855, Utica Public Library, Utica, N.Y.
7. Mortgage and purchase of Koob premises at 706 Schuyler Street, Utica, N.Y.: *Book of Mortgages*, 1842, pp. 437–38, Oneida County Office Building, Utica, N.Y.
8. Mother Marianne's younger brother was married to Rosalia Fagant on August 5, 1873, at St. Joseph's Church in Utica, N.Y. The couple moved to Newark, N.J., about 1877. Eight children were born to them.
9. *The Census Record of Oneida County,* N.Y., of June 1855, preserved in the Utica Public Library, is the only official document available to indicate the naturalization of Peter Koob. On September 16, 1984, John J. Walsh, Oneida County Judge and Utica City Historian (N.Y.), reviewed this record and its particular circumstances. He ruled there is a valid presumption that Peter Koob was a naturalized citizen of the United States in 1855; therefore, his daughter Barbara (Mother Marianne) automatically became a citizen upon the naturalization of her father. (Naturalization Act of Congress, April 14, 1802.)
10. Barbara Koob's schooling and First Holy Communion: *Record of Perpetual Vows I,* (1861–1883), p. 30. Concerning Confirmation: no records are available from St. John's Church, Utica, N.Y., where the children of St. Joseph's Parish received the sacraments in early days. According to Rev. Clarence O'Shea, O.F.M. Conv., the sacramental record books of St. Joseph Parish, which begin with 1862, show that "It is very clear" that in the early days of the parish the sacraments of Confirmation and Holy Eucharist were received on the same day, and perhaps in the same ceremony. Thus, Barbara Koob would have been confirmed on the same day in 1848 as the one on which she received her First Holy Communion at St.

John's Church in Utica. Although no relevant records at St. John's Church are extant for that period, the year of her First Holy Communion is noted in *Record of Perpetual Vows I.*

11. Mother Marianne's eyes: although Sister Leopoldina often mentioned Mother Marianne's "merry eyes," neither she nor anyone else ever described their color. Photographs suggest that they were either jet black or very dark blue.

12. "Barbara . . . undoubtedly, contributed all her wages": The quitclaim deed to the family property on Schuyler Street that was settled in 1871 gives additional evidence that Mother Marianne contributed her salary to the support of the family while living at home. Apparently, the division of the small estate was agreed upon harmoniously among the Cope children almost a year before their mother's death in July 1872. Mrs. Barbara Cope, widow, who had dower ownership of the home, gave five of her children an equal amount of money [$40] on August 31, 1871. In a separate claimdeed, dated the same day, she gave "Marianne Cope, Syracuse, N.Y." more than double the amount given to the others [$100]. John Cope purchased the house from his mother in late 1871, a few months after the settlement. One year later on 27 August 1873, after his mother's death, he sold the property. Interestingly enough, the deed of 1871 presents the only reference found so far concerning Elizabeth Cope as an adult; that is, her name is given as Mrs. Elizabeth Miller. Records of deed are kept at the County Clerk's office in the Oneida County Building in Utica, New York.

13. Founding of American branch of Sisters of the Third Order of St. Francis, in Philadelphia: (a) Manuscript in German, belonging to Mother M. Bernardina Dorn (translation by Mother M. Margaret Haskin); (b) translation of "Description of Beginning of Foundation" written by Father John Hespelein, spiritual director of the Sisters in Philadelphia; (c) Mother M. Carmela Prandoni, 1960: *Greater Love*, pp. 28–29.

14. Death of Peter Koob (and sons Leonhard and Adam): *Record of Deaths,* 1842–1897, St. Joseph's Church, Utica, N.Y.

15. Application and admission of Barbara Koob: *History and Chapters of St. Clara Convent,* Utica, N.Y.

Chapter II

THE NARROW PATH

TWENTY-SIX years later, in a letter she wrote to Mother Bernardina Dorn from the Leper Settlement on Molokai, Mother Marianne remembered once again the kindness of her counsellor: "Accept, dear Mother, my heartfelt thanks for all you have done for me—many, many years ago—I believe only for your kind influence I would not have been received into the Order. So if I have done a little good during those years, that have passed into eternity, you share the reward of it. . . ."

The convent doors opened for Barbara Koob not in Utica but in Syracuse, about 70 kilometers to the west. Because the four sisters in Utica were not able to train novices in the tiny Convent of St. Clare, Mother Bernardina arranged for Barbara to enter St. Francis Convent in Syracuse.

On November 19, 1862, the feast day of St. Elizabeth of Hungary, Barbara Koob and several other postulants were invested in the habit of the Order of the Sisters of St. Francis. The Right Reverend Father Leopold B. M. Moczygemba, Commissary General of the Order of Friars Minor Conventual, presided at the ritual in the Church of the Assumption of the Blessed Virgin Mary—a little wooden building with the letters DEO painted upon the façade above the front door. At the conclusion of the ceremony, the novices filed through the portals of St. Francis Convent, opened briefly for them.

Known now as Sister Mary Anna, she spent the prescribed year of probation that is called the novitiate. During this critical period a novice, a newcomer in every sense of the word, is instructed and observed by sisters who have preceded her along that narrow path. They must ascertain if she is in good health, both physically and emotionally; and they must decide whether or not she will be able to

16

endure the sacrifices of self, the demands upon spirit and body, that life in a convent exacts. The novice herself, during the period of trial, is given the time to learn whether or not she can submit in good heart to the rigorous discipline by which every minute, every act, and almost every thought of her life will be regulated. Regret for the world shut out, for all its insidious charms and comforts and deceits, must be uprooted in that short year; and so must all the little willfulnesses of pride, and sloth, and malice, and earthly love, and a myriad other evidences of selfishness that can be aroused so easily in an individual who is immured among others who also are individuals. "The Lord wants converts, not victims," as St. Francis said. Not without reason do the vows professed by a priest or a sister promise perpetual poverty, chastity, and obedience. Until the new rite of reception emphasizing the Baptismal commitment was adopted, a postulant could present three names to the community by which she preferred to be known in the religious life. In 1862, however, professed sisters allowed postulants no such liberties. Barbara Koob's name in religion could hardly have been given her without much forethought: Anna was Mother Bernardina's name in the world, before she entered the Franciscan community.

Mother M. Antonia Eulenstein, superior of St. Francis Convent (and one of the first American women to join the Order in Philadelphia) served as directress of novices. Early in November 1863 she informed the bishop of the diocese, who lived in Albany, and the commissary general of the Order, who lived in Syracuse, that five young women were about to complete the novitiate: Barbara Koob and Catharina Sprattler of Utica; Catharina Buchmeier of Rome; and Maria Zimmermann and Maria Wirges of Syracuse. Upon receiving official approval from Albany, Mother Antonia made preparations for the novices to pronounce their vows on November 19.

During the day before that climactic event, each novice signed her last will and testament, as is required by the Rule of the Order. "For he that will save his life, shall lose it," St. Francis had admonished, when he explained that a follower who "does not renounce all he possesses cannot be my disciple." Sister Mary Anna bequeathed the little she had, which surely could not have amounted to much: "Any and all of the property, both real and personal, of every name, nature, and kind . . . to the two incorporations of the Franciscan sisters" in the state of New York—that is, to the convents in Syracuse and Utica. At the foot of her will the novice who had begun life as Barbara Koob wrote legally for the first time the name the community had chosen for her: Sister Mary Anna Cope.

Early the next morning, on the feast of Saint Elizabeth, exactly one year after the novices had been invested in the Franciscan habit, they went in procession to the Church of the Assumption. Each novice, still wearing the white veil denoting her station, carried a lighted taper in her right hand, signifying that she cherished and guarded the Light of the World. Father Leopold conducted the rite in which each one pronounced her vows, in the presence of relatives, friends, and religious.

Having made that profession, in what must have been the most solemn moment in her whole life, Sister Mary Anna was a novice no longer. In sign of that change, Mother Antonia hung about her neck the chain with the heavy cross that represents the devotion each sister brings to her life and the burdens she is willing to assume in the name of Christ. Whereupon two older sisters laid upon her head the black veil of the professed sister, covering the white veil of the novice. Thenceforth, in apparel and demeanor, Sister Mary Anna would be no different from all her companions in the Third Order of St. Francis. Yet, such are the wondrous complexities of the human spirit, in mind and devotion she would be very different from all others in her community.

The page in *The Record Book of Perpetual Vows* that preserves the notice of her profession adds one further interesting detail: "Sister Marianna has the intention of doing school work in the Order." Apparently her duties as a teacher began immediately, in the Assumption Parish School in Syracuse, not far from the Convent of St. Francis.

The note also indicates that already people were spelling her name in its several variations. As the signature on her will attests, she was supposed to be called Sister Mary Anna, in conformity with the custom of the Order, whereby each professed sister automatically received Mary as a first name, because that is the name most dear to Catholics who revere the Mother of God. In that German community, however, Mary Anna soon became Marianna. Later, other people heard it as Marianne. For many years letters addressed to her bear any one of the three names. For a while she signed herself with one or the other of the variants, apparently spelling it according to the identity of the person to whom she happened to be writing. Eventually she settled upon Marianne, probably because it was the version most suitable for all eyes and ears, possibly because an older Sister Mary Anna also lived in St. Anthony's Convent. By 1871 she was using Marianne almost exclusively. Other people, however, especially newspaper reporters, continued to employ the variant spellings until the end of her life.

About six months after Sister Mary Anna professed her vows, a young man from Belgium, Joseph de Veuster, was ordained a priest in far-off Honolulu, the capital city of the Kingdom of Hawaii. Mother Marianne and he would meet in time, under circumstances that neither one could have imagined in 1863. For his priest's name the young man chose to be called Damien.

Sister Mary Anna quickly demonstrated the abilities that Mother Bernardina had perceived in Barbara Koob, the young factory worker. At a chapter meeting held on June 10, 1864, seven months after her profession of vows, the Reverend Commissary General appointed her to membership in the Definitorium of the community. A definitorium, in modern terms, is the governing council that decides upon points of discipline and other minor matters in the internal affairs of a religious community. At that time, the Definitorium in Syracuse consisted of Mother Bernardina, who had been a consultor in the Philadelphia community (and co-foundress); the superiors of the several missions; and five "school-sisters," who were appointed by the Commissary General of the Order, apparently upon recommendation of their chapters.

The next morning the chapter elected Sister Antonia Eulenstein to be "Mother Superior of the Mother or Centralhouse for the space of three years." She and a number of sisters were moving that day to larger quarters, set down amid twenty green acres of farm land at the northern end of the city of Syracuse.

At the same chapter Sister Mary Anna was elected vicaria, or deputy, to Mother Antonia. In that position she would supervise a small group of sisters who would remain in St. Francis Convent, near the Church of the Assumption in Northside Syracuse.

The new convent in the country was dedicated to St. Anthony of Padua on his feast day, June 13, and became the Order's first Motherhouse. Originally built as the residence of a prosperous farmer, it had walls made of concrete mixed with riverbed pebbles of varied sizes and hues, which the sisters called "cobblestones." The "cobblestone house" rose two-and-a-half stories to peaked roofs covered with shingles. Two pointed dormers emerged from the steep roofs at the front of the house, and two slender red-brick chimneys at the rear. Fret-work decorations, resembling flattened lozenges, hung from the eaves of the gable above the main entrance. Fruit trees and flowering shrubs grew in the big yard, a rambling vine clung to the façade above the front door.

The farmer's house needed very little renovation to prepare it for the sisters' use. The most important alteration was the remodeling of the former living room into a small chapel. To people of today the building would look cramped and dark and grim. For the sisters who in 1864 escaped to it from the crowded quarters at St. Francis Convent in Syracuse, it must have been an abode both beautiful and spacious.

A year later, in 1865, Sister Mary Anna was elected vicaria of St. Anthony's Convent, while still keeping that same office at St. Francis Convent. The duties of vicaria took only a small part of her time. She spent most of each day's working hours in a classroom at the parish school, the early mornings and evenings at prayers in the chapel or in performing the chores of housekeeping. In those quiet years, when all schoolchildren were tractable and all sisters were obedient, the role of a teacher in an elementary school was relatively pleasant, the duties of a vicaria were relatively uncomplicated. Sister Mary Anna spent her life just as she had hoped she might, within the sheltering embrace of classroom and convent, shielded by superiors and by rules from the encroachments of the world outside. During recitation of the Little Office of the Blessed Virgin in the chapel, or in the tiny cell in which she slept for the few hours the Rule allowed, even in school rooms, filled with uncorrupted children, or in the convent's refectory, filled with sisters observing "salutary silence" as they listened to spiritual readings, she could believe that she had gained at last the haven she sought and in it had found the peace that surpasses all understanding.

The peace could not endure. As she herself would have said, the God to Whom she had dedicated her life had other plans for her.

The talents so valued by the world she expected to leave behind— efficiency, good judgment, devotion to work, and especially the ability to direct people without arousing their resentment—drew the attention of superiors among both the sisters and the priests who administered the Franciscan Order's temporal affairs. They saw that her abilities, although useful in keeping the peace in a convent, could be used to better advantage beyond so limited a setting. Even while the sisters of

St. Anthony's continued to elect her to positions of trust, the administrators who struggled with hard realities outside the convent's walls plucked Sister Mary Anna out of that refuge and sent her forth again into the world.

In January of 1866 a second phase began in her religious career. It would last for seventeen years. If, during this period, she had been merely an able administrator, or even a brilliant one, few people today outside the Order would remember her. The positions she held were not remarkable in themselves, were not even extraordinarily exacting. They are worthy of attention for two reasons only: because they prepared her for the mission she would choose to take to Hawaii; and because, ultimately, she renounced their temporal authority for the supreme position in which she wielded no power at all.

From one point of view, the common one which measures all jobs in terms of opportunities for advancement, those successive positions were like stages in a career that might have led her in time to the very top of the female hierarchy that administered the Sisters of St. Francis. Yet the hierarchy itself, like the Order, was not important within the vast edifice of the Roman Catholic Church. She belonged to a struggling new congregation, little more than five years old, which claimed few members, owned little property (while accumulating a full complement of debts), commanded no power in or out of the Church, and was all but unknown except among German Catholics in central New York State. In those difficult years the Sisters of St. Francis could have had little more than a sublime faith to sustain them.

But faith is a powerful weapon, as many a sinner, countless heretics, and hosts of infidels have discovered, the earth around.

The presence of those few Sisters of St. Francis in Syracuse and in Utica, most especially the example of their good works as teachers of children and attendants upon the sick poor, attracted an increasing number of novices to the Order. By the end of 1861 the superiors of the community, after conferring with the commissary general, decided to send out small groups of sisters to establish convents in nearby towns. In mid-January 1866 Father Leopold Moczygemba, as Commissary General, appointed Sister Mary Anna as "temporary superior" for Immaculate Conception Convent in the little village of Rome, about 50 kilometers northeast of Syracuse. Whatever regrets she may have felt about the need to leave St. Anthony's shelter, Sister Mary Anna could only obey the order to go to Rome.

Less than eight months later, at a meeting held in Syracuse on

August 3, 1866, the general chapter elected her superior of the new Convent of St. Teresa and principal of St. Peter's School in Oswego, New York, a small town on the shores of Lake Ontario, about 50 kilometers northwest of Syracuse.

Two years later she returned to her home town, Utica. On August 14, 1868, Right Reverend Father Fidelis Dehm, successor to Father Moczygemba as Commissary General of the Order of Minor Conventuals, appointed her superior of St. Clare's Convent to take care of the welfare of the sisters who were teaching at St. Joseph's and St. Patrick's parochial schools.

Two weeks earlier, while visiting St. Clare's Convent, Father Fidelis had written her—in confidence and in Old High German. A hugely corpulent man, with flaxen hair, full cheeks, and a small sharp nose, he looked surprisingly like an overgrown and very worried boy. Sometimes he could be almost tyrannical in his treatment of the sisters he governed, but on this occasion he wrote with something of the simplicity of a trusting boy: ". . . Mother Bernardina (on account of sickness and other concerns) laid her office as Superior in my hands. . . . To this office I have chosen you venerable Mother. . . . Do not be shocked by this message—but, with child-like confidence trust and put all your cares in Divine Providence . . . you will accomplish a lot of good here, and with the help and grace of God also experience much consolation. . . ."

This assignment to Utica would have permitted Sister Mary Anna a reunion with her mother and with brother John Peter, then 19, still living in the house on Schuyler Street. John worked in a "woolen mill," as census records indicate. No doubt she met her younger sister, Elizabeth, and Catharina, too, although that sister had left home a year or so before, as wife to Thomas Murphy. Older sister Eva also was living in Utica, as wife to Francis Lehrscholl and mother of the first seven of her eight children.

Mother Bernardina remained in Utica and after a few months' relief given by Mother Antonia, she resumed her duties—as Superior of St. Elizabeth's Hospital. This unconquerable woman, not weary after teaching all day at St. Joseph's School, had spent the rest of her time in caring for the sick poor in their homes—ignoring her own failing health as she did so. In 1866 she requested permission from the Franciscan Fathers to use a small tenement house next to St. Joseph's Church, and converted it into a home for the sick. Called St. Elizabeth's, it was the first privately owned hospital in Oneida

County, New York, and received its first patient on December 12, 1866.

Sister Mary Anna's service in Utica continued until November 10, 1869, when once again the Definitorium elected her superior of St. Teresa's Convent in Oswego. Mother Bernardina and Mother Antonia convinced Father Fidelis that Sister Mary Anna was needed there more than in Utica, and so he released her to Oswego for a term of three years.

Her second stay in Oswego was shorter than the first. In June 1870 Father Fidelis thrust her into a brutal reality such as she had never anticipated. The harried Commissary General, desperately in need of a good administrator, "intervened" (as tactful Franciscan sisters say), and installed her as Superior of the recently opened St. Joseph's Hospital in Syracuse.

Once again he wrote to her in Old High German, this time from Syracuse. This is a most mystifying letter, full of vague references to people and to problems that are beyond identifying today. But it does show how Father Fidelis turned to Sister Mary Anna for help in resolving a difficult problem: "It cost me a great deal to overcome and accept the fact that the known change must be made here at the hospital. The reasons for it are of such nature that I could find no rest until the decision was finally expressed this morning after Holy Mass. Tomorrow I will make the decision publicly known before the Sisters . . . and then procure [Venerable Mother Dominica] her appointment as Superior of Oswego until further notice. Enclosed I send you your renewal as Superior and congratulate you as Mother of St. Joseph Hospital.

"Since you take upon yourself this great responsibility and concern in the spirit of Holy Obedience, I can only repeat the words in the testament of our holy Father St. Francis—'cast all your cares upon the Lord.'"

The reasons that prompted Father Fidelis to relieve Sister Dominica Cumming as head of the hospital are no longer known. But her story is worth the telling because it reveals another and unusual aspect of Mother Marianne's career: in her long life, Sister Dominica stands out as her one and only declared antagonist.

Father Fidelis probably acted as he did because Sister Dominica seems to have been a crusty character who stirred up conflicts in the people around her, both religious and secular. Indeed, as certain vaguely worded letters to and from Father Fidelis and church officials attached to the diocesan bishop in Albany imply, she may even have assailed the "tyrannical" Commissary General himself, calling him "both accuser and judge" for the Sisters of St. Francis.

Photographs present her as a short, solid woman with heavy features, looking very much like a battered Irish pugilist dressed in the garb of a nun. Hardworking, efficient, forthright to the point of being harsh, Sister Dominica obviously compensated for her lack of feminine beauty by being more masculine than many of her associates could tolerate. The few surviving references to her personality support this impression. In 1977, a senior sister, remembering Sister Dominica from her mellowed age, said "She wasn't a person you told much to." Her contemporaries in the community at the time when she was most abrasive, calling upon wit as well as perception, referred to her as "Sister Dominic." She herself, in a letter written to Mother Marianne in 1883, acknowledged the cause of much of her difficulty by admitting ". . . I was always stormy in my manner. . . ."

Contentious she might be, but no one doubted her devotion to the Order, not even Father Fidelis. Even so, Sister Dominica had not yet learned the most difficult of all forms of self-discipline that are exacted of a religious—complete humility and unquestioning obedience. She seems to have been much wounded in her pride when Father Fidelis removed her as superior of St. Joseph's Hospital. He did not ease the strained situation when he sent her to Oswego, to exchange places with the very sister whom he had selected to take her former position in the hospital at Syracuse. Sister Dominica, three years older than Sister Mary Anna, two years senior to her as a member of the Franciscan community, experienced in running a hospital and caring for patients, had good reasons for feeling hurt.

Following the transfer from Syracuse, Sister Dominica continued to serve in responsible positions, first as superior in Oswego, and then as head of St. Elizabeth Hospital in Utica. After nine effective years there, she was elected—during the very important general chapter convened on July 14, 1881—to be superior of St. Joseph Hospital in Syracuse. The return to St. Joseph's led to a time of great unhappiness for her, of distress for Mother Marianne, and of dismay for the whole community.

When, in 1870, Sister Mary Anna assumed her new position at St. Joseph Hospital, she must have done so with some trepidation. A characteristic letter she wrote in 1882, as Mother Provincial, suggests how some sisters reacted to orders assigning them to duty in the big hospital. The message she sent to Sister M. Bonaventure Caraher is, clearly, one that she had learned for herself, twelve years before: "For Jesus' dear sake take up your cross and follow Him on the thorny path his blood stained feet have traced for you. Follow Him cheerfully and patiently even though it be in the performance of Hospital duties...."

St. Joseph's Hospital, the first such institution to be created in the Syracuse area, was opened in 1869, only three short years after the Franciscan sisters had founded St. Elizabeth's Hospital in Utica. The Franciscans' concern for the sick led them naturally to establishing these first hospitals for the care of patients drawn from the general population of central New York State.

In expressing this concern in so practical a way, the Franciscan sisters of New York were following the example of the three women who, in Philadelphia in 1855, established a foundation of the Third Order of St. Francis in America. The founding group in Philadelphia was encouraged and assisted by St. John Neumann, then the bishop of that important diocese (and, with his canonization in 1977, the fourth man from the United States to be recognized as a saint). After their organization as a Franciscan community, the sisters devoted much time to caring for "the poor sick in their homes." Sister Bernardina Dorn, who later would become Barbara Koob's counsellor and sponsor, was one of the members of that original group.

In 1860 Mother Bernardina and three other sisters moved from Philadelphia to Utica, to serve as teachers at St. Joseph Parish School. After classes each day, and on weekends, these tireless sisters gave nursing care to sick people in West Utica. By 1866, inspired primarily by Mother Bernardina, they decided to build a hospital.

Inasmuch as Peter Koob and his family on Schuyler Street lived only a short distance from St. Clare's Convent, Barbara Koob undoubtedly saw the Franciscans quite often as they went through the city on their errands of mercy. They may even have brought their help into the home of such good parishioners as the Koobs, especially during Peter's last illness.

By 1866 Barbara Koob, having herself become a Franciscan, was a member of the Definitorium in Syracuse which approved the creation of St. Elizabeth's Hospital in Utica. And in 1869, as a member of the Franciscan community's Board of Directors, and as superior of St.

Clare's Convent where a decisive meeting was held, Mother Marianne participated in the discussions which led to the founding of St. Joseph's Hospital in Syracuse.

The decision was made on April 8, 1869. The need was great: cases of typhoid fever and malaria were numerous, among rich and poor alike. Undaunted by lack of funds, the sisters, imitating St. Francis himself, "walked the streets, gathering funds and supplies." They collected $6,000 in donations and received "an equal sum" from several wealthy residents of Syracuse and its suburbs. On April 12, 1869, the sisters bought three contiguous pieces of property on Prospect Hill, in a section of town which more genteel citizens referred to as "an amusement park." Upon the corner lot stood a two-story brick house that had been used as "a lager beer saloon." The adjoining strip of land was empty. The third lot was occupied by "a large and disreputable Saturday-night dance-house." With amazing speed, a newspaper reporter wrote approvingly, workmen "transformed a source of crime and sorrow into a temple of healing." On May 6 the hospital opened for "reception of patients." The former dance hall, converted into a ward, accommodated about fifteen patients. Five nurse-sisters of St. Francis, under the supervision of Sister M. Dominica Cumming, lived in quarters prepared for them in the house that had been a saloon.

A new edifice was constructed in the empty lot between the two refurbished buildings. Made of red bricks, it was three stories tall, the topmost floor having a Mansard roof. With the completion of this new building, toward the end of 1869, the capacity of the hospital was increased to "more than 50 patients"—and the institutional debt had been raised to $18,000. The first floor of this new structure held a reception room, nurses' office, doctors' lounge, pharmacy, and at least one operating room. A low, neat picket fence, whitewashed, enclosed the three buildings except at the portal through which people entered the central one. Female patients were safeguarded on the second and third floors, while male patients were segregated in the former dance hall. By the end of the year, 123 people had been admitted to St. Joseph's for treatment.

The only hospital in the area of Syracuse, St. Joseph's accepted patients from the general public. Even at that early date, the Sisters of St. Francis expressed their own philosophy toward the sick—as well as the seraphic saint's—when, in the charter they were required to present to the State of New York in 1870, they declared: "In the admittance and treatment of patients, no distinction shall be made because of theological belief, nationality, or color."

Given such examples of heroic virtue as were provided by the lady founders of her community, Sister Mary Anna could not falter when, in 1870, Father Fidelis summoned her to St. Joseph's Hospital. Even if she had not already become acquainted with sickness and death, from attending her aged father and ailing brother Leonhard as each lay dying at home, Sister Mary Anna would have remembered the charity of St. Francis toward the sick and needy, as well as she recalled "the thorny path" of Christ.

Sister Mary Anna performed her duties as nurse and administrator so well that Father Fidelis would not release her when, at the end of 1871, the sisters of the community imposed new offices upon her. At the Order's first General Chapter, held on December 27 and 28—with a General Visitator from Rome presiding, Commissary General Father Fidelis Dehm as secretary, and Father Bonaventure Keller as concilarius—the sisters elected Mother Bernardina to be their first Provincial Superior. The number of sisters, novices, and convents had increased to the point where the hierarchy in Rome and in the United States approved the creation of the higher office—and promotion for the wise and benevolent woman who led the group.

To assist Reverend Mother Bernardina the chapter elected Sister Mary Anna to be secretary-general of the province and directress of novices at St. Anthony's Convent. Considerate of Reverend Mother Bernardina's needs, and obedient to Father Dehm's will, Sister Mary Anna held all three positions for three exhausting years. As incumbent in those offices, she also served as a member of the Definitorium.

Beyond any doubt her duties as superior of the hospital were the most demanding. She administered it, from top to bottom, in every department, watching over sister-nurses, lay servants, physicians, patients, visitors, the buildings themselves and all their furnishings. She prepared the annual reports—based, of course, upon daily, weekly, and monthly accountings—that presented "The Board of State Commissioners of Public Charity" with all the pertinent information they required. This included the number of patients admitted and treated at St. Joseph's, and their several categories with respect to sex, age, condition at time of entry and time of release, and the sources of funds that paid for their care. Other figures told about the value of the land, buildings, personal property, and furniture; the size of the inevitable debt; the sources of income; the expenditures approved during the year by the hospital's Board of Trustees. And, when the balance sheet had been drawn, the amount of cash she had on hand. In her Annual Report of October 1, 1871, the first she prepared, cash on hand amounted to $36.25. Total receipts for the year had been $9,689.76, and total expenses, $9,653.51. Total indebtedness, as usual, far exceeded income: in 1871 it stood at $14,005.33, an encouraging reduction from $18,000 incurred in 1869. "Donations and voluntary contributions" amounted to only $381.54.

As usual, the hospital always needed money—and she was forever trying to find ways to bring in the needed silver and gold. She encouraged willing benefactors to organize fairs, bazaars, plays, concerts, and more popular entertainments at Shakespeare Hall, the Opera House, and other places of good repute. The cause of St. Joseph's, as a historian of Syracuse remembered half a century later, "hallowed the day after Thanksgiving as Donation Day. It came to be a time when hundreds gave, irrespective of creed, supplies of many kinds as well as funds to the charitable work." And, perforce, she addressed the necessary deferential letters to "the Right Reverend and Dear Bishop" in Albany, "asking permission from your Lordship to hold a Fair for the benefit of our Hospital." She wrote letters of thanks to His Lordship after the fairs had been held. And, with "Cards of Thanks" and letters to newspapers, she expressed gratitude to all the responsible people who, by their efforts, had made the affairs successful: "To the ever generous and liberal citizens of all classes who vied with each other in this friendly Sympathy for a charitable object, and which unity produced the success that has been realized, our thanks are due; and for them many a prayer will go up to the giver of all good from the hearts of those suffering creatures, who will be in future consoled by the comfort and attendance secured to them, through the results of this Fair."

She wrote personal letters of thanks to individual donors of gifts in money or in kind: to Mr. E. Eckett of Skaneateles, N. Y. (this one surely without sarcasm) for his "truly noble act of charity" in contributing a barrel of crackers to the hospital larder; and to "the kind-hearted" James Lighton for a "very generous donation of five barrels of flour." She thanked the members of the Syracuse Fire Department for a gift of $200; and Mrs. Doctor Pease (as Madame President and founder of the Hospital Ladies Aid Society) for the receipt of $400 earned at one of the society's functions. The Ladies' Aid Society also provided the hospital with innumerable articles needed in the care of patients, such as bed linens, towels, and bandages.

Every cent counted, in that straitened budget, and Mother Marianne never overlooked an opportunity to enlist the help of Syracuse's people. But neither did she forget to tell them of her appreciation for their help in whatever form they gave it. Some of her letters of thanks were composed according to forms which, like every busy administrator, she prepared once and thereafter kept on file in her desk, for copying in the future. Others, however, were originals, written for a special person alone. Many bear the marks of haste—as if she simply sat down, whenever she could spare a moment, picked up her pen, and wrote out the message, straight from the heart, without having time to think about niceties of composition or to read and revise whatever she had written. The letter of thanks she sent to the newspaper that has been quoted earlier is an example of work done in a hurry. It is also an unusual instance of her resorting to a rather turgid style, imitating the pompous mannerisms used by most writers of letters to editors in those days. For ordinary people, she trusted to the simple phrases and direct statements that made her letters both brief and clear.

Her letters of introduction certainly are models of brevity and clarity. She wrote them for trustworthy patients or parishioners who were seeking jobs in Syracuse or moving to other cities. And always, fulfilling a most melancholy duty, she sent letters of condolence to relatives of patients who died in the hospital.

When she was not busy caring for sick people or managing the routines of the hospital, she did not need to wonder what to do with her free seconds: upon that overladen desk a stack of memoranda, notes, requests, reports, requisitions, petitions, and unanswered correspondence always awaited her attention. And another stack of letters, concerned with another set of responsibilities, awaited her when she went to her tasks at St. Anthony's Convent. A directory of the period indicates that she lived at the hospital most of the time, along with the nurse-sisters under her charge. In going to and from the convent, she often walked, along poor roads and through fair weather or foul, over a distance that sisters today estimate would have taken about thirty to forty minutes of her valuable time. She did not need the exercise, but she would have welcomed the chance to think in relative peace and quiet.

During this hectic session of triple responsibility, Sister Marianne learned that her mother died in Utica on July 9, 1872, at the age of 69. Barbara Witzenbacher Koob, as devout a believer as her daughter, received the Last Sacraments from a priest of St. Joseph's Church. Her body was buried in St. Joseph's cemetery, near the grave of the husband she had survived for ten years. She was more fortunate than Peter Koob's first wife had been: of the ten children she bore, six still lived to mourn her.

Soon after she took up the duties as supervisor of St. Joseph's Hospital, Mother Marianne engaged in negotiations with far-sighted members of the medical profession in Syracuse and nearby Geneva. St. Joseph's provided both physicians and patients with the only genuine hospital facilities in a large part of central New York. The only medical college in that area was located in the village of Geneva, about 65 kilometers southwest of Syracuse. The college's faculty saw in St. Joseph's a means for improving the training of future physicians—and, almost as a secondary benefit, for providing patients with better care. Preliminary discussions with Franciscan officials favored a close relationship between the two institutions. Accordingly, in 1872 the entire Medical College of Geneva—faculty, students, library, museum, and such modest bits of equipment as a medical school needed in those uncomplicated years—was transferred to Syracuse and became the College of Physicians and Surgeons of that city's young university.

On October 23, 1872, soon after the start of the academic year, Mother Marianne wrote to Dr. John Van Duyn, "Registrar of the Medical College," concluding subsidiary arrangements concerning its students: "I am happy to inform you that the sisters of St. Joseph's Hospital cheerfully grant the medical students of the Syracuse University the privilege of having admission to the Hospital for clinical instruction."

She tactfully reminded Dr. Van Duyn of the need to discuss with the hospital's staff physicians the times at which medical students might visit St. Joseph's wards. In her exercise of cheerful charity she was also correct and diplomatic, having learned to be thoroughly aware of all the conflicts of personality, profession, and rank that are so easily set to quivering if the people involved are not treated with the respect they think is their due. This ability to smooth the way and to soothe the ego, by anticipating all sorts of problems, was one of her great strengths as an administrator, whether of the hospital or of a convent.

That same concern for fairness in personal relationships entered into her thoughts about institutional associations. When the need arose to consider costs, she did not hesitate to ask the medical college to bear a proper share of expenses for the clinical instruction of its students. In October 1874, in a letter to Dr. William T. Plant, "Registrar, College of Physicians & Surgeons," after telling him that "the privilege you ask for is cheerfully granted," as before, she went on to say: "It will not, I hope, be asking too much to request the medical department of your University to help us in the construction of the benches that may be needed for the accommodation of the students."

In establishing these cooperative arrangements between St. Joseph's and the medical school—a relationship by no means common in America at that time—Mother Marianne understood from the beginning how valuable the hospital's participation would be to her nurse-sisters as well as to physicians, students, and patients. The cooperation meant much more work for herself and for all members of the hospital staff. But to her the rewards of the association far exceeded the weight of the labor.

Most European and American hospitals in those days provided a patient with little more than "a bed to lie in and to die in," as many people said. With the bed came a small amount of nursing care, an occasional inspection by the patient's attending physician, and a bewildering pharmacopeia of "medicines"—almost all of which were utterly valueless in relieving pain or controlling infections. A patient recovered because his body's defenses, not his physician's therapy, enabled him to do so. And almost everyone said—and believed—that the sick one recovered or died because "God so willed it."

Mother Marianne knew that the kind of care St. Joseph's Hospital offered was better than nothing at all, but she also felt that it was not good enough. Being practical, rather than visionary, she achieved a synthesis of attitudes that was unique in a nursing sister of her time: she could be both charitable in the religious context and scientific in the medical approach.

In the interests of St. Joseph's patients, she took every available opportunity to improve the hospital's services. In this pioneering she was guided by the recommendations of the physicians who served on the hospital's staff or who taught in the medical school. When their suggestions for improvement required new techniques, she established them as soon as she could train her staff in the methods or could afford to buy the equipment or the material needed. Apparently she introduced the new concepts of sanitation, only then being practiced in Europe by Lord Lister and the few enlightened physicians who were aware of his work. In 1872 Louis Pasteur and Robert Koch had not yet completed the researches by which they would establish the fact that infectious diseases are caused by certain kinds of microorganisms. In 1872 a few physicians had learned, from Dr. Ignatz Semmelweiss's observations in Vienna and Dr. Oliver Wendell Holmes's in Boston, that if a doctor would only wash his hands thoroughly with soap and water before he assisted a woman in childbirth, he could reduce remarkably the chances that she would suffer from child-bed fever. And some surgeons were aware of Lister's spectacular achievements in antisepsis, by which he almost eliminated infections of surgical wounds by using diluted carbolic acid, applied to the skin before the incisions were made and sprayed as a fine mist in the air above the wound, while the surgeon performed the operation. The sharp clean odor of carbolic acid would have been detectable in the wards and operating theater of St. Joseph's Hospital. And the clean floors, walls, bedding, equipment, furnishings, nurses, patients, and physicians amazed both patients and visitors at St. Joseph's.

Compared with the glittering, palatial medical centers that Americans nowadays take for granted, St. Joseph's Hospital would be astonishingly primitive, in every respect. But a newspaperman who wandered into it in late 1874, when Mother Marianne was directing the institution, admired everything he saw:

"There is a laboratory, well stocked with medicines, the attending physician's private room, where he lodges overnight in case his services are required. The hospital wards with their clean, well-aired beds, and the excellent ventilation; the lime-whitened walls and ceiling, and the healthful location of the institution presenting all that is advantageous . . . the same cleanliness, good order, care and attention pervades every department throughout the hospital."

In that era, opium in its several forms—such as chandoo, laudanum, and morphine—was the only effective palliative for pain. Medicines for the *cure* of diseases of any cause simply did not exist. Nonetheless, hopeful men the world around had contrived to make innumerable preparations of every conceivable composition and texture in their attempts to find medicines to ease the ailments of mankind. Mother Marianne developed a great interest in the uses of whatever salves, emollients, lotions, electuaries, elixirs, infusions, tinctures, carminatives, purgatives, and other preparations the medical profession in Syracuse was recommending at the time. She herself learned how to compound many of those apothecary's concoctions and to relate them to the illnesses for which they should be employed. Her knowledge of this almost alchemical lore, considered as being even more magical in isolated Hawaii, so impressed several observers in the islands that they regarded her as "a professional druggist," and so described her in a Board of Health report. Such praise was exaggerated, of course; and she never claimed that degree of competence. But the fact that knowledgeable people expressed it in those complimentary terms indicates that she was interested in the *materia medica* employed in caring for sick bodies as well as in the spiritual consolations she brought to frightened souls.

And yet charity, Christian love, always found fuller expression in this sister who had renounced the world only to be called back into it at its miserable worst. The knotted rope around her waist, the weighted cross upon her bosom, declared that she had chosen to be penitent, humble, compassionate. But the fearlessness with which she went among the diseased and the dying, bringing the solace of a touch, a comforting word, a prayer, proved that she was no shallow pretender, hiding behind a dark habit and a vapid smile.

To her the dignity of an individual—that precious right that Americans had so recently gained for themselves—was most important. The dignity of an individual, she knew, was not incompatible with the Will of God. She protected her patients from those other afflictions that all too often are visited upon hospitalized people: the dangers of being looked upon as mere illustrative cases, rather than as persons, by eager students and insensitive professors of medicine. In the same letter in which she assured Dr. Plant "that we will strive to accommodate as many students as possible," she made another of her firm declarations: "I would merely add that the wishes of the patients with regard to their being brought before the Medical Students should be respected in every case." Throughout her long life, especially among the lepers of Hawaii, forsaken by all others, she did not relax in this concern for safeguarding the dignity of her patients.

Nonetheless, this cheerful and charitable executive could be very strict when the circumstances warranted. Such a need arose in 1876. A physician who had the privilege of admitting patients to St. Joseph's committed some offense which earned the disapproval of his colleagues. He may have committed an error of judgment, or he may have behaved "unethically," as physicians say among themselves; the facts of the case are not known. Sister Marianne's response to the problem caused by the erring doctor was immediate and clear: "... as one unfortunate case exactly resembling this has already occurred in the hospital, and has given us much trouble, we have decided not, under any circumstance, to permit it to occur again. Dr. _____ acknowledges his error to me. Why try to persist in shielding himself, when truth and honesty are against him. If he had been as frank with the Attendant Physicians at the hospital as he has been in his note to me, I have the charity to believe that they would have tried to shield him from blame.

"But under the circumstances he has no other way to do than to act as the etiquette of his Profession dictates."

This letter reveals another face of Mother Marianne, one not often shown. Here she is the formidable judge who, having been presented with evidence of guilt, must render a verdict upon the offender. The need to do so saddens her, hardens the very tone of her voice, causes the instinctive retreat into addressing him in the third person. She decrees that the "recreant" (to use her term) must be cast out. But in stripping the unfortunate physician of his privileges at St. Joseph's Hospital, she is kind enough not to rob him of his dignity as a man.

While all the chores and problems of running the hospital demanded her attention there, two other jobs used up the rest of her waking moments. Mercifully, her duties as directress of novices were relatively light, the community's system for managing them having been perfected by then. Even so, she would have had to supervise the course of training and the sisters to whom she delegated that responsibility; and she would have examined the novices at regular intervals the while, at all encounters, she cast an elder sister's appraising eye upon their persons and deportment. She had to write about them, too, informing parents when a daughter fell ill or reassuring them when a novice did not write home as often as they wished. And the report must be sent to the bishop when the novitiate approached its end and she recommended the young ladies for permission to profess their vows. In general, however, being novice mistress must have been something of a relaxation, compared with the continual distresses of the sick awaiting her at the hospital.

Serving as Mother Provincial Bernardina's secretary would have been both instructive and interesting. Managing the affairs of a whole province of the Order required an enormous amount of correspondence; a profound knowledge of the psychology of women (as well as of commissary generals and bishops); a thorough acquaintance with the rules by which Church and Order were maintained; and a limitless fund of patience and tact. By all accounts, Reverend Mother Bernardina and her principal assistant made an able team, who supervised the affairs of the expanding Order with a high degree of success and—as far as can be determined now—with only one serious embarrassment over a conflict of personalities and policies that they should have anticipated.

As secretary, Sister Marianne wrote most of Mother Bernardina's official correspondence in English. Sometimes she translated the Superior's letters, composed in German, at others she wrote directly in English after having learned Mother Bernardina's thoughts and decisions about a matter. And once in a while she sent out a letter or a directive written in High German, using the cursive Gothic script employed at the time. The amount of paper work she had to do, in that age before typewriters were in general use and carbon copies could be readily made, must have taken a great deal of time. And yet there is no evidence that she ever had the help of a copyist: all surviving documents are written in her own hand.

At Mother Bernardina's direction, she prepared the orders that summoned superiors from other convents to general chapters convoked in Syracuse. In several instances she surprised a sister in some distant convent with the news that the startled one had been elected to be a mother superior in yet another house—"to which you will proceed," Sister Marianne would conclude, in the accepted militaristic style, on a date she carefully specified. She notified parish priests, whether they belonged to the Friars Minor or to other orders, of decisions reached at meetings that concerned their relationships with the Franciscan sisters' convents and schools.

And always, of course, she transmitted required information to His Lordship in Albany.

In the summer of 1875 several of Mother Bernardina's charges gave him reason to make an inquiry. Between January and August five sisters of St. Francis departed from the Order. Several accused Mother Bernardina of "injustice" in one guise or another. Three fled from St. Teresa's Convent in Oswego. Of those, two actually descended upon Albany, to present their grievances in person to the bishop. Thus disturbed, he demanded explanations from Mother Bernardina.

"It is a very painful disturbance" indeed, Mother Bernardina (and her secretary) acknowledged in a preliminary reply to his Lordship. "The whole affair is so dark and complicated," they added, as they asked permission "to defer an explanation of the matter until after the Retreat." That respite was scheduled for a week early in August.

"The whole affair" was one of those complications that sooner or later happens in any religious community. Naturally, it gave scandal to the unimaginative, delight to the ribald, and anguish to Mother Bernardina.

The explanations the two ladies in Syracuse addressed to their bishop, late in August, was forthright, detailed, and convincing. They explained how Sister M. Agnes Spang, "unhappy" with having been St. Teresa's organist and choirmistress for nine boring thankless years, had rebelled against the "injustice" of Mother Bernardina, who would not allow her to move on to other tasks. They told how Father Joseph Wibbe of Oswego, apparently an autocratic priest and a virulent misogynist as well, encouraged Sister Agnes by "insulting [Mother Bernardina] and the Community in the roughest manner." Not content with detractions, he urged the disgruntled one to run away. She did so—and took her own sibling, Sister M. Clara Spang, as she went.

Some of the distress that can be introduced into convent life by mismatched women, who break down after spending several frustrating years in a community, can be glimpsed both in the incident itself and in Mother Bernardina's opinion of the reasons leading up to it. The five sisters who have left, she told the bishop, "are not indeed the best members, as has been reported to you, but only such who have been for years a source of grief and painful anxiety to their Superiors."

His Lordship must have agreed with Mother Bernardina's opinion. The Order's archives contain no more correspondence with the bishop about four of those defectors.

One of the troublesome five, however, did depart honorably and—happily for Mother Marianne—was not lost permanently to the Franciscans. Sister M. Bonaventure Caraher, whom another busy interfering reverend gentleman than Father Wibbe had persuaded to leave her position as superior of a new Franciscan convent at Burlington, N. J., came to the Motherhouse in Syracuse to apply for dispensation of her vows, saying she wanted to enter the community of the Sisters of Mercy. Her request was granted and she left St. Anthony

Convent on May 21, 1875. By August she regretted the move, asked to be readmitted to the Franciscan Order, and returned to Syracuse on September 2, 1875. She could not escape her destiny: to be a Sister of St. Francis, a loving disciple of Mother Bernardina, and—in the fullness of time—an invaluable member of Mother Marianne's mission in Hawaii.

Inevitably, in her role as secretary to Mother Bernardina, Sister Marianne also became confidante and adviser as well. She learned all about the affairs of the Order, and helped to find ways to manage it and the disparate personalities among the sisterhood. In the perennial contesting between religious women wanting to manage their own business and wilful men determined to mind it for them, she learned how to appease superiors in the masculine hierarchy without ever yielding too much control to them. Always protocol was observed, always daughterly obedience was expressed, and almost always the ladies won their points. By moving swiftly to prevent discord among the sisters, she succeeded in forestalling any more such embarrassments as the defecting five had caused Mother Bernardina just that once. If she had not known this maxim before then, she learned in 1875 that vigilance before dissension breaks out, not correction after it, is the mark of a good administrator. This decisiveness in all matters probably caused some sisters to consider her too "despotic," as Sister Dominica Cumming would charge, before many more years passed.

Reverend Mother Bernardina and her secretary were re-elected to their supervisory offices during a general chapter held at St. Anthony's Convent in December 1874. This time Mother Bernardina succeeded in persuading Father Fidelis Dehm to release Sister Marianne from her duties at St. Joseph's Hospital. He yielded, although reluctantly. And, as he feared, before long the hospital suffered from her absence. After serving for four months, the newly appointed supervisor resigned, for reasons of health. Apparently she was suffering from the illness that would take her life in two more years. Father Fidelis called Sister Marianne back to manage the hospital, and Mother Bernardina assigned her to that position. On April 26, 1875 she took charge of St. Joseph's for the third time. On this occasion Mother Bernardina made the concession: she relieved Sister Marianne of duties as directress of novices, but kept her as secretary-general to the Order. The load, although lightened somewhat, was still heavy.

It is possible that, during those years of incessant work, unremitting fatigue, inadequate diet, and continual exposure to consumptive patients in the hospital, if not to phthisic sisters in the convent, Sister Marianne herself contracted the pulmonary tuberculosis that would add to her trials in the years to come. On the other hand, it is also possible that she may have acquired the infection in childhood, as was the common experience in those years. Certainly she could have shown no overt signs of the disease during her novitiate, else she would not have been accepted into the Order.

Even without suffering from active tuberculosis she had causes enough to be weary. By December of 1877, when she wrote the letters summoning mother superiors from other convents to a general chapter to be held at St. Anthony's in Syracuse, the body, if not the spirit, was weakening. She ended at least one letter, addressed to Mother M. Helena, with a plea not seen before in her correspondence: "May I ask you to have the charity to remember me in your prayers. I have hard trials, and stand much in need of prayers." Not a complaint, certainly not a whimper, it is a call for strength from a servant who sees how much more work must be done before her labors for the Lord are ended.

Late in 1877 Mother Bernardina approached the end of her second three-year term as Provincial General, the last that would be permitted her according to the Order's constitutions at the time. She knew exactly whom she hoped would take her place. For thirteen years this spiritual daughter had been a great comfort to her, and for six years an invaluable aide. Nonetheless, because elections at Franciscan chapters in republican America are supposed to be reasonably democratic affairs, in which each sister votes according to the dictates of her conscience as it is instructed by Divine Providence, Mother Bernardina did not presume to tell her charges whom they should choose. She had asked Sister Marianne to write the proper instructions in that summoning letter: "You are . . . requested to pray with your Sisters daily, from now till then, that the good God may direct us all, to do what is best for our Community, and for His greater honour and glory."

At the general chapter on December 27, 1877, held "in the morning immediately after Mass," Reverend Mother Bernardina had the great satisfaction of seeing Sister Marianne elected to be the second Provincial Superior of the Sisters of the Order of St. Francis. Mother Marianne received a majority of the votes cast, in a nice demonstration that the democratic process had been observed. At the same meeting her sisters elected Reverend Mother Bernardina to be the superior of St. Joseph's Hospital.

Mother Bernardina bequeathed a thriving community to her successor: sixty-two professed sisters (an increase of twenty-three since 1871), nine school missions (instead of five), and two valued and expanded hospitals.

Three and a half years later, on July 14, 1881, at a general chapter, the assembled delegates voted unanimously to elect Reverend Mother Marianne to a second term as Provincial Superior. The first election in 1877 might have been a submitting to Mother Bernardina's implied wishes. The second election was a tribute to Mother Marianne alone.

During Mother Marianne's administration, the community added two new schools, one in Trenton, N. J., the other in Albany, N. Y.; purchased property for a further expansion of St. Elizabeth's Hospital in Utica; and replaced the inadequate chapel at the Motherhouse "with a beautiful Gothic structure of red tapestry brick." In 1883, before she left Syracuse, Mother Marianne was instrumental in planning the first large addition to St. Joseph's Hospital. (This new wing was completed in 1884.)

The general chapter of 1881 that gave such a vote of confidence to Mother Provincial Marianne also brought Sister Dominica Cumming back to Syracuse, as superior of St. Joseph's Hospital. In doing so, the chapter set the stage for the most serious conflict of Mother Marianne's career as provincial in Syracuse. Those two strong-willed women worked best when they lived far apart. In Syracuse they were simply too close for comfort. Given Sister Dominica's paranoia—and, we can suspect, Mother Marianne's watchful scrutiny over the hospital that, by then, she must have regarded with a special concern, not only because she was president of its Board of Directors—the proximity proved to be explosive.

The break came on August 3, 1882, "on the vigil of the Feast of St. Dominic," as the Chapter Records observed. Apparently it came as the culmination to several months of disagreement between the principals. Sister Dominica, in a burst of rage and despair, forgetting her vows, forgetting her love for the community, throwing away everything to which she had devoted herself for nineteen years, "left St. Joseph Hospital, telling the sisters she is going on a visit to the Motherhouse, but instead of doing this, she left the city to seek her happiness elsewhere." She sped to the home of relatives in Utica, and from there sent a letter to Syracuse in which "she begged Rev. Mother Provincial for Dispensation of her vows."

Mother Marianne's answer is not preserved. Whether it was placating in tone or chastising, it drew from Sister Dominica a strong reply, as brusque and direct as she was in person. During her entire career as Provincial, Mother Marianne could not have received another letter like it.

Using borrowed paper and a purple pencil to spell out her meaning, Sister Dominica began her rebuttal with heavy sarcasm, and rushed from that into recrimination:

"Yours was received—*many thanks*.

"I sorely regret that your conduct since Provincial has forced me to take the step I am about to take. My love for M. Antonia and the Sisters would not allow me to act otherwise than I am acting—I selected this time that I would not be obliged to say Goodbye. Therefore I retire, try to get my dispensation as soon as possible—I asked for it at Christmas—but did not receive it. . . .

"Wishing the dear Community God's blessing and that you may not continue to treat the members with despotism, as you are doing and as you have treated me. May God forgive you M. M. Ann but I must let you feel that the consequences of others as well as me, rests on your *conscience*. You say that I have been working for Satan since in the Convent—well now I must try to spend the remainder of my days for God. My soul I shall serve no matter where. . . ."

Mother Marianne's written response to Sister Dominica's accusation is not available. Although she herself preserved most scrupulously, for the Order's files, all the letters she received from Sister Dominica, the rebellious one did not save the communications addressed to her. More than likely Mother Marianne was not surprised by the charge, although as a good Franciscan and a woman of sensibility she would have been distressed by any hurt she may have caused a sister. After Mother Provincial Bernardina's softer regime, and the embarrassments of 1875 (when those four unhappy sisters left the Order), Mother Marianne probably had tightened discipline considerably and emphasized a more rigorous observance of the Rule. Now, by her flight and with her challenge, Sister Dominica presented Mother Marianne with a serious problem.

The easiest and quietest solution would have been to let the truculent sister go, indulging in the feeling that the Order would be well rid of her. But Mother Marianne did not take that course. Superiors in a Franciscan community are instructed to learn compassion and humility from the mistakes their charges make—or, as St. Francis himself said more than once, from their own mistakes, to which their companions are supposed to call their attention. Even though her letters are not available, other pieces of evidence—found in minutes of chapter meetings, correspondence pertaining to the case, and especially in Sister Dominica's own letters—all show that Mother Marianne was most sincerely concerned to rescue the distant sister from the consequences of her stormy departure.

The one-sided feud did have a happy ending, eventually. Sister Dominica's temper cooled, in time and with distance. Sober second thoughts, as they usually do, caused her to regret both haste and anger. A yearning for the life of the Rule, for the devotion to duty, grew stronger with each passing week. She asked to be allowed to return to the community.

Mother Marianne, with a generosity that Sister Dominica did not reject, recommended that the absent sister be accepted back into the fold. She skillfully directed the series of chapters, conferences with priest-superiors, and votings upon the proposal by members of the community. Of fifty-two sisters who had been professed for five years or more, fifty voted to restore Sister Dominica to her place. Finally, after more than a year of separation, with its attendant admonishments, corrections, and acts of penitence, Sister Dominica returned to the Motherhouse in Syracuse.

During the summer of 1883 apparently (Sister Dominica, unfortunately, never dated her letters), she wrote Mother Marianne a letter of thanks combined with explanations that set everything aright between them: "... I want you to put confidence in me, and do not think, she will do the same again. No; I shall not.—This foolish step had to be taken—it seems for my own good although for my great humiliation—.... I felt as though you hated me, despised all my doings, and sayings—in fine I became so desperate I could not help myself—for I was trying to do and work for the Community with the best will. You know how you felt. I admit—I acted foolish—consequently, I only look on my own side, and will try to make up for what I did wrong—humility would have overcome all, that came too late, to avoid my rash act..."

In another letter, probably sent soon after she stormed out of St. Joseph's Hospital, Sister Dominica gave another clue to Mother Marianne's method of guiding the community. After expressing concern about the sisters for tattling about her peccant self to priests, who thereupon carried the gossip to newspaper reporters, Sister Dominica conceded: "... I always blamed you for been so secret about things. Now I see the necessity of this and give you credit for it...."

Sister Dominica, better schooled in humility, reconciled with companions and superiors, returned in dignity that Mother Marianne was careful to safeguard. During the remainder of a long and useful life she caused no further scandal to the community.

Early in June 1883, during the second year of her second term as Provincial Superior, Mother Marianne received a letter from a priest assigned to the Catholic Mission in the Kingdom of Hawaii. He wrote from St. Mary's Institute, in Dayton, Ohio, where he had found refuge while making his quest:

Reverend Mother Superior:

I have passed 29 years of my life as a missionary in the Sandwich Islands. At present I am in America. My Bishop, Right Rev. Hermann requested by the King of the Archipelago and his government sent me to this country to look for Sisters, who would take charge of our Hospitals, and even of our schools, if it were possible. The King, remark it, and his counsellors are protestants.

I take, therefore, Reverend Mother, the liberty of addressing myself to you and begging you to assist us in our work. Yes, help us to procure the salvation of souls and to promote the glory of God and the interest of our holy religion by showing that the Catholic Religion alone is able to inspire her children with such devotedness, the fruit of true Christian Charity. It is this devotedness, that decided his Majesty the King to entrust to us the care of the Hospitals. Now, since our Sovereign is so well disposed, it would be a very sad case for the mission to disappoint him at present.

I am supplied with full power to transact business. My Bishop, the President of the Board of Health and the King chose me as *Special Commissary* to settle this affair. Besides I deposited in the California Bank of San-Francisco enough money to pay all the travelling expenses of the Sisters. One Hospital is already built at Honolulu, the capital of the Islands; and arrangements are taken to build two others.

With regard to the other conditions I find it very difficult to develop them in a letter. If you give me some hope to get the sisters I will at once pay you a visit, and explain verbaly the matters to you.

Have pity, Reverend Mother, on our poor sick, help us. Almighty God through the intercession of the Immaculate Virgin Mary will not fail to reward your charity.

Hoping a speedy and favorable answer, believe me to be, Reverend Mother, your devoted servant in the SS. Hearts of Jesus & Mary.

F. Leonor Fouesnel
Miss. Ap. des SS. CC.

When Mother Marianne sat down at her desk to answer him, she did not know how she could help the pleading priest.

But she did know that his cry for help must not go unanswered.

NOTES on Chapter II

1. Novitiate for Sisters of St. Francis: in 1862 the period of the novitiate lasted for only one year, and terminated with pronouncement of vows for life. A brief period of candidacy spent in a convent of the community, and lasting only a few months, preceded the novice status. See *Monthly Meetings: St. Francis and St. Anthony Convent* (Syracuse, N.Y.), for more details about acceptance/novitiate of Mother Marianne.

2. Ceremonies of investiture and of profession: names of participants, times, dates, and places are drawn from records in AS.

3. Mother Marianne: Profession of Vows and subsequent career: *Record of Perpetual Vows I.* (1861–1883). pp. 30–31. On these pages are entered, according to date, the succession of offices and duties which marked the course of Mother Marianne's career in the Order. *Record of Perpetual Vows I* is the current title used for the original book in German which contains the written vows and subsequent appointments of members of the early community in Syracuse. In the 1880s, the contents of this book were copied and continued in a larger book entitled *Record of Professed Sisters. Book I.* (1861–1900s). In the latter book, entries are written in English after July 1883. In 1942, Mother M. Margaret Haskin translated the earlier record book written in German, transcribing the information in a book which she entitled *Record of Professed Sisters. Book I. English Translation.* (1861–1883). Therefore, the same facts are found in two and sometimes three official record books of the Community. For the career of Mother Marianne, the first book is noted here for reference because it is the one containing her written Vows in her own handwriting.

4. Founding of the Order: In 1851 Mrs. Marie Anna Bachman, a widow, started a ministry in Philadelphia by opening a home for working girls. In that charitable endeavor she was assisted by her own younger sister, Barbara Boll. In 1854 Anna Dorn (later known as Mother Bernardina), a young woman from Bavaria, joined them in their work. When the three women agreed that they were called to form a religious community, Anna Dorn urged that they accept the Franciscan way of life. With the help of St. John Neumann, then Bishop of Philadelphia, they established the Philadelphia Foundation of Franciscan sisters. Mrs. Bachman, as

Mother Mary Francis, was the first superior general. Her sister, Barbara Boll, took the religious name Sister Mary Margaret (and in 1861 became the first superior general of another independent branch of the community, located in the Diocese of Buffalo, New York). In 1860, for legal reasons, Bishop James F. Wood, who succeeded Bishop Neumann to the See of Philadelphia, caused a separation of the sisters serving in Central New York State from the foundation in Philadelphia. With the approval of the Most Reverend John McCloskey, Bishop of the Diocese of Albany, the smaller group of sisters in New York formed a new community, under the direction of the Franciscan priests at Syracuse.

5. Mother Bernardina and founding of St. Elizabeth Hospital, Utica: (a) *General Chapters, Book I.* (1863–1876), p. 31; (b) Prandoni, 1960: *Greater Love,* p. 78.

6. Sister Dominica Cumming: (a) photographs; (b) letters to Mother Marianne 1882–1883; (c) *Record of Professed Sisters. Book I. English Translation* (1861–1883), Entry no. 8; (d) *General Chapters. Book I.* 1863–1940, p. 81; (e) *St. Joseph Hospital Minute Book.* p. 10; (f) *Council Meetings* 1891–1905, p. 18; (g) *Acta. Prov. Imm. Con. BMV 1871–89: Ad Historiam Provinciae, Bk.* 2, Archive of Friars Minor Conventual, Immaculate Conception Province, St. Anthony on Hudson, Rennselaer, N.Y.

7. St. Joseph's Hospital, founding and early years: (a) *General Chapters,* Book I, Insert pp. 40–41, written by Father Fidelis Dehm, April 6, 1869, and Minutes pp. 40–41, April 8, 1869; (b) *Onondaga County Medical Society 1905–1956,* Sesquicentennial, pp. 58–59; (c) Several hundred newspaper articles of 1869, 1870s, 1880s kept in a reference file for St. Joseph Hospital at the Onondaga Historical Association in Syracuse evidence the early trials of Mother Marianne at St. Joseph Hospital; (d) Prandoni, 1960: *Greater Love,* pp. 88–89.

8. First Provincial Chapters: (a) *General Chapters, Book I,* pp. 56–65; (b) Prandoni, 1960: *Greater Love,* p. 27.

9. Death of Mrs. Peter Koob, mother of Sister Mary Anna: *Record of Deaths 1842–1897,* St. Joseph's Parish, Utica.

10. Growth of the sisters' community: (a) Prandoni, 1960: *Greater Love,* pp. 29 and 31; (b) *Corporation Meetings III Franciscan Order 1862–1893; (c) General Chapters, Book I.*

11. Chapel at Motherhouse: In 1879, during Mother Marianne's first term of office as Provincial Superior, the small chapel in the little cobblestone Motherhouse was replaced by a new and larger one made of red brick, attached to the front of the convent.

12. At the time Mother Marianne left for Hawaii, St. Joseph Hospital was being expanded for the first time since it opened in 1869. In late 1883 and early 1884 the hospital was more than doubled in size by a large three-story wing added to the west side of the building and by other changes in the older wards.

13. Sister Dominica's last years: Although her demeanor may not have changed completely (even as late as 1895 she was being reprimanded for her quick temper) most of the inner rage was quieted, most of the time. For many years she worked "loyally and faithfully" as superior at St. Elizabeth Hospital in Utica. When age made her unfit for that responsibility, she served at St. Joseph Home in Beverly, N.J., as a teacher of religious instruction to children. She died in St. James Hospital in Newark, N.Y., at peace at last, on 4 December 1916, in her eighty-first year.

Chapter III

AN IRRESISTIBLE FORCE

AT HER DESK in the Motherhouse she answered Father Leonor's disturbing letter on June 5, 1883: "... I hardly know what to say. ... Shall I regard your kind invitation to join you in your missionary labors, as coming from God. This is a question that has been constantly on my mind. ... My interest is awakened and I feel an irresistible force drawing me to follow this call. ... "

Having confessed so much, she drew back as prudence raised its hand. She knew nothing of the Sandwich Islands, so remote from Syracuse that she must wonder where they lay and what they were like. And what of the poor sick, who needed care? She asked for details about "the place and its conditions." How will the hospitals be supported? Would the sisters be expected to collect money for operating them? Remembering her unending worries about St. Joseph's perpetual need for money, she inserted a frank objection: "(I would not like that.)"

She remembered as well many earlier and closer claims upon the services of her Order: "I see too many difficulties or rather impossibilities that could not be overcome, just now. We have already more work than we can do. ... "

Well aware of constraints upon her freedom of action, she warned—and, in the same sentence, encouraged: "Our Rev. Father Superior is at present in Europe, and without his approval I could not give you any hope of coming to your assistance although my heart and hands are more than willing to be at your service."

At the last, because compassion would not allow her to close the doors that St. Francis had opened, six hundred years before, she gave herself away: "I would beg the favor that you write me again about the matter. I may be of some help to you, if not now, it may be later."

She was caught, like a fish on a hook.

At the other end of the line, Father Leonor, thinking that he was the Fisherman, began to draw it in.

Of all the replies to the very artful letter of appeal he had sent out to heads of more than fifty Catholic institutions in the United States and Canada, Mother Marianne's was the only one that offered him some hope of help.

If ever Father Leonor Fouesnel had been a humble priest, very soon after his ordination, by 1883 he had elevated himself above that beginner's station. He liked to take the grander view—especially about himself. His many assorted talents (and they are not denied) helped him to rise in the hierarchy of the Congregation of the Sacred Hearts of Jesus and Mary, a European order, whose priests had been assigned as apostolic missionaries in the scattered isles of Polynesia. Among those scenes of endeavor were "the Sandwich Islands," as Father Leonor (and a great number of other insensitive folk) persisted in calling them, long after enlightened governments and instructed people referred to them as the Hawaiian Islands, in accordance with the wishes of their native inhabitants. In 1883 Father Leonor was transferred from his parish of Wailuku, on the Hawaiian island of Maui, to serve the diocesan bishop in Honolulu, capital city of the Kingdom of Hawaii. He assisted the prelate's aging executive secretary and, even more important, he helped His Lordship to plan the campaign by which nurses belonging to a Catholic order might be recruited for Hawaii's hospitals.

In both those capacities Fouesnel became a priestly politician, a vain and crafty man, given to vaunting his own part in any successful deal, to boasting of his connections with the great personages who dwelled in the infinitesimal pond of Honolulu. Jealous of his position, a martinet in enforcing the hierarchy's regulations, he fretted when a mere priest in Hawaii neglected to heed him. And he harassed when an underling failed to obey his rules to the letter. Inevitably, Fouesnel by his harsh words and actions became the archvillain in the life of Father Damien, one of those mere priests. And heaven, in achieving its wondrous ends, appointed Father Leonor to be the catalyst in changing the life of Mother Marianne.

In Nazareth of Ohio he leaped into action, playing out the Fisherman's line: ". . . your kind and welcome letter was like balsam for my heart," he burbled. "Your sentiments of devotedness and charity moved me to shed tears. . . . Oh would to God you could help us in our distress!"

He made a great show of telling her everything she wanted to know about the wonderful, the enlightened, the idyllic Sandwich Islands— and much else besides: "The government supports the hospitals and defrays all expenses. . . . The Sisters [will] direct the hospitals, the government will not interfere with their way of doing. . . . The Sisters will be helped and assisted by as many hands, as many servants as they would want, besides each Sister will receive from the government a salary of at least $20.00 per month. . . . The Sisters will be allowed to keep the Blessed Sacrament in their little chapel: but they will be obliged to go to Mass in the parish church. At Honolulu . . . a carriage will be ready to bring them to holy Mass every morning."

He extolled the climate: "delightful . . . the heat is temperated by the sea breeze; there is no frost, no snow in winter. As far as nature is concerned, you will find a kind of earthly Paradise in the Sandwich Islands."

He appealed to purest compassion and ignoblest ambition in the same breath: "Many [hospitals] are necessary and a vast field is open for your charity. May our dear Saviour wound your heart and influence it with still greater charity for the poor & weak."

He conjured up horror at the peril of encroachment by heretics: "a protestant government has sent me, if I should not succeed, very probably the same government would apply for Sisters at an Anglican Sisterhood and then our case would become almost hopeless."

He urged haste: "Write then, dear Sister, immediately, to your Rev. Father Provincial, and if he can send a favorable answer let him send a dispatch. I will pay all expenses. . . ."

He promised that soon, very soon, he would call in person upon her in Syracuse.

He ended this breathless effusion with appeals to "the name of Jesus, our Saviour, who cured the sick," and with the kind of glib promise that comes easily to wily persuaders but is never theirs to make: "Your crown shall be beautiful and your place in heaven will be in the company of Jesus and Mary."

No doubt Father Leonor was imbued with the noblest of motives and the most compelling of needs. He was also a churchman and a Frenchman, who used the pious expressions of the one with all the suavity of the other. That letter to Mother Marianne was full of untruths, half-truths, and subtle distortions of fact that he must have recognized as he put them down on paper. It gave as honest an appraisal of Hawaii in 1883 as does a tourist-baiting travel brochure about Waikiki today. After having lived for twenty-nine years in the Kingdom of Hawaii, for several weeks of those as an actual inter- mediary between his bishop and the nation's high officials, he must have known how timorous was his church, how weak was the coun- try's government, how empty its treasury, how unstable its ministries, and how reckless were the assurances he was showering upon Mother Marianne. In that letter full of guile, the only promise that he and Hawaii would fulfill without difficulty and delay was the one concern- ing the Blessed Sacrament. That indeed the Sisters would be given— eventually—to keep in their little chapel, but only because neither government nor church would have to spend a penny to buy it with.

And yet all those untruths told to Mother Marianne are as pleasant fables compared with the one great truth that he very carefully with- held. He did not tell her that he had come to America to find nurses who would minister to lepers.

Father Leonor invites sarcasm, caricature, even ridicule and rage. His verbosity, his utter inability to abide silence, either in person or in correspondence, make him sound like a buffoon. And, indeed, he is welcome as a kind of comic relief in what otherwise would be a rather somber chronicle of miserable lepers and willing martyrs. Nonethe- less, although he may have chosen to act the part of a buffoon, in reality he was no fool. In fact—as his determination to stretch the truth to suit his purpose indicates—he was a dangerous man. How- ever, to do him justice, in the matter of telling Mother Marianne—or any other mother superior—the truth about his mission, he was simply being cautious. How could he dare to mention the word leprosy in a letter of inquiry addressed to any convent and expect to be made welcome there as a seeker of nurses? Only too well aware of the horror built into that word, he hid behind a subtle evasion: "With regard to the other conditions I find it very difficult to develop them in a letter. If you give me some hope to get the Sisters, I will at once pay you a visit, and explain verbaly the matter to you."

Like all successful traveling salesmen, Father Leonor had learned that a man has to get his foot in the doorway first, before he can hope to make a sale.

Father Leonor had been sent upon this mission to America by his superior, Right Reverend Hermann Koeckemann, titular Bishop of Olba and Vicar Apostolic to the Sandwich Islands. Bishop Hermann (who had been elevated to that high position only in June of 1882) accepted the request to find nurses very reluctantly, and only after months of "discussions," not because he disdained lepers, but because he held serious doubts that the Hawaiian government would support the proposal for bringing nurse-sisters to the islands or for sustaining them once they had been imported. His Lordship, with the experience of the oppressed, had good reason to entertain those doubts: always he and his church suffered from being late arrivals in a country dominated by the most certitudinous of Protestants.

Congregational missionaries from America had reached the islands in 1820. Young and resolute New Englanders, they were full of evangelical zeal and that terrible Christian love which is determined to save the souls of heathens at any cost, even if the price of salvation is inhibition of the spirit and annihilation of the body. The American missionaries came just at the time when native Hawaiians—having been exposed to the mores and the immorality of the western world since Captain James Cook's expedition discovered their islands in 1778—had rejected their ancient deities and overthrown the established system of god-given taboos by which their society had been governed. In itself this rejection of the past was an admirable act of the intellect, achieved by the very priests and aristocrats whom that system had been designed to support. Unfortunately for them and the nation, however, they lacked the experience and the foresight to devise a new system of taboos to replace the one abandoned. In consequence, they lived amid the ruins of a shattered and disintegrating society, unfixed to a necessary code of conduct, and as adrift morally as is flotsam upon the open sea.

The Congregational missionaries and their families presented Hawaiians with worthy examples of a new code of morality. Even though it was rigid, demanding, and utterly intolerant of almost all their ancient customs and beliefs, the Hawaiian nobility recognized it as being better than no code at all, and far superior to the lawlessness of alien sailors, whalers, traders, and other wanderers who came to them across the Pacific Ocean. Within a decade of their arrival in the islands the American missionaries had won the ruling chiefs to Calvinism—and with them the masses of commoners who, perforce, followed the dictates of their lords. The Calvinists, by their influence over the native people, shaped the religious, political, intellectual, and cultural future of Hawaii. By 1850 they made it, in name at least, "a Christian nation." In doing so they also made Hawaii, until World

War II changed everything, more Puritanical and more conservative than New England itself had ever been since the end of the seventeenth century.

The first Roman Catholic missionary priests arrived in Honolulu in 1827. They were Frenchmen, members of the Congregation of the Sacred Hearts of Jesus and Mary, which operated out of its Motherhouse in Paris. They came too late to be welcomed by the ruling chiefs with the casual and generous aloha that would have been offered them before 1825. By 1827 the ruling chiefs had become Calvinists in attitude, if not always in spirit. They thought they saw in Catholicism's holy images and ancient rituals too many resemblances to the idols and the taboos of the old rejected pantheism. They were confused, too, by the mutual antagonism in matters of theology and nationality immediately displayed between Calvinist Americans and Catholic Frenchmen. Not for reasons of theology, but rather because they did not want to add another cause for divisiveness to their already confused existence, the ruling chiefs expelled the Catholic priests from the islands in 1831 and forbade their subjects to listen ever again to those preachers of "a false faith."

In best missionary tradition, Catholic priests—supported by strong representations from captains of visiting French and British warships—came back to the islands in 1837. The more bigoted among the ruling chiefs arranged a desultory persecution of Catholic converts, which consisted primarily of imprisonment, under one pretext or another, and enforced labor upon public works. Although this attempt at suppression was very mild, compared with the excesses in which bigots in other countries indulged, it was nonetheless a persecution. All American missionaries opposed the corporal punishments as such, but some condoned the philosophy that hoped to eradicate "Papistry," root, stock, and branch, from the vineyards in which they wanted to be the only workers for the Lord.

Fortunately, wiser counsellors among more sensible Protestant missionaries and Honolulu's merchants persuaded the ruling chiefs to end the persecution. A healthy fear of intervention and rebuke from captains of French frigates also helped to restrain the zealots. In 1839, with a model Declaration of Rights, young King Kamehameha III proclaimed freedom of worship for all his people.

By 1883 both Calvinists and Catholics had made accommodations to each other and to the larger world impinging upon them. Catholics were more than tolerated, having become the second largest Christian sect in the nation. But complete accord was far from being attained: ecumenism was something so remote as not to be imagined. Mormons, whose missionaries arrived unasked in 1852, and Episcopalians, whose priests came by invitation in 1862, were still sects too small to be threatening. But, of course, both Calvinists and Catholics opposed them as unwelcome interlopers.

Catholics still suffered somewhat because their priests had not come first. They were poorer in numbers, in wealth, social standing, political power. The dominant faction in government, business, society, and prestige was Protestant in both name and intention. Nowadays, the controlling clique of those years is mislabelled, with a sneer, "the missionaries." In fact, the missionaries as such—who most certainly had wielded moral and social power in the 1830s and 1840s—were long since dead by 1883, or so pushed aside by much more ruthless successors as to be without any political influence at all. Most of the men who ruled Hawaii in the 1870s and 1880s were the sons, grandsons, and sons-in-law of missionaries, and their employees. A wholly new breed of men, most of them had been born in the islands or had moved in from the United States. A very few came from England, Scotland, Germany, or Sweden (which in those years included Norway as well). They were the entrepreneurs who established the assorted businesses—especially the sugarcane plantations and "the service industries," as these are called today—which sustained the economy of Hawaii. Those businessmen were not really religious, as their parents may have been (and as their wives continued to be). They paid token respect to religion, but they were really interested in property, money, efficiency, security, and the comforts that all those advantages could gain. Bishop Hermann took their measure exactly: "The general spirit which prevails here," he wrote to Father Marcellin Bousquet, Superior General of the Congregation of the Sacred Hearts, in Paris, on July 2, 1883, "is one of a kind of liberalism of Free-masons, slightly aggressive, a combination of much religiosity more or less hypocritical."

Bishop Hermann, much as his Catholic mind and heart might disapprove of their spiritual state, had learned to respect those efficient Calvinists. He knew very well that they were the rulers of Hawaii. King Kalakaua, to his misfortune, never did learn this hard truth. Bishop Hermann sensed that, for the time being, but not for much longer, the men of power would allow Kalakaua the semblance of kingship, the expensive foolishnesses of royal estate according to European models, and the grandiose pretensions of "his lackey," Walter Murray Gibson, "the prime minister." The managers of Hawaii, not the king nor yet his premier, were the men about whom Bishop Hermann worried. He did not know how they would treat him and his church if ever they seized the power completely and forced the king from his throne.

His Lordship did not have a high opinion of either His Majesty or Walter Murray Gibson—whom he called "the old fox." "Between us," he confided to Father Bousquet in a Frenchman's balanced epigram, ". . . the word of the King has no great value, and the prime minister has too evil a past to be able to count on an assured future." He returned to this theme a month later, in January of 1883: "The King and his Prime Minister do not seem to have any great devotion for any religion whatsoever, but they wish to serve themselves for their own ends, by all religious denominations. This is modern politics. . . . The King has chosen the new Minister [who is] more crafty than honorable according to his personal history, in order to try to escape from servitude under the yoke of the Puritan clique who desire to dominate him absolutely. The King and his Minister were consequently unpopular through the intrigues of the members of the sect and also a large number of natives." The astute bishop recognized that King Kalakaua cultivated Catholics in hope of counteracting Puritans; but he also understood that "at a fatal moment He would sacrifice us to our enemies to appease their anger."

Bishop Hermann was far from blind to weaknesses in his own establishment. "Our principal sufferings come from obstacles—systematic secret persecutions on the part of heretics, and the weakness in the faith of our Catholics, white and native, with some commendable exceptions." But Puritans and Episcopalians, he added, "are always in sufficient accord against Catholicism, their common enemy."

By 1883, then, relationships between Catholics and Protestants had settled down to the kind of gossipy backbiting that is so typical of insular communities, and to a more hurtful sort of financial warfare in the national legislature. Very few Catholics ever got elected to that strident and undisciplined body, and consequently Catholic enterprises did not receive their fair share of public funds. The "persecutions" that Bishop Hermann complained about were not physical torments but financial slights and social insults. The Puritan members of the legislature, for example, found many "justifications" for denying public funds to Catholic schools, but applied none of the same logic to appropriations granted to several institutions run by Congregational missionaries which were included among the so-called government schools. Protestant newspapers either completely ignored Catholic events and persons, or used them as occasions for scolding native "Papists" for sinking to idolatry, bigotry, superstition, and (worst of all) subservience to Rome.

In this sort of psychological warfare, however, Catholics gave almost as much as they received. They, too, sniped at the heretical opposition from the jungle cover of legislative committees, press, pulpit, social gatherings, and private correspondence. In this sport, as his letters to Mother Marianne show, Father Leonor took a partisan's delight. Bishop Hermann, by nature more charitable and by position more judicious—or "prudent," as he wrote so often—indulged in none of Father Leonor's captiousness. But Bishop Hermann seems also to have been more sensitive about weaknesses in the Catholic position than in fact he needed to be. He remembered the difficulties that Catholic priests and converts had had to endure in the 1820s and 1830s, and he did not realize how in the 1880s materialism and liberalism were already corroding away the pillars of Protestant opposition.

Because he understood the past better than he foresaw the future, Bishop Hermann worried about holding his church's position in a country where an enemy *might* lurk behind every potted palm. Quite naturally, then, he did not respond with enthusiasm to a request from Walter Murray Gibson that he invite some "Sisters of Charity" (as Gibson loved to call them), to care for the lepers whom every white man and woman in Hawaii shunned in fear and revulsion. How could Bishop Hermann believe that Gibson, this Mormon turncoat, this heretic twice over, this profligate sinner and conniving man, was really serious in making such a proposal? And how could he possibly believe that, as Gibson so grandly promised, the government would pay all the expenses incurred by a program so costly, and withal so Catholic?

Despite his doubts, Bishop Hermann consented to listen politely After all, sinner and heretic though Gibson might be, he was the Prime Minister of the realm because he was the Minister of Foreign Affairs. He was also President of the Board of Health, President of the Board of Education, and holder of heaven only knew how many lesser dignities, in this Court of the *Opéra Buffe*. Much as the bishop might recoil from Gibson's "evil past," and question his claim upon any future, he conceded that no one in the kingdom was more concerned than Gibson about the health and well-being of the dying Hawaiian race. Gibson was Hawaii's conscience in matters of public health. No, he was more than just a conscience: where others talked, he *did* things to help the ailing discouraged natives. The man had written a book most excellent, *Sanitary Instructions for Hawaiians.* And, after he entered the government as a member of the legislature, he arranged to have that book printed, in two editions, one in English, the other in Hawaiian, in an effort to teach natives the modern ways to stay alive in a world that seemed so determined to destroy them. He introduced numerous bills in the legislature that were directed toward improving the medical and public health facilities of the country, for the benefit of all its residents. And, moreover, Gibson had made many friends among the natives, and quite a few enemies among the foreigners, because he fought for the rights of Hawaiians, urging them to direct their own destinies before the increasing numbers of white men decided to do that for them.

Gibson, this intruder into the businessmen's preserve, this poseur who was to play so flamboyant a role in the drama of Mother Marianne, was like a fox, as Bishop Hermann said, a sly renard come among fat sheep wanting only to graze safely in lush pastures. Beyond all compare, he was the most brilliant, complex, and imaginative man to live in Hawaii during the nineteenth century—and possibly in the twentieth as well. Hawaii desperately needed such a stimulating intellect, if only to excite the sheep, so to speak, to arouse thoughts in the minds of natives and foreign residents who were much too willing to go on existing as before, satisfying the body's demands without giving much consideration to those of the mind. Such provokers of thoughts are never welcome anywhere; and in Hawaii, as elsewhere, the old story was repeated. Gibson proved to be too provocative a personality for his time and place, too maddening to bear because he was too unpredictable, too self-centered, to control or to comprehend. In expressing his opinions, the better to stimulate those ruminative sheep, he alarmed the leaders without inspiring the flock. The leaders, shoulder to shoulder, glaring at this interloper, decided that such a dangerous foe could not be tolerated. He, for his part, entertained until too late a trickster's indifference to the opinions of such kind. He forgot, until too late, that even docile sheep will turn upon a predator.

In 1883, however, he had not yet alarmed the herd, although for at least twenty years its leaders most certainly had been regarding him with extreme suspicion.

Probably he would have been punished for his talents no matter where in the world he settled. Such is the fate of the superior man in any community—especially if, during the time of his thriving, he laughs at his enemies. From the beginning of his life to the end of it, Gibson sought excitement, controversy, provocation, confrontation, entertainment and, above all, preeminence. In deeds as well as in thoughts, he was a genuine romantic of the type his century created in such profusion. The whole course of his life was marked by cycles of achievements followed by defeats, of risings to heights and fallings into depths, of searchings for lofty ideals always rewarded by disappointments. The ups and downs in his life before 1883 had given him a past of the sort that Victorian novelists called "checkered." And Hawaii's Calvinists, in 1883, devoutly believed that it was being matched by a present far from spotless. Hawaii's Catholic hierarchy reserved judgment, not so much out of charity as from a fascination with the manner in which Gibson handled the ruling party—and, to be sure, from the ingrained wariness that marks the possible victim.

Gibson's earlier past, we can suspect, was more imagined than real. As he disclosed it, his story is a fabrication of contrived obscurities, attested accomplishments, and—alas!—of documented embarrassments. He told so many tales about himself—partly to confuse opponents, partly to beguile admirers, and mostly to protect his privacy—that separating fact from fancy has provided a game for historians ever since. He claimed that he was born aboard a ship at sea, during a perilous storm, and, naturally, of parents most noble. For reasons he never made quite clear, the infant babe, a changeling child, was brought up by a farm family in England. Perhaps he told the truth, perhaps he preferred to believe the pleasing delusion—which, after all, is a necessary component in legends about all the world's great heroes. More than likely, however, as diligent biographers have stated, in truth he was the infant born to a farm family in Northumberland, who was baptized Walter Murray Gibson in the village church at Kearsley on March 9, 1822.

During the early 1830s the Gibson family migrated to North America. They settled first in Montreal and then in 1837 moved to New York City. When he was fifteen Walter left home, to make his fortune. In South Carolina he met Rachel Lewis. If his account can be trusted, she was the daughter of a prosperous planter, "a fair gentle girl of my own age. . . . We rambled hand in hand to gather wild grapes and muscadine, then we would rest . . . at the foot of some great tree, and talk of our . . . fancies; and then without any thought as to mutual tastes, character, or fitness . . . but listening only to the music of our young voices, to the alluring notes of surrounding nature, and having only our young faces to admire—we loved; and long ere I was a man, we were married." So did the man Gibson, at the age of thirty-three, limn the portrait of the tender and innocent youth he wanted the world to see. In fact, as researchers have discovered, Rachel was several years older than he.

Six years after that precipitated marriage Rachel died, leaving Walter a widower with three children. He never married again—but whether he stayed unwed out of enduring inconsolable sorrow or out of sheerest relief at being a free man once more, is a question he was too subtle ever to answer.

Boredom, if not grief, drove him from that southern home. Entrusting his children to Rachel's kin, he returned to New York City, and found a job as "a commission agent and manufacturer." Although "wealth was eked out of this dull toil," he soon became bored with "the drudge and routine of the daily life of trade." Casting aside the constraints, but not the wealth, he joined the horde of gold hunters heading for California. Finding that sort of grubbing not to his liking, he traveled through Mexico and Central America. Apparently the plight of Spanish America's oppressed peoples aroused either his sympathies or his awareness of another and easier way to make a fortune. He hastened back to New York in 1851 and bought a schooner, intending to use it in smuggling a cargo of guns and ammunition to rebels in Guatemala. When revenue agents of the United States government foiled that scheme, he loaded his schooner with harmless ice for ballast and set sail for a destination he refused to divulge, probably because he himself did not know where he was going. Even though mutineers in his crew beset him, along with the hazards of the sea and other misfortunes, the valorous owner took his ship safely to the Cape Verde Islands, Brazil, the Cape of Good Hope, and eventually to the Netherlands East Indies. At Palembang in Sumatra he made a reckless offer, in writing, to supply armaments, ships, and sailors for a dissident sultan planning to rebel against Dutch rule. Dutch officials intercepted the letter, seized his ship, arrested Gibson upon a charge of "fomenting rebellion," and cast him into the infamous prison of Weltevreden at Batavia. The book he composed and published in 1855 about his experiences in the Netherlands Indies is as well written, fabulous, improbable, untrustworthy, romantic, and entertaining as is anything in the genre published by other adventurers of the era.

His fulsome apologies to those Dutch captors—"I have been but too often led away in life by some high-colored romantic idea. . . . I committed grave errors. . . . I make no defense . . . hoping that there will be found a sufficiency of extenuating circumstances to mitigate the sentence I may strictly deserve"—did not soften their hearts. They condemned him to a term of twelve years in Weltevreden—a sentence which, in that pest-hole, would have meant early death for the culprit. Somehow, probably with the connivance of the very officials who had sentenced him, and certainly with the assistance of "the beautiful princess" who taught him both Dutch and Javanese while he languished in that extraordinary jail, he managed to escape from Batavia just in time to avoid paying the exacted penalty.

During the return voyage to America, Gibson—full of smarting pride, fevered schemes, and a need to recoup his losses—transformed himself into an outraged American citizen, protesting ill treatment by a repressive and undemocratic foreign government. In Washington, D.C. he actually persuaded the Secretary of State to demand $100,000 from the Netherlands government as compensation for the loss of his ship and for false imprisonment. The Hague's rejection of Gibson's claims provoked a serious diplomatic crisis. Fortunately for the two countries, if not for the plaintiff, Gibson himself, hovering about the negotiators in Washington and in Paris, ruined his case: they recognized in him a deceiver, unscrupulous and unreliable. American diplomats withdrew their support, and Gibson's pretensions collapsed. Poorer in pocket, bruised in pride but undaunted in spirit, he set out for home, once again, to pick up the pieces.

Nathaniel Hawthorne, United States consul in Liverpool at the time, had met him on his first long slide back to America, on the way from Batavia. Gibson's charm entertained the novelist, but did not fool the consul: "A gentleman of refined manners, handsome figure, and remarkably intellectual aspect . . . he had the faculty of narrating [his] adventures with wonderful eloquence. . . . In fact, they were so admirably done that I could not more than half believe them. . . . There was an Oriental fragrance breathing through his talk, and an odor of the Spice Islands still lingering in his garments. . . ."

In New York Gibson looked about for new outlets for his talents.

He wrote his romantical book, gave lectures, was much seen about the town. By 1859 he decided to employ his abilities in promoting the cause of Mormons, then being harassed by the Federal government and its scandalized orthodox constituents. Still dreaming of the alluring East Indies and their engaging people, he offered his services to Mormon leaders in Utah, expressing interest in establishing "a colony upon an island of Central Oceanica." The elders of the church, thinking they had taken his measure and liking what they saw, sent him to help converts in the nearest thing to Oceania they had at the moment—the Kingdom of Hawaii, a Mormon mission field since 1852. In compliance with orders, Gibson, a dutiful convert to Mormonism, reached Honolulu on July 4, 1861. His daughter Talula accompanied him.

He took charge of "the City of Joseph" on the little island of Lanai, an agricultural colony that native Mormon converts had been struggling to develop since about 1853. If the island itself had been more habitable, the colony might have succeeded. But lack of rainfall denied settlers the water they needed for growing crops of wheat, cotton, and kitchen vegetables, and for raising herds of sheep and goats. Insect pests attacked the plants that did survive prolonged droughts, but no sea gulls came to the settlers' rescue, as they had done not long before near Salt Lake City in Utah. Inevitably, physical hardships mounted, to be further complicated by difficulties with personalities and policies. Soon the enterprise failed. Gibson's worldly ambitions and "heretical" attitudes may have been important factors contributing to the colony's decline. He made everyone work hard, including himself, saying that Hawaiian Mormons spent too much time in prayer and at meetings, not enough at laboring in the fields. He did seem to be less interested in being the devoted leader of a religious flock than in becoming the undisputed lord of Lanai's demesne. Whatever the reasons may have been, most of the 180 unhappy colonists departed, complaining about Gibson's "preaching false doctrines" and his "unwillingness to submit to the authority of the church." Gibson, always happy to welcome opportunity at her first knock, kept the land, turned the fields and streets of the ghostly City of Joseph into pastures for sheep and goats, and thereafter presided like a tribal patriarch over his own dusty barony. For his defects in dogma the Mormon elders excommunicated him in 1864. But they decided not to demand that he return the lands of the City of Joseph, inasmuch as the funds for leasing them from the Hawaiian government had been contributed by Gibson himself and the settlers, rather than by the church in Utah.

Honolulu's gossips and newspapermen never forgot this "scandalous" period in Gibson's progress. Later, when he was much in the public eye as King Kalakaua's prime minister and crony, they delighted in jeering both at him and at suspect Mormonism: "the Shepherd Saint of Lanai" they dubbed him, thinking that with the epithet (and a fifty-page tract documenting it) they revealed his villainy and the gullibility of Mormons everywhere. They did not realize how little such adolescent taunts bothered their target. He was not so stupid as not to know that enemies assailed him from all sides. But he was smart enough to have risen above them—most of the time. He had learned from his youthful mistakes, he did rise again after each fall. He was a man of invincible confidence in himself, of eternally renewed hope. And he had a sense of humor to sustain him that, predictably, too many of his sour antagonists lacked. Besides, he could comfort himself, the jeers of the envious are easier to bear when a man is getting what he wants.

In 1864, the first of those years of enjoying the simple life on Lanai, Gibson's two sons, John and Henry, joined him and Talula at the ranch. During the time he spent on Lanai Gibson learned to know and to like the Hawaiian people who were his employees or neighbors. He studied their language, customs, thoughts, hopes, sorrows, and frustrations. They responded to aloha with aloha. One day, when he was in danger of being drowned, a group of natives saved his life, at great risk to their own. Friendship evoked sympathy. His youthful concern with "the poor and the oppressed" of Central America was revived, and devoted to their counterparts in Hawaii. Now at last, after three decades of searching, he found his proper place, not only in Hawaii but also in life: he cast himself in the starring role that he would play for the years that were left to him.

In September 1872, in order to fulfill his purpose, he moved to Honolulu and founded a newspaper printed in both Hawaiian and English, naming it *Ka Nuhou,* or *The News.* On its masthead he set the legend, "a friend and champion of the Hawaiian people." It was both a promise to the Hawaiian people and a warning to the foreigners in their midst. In 1874, following the death of King Lunalilo, Gibson and his newspaper supported High Chief David Kalakaua's candidacy for election as the nation's next sovereign.

Among the many causes he supported in *Ka Nuhou's* columns were those concerned with the proper care of lepers who had been exiled to the isolated settlement on Molokai. In the issue of April 15, 1873, he printed a plea that would have profound consequences, not only in Hawaii. "If a noble Christian priest, preacher or sister," he declared, "should be inspired to go and sacrifice a life to console these poor wretches, that would be a royal soul to shine forever on a throne reared by human love." The style is unmistakably Gibsonian. But so, also, was the idea: like much else that he advocated, it was original, generous, thought-provoking—and timely.

Early in May 1873, Bishop Louis Maigret, first Vicar Apostolic of the Holy See in Hawaii (and the indomitable missionary priest who established the Catholic Church in these islands), met with most of the priests of his diocese. They gathered at Wailuku, on the island of Maui, for the consecration of St. Anthony's Church. Inevitably, they talked about Gibson's appeal in *Ka Nuhou,* reminding them of cries for help they had been hearing for years from Catholic patients confined in the Leper Settlement at Kalawao, on the island of Molokai. Several of the fathers expressed their willingness to go to Kalawao, to join the lepers segregated there. But Bishop Louis, sharing the general horror of the disease and the place, refused to assign anyone to a permanent station in the Settlement. He did agree, however, to sending a succession of priests, each to serve for a short period, perhaps for a term as long as three months, but no longer. The willing man Bishop Louis chose to start the cycle of visits was Father Damien de Veuster, a young and vigorous priest he himself had ordained at the Cathedral of Our Lady of Peace in Honolulu, almost nine years earlier.

Bishop Louis and his chosen companion landed at Kalawao on May 10, 1873. The *Kilauea,* the interisland steamer that brought them, also unloaded fifty lepers from Maui and several head of cattle. Aboard the same ship, a few hours later, Bishop Maigret, "sick at heart," resumed his journey to Honolulu. But Damien had come to stay. Two days after he arrived he wrote to his superior in Honolulu, asking him to intercede with the bishop: "I am willing to devote my life to the leprosy victims. It is absolutely necessary for a priest to remain here. The harvest is ripe. The sick are arriving by the boatloads. They die in droves!"

Gibson heard the news about Damien's having gone to Kalawao almost as soon as the *Kilauea* delivered Bishop Maigret in Honolulu, and many days before ever Damien's request reached his superiors. Excited as well as misinformed, Gibson published an article in *Ka Nuhou* on Tuesday, May 13. It rather settled the problem for everybody:

"*A Christian Hero.* We have often said that the poor outcast lepers of Molokai, without pastor or physician, afforded an opportunity for the exercise of a noble Christian heroism, and we are happy to say that the hero has been found. When the *Kilauea* touched at Kalawao last Saturday, [Bishop] Maigret and Father Damien. . . went ashore. The venerable Bishop addressed the lepers with many comforting words, and introduced to them the good father, who had volunteered to live with them and for them. Father Damien formed this resolution at the time and was left ashore among the lepers without a home or a change of clothing except such as the lepers offer. We care not what this man's theology may be, he is surely a Christian Hero."

By 1878 neither the rustic attractions of Lanai nor an editor's career in Honolulu appealed anymore to Gibson's restless mind. In search of a constituency, he moved briefly to the port town of Lahaina on the island of Maui, just across the narrow channel from Lanai, and stood for office as a legislator. Natives elected their white champion to represent them and reaffirmed their trust, in impressive numbers, in 1880 and 1882. In May 1882 King Kalakaua appointed Gibson Minister of Foreign Affairs, making him in effect premier of the cabinet. Gibson, proclaiming "a new departure in Hawaiian politics," declared his intention to appoint more natives to higher positions in government and supported it by including one in his first cabinet. While most enfranchised Hawaiians rejoiced over Gibson's rise to power, Honolulu's businessmen shuddered. As United States Minister J. M. Comly reported home to Washington, Gibson himself and his cabinet were "looked upon with apprehension and dread by the foreigners who do the business and pay the taxes of the country."

In 1882, when he initiated a search for Sisters of Charity, Gibson would have been about sixty years old. He was tall and lean, almost gaunt, being both consumptive and hectic. He could not be considered handsome in the usual sense, yet he was attractive in a thespian sort of way. Although Bishop Hermann and many other townsfolk, thinking of his mind, called him a sly fox, in person he resembled a goat much more: he had the long narrow head, the curved nose, heavy-lidded eyes, and tapered white beard of a sexagenarian Pan. Probably more to sustain his reputation as a devilish fellow than out of concupiscence, he cultivated a certain reputation to match the satyr's guise. "My hair may be white," he would allow, in all the improper places, "but my heart is still green." Thus forewarned, and always looking for the worst in every one, Honolulu's Puritans fully expected to find a pair of horns hidden beneath those hoary locks, so artfully arranged, and cloven hooves within the polished boots. Had they known Hawthorne's description of him, they would have laughed at the reference to "the Oriental fragrance breathing through his talk . . . the odor of the Spice Islands still lingering in his garments." Honolulu's Calvinists preferred to believe that "the Old Devil" reeked rather of hell-fire and brimstone.

And yet, much as his enemies would have relished the chance to smear him with the pitch of scandal, they could never really find any to hurl at him. Either the old goat was cleverer at hiding his spoor than they were at tracing it, or else—the inimitable showman!—he deceived them with easy stories presented as performances. Yet in all this busyness on Gibson's part, a perceptive observer would have seen not a capering Don Juan but a lonely Don Quixote, somewhat out of touch with Philistine reality because he was so full of imaginings—and therefore somewhat ridiculous and, despite all his show of good cheer, more than a little saddening.

Whether consciously or not, Gibson had fashioned himself in the style of the romantic heroes of his era, as they were revealed in such sources as Sir Walter Scott's novels and Alfred Lord Tennyson's poems. His speeches, letters, courtly manners, and public deeds all declare his models. Unlike those of his adversaries, his letters, articles, and speeches are pleasures to read because they are the works of a literate man, because he knew the meanings of words and loved to use them in the service of wit as well as of policy. Like those heroes of yore, he was driven more by the needs of the spirit than by the tumults of the body. The body's imperatives he could have appeased readily enough in the free and easy quarters of Honolulu. The fact that he did not seem to do so eventually caused his enemies to conclude that he was beyond their reach on that score. Until near the end of his career, they were forced to attack his public policies rather than his innocent private indulgences. His political maneuverings gave them reasons aplenty for resenting him.

His questing intellect had not been easily satisfied in this insular setting. For its sake, he plunged into politics as the best forum for his talents that Hawaii could offer. He reveled in the maneuverings and machinations employed by politicians, both in and out of the legislature. He enjoyed the writing of articles for newspapers, couched in the flowing rhythms and convoluted sentences of the time, equally fluent in English or in Hawaiian. He delighted in those public occasions when he might deliver, not mere speeches but long, flowery, grandiloquent *addresses,* which displayed his mastery of both languages as well as an admirable skill in arousing the emotions of all listeners, whether friendly or inimical. He enjoyed the sheer fun of stirring people up. He transformed with touches of beauty the tawdry, grimy, mildewed town in which his stolid contemporaries seemed perfectly content to abide. With his remembrances of beauty seen in Paris, London, Washington, New York, he persuaded the government to tear down a score of ancient sagging residences in Honolulu's very heart and to raise in their place a faëry palace, fit for a king to dwell in.

Like that other mad haole in Hawaii's royal history, Robert Crichton Wyllie—who, a generation earlier, while serving as a cabinet minister to Kamehameha III and Kamehameha IV, introduced the protocol of the Congress of Vienna into Hawaii's tiny court—Gibson loved the panoply and the pomp of high position. In the palace, in the legislature, at a ball held in one or another of Honolulu's few worldly mansions, he liked to be the center of attention. He hated to yield the stage to anyone—except, of course, to his patron, the king. He succeeded so well in serving king, country, and himself that, toward the end of his career, he had elbowed almost everyone else aside and was managing almost all the business of government, both domestic and foreign. The few islanders cultivated enough to have heard about "The Mikado" were enchanted to discover that Gilbert and Sullivan in their operetta had created the veritable model for Walter Murray Gibson. Snickering among themselves, those adversaries in Hawaii referred to him as "Pooh Bah, Lord High-Everything-Else." None of them realized how, against their chorus of nonentities, Gibson with his florid arias and witty recitatives quite stole the show.

Humorless enemies, unable to appreciate their local Pooh Bah, accused him of being unscrupulous and unprincipled, if not utterly immoral. They did not admire his capacities, imitate his virtues, accord him worth. They called him villain, rascal, Machiavelli, Mephistopheles, trouble-maker, scoundrel, renegade, hate-monger, fool, traitor, charlatan, kanaka-lover, and half a dozen coarser epithets. To be sure, he did not play the game of politics according to the rules of conduct that most other haoles professed to follow. They smarted and writhed and cursed when, time after time, Gibson's "tricks" won still another prize of which they did not approve. But a man should be known by the testimony of his friends, as well as by the attacks of his antagonists. Gibson's friends, while he lived and after he died, were given little chance to express their opinions in lasting print. Yet his friends were numerous, and represented all of Hawaii's classes and races. Their misfortune, and his, lay in the fact that, in the end, they belonged to the losing side.

He did not deserve his enemies' unqualified condemnation, if only because he was too shrewd, and also too kind, to be the complete villain all the time. Of course he maneuvered and manipulated, schemed and cajoled and pressured, to win his goals. So did his rivals—but they resented his ability to manage people and facts so expertly as to win much more often than they did. To them he must have been, all the time, a cause for fury and execration. Most of all, they hated him because he was the one strong man in all Hawaii who stood up and opposed their burghers' complacencies and exploiters' plans. Moreover, forty years of experience with people and governments half the world around had made him wiser: until toward the very end, he knew when to veer off from pushing a campaign designed to promote a special cause, when to yield in a legislative debate or a showdown over votes. He loved to win, but he also knew how to lose gracefully. And when he did win, he treated his opponents with greater generosity than ever they accorded him in their times of triumph.

As did many another man who sought power in Hawaii, Gibson sincerely believed that he labored to help the country and all its people. He did not enlarge his personal estate nearly as much as did most of the kingdom's sugar planters and businessmen. He amassed no great fortune, lived in no ostentatious manner. He seemed to be content with the income from his ranch on Lanai and with the salary of $12,000 a year he earned as minister to the king. They kept him in comfort and enabled him to make modest gifts to relatives and to friends. He was a good family man, enjoying the affections and the company of children and grandchildren. Because they were not so generous, or so flamboyant, Gibson's adversaries hinted that he had his hand in the government's till, or accepted bribes from foreign entrepreneurs, such as Claus Spreckels, the Sugar Baron from California who wanted to be the Sugar King in Hawaii. These accusations, frequently raised though never proved, kept Gibson's reputation perpetually tarnished and, as his diaries show, distressed him more than he cared to admit in public.

In summary, he seems to have liked best the playing with power, not the acquiring of wealth. He preferred to dazzle people, not to use them to further his ends. He enjoyed envisioning great goals, not organizing the boring details by which they might be attained. He thought of himself as a lion, stalking through Honolulu's social jungles, not as the fox or the goat—or the Devil—his adversaries imagined. In many instances the actions he proposed to the government, the bills he introduced in the legislature, were concerned with benefits too long withheld from the public, such as the beginning of a sewerage system for Honolulu (whose citizens were frequent victims of intestinal infections caused by microorganisms in water supplies and foodstuffs polluted with fecal material not properly removed from the community). He recommended programs to achieve other improvements in public health, such as hospitals on outlying islands and the importing of nurses to care for lepers. He advised government-sponsored immigration of "cognate peoples" in order to fill the empty land left desolate by the destruction of the Hawaiian race. Because they still lingered among his memories, he thought the handsome people of Sumatra would make ideal settlers in the Hawaiian realm. He supported building the graceful new Iolani Palace and holding King Kalakaua's belated coronation, with all its "extravagant entertainments," because he believed they would help to raise the morale of native Hawaiians even more than they contributed to the self-esteem of the king. About the palace he declared, forthrightly, "it is essential to the dignity and security of a throne that it should be upheld by appropriate surroundings of domain and mansion."

The very flair with which Gibson spoke and dealt, and, always, his championing of the rights of natives (much too silent) against the intentions of businessmen (much too vociferous), earned for him the antipathy of many residents who approved neither his expensive proposals nor his unorthodox methods for realizing them.

In their eyes his greatest crime was something they called "fiscal irresponsibility." With his free imaginings and romantic illusions (and Hawaii's empty treasury), Gibson—like certain other ministers to extravagant monarchs in larger countries—had discovered the principle of deficit-financing. He recognized that in order to make money a country must spend money—even if it doesn't have much of that commodity to expend. And so he persuaded his government to spend freely, even lavishly by contemporary standards, using borrowed money for its programs. His businessmen-adversaries—bookkeepers and budget-balancers to a man—recoiled, aghast at such madness.

For this "irresponsibility," and for some other fantastic notions much more foolish, which toward the end he and King Kalakaua conceived between them, Gibson's enemies would bring him down at the last.

Gibson allayed Bishop Hermann's suspicions about the government's intentions when he said that the king and the queen strongly supported his proposal to bring Sisters of Charity to Hawaii. Indeed, the queen herself may have been the first to think about bringing in hospital sisters, and, having done so, asked Gibson's help in making the necessary arrangements.

Their Majesties, too, were much distressed by the plight of the lepers—as they were appalled by the rate at which their people were dying away. Although no one could really say how many Hawaiians lived in these islands in 1778, when Captain James Cook discovered them, most estimates placed the number at a figure between 200,000 and 300,000. The most recent census, taken in 1878, had counted only 44,088 living Hawaiians. The infectious diseases of foreigners, to which Hawaiians had not been exposed before 1778, had been killing them, in waves of epidemics and in insidious smolderings of chronic ailments, ever since that fateful year. Of all those pitiless plagues, leprosy was one of the more recent to arrive—and, by every standard, the most horrendous. No one knew what caused it, where it came from, when it was introduced, or how it was spread. The first case of leprosy to be seen in a native Hawaiian was recognized only in 1840. By 1882 the epidemic had afflicted thousands of Hawaiians, as well as a few scores of immigrants of other races. It gave no sign of waning. And, even more frightening, no one anywhere in the world knew how to cure it.

Weeks of discussions and of pondering followed Gibson's first conversation with Bishop Hermann. They held other meetings, sometimes at Iolani Palace with the king, or with the queen, or occasionally with both. More often Gibson went alone to the diocesan chancery adjoining the Cathedral of Our Lady of Peace. Always His Lordship weighed the need to safeguard his church against the undoubted value of bringing in Catholic nurses who would minister to neglected lepers. Father Leonor, and others, pointed out the obvious: what a blow to Protestant pride that would be! To have Catholic sisters step in where Protestants feared to tread. But, His Lordship cautioned them, how can we be sure that the government will support this proposal? Whatever the king and Gibson want, the Puritans too often will deny. And who will pay the expenses for bringing those sisters to Honolulu? And for keeping them here? Assuredly we cannot, the bishop mourned, because we do not have the money....

Meanwhile, Gibson had been directing his powers of persuasion upon influential members of the Board of Health and of the legislature. On January 4, 1883, as recently appointed President of the Board of Health, he brought all these preliminary explorations to an official conclusion in a formal letter, written upon Department of Foreign Affairs stationery, and addressed to "the Lord Bishop of Olba."

It is a dignified presentation of the country's need for "trained faithful nurses" and of Gibson's belief that "no where could this invaluable assistance be obtained so readily as within the ranks of the blessed Sisterhoods of Charity who have in various parts of the Earth devoted themselves to the care of the sick and the needy."

He has received authorization from the Board of Health "to invite eight or more Sisters of Charity to come to the rescue of our sick people," and to pay for their "travelling expenses in first class accommodations" as well as for their "comfortable lodgement and subsistence" after they arrive in Hawaii.

The last paragraph of this document presents Gibson at his rolling orotund best: "Now, my Lord, as I am aware that eminent Institutions of Charity such as I have referred to, and this Country needs, abound in the Catholic Church, and as I feel assured that your representation of our needs would be all influential, I make an appeal, and offer an invitation through your Lordship, to Sisters of Charity of the Catholic Church, to come to the help of the sick of this country, and I doubt not I may proffer to them in advance the profound obligation and gracious recognition of Their Majesties, the thanks of His Majesty's Government, and the blessings of the Hawaiian People."

At last Bishop Hermann was persuaded that Gibson and His Majesty could keep their part of the agreement. "The middle class"— by which he meant the tax-paying businessmen and their representatives in the legislature—"have already declared their approval for the undertaking," His Lordship wrote to Father Bousquet on February 8, 1883, "but they wish to let the government act.... Mr. Gibson... wants to give us all guarantees desired that we should not have the slightest doubt about the establishment of the Sisters required, and wishes to deposit a sum of money in my hands." His Lordship nimbly sidestepped that possible fiscal trap by leaving the matter of financing entirely in the hands of the capable President of the Board of Health.

Bishop Koeckemann agreed to begin a search for "hospital sisters," as he preferred to call them. From Paris, Father Bousquet sent a letter suggesting that Father Leonor be chosen as the emissary to go in search of the sisters. Inasmuch as, during a journey to America in the previous year, Father Leonor had persuaded the Society of Mary to send a group of brothers to teach in Catholic boys' schools in Hawaii, Father Bousquet believed that his experience would make him equally successful in a search for hospital sisters.

Father Leonor would depart with high hopes, many ideas, "a double commission," and a long list that a visiting Jesuit priest and Bishop Hermann had helped him to compile. First he would ask help from the Sisters of St. Vincent de Paul. If they were not interested, he would approach the Sisters of St. Joseph. If they said no, he would turn to the Little Sisters of the Poor. In the event that not one of those well known orders responded, Father Leonor was empowered to approach "some other Congregation already established in America." The three consultants in Honolulu agreed that sisters from America would be best, for this essentially American community. Sisters from Ireland would not be good, because they had a tendency "when they are prevailing to become ill adapted, not to say unmanageable."

Gibson, a skilled publicist whom Father Leonor must have admired for that virtuosity if not for other talents, planted articles in island newspapers he controlled, expressing hope that some Sisters of Charity might be persuaded to come to Hawaii. And, always alert to ways of capturing the public interest anywhere, he equipped Father Leonor with a commission from the king, written in impeccable Hawaiian. Armed with this esoteric document, letters to the several Hawaiian consuls stationed in seaports of the United States, his list of Catholic institutions in America, and government gold sufficient to meet all expenses, Father Leonor sailed from Honolulu on April 11, 1883, aboard the S. S. *Australia.*

Neither he nor Bishop Hermann forgot for a moment that, wherever he might find them, the hospital sisters were going to be valuable pawns in the unceasing struggle being waged against the Puritans. Because Catholics were second in this contest for supremacy, they must try harder—and worry more. But, unlike the heretic leaders, Catholics would count upon an invincible ally: "As we have God on our side," the bishop assured his Superior General in Paris on May 2,

1883, "we hope for real success with time, without glamour, by patience and perseverance. . . ."

Father Leonor, as he enjoyed doing, took a gloomier view of prospects. On April 13, two days out to sea, he wrote "Mon Cher Reverend Père" (probably Father Bousquet) a protracted plaint, recounting at length the woes afflicting his brother-priests, and bemoaning his own tribulations, present and future: "I am of age," he began, in English, before reverting to his native French. He was 61 years old in 1883, overworked and weary, like all priests, and he did not look with pleasure upon this second expedition into alien and alarming America. ". . . the great uncertainty of succeeding in the searches I am going to make," worried him. So, also, did the attitudes of certain Calvinists at home in Honolulu: ". . . *this* voyage, made in the name of the government of His Majesty (Protestant), to get Catholic sisters who can only draw great credit to Catholicism—this is something they will not forgive me for . . . I have been challenged in the streets of Honolulu by Protestants who [formerly] seemed almost friendly and who now grind their teeth and shake their fists at me. If I succeed they will be obliged to [line illegible], but if I fail it will be a day of public rejoicing for them. . . ."

In Syracuse events moved swiftly under the joint impetus of Father Leonor's insistence and Mother Marianne's interest. The development of their history is revealed in the letters they exchanged. It becomes even more complex, more episodic, as the third party in their negotiations, Father Joseph M. Lesen, is drawn into the planning.

Early in July 1883 Father Leonor called upon the Sisters of St. Francis in Syracuse. "The person whom you will send for me," he instructed Mother Marianne, "will recognize me at my large white beard." That adornment was unmistakable, the personage behind it vastly imposing. Mother Marianne's emissary could not have missed him among the crowds of people pushing through the depot in Syracuse. He was short and stocky, his bulk somewhat reduced in consequence of "the violent colics" from which he, the tourist in a strange land, had been suffering since early in June. A veritable St. Nicholas, he was bedecked with an enormous fluffy white cascade of a beard that flared out from cheekbones to chest, and a cavalryman's full brush of a mustache to go with it. Tiny oval spectacles in gold wire frames rode upon the fleshy nose. The pale eyes behind them were small and shrewd. They could twinkle, when he allowed them to, or weep when he called for tears, or blaze with wrath in a calculated tantrum. Above the high smooth brow the hair on his head, closely trimmed and forcefully brushed down, deferred in every filament to that exuberant beard. Father Leonor's photographs, letters, performances present a man who was altogether pleased with himself.

In Syracuse he was both busy and ill. He spent several days as a patient of Mother Bernardina's in St. Joseph Hospital, and seems to have used the hospital as his base of operations.

He departed the city on July 9—provided that a long article about him published that same day in the Syracuse *Evening Herald* can be trusted any more than its contents can be. The clever public relations man, exuding charm in all directions despite his sickness, Father Leonor had granted the press an interview.

Headlines proclaimed an exotic novelty:

FROM KING KALAKAUA

SISTERS OF CHARITY INVITED TO THE SANDWICH ISLANDS

The reporter led off with a long excerpt in Hawaiian, much misspelled. It is the introduction to King Kalakaua's letter presenting Father Leonor Fouesnel as his Special Sanitary Commissioner. Presumably the reporter—enchanted by those strings of lovely vowels, the paucity of obstructive consonants, the absolute unintelligibility of this specimen of what (with the typical white man's superlative insensitivity) Father Leonor called "the Kanaka language"—wanted to share this evocative bit of barbarism with the *Evening Herald's* readers.

Ever theatrical, even in the heat of summer, Father Leonor grabbed attention from the very start. "'I am not yet acquainted with your climate,' said Father Leonor, as he sat this morning in the cheerful reception room at St. Joseph's Hospital, and asked to have the window closed on account of the cool breeze." Whereupon Father Leonor proceeded to discourse about Hawaii's climate, people, himself, Catholics (and uncapitalized protestants by omission), himself, the sugar industry, sugar magnates, laborers and wage scales, laws, himself, King Kalakaua ("who is a good friend of mine"), and, finally, about himself and the reason for his presence in Syracuse: "to secure, if possible, the services of sisters to work in the government hospital. . . . I have been in several states and in the Canadas, and have met with more encouragement in Syracuse than anywhere else."

The article, in all that it says about Hawaii, is just such a collection of misstatements as every uncomprehending reporter always extracts about any place from the briefest of interviews with any garrulous celebrity come to town. And, as usual, the celebrity maintained later that he was much misunderstood: "he did not correctly copy my papers in Kanaka, commited in the rest some inexactness, and inserted things I did not tell him. It is disagreeable. His intention was good, and I thank him for it; but he did not reach his aim."

Missing from that record of an amiable, expansive conversation, however, is the one word that would have galvanized the reporter into a frenzy, and thrilled his readers with horror.

Father Leonor, although he loved to talk, also knew when to keep a secret. But when he met Mother Marianne, perhaps in a room at the hospital, possibly in the parlor at St. Anthony's Convent, he had to tell her the truth.

And, in telling the truth about the plight of Hawaii's lepers, he won her for their need.

More than forty years later, on Molokai, Sister Leopoldina Burns was asked to write her memories of Mother Marianne and of the beginning of the Franciscans' mission in Hawaii. Sister Leopoldina, as a Franciscan historian has said recently, "could not spell or punctuate very well, but she certainly could tell a story." She began her reminiscences with an account of the day when Father Leonor spoke to the sisters and novices in St. Anthony's Convent:

". . . His story was sad, how he had gone from one community to an other begging for workers but not one community would accept the work. Our gentle Mother said she would gladly accept the work if the sisters would be willing so she called the Sisters and Novices . . . so we all heard the good Father's sad story. His voice chocked and tears were in His wonderful kind eyes as he told us of the sad need of Sisters in the Islands and of what little success He had until He came to us and now he said your good Mother has given me great hope. We returned to the novitiate and the next day Sister Boneventure came to write the names of the volunteers and nearly all the novices volunteered to go . . . many Sisters requested for the work in the Islands. . . ."

Very much encouraged by the sympathetic reception he had won from the Sisters of St. Francis (if not from their acting Provincial Minister, Father Francis Neubauer, with whom he had had an unproductive interview), Father Leonor returned to St. Mary's Institute at Nazareth, near Dayton, Ohio. Although he had already concluded negotiations with officials of the Society of Mary for sending a party of teaching brothers to Honolulu, he needed that sanctuary. The poor man still suffered from those attacks of colic.

On July 12 Mother Marianne sent her answer to him at Nazareth:

". . . I am hungry for the work and I wish with all my heart to be one of the chosen Ones, whose privilege it will be, to sacrifice themselves for the salvation of the souls of the poor Islanders. . . . I am not afraid of any disease, hence it would be my greatest delight even to minister to the abandoned "lepers." . . . Waking and sleeping, I am on the Islands. Do not laugh at me, for being so wholly absorbed in that one wish, one thought, to be a worker in that large field. . . ."

Surely, as she wrote this letter of promise and personal commitment, she was remembering the injunction of St. Francis that is reported by Thomas of Celano: "He wished that all things should sing pilgrimage and exile."

Even so, she knew that the decision was not entirely hers to make. She began this revealing letter to Father Leonor with mention of "our own good Father Provincial." She has just learned that he "has arrived in New York. . . . We look for him every day and I hope his good heart will approve my wish to accept the work in the name of the great St. Francis. . . ."

Too late to save his lambs from the marauder, Father Joseph M. Lesen returned to Syracuse on July 11, after having been in Europe for more than a year. Since the death of his predecessor, about three years before, Father Lesen had been serving as Acting Provincial Minister of all the Minor Conventuals of St. Francis in the United States. Although his motherhouse—which included a seminary and a monastery—was located in Syracuse, the duties involved in administering his vast province often took him away from home.

Mother Marianne promptly informed him of Father Leonor's quest for nurse-sisters, and of her own interest in responding to it. Father Lesen immediately called a special chapter at St. Anthony's Convent, scheduling it for July 16. Nine sisters attended, among them Mother

Provincial Marianne, Mother Bernardina, and Mother Antonia. Father Lesen presided, a superior without a vote.

The minutes of that chapter are very brief, as they always were in those efficient days. "The usual prayers were said." Father Leonor's letter was read, "in which he made application for Sisters to take charge of Hospitals and Schools" in the Sandwich Islands. "The matter was fully discussed, after which ballotation took place." When the ballots were counted, "8 were in the affirmative, 1 in the negative."

As Father Lesen looked around him, upon those nine naive women, as untouched by the ugliness of the world as their coifs and collars were unspotted by Syracuse's dirt, his heart must have softened with wonder. They could never have seen a leper, mutilated, loathsome, stinking, revolting—and pitiable. Yet, having merely heard about the plight of those miserable creatures, eight of these earnest women ignored the horror and thought only of the pity. They wanted to minister to hundreds of lepers, dwelling in a foreign country half a world away, when they had work enough to do here at home, for several lifetimes, among the sick and the poor of central New York. And yet, in a casual balloting that lasted for only a few minutes, after a superficial discussion that took scarcely an hour, they willingly gave their lives away, to an alien people in a distant land they'd never heard of before Father Leonor came among them, purveying his message of holy martyrdom. They had no idea what perils awaited them, what trials of body and spirit, before ever they reached the Sandwich Islands. They had not the faintest notion about the dangers that might beset them there, once they were installed in those promised hospitals. Nor did they understand in the slightest the ghastliness of a lazar house in which they would see nothing but the devastated faces, the spreading sores, the decaying limbs of men and women whose flesh had died long before their hearts ceased to beat. . . . And yet these women voted, calmly, eight to one, asking for pilgrimage and exile, as if they were deciding upon the kind of tea to be offered to guests in the visitors' parlor, rather than resolving to sacrifice their lives to the lepers for whom that interloper had pleaded so affectingly. . . .

Mother of God, sighed Father Lesen. Blessed Virgin, help them, he prayed. Father Lesen, unlike the visitor from Honolulu, did not perform upon his little stage. A neat, clean-shaven, tight-lipped, pale little man, who wore the same kind of wire-rimmed spectacles that adorned Father Leonor, and who slicked down his fair hair in precisely the same way, Father Lesen looked the very picture of a grudging martinet. But he was far from being one in fact. He guarded with a paternal benevolence the welfare of the Franciscan priests, brothers, and sisters for whom Rome made him responsible; and always he was most especially concerned about these innocent sisters in Syracuse. A scholar before he became an administrator (he had learned seven languages in the course of earning the degree of a doctor of philosophy in philology), Lesen was also a man of the world and a bureaucrat in the church.

With a fine awareness of the deviousness of villains (for, despite his Germanic name and appearance, he was an Italian by birth and association), and with due regard for protocol, Father Lesen raised some fundamental questions about Father Leonor's propositions—and, by inference, about the credibility of the jolly persuader himself. He offered some further words of advice and caution to his unworldly daughters in Christ. Only then did he adjourn the chapter, after "the usual prayers."

The very next morning Mother Marianne sent a telegram to Father Leonor, then in Chicago, rushing back to Honolulu. Her telegram told him the sense of the chapter's vote, perhaps even mentioned Father Lesen's conditional consent, but also must have indicated that the matter was not yet settled in Hawaii's favor. A letter written the same day explained why: "after an hour's deliberation it was resolved that we send Sisters to your assistance." However, although Father Lesen has expressed "a deep interest" in the call from Hawaii, he "cannot permit or sanction our going so far from home until he receives letters from your good Bishop. The import of these letters, yourself and the good Bishop will understand."

She added a paragraph that, in view of her intense desire "to be a worker in that large field," revealed an awareness that obedience to higher authority might yet prevent her from answering the call: the chapter "deemed necessary ... that either myself, or another older member acompany the Sisters to the Island to see them established, as also to learn more about the place and its requirements so we may be better able to supply the mission in future with proper subjects."

Even as he rolled off into the wide and dangerous West, Father Leonor could not go quietly. In Syracuse, during their conversations, Mother Marianne must have mentioned the possibility of sending six sisters, at the most, for the mission in Hawaii. From Chicago, on July 18, after receiving her telegram of the seventeenth, he sent a letter of joyful gratification—in which he promised to sign the protocol of conditions the sisters had discussed in Syracuse, if she would send the document to him in San Francisco. In closing, he asked for "*seven Sisters instead of six,*" underlining the words for emphasis. Eight days later, in San Francisco, having envisioned an empire of his own while crossing the continent, he repeated his promises and raised the bid: "I beg of you most earnestly not to send me less than 7 or 8 Sisters, one or two of whom should be competent to teach school." Relative pronouns he managed perfectly, but relative proportions he could never keep straight.

On July 31 Father Leonor returned to Honolulu in gladsome triumph, with two achievements of his "double commission" to report to Bishop Hermann: the imminent arrival of a company of Brothers of Mary, coming to revive a languishing Catholic school for boys in Honolulu; and the strong probability that soon a company of Sisters of St. Francis would be coming to take charge of the hospital for moribund lepers.

Despite his volubility in person and on paper, Father Leonor did keep the few promises which he had the power to fulfill. He (and Mother Marianne) knew very well what Father Lesen was thinking about when he asked for "letters from your good Bishop."

He lost no time in putting his good bishop to work. "On the very day I arrived here," he wrote to Mother Marianne from Honolulu, "I availed myself of the first opportunity to settle the affair which interests us so much and I called on His Hawaiian Majesty, with His Lordship the Vicar Apostolic, and the President of the Board of Health. The result of our visit was that all your conditions were accepted."

After that conference at the very summit of power in the Lilliput of Hawaii, the modest machinery of both Catholic Church and Protestant State began to turn, at a speed almost without precedent in this abode of procrastination. His Lordship instructed Father Leonor to prepare the letters that welcomed the presence of the Sisters of St. Francis in his diocese and promised them his protection. Into the same packet of documents Father Leonor slipped two authenticating portrait photographs. One presented his grandly opulent self, the bearer of that magnificence of a beard. The other depicted Bishop Hermann, sitting like a shy peasant frightened of the camera. If, in those simpler times,

Rome had chosen bishops according to the authority evidenced in their photographs, Koeckemann would have lost to Fouesnel on all points.

His superior in Paris valued him as much as did his bishop in Honolulu. The very same ship that returned Father Leonor to the bishop's side also brought the official document from Father Bousquet that elevated him to the position of vice-provincial. He did not announce this promotion in his letter to Mother Marianne. He simply signed himself "Fr. Leonor Fouesnel, Miss. Ap. Vice Prov."

And added an unnecessary postscript: "With the photographs of the Bishop Hermann and mine."

In Trenton, New Jersey, where business of the Order engaged him, Father Lesen received a nunciatory communication from Father Leonor in Honolulu, presenting unofficially the assurances of esteem and identification that soon his bishop would be making formally. On August 22 Father Lesen, in his indubitable Italian voice, sent instructions to Mother Marianne: "Call together the Chapter, and write down the conditions under which you intend to accept definitively the mission. . . . Think to what may seem necessary to insure the future state of the mission and of the Sisters, and then send to me the conclusions which you will have arrived to."

He worried still about the welfare of the sisters who might be going to Honolulu. Several of them believed, as they had told him, "that they could come back from the Mission after some number of years. If this is the case, it must be one of the conditions of acceptance. As also any Sister that at any time should become unfit to remain, should also have the right of returning to her Community by expense of the Missions."

Lesen also expressed concern about "the right of opening schools"—the secondary interest that Father Leonor was pressing more vigorously from Honolulu than ever he had done in Syracuse. "This is a point which now has to be acted upon and not left to future good will . . . in order to avoyd future misunderstanding."

In Honolulu Father Leonor, on August 27, contrived a progress report to Mother Marianne that managed to be fuller than usual of ambiguities: ". . . I take my time, before I tell you start, come because I want you to find everything in good order on your arrival, and in this country with the best will in the world, things go so slow, that I think it rather safe, to advise you, not to hurry your voyage. I have no doubt, in two weeks from here, I will have the pleasure of telling you to come. . . ."

He relished the prospect of seeing hecatombs of Calvinists writhing in Honolulu's streets as—by his arranging—salt was heaped upon their raw wounds: "As for the reception, everything is settled. The royal carriages will meet you at the steamer etc. . . ."

In parting he made his contribution to ecumenical good will: "People longes for your arrival, with the utmost impatience, save however the protestant ministers, who, I suppose, would rather see you wrecked on the way. . . ."

Late in August the official documents from Father Leonor's bishop in Honolulu reached Father Lesen in Albany, New York. Lesen, on August 27, dashed off a note to Mother Marianne: "We need to let the Bishop know what the Community intends to do, and when."

Mother Marianne knew quite well what the Community intended to do, if not exactly when. On September 1 she wrote to a travel agency in New York City, asking "for information regarding the rates from New York to San Francisco for 5 or 6 [and] from there to the Sandwich Islands." She also inquired about the possibility of "a reduction on the ordinary rates" (which certain railroads accorded recognized representatives of the several religions) and requested "the favor of an early reply."

The following day, more than a week after the chapter had been held, she replied to Father Lesen, in one of the longest letters she ever wrote. She challenged him upon one point after another in the understanding that she believed she had concluded with Father Leonor.

"In compliance to your wish," she began, in the language of obedience and yet with just the slightest suggestion of impatience, "I called a meeting of the Chapter to consider, again, the already well considered question of accepting the invitation to go to the 'Sandwich Islands.' The result was the same as in the previous Chapter."

Several years later, in Honolulu, when she prepared a very brief account of the beginning of the Franciscan mission to Hawaii, she remembered that this chapter was held on August 26, 1883. The support of the community was overwhelming: "Previous to the holding of the Chapter thirty five Sisters cheerfully volunteered to go to the Islands."

Now, in her letter to Father Lesen, she listed once again the proposals from Father Leonor that the chapter had accepted: how the Hawaiian government would support the hospitals which the sisters would manage, underwrite all expenses of their journey to Honolulu, pay each sister a salary of $20 a month, and provide them with all the servants they might need. Therefore, she declared, "the temporal welfare of the Sisters is as favorable as can be desired, and I do not see any more conditions to make unless it be to ask the kind protection of the King and his government."

She did not presume to be as certain about the sisters' spiritual welfare. After pointing out that they would keep the Blessed Sacrament in their chapel and would go each morning to hear Mass at the parish church, she transferred the problem to Father Lesen: "I do not know what your idea is about [these spiritual needs]. I beg you to make the necessary conditions. You know better than we do how to express yourself to the Bishop, and you also know what rights we are entitled to as regular religious."

Lest Father Lesen be suspecting that the Bishop of Olba in Honolulu would take the Franciscan sisters under his jurisdiction to the disadvantage of the Franciscans, she tried to reassure her Provincial Minister: "We wish the Sisters, who may go there, to remain united to the Community here, and they must in all matters of importance depend on the decisions of the Superiors here. . . . I do not know what else to say in the matter—Please Father, if I may ask the favor, have all the conditions that you may deem necessary written out. . . ."

She reminded her Provincial Minister of an accomplished fact which he may have been trying to forget: "We have already given our word that we accepted, and would come as early as possible. Therefore it is too late to exchange letters. By the consul's letter you will see that the Sisters are expected to leave San Francisco on the 24 or 25 of this month, consequently they would have to start from here on the 13 or 14. Please give us full instruction what to do."

But at the last, as she must, she bowed before her superior's will. ". . . As for myself going, I would wish a written permission from you as my Superior. It was a decision of the Chapter that I should accompany the Sisters and see them established. However, if you think otherwise, I am your humble subject, and shall cheerfully submit to anything you say. Should it be your wish that I go, then please state, in the written permission, how long I may remain. In case you do not approve of my going please appoint some one else."

This is a strangely disturbing letter, because it is unlike all the others that Mother Marianne composed during her career as Provincial, whenever she wrote, with respect, to a superior. The more one reads it, the more one can read into it. The measured pace, the soft tone, the placating words, and the conventional phrases, all perfectly proper, are just what one would expect of a dutiful woman, commanded to obedience, who is addressing her powerful superior in an authoritarian and masculine hierarchy. And yet the logic, the persistent flow of counterargument, the stubborn unwillingness to accept without question a superior's will are there as well, and all are signs of a deep-seated hope. This letter cannot be read as having been composed by a member of a religious order at her patient and acquiescent and unthinking best. It is, rather, the work of a strong-willed, tenacious, indomitable woman who is striving to gain her goal with all the weapons that she can employ. She who wants desperately to be "a worker in that chosen field" is not willing to give up her great hope without a struggle.

In the manner of holy men and holy women who recognize at last their true vocation, she has identified her hope with God's will. And, in order to fulfill God's will, she tries to convey her hope to a superior who is not yet able to recognize what God is requiring her to do.

In responding to that intense conviction, she is willing to throw away the high position and the great power she has gained after seventeen years of hard work and completest dedication to the purposes of the Sisters of St. Francis. Whether or not she realized this, she is telling Father Lesen that many another sister can be just as good a provincial superior as I am. But only I can be the mother to those pitiful lepers, Only I can establish a community of our sisters there, in that suffering land. . . .

Moreover, this long letter is even more troubling in another sense. It is confounding because of what it does *not* say. She could manage a busy hospital, a motherhouse, a whole province of convents and schools, with exemplary efficiency and conspicuous success. The fact that she did so, to the satisfaction of superiors and colleagues, means that she thought of all the factors involved in administration, anticipated all needs, prevented all organizational crises, and kept almost all her human charges under control, if not blissfully happy. But she applied none of her abilities as organizer and planner and manager of projects in New York to defining the details of the mission that she yearned to establish in Hawaii. Despite Father Lesen's frequent adjurations to think ahead, to stipulate all the conditions under which she and her sisters would agree to work in Honolulu, she did not add a single one to those that Father Leonor presented in his first letter. And despite her recognition of that pompous little man's weaknesses of character—for surely she was shrewd enough a judge of people not to have been fooled by him for a minute—she accepted everything he said without question or qualification. Not once, in the several letters concerning the mission to Honolulu that she wrote to Father Leonor or to Father Lesen did she indicate that she was thinking about even the most basic circumstances under which she and her company would live. For a woman of her intelligence and efficiency, this lack of interest in the practical aspects of maintaining a mission is nothing less than astonishing.

Until one remembers that, for a woman of her great faith and utmost dedication, those matters were unimportant. To worry about such details was to bargain with God. For a mission of such worth, she believed—with the same trust that moved St. Francis and St. Clare and all their poor brothers and sisters—faith must be enough. She did not put her trust in Father Leonor, nor even in his bishop. She cast all her cares upon the Lord. And God, she knew, would sustain her.

While Mother Marianne's letter traveled toward him, Father Lesen returned to Trenton, New Jersey. From there, on September 3, he wrote to her, almost gaily: "It is time to give an answer to the Bishop of the Sandwich Islands. Let me know then something about what you have resolved. I commence to fear, that, when the conclusion had to be made most of the great-courage-showing Sisters demurred, and you have now difficulty to make up the gang. Any how let me know how matters stand, that we may see what to do, not to blame ourselves. . . ."

When, a day or so later, her long letter reached him, he understood at once that he could not keep her from going upon that perilous mission. She herself had become an irresistible force, beyond stopping. He could have ordered her to stay at home in Syracuse, by arguing that she was needed there, or even by simply refusing to give her permission to depart. He did not even point out, once again, how she had not yet obtained a contract from Hawaii, in which all the details of her mission's duties and reimbursements were properly specified.

But he did nothing of the sort. He capitulated, perhaps because he trusted in her good sense, demonstrated so often before, probably because he thought that, in any event, she would be gone for only a short while. He let her go, with his blessing—and in doing so lost her to a higher cause.

He did not know, just as she herself did not know, how strangely confused she was, in heart and in mind. In her statements to him, and to companion sisters, she declared that she would be absent from Syracuse for only a short time, just long enough to establish the mission in Honolulu. Yet, from the very beginning, her letters to Father Leonor reveal a passionate commitment to the new kind of life he has offered her. In her heart, she has already made the sacrifice, by which she will remain in the islands, "working for God."

But the heart, as it must, kept its secret. She could not lie to herself, as she could not lie to Father Lesen or to any one else. And so she suppressed this knowledge, admitting it rarely, if ever, to her consciousness. Saints and sinners alike can do this easily enough, as circumstances demand. But saints are strengthened by the certainty that God himself will decide the issue, when the time comes.

On September 9 Father Lesen sent her the *nunc dimittis* she so earnestly wanted, along with "the letter of the Consul and the travelling papers." Still concerned about lesser matters, he added suggestions for other stipulations in their contractual understanding with the bishop in Honolulu. He urged her to make provisions that would allow the Sisters to return to their Community in America, if they wished, or in case of necessity or at the end of a specified time, such as twelve years, at the expense of the government.

In answer to her question about how long she could stay in the Sandwich Islands, he gave her completest freedom: "Use of your prudence and come back when You see matters settled."

With a tenderness that bares the heart of this good man, he bade her and her company a father's farewell: "My blessing be upon You and the other Sisters and accompany you all in your way, and home safe. I shall daily remember you in the Holy Sacrifice, and pray God that He bless your undertaking. I hope it will be for the greater glory of God, and the salvation of souls, which is our paramount end, and do not see any real danger that it shall not succeed. Certainly those Sisters that volunteered to go should not think that they are going to a place of rest or joy, but to a field of labor and privation. If they wish to make this sacrifice to God, let it be perfect cheerfully accepting what bitterness be in it. . . .

"Write when you leave even if only a postal card. Do the same when in San Francisco, as also as soon as You are in Honolulu.

"I put you all under the protection of Jesus, Mary, Joseph, and St. Raphael, and giving you again my blessing I remain Yours in Christ. . . ."

Mother Marianne chose six sisters to go with her to the Sandwich Islands. She could not spare even one more from labors at St. Joseph's Hospital or from other missions of the community. The courageous seven became subjects for admiration, or envy, or grieving to the sisters and novices who would remain at home.

During this extremely busy time, the whole problem of arranging Sister Dominica Cumming's return to the community also demanded much of Mother Marianne's attention. She must have drawn some comfort from the concluding paragraph of the letter Sister Dominica wrote her about then, asking for her confidence and trust. Sister Dominica, still living in Utica, had heard about the mission being planned for Hawaii. No better proof of her complete submission can be found than in her plea to be chosen as a member of that company: ". . . You write to Rev. Joseph [Lesen], ask him about me going with you. if you and M. Antonia say so, you can coax him. I can do the cooking for them. I can carry your satchel, too. Pray for me, answer soon. Believe me very sincere in all my resolutions. M. E. C."

Mother Marianne told the members of the mission that they would depart from Syracuse as soon as the signal came from Father Leonor. His most recent letter, and the Hawaiian consul's communication from San Francisco, mentioned that a steamer would be sailing from that port on September 23 or 24. The consul said, further, that he had been "instructed to secure convenient staterooms" aboard that vessel, and enclosed in his letter a draft for $1,200 to cover expenses incurred in traveling across the continent. Accustomed to her level of efficiency, not yet aware how slowly progress can be made in Hawaii, Mother Marianne instructed her companions to be ready to leave by the twelfth day of September.

A day or two before that time, in the inevitable anticlimax, Father Leonor's letter of August 27 arrived, telling them to postpone their departure until further notice. "Two weeks from here," he dared to add, "I will have the pleasure of telling you to come."

And so, as expectations and excitement mounted, they waited, and waited.

NOTES on Chapter III

1. Letters from Bishop Hermann Koeckemann and Father Leonor Fouesnel to Father Marcellin Bousquet (and others): originals are in Archives of the Congregation of the Sacred Hearts, in Rome; authorized copies are in AS.
2. Facts about Walter Murray Gibson: (a) his own book, *The Prisoner of Weltevreden,* published in 1856: (b) *The Diaries of Walter Murray Gibson, 1886, 1887,* Jacob Adler and Gwynn Barrett, editors, published in 1973; and (c) *Board of Health Reports,* Honolulu, 1880–1887.
3. Father Leonor's trip to America: more details are found in the Journal of Brother Bertrand, now in the Archive of the Roman Catholic Chancery in Honolulu, and in the letters of Brother Bertrand preserved in Rome.
4. Search for the sisters: a letter of Bishop Koeckemann of April 5, 1883, and an extract of a letter written by Brother Bertrand on January 6, 1884, demonstrate that some efforts were made by Père M. Bousquet, Superior General of the Sacred Hearts Congregation, to find sisters in France for the hospitals in Hawaii. Bishop Koeckemann called the failure to find such assistance their "first defeat." Later, while in America, Father Leonor, frustrated in his attempts to find sisters, on June 4, 1883, wrote to Père Bousquet urging him to plead Hawaii's cause with a specific community in France.

Chapter IV

THE JOURNEY

FATHER LEONOR'S signal from Honolulu, dated September 8, finally arrived on the twenty-fourth—the very day when Mother Marianne and her "first brave soldiers" had expected to sail from San Francisco.

"I am at last able to give you full directions for your trip," he began. Upon which he proceeded to give her four full pages of detailed information about routes of travel across the continent, the methodology of obtaining reduced fares, the transferring of baggage when they changed trains, the manner of arranging for "sleepers," and how much to pay for those conveniences. Terminal by railroad terminal, he conducted them from Chicago to Council Bluffs and Omaha and Ogden to San Francisco. He dropped the names of priests along the way who could assist them in time of trouble. Much of this information would be helpful, to be sure. But the one important fact that she wanted most of all to learn he buried in the very last paragraph of this chatty epistle:

"You may leave on the first steamer *after* the 15th of October, and everything will be ready for your reception." Typically, he shifted to her the responsibility for deciding upon the date: "but I beg you to write to me by the end of this month, telling me when you intend to leave.... As soon as we know the day of your departure... we will join in public prayer that God protect you during the trip."

Mother Marianne, well informed about time tables for westbound trains and sailing schedules for ships, decided to book passage aboard the vessel leaving San Francisco on November 1.

In 1883, if all went well and acts of neither God nor fallible man supervened, a brave traveler in good health could cross the whole continent by riding trains from New York City to San Francisco for six exhausting days and six distressful nights. Just to be sure—and allowing for accidents, derailings, missed connections, and other possible interruptions along the way—Mother Marianne told her "gang of great-courage-showing sisters" to be ready to leave Syracuse on Monday, October 22. From among the volunteers at St. Anthony's Convent and St. Joseph's. Hospital she chose Sister M. Bonaventure Caraher; Sister M. Crescentia Eilers; Sister M. Renata Nash; Sister M. Rosalia McLaughlin; Sister M. Ludovica Gibbons; and Sister M. Antonella Murphy. Miss Catherine Caraher, a cousin of Sister Bonaventure's, would be going with them all the way to Honolulu.

Interestingly enough, from that quintessentially German community of religious, Mother Marianne chose not a single German sister for the mission. Five of her company were daughters of Irish parents, and one—Sister Crescentia Eilers—was Dutch. Obviously, and even after her experience with Sister Dominica, Mother Marianne did not share Bishop Hermann's fears about strong-minded Irishwomen.

While they waited, Mother Marianne still performed the duties of Provincial Superior, managing the affairs of the Order and preparing Mother Antonia Eulenstein to act in her place during her absence.

Early in the cool morning of October 22, the chosen ones set forth upon their pilgrimage. They attended Mass at dawn, broke their fast with the convent's usual light fare, said tearful farewells—mingled with promises to return soon—to sisters, novices, and servants crowding into the vestibule. The lone handyman had already taken trunks and valises to the railroad depot. Each traveler carried a big bag fashioned of black serge lined with percale, holding personal articles for use on the way. And several carried also small wicker hampers filled with some of Sister Anna Dorn's jars of catsup and pickled peaches, packages of buttered bread and roasted chicken, and ripening fruits harvested from St. Anthony's orchard.

A few older sisters from the convent and from St. Joseph's Hospital accompanied them to the railroad station, where friends from among the laity joined the group. Just before 7 o'clock the express train from New York City came hissing in. With last embraces, tears, and prayers the seven Sisters of St. Francis and Miss Caraher bade farewell to their dearest friends. Conductors helped them to enter the car. At 7 o'clock the train began to move out of the station. Kneeling at the coach's open window, looking back, Sister Crescentia saw a picture of grief that she would never forget: Mother Bernardina reaching out her arms, "her dear face so white and drawn like the agony of death." And weeping sisters gathering around, to comfort her.

In all the excitement, Mother Marianne had forgotten her purse at the convent. She missed it soon after the train left Syracuse. Inasmuch as they were riding aboard an express, she could not leave the train until it reached Buffalo. From there she took the eastbound express back to Syracuse. She entered St. Anthony's while some of its residents were still talking about her departure. Sister Leopoldina remembered the scene, as they fluttered about in surprise: " 'I told you,' she said with her bright smile, 'I would come back and here I am!' " With the purse firmly in hand, she sped off again, alone this time, boarded the next westbound express, and met her company in Chicago.

The incident of the forgotten purse is most uncharacteristic of this woman who, during all the years until that day, seems never to have forgotten anything else at any other time: it is a lapse of memory for psychologists to ponder. Sisters of the community probably are not mistaken when they think of it as being Mother Marianne's way of keeping her promise to return. The real question, however, must ask whether or not she herself recognized this at the time.

Among the tickets, documents, addresses, money, St. Christopher medals, and other items she carried in that heavy purse would have been a letter from Father Joseph Lesen, sent earlier but dated that very day, in Syracuse. "TO WHOM IT MAY CONCERN," he wrote in large letters across the top, as he commended Mother Marianne and her companions to the charity of strangers they might seek out in times of need.

Often, before leaving Syracuse, Mother Marianne said that she expected to return "in a few weeks," just as soon as she had set up the Franciscan mission in Hawaii. She went to Honolulu as Mother Provincial of her community, with full permission from Father Lesen and a clear understanding on the part of everyone in the Franciscan Order that she would resume her duties in Syracuse when those in Honolulu were completed.

The six sisters who accompanied her also expected to return to the Motherhouse in a few short years, when their labors in Hawaii were done.

In those naive expectations, the seven sisters deceived themselves most of all.

They were as deluded as are young men who, laughing and jesting and singing, think they are marching off to a summer's war from which all of them will return.

Among all the Franciscans in Syracuse only Mother Bernardina may have foreseen the bitter truth.

Of the seven sisters who went forth from Syracuse that day, not a one would come back to live in St. Anthony's Convent. Only two, Sister Ludovica and Sister Rosalia, would return to die in America. And Sister Rosalia would be mad.

Six days and five nights later, on Saturday October 27, the pilgrims—"so tired that we could scarcely stand"—arrived at the railway terminal in Oakland, California. Father George Montgomery and his sexton met them and escorted the weary group, with their baggage, by ferryboat across the bay to San Francisco. He deposited five of the ladies (Miss Caraher among them) in the convent attached to St. Mary's Hospital, and three in the Convent of the Sisters of the Presentation.

During the afternoon of All Hallows' Day Sister Bonaventure Caraher wrote to Mother Bernardina, at home in Syracuse, telling about the respite they were enjoying in the city named for their own St. Francis. Five sisters and Miss Caraher had recovered from their fatigue, but Sister Bonaventure and Mother Marianne still felt the effects of a bad cold. While one of San Francisco's young ladies took all the other visitors for a ride, to see the sights of the great city, Sister Bonaventure preferred to sit beside a pleasant fire in St. Mary's Convent, nursing "a headache and neuralgia," the while she sent a message to her beloved Mother Bernardina. The two women looked so much alike that they might have been born to the same parents.

Sister Bonaventure said very little about the hardships of the trip across the continent. But they are implied in her remark that, for two days after they reached San Francisco, "we would wake up imagining we were still on the cars and are yet so dizzy that we sit down." Sister Anna's catsup and pickles "had something the matter with them," but the cold chicken and the bread and butter were so tasty that "we licked our fingers after them."

On Sunday they did little more than go to Mass early in the day and to Benediction of the Blessed Sacrament in the evening. Father Montgomery called at 10 A.M., "to see what he could do for us," but they asked for nothing. In the first vacation that any of them could have been granted since she entered the novitiate, each felt guilty about passing the time so uselessly. Sister Bonaventure all but apologized for being lazy: "One would think that after sitting still from Monday until Saturday night we would not want to sit for a month, but it is surprising that it is not so."

The great event came on Tuesday morning, when Mr. W. H. Severance, the Hawaiian consul, took the whole party down to the Embarcadero, to see the vessel that would carry them to Honolulu. The coal-black *Mariposa*—low in the water, narrow in the beam, slightly more than a hundred feet long, with only one level of cabins below her maindeck—was no luxury liner by modern standards. In 1883, however, her owners, the Oceanic Steamship Company, advertized her as being "new and elegant." The sisters from Syracuse were much impressed: "it is splendid," Sister Bonaventure pronounced, "is of iron & everything about it in first class style. We saw nothing we would change for [Consul Severance] had studied everything for our comfort. We are together that is our staterooms & are on the lee side in the best part of the steamer." They met "Captain Howard, a fine man, and the Stewardess a good woman & a Catholic. Although that would make but little difference for all we met, passengers, conductors, etc. were Protestants & they vied with each other (seemingly) to make us comfortable."

On the way back to St. Mary's they visited the Consul's office and saw "large portraits of their Majesties. Then the Consul gave orders to the Coachman to take us through the principal parts of the city, & to St. Ignatius's Church (the Jesuits). Oh! what a church! perfectly grand."

"Today," Sister Bonaventure continued, coming quietly to the moment of shock, "we went to Confession at 10 A.M. & Mother & some of the Sisters are riding. tomorrow at 2 P.M. we must be on the vessel & at 3 P.M. we sail."

Tomorrow the long exile would begin.

With that prospect fixed now, on paper as in her consciousness, poor Sister Bonaventure's longing for home welled up. In a flood of nostalgia (and probably of tears), she remembered by name all her favorite companions at the convent and in the hospital, many of her patients there, even "my Jim," the urchin paper boy, whom she would see no more.

"Please give our fondest love to all the Sisters," she finished, "accepting a large share for your own dear self." Remembering a charge from her leader, she added, "with fondest love to you & all the Sisters from Mother Provincial."

At 3 P.M. on November 1, keeping to schedule, the *Mariposa* backed from her berth near the foot of Market Street and turned her bow toward the west. She may not have been large, but she was a steamship, relatively new and wonderfully self-sufficient. Under her own power, indifferent to winds and tides, she moved as her captain directed across San Francisco's great bay. On the maindeck the first-class passengers gathered at the rail, to bid farewell to the city, spreading over its fabled hills, to look upon this westernmost edge of the vast continent of America. The thirty-two steerage passengers, confined below decks, saw nothing. Like the 1,330 tons of merchandise the *Mariposa* carried in holds around them, steerage passengers were considered to be a kind of freight that had no need for comforts.

The thirty-one passengers on the maindeck, having introduced themselves earlier, chatted sociably. Most were citizens of the United States, sailing for the first time to the Hawaiian Islands. Some were kamaainas, residents of the kingdom, "going home" as they said with evident pleasure. A few passengers came from Europe and Australia.

One of the Europeans was a slight pallid golden-haired young man, who appeared to be more youthful than his years and title warranted. He affected a blonde mustache, clothes of the latest cut, and pince-nez affixed to the lapel of his jacket by a long black ribbon. The limp mustache and the spectacles made him look prim rather than scholarly. He signed himself Dr. Eduard C. Arning, had been born in Manchester, England, and educated as a physician in the new Imperial Germany. As a dermatologist and venereologist (the usual pairing of specializations at the time), he had sought training in the new science of bacteriology with Dr. Albert Neisser, one of Germany's most brilliant (and least principled) younger scientists. Dr. Arning, too, had been invited by Walter Murray Gibson to work with the lepers of Hawaii. The Sisters of St. Francis would see him often in Honolulu.

Almost as soon as the *Mariposa* emerged from the Golden Gate, and met the long rolling swells of the open sea, many passengers became sick. All the sisters from Syracuse took to their bunks, and all except Mother Marianne recovered by the third day. She kept to her bed for the entire voyage. This first encounter with the sea since childhood exposed a weakness that she had not expected—and one that no act of her will could ever control. She would suffer from seasickness, that most treasonous of afflictions, whenever she traveled aboard ship among the islands of Hawaii.

Soon after daybreak on the seventh day out from San Francisco, the excited kamaainas and other early-rising passengers caught their first glimpses of the islands of Hawaii. Blue in the distance, they looked like huge clouds pressing down upon the horizon. Far to the left, the sun set fire to the snowy peaks atop the immense mountains of the great island that is called Hawaii. Not quite so far to port, it touched with pink the high rounded bulk of Haleakala on Maui. Later, as the *Mariposa* wallowed along on its course, the pinnacles of Oahu rose up, straight ahead. A kamaaina pointed out to the sisters the long gray shape of an island off to the left, low only by contrast with its neighbors, Maui to the larboard, and Oahu, off the starboard bow. "That's Molokai." Although it was too far away and too low to be seen, he would have told the sisters about the little leaf of land called Kalaupapa, lying at the foot of the rampart of tremendous sea cliffs that form the whole northern face of Molokai. "Kalaupapa. That's where the Leper Settlement is.—You've heard of Father Damien, I suppose? That's where he lives."

The *Mariposa*, plunging ahead as if swept along by fresh trade winds like a clipper ship under full sail, entered the rough channel between Molokai and Oahu. Winds and currents, rushing through the narrow straits, make seas so boisterous there that ships of all sizes will toss and roll, and sick passengers must groan in anguish. Now the hardy observers on deck could remark the surf crashing against Oahu's sides. Black and brown, yellow and red, carved by winds and waves, they withstood for yet a while the unending assault of the sea. And the malihinis (as kamaainas called them), the newcomers who were approaching Oahu for the first time, could marvel at the almost vertical ridge of mountains that, thrusting their sharp peaks into the sky, rose like a flying fish's open fin above the narrow coastal plain.

At midday the *Mariposa* rounded the point of a huge crater lying at the very southern edge of Oahu. Its top had been blown apart thousands of years ago, but its base was perfectly preserved. This tawny remnant lay crouched like a lion with its forepaws in the sea. "That's Diamond Head," islanders informed malihinis an hour earlier, when the ship was still off Koko Head.

Beyond the point of Diamond Head they came upon the southern coast of Oahu, stretching off into the distance, toward another range of sculptured mountains far to the west. Immediately to their right lay Waikiki, a long arc of beaches covered with golden sand and fringed with feathery coconut palms. They came abreast of Kewalo, a stretch of swamplands, green with bulrushes and low shrubs, protected by coral reefs that kept the surf at a distance from the land. Beyond the wide plain stood the mountain wall that earlier they had seen from its farther side. Here it was cleft by great valleys and buttressed by long sloping ridges. Inland, at the heads of the valleys, the crags and cliffs were green and cool, covered with trees and shrubs that refreshed eyes weary of looking at blue sea and bluer sky. But closer to shore the slanting ridges were brown and dry, baking in the bright sunshine, robbed of moisture by the warm winds and stripped of vegetation by cutters of wood for the kitchen fires of Honolulu. In many places nothing grew on the ridges at all, not even tufts of grasses among the boulders. And wind devils, swirls of brown dust, skittered across the plain.

In the lee of Oahu, in this bay of Waikiki, the sea was almost tamed. The *Mariposa* settled into a pace as seemly as a nun's. Victims of seasickness lifted their heads, thinking that now they might manage to live. Mother Marianne's companions, who had been on deck for hours, rushed to her stateroom. They helped her to don the heavy black serge robe, the coronet and band, the white collar, and the double veil. They handed to her the cord with the three knots, to bind about her waist, and the rosary of seven decades, to fix to it. And at the last they put upon her bosom the heavy cross. Then they took her up the narrow companionway leading to the maindeck—and to her first view of the land that had drawn her so far away from home.

She gazed upon the dramatic mountains beyond, the forests of coconut palms leaning out over the sands of Waikiki, the hills and valleys and beaches almost empty of people, lacking even the signs of their presence. A few beach cottages, whitewashed and weathered, all seeming to be abandoned, squatted among the palms of Waikiki. A few fishermen's huts littered the shore of Kewalo. Honolulu, the capital city of this kingdom in the middle of earth's largest ocean, lay almost hidden behind a screen of trees. Some were coconut palms. Others were decked with large glossy leaves. Most had foliage so fine that their branches seemed to be swathed in green mist. All were strange. Eight steeples lifted crosses or weathervanes into the clear air. From tall flagstaffs atop the mansard turrets of a great high building red, white, and blue standards waved in the fresh breeze. "No, that is not the British ensign," the patient kamaainas explained to more than one startled American. "Nor the American," they said to the Europeans. "That is the flag of Hawaii."

The *Mariposa* drew near the narrow channel that had been dredged through the reef. It afforded the only entry to Honolulu's pocket of a harbor. Just before the ship turned in toward the channel, the kamaainas lifted fingers to point at a clutter of cottages upon the shore, enclosed by a fence of weatherbeaten wooden planks. Between the palisade and the open sea lay a stretch of shallow water and coral flats carpeted with seaweeds of varied hue.

"That's Kakaako." said kamaainas, not looking at it. "The Branch Hospital. For lepers."

Sister Leopoldina, who was not present that day, heard about the next event in this approach to Honolulu: "And then they had a great surprise. They were far from the Island when the pilot's [boat] met them and it was flying the royal collers. The passangers and the ships crew were staring with wide eyes and open mouth. What does this mean? they said. we have no royal people on board, and as the pilot drew near somebody said oh, there is Father Leonor. When the pilot reached the Mariposa Father called out are the Sisters aboard? and when he received the answer Yes, the little pilot [boat] whirled around and was soon out of sight returning quickly to the city to announce to the good King and Queen that our Rev. Mother and Sisters were on board. . . ."

One of the sisters in the first company wrote a long letter home to her friends at St. Anthony's Convent. The letter has not survived, and the writer cannot be identified with certainty, but internal evidence suggests that she was Sister Bonaventure. A reporter from the Syracuse *Evening Herald* quoted portions of it, and reduced other parts to a rather bald narrative, much too deficient in detail, that was published on January 19, 1884. Inadequate as it is, this account of the arrival does seem to relate what actually happened. Father Leonor, rowed by two native men, actually did venture out in a little boat, to hail the ship off port. Upon learning that the sisters were aboard, he hastened back to shore and put his well-laid plans into operation. As he had written Mother Marianne several weeks before, "the reception is all arranged." By telephone, by messenger, by jubilant ringing of the

Cathedral's bells, and in breathless person, he alerted the people who were to take part in that gala spectacle.

Six days and twenty-two hours out from San Francisco, the *Mariposa* tied up at the pier about 1 o'clock, a convenient time for Honoluluans. They turned out in happy crowds to greet each arriving ship, and to wave goodbye to each departing one, just for the excitement that such comings and goings offered townsfolk provided with few other entertainments. On this special day, loyal Catholics augmented the usual throng. So also did astute Protestants and hold-out pagans, intrigued by the sight of all those Catholics wearing their best clothes, and by the unparalleled spectacle of five royal carriages in fine trim, even if unoccupied, dashing from the palace stables to the pier.

Weeks before this festive day, Father Leonor had requested the presence of Her Majesty, Queen Kapiolani, and she had promised to come. But the serious illness of her sister, Princess Kekaulike, Royal Governess of the Island of Hawaii, caused the queen to remain in seclusion. In her place she sent a beautiful Hawaiian lady in waiting, Mrs. Frederick W. Beckley, wife to King Kalakaua's chamberlain. The king, keeping the promise he had given Father Leonor, sent five carriages of state. He himself decided not to attend, for reasons of policy, in which, for once, both Catholics and Protestants concurred.

From the *Mariposa's* rail, as stevedores warped her into the pier, the Sisters of St. Francis studied with great interest the people standing on the wharf below them. Such a variety of faces, such a range of complexions! The Franciscans thought they recognized the usual array of features given to the people of America: Germans, Irishmen, Scandinavians, Britishers, even Portuguese and Frenchmen. They detected a number of Chinese, looking somewhat like American Indians even to the braided queues, because they had seen representatives of that mysterious race in the railroad towns strung out across the continent and in San Francisco. The large-bodied men and women, the sisters inferred, those handsome people with the brown skins, and the great brown eyes, and the bright white teeth flashing as they smiled: these must be Hawaiians.

The others of the *Mariposa's* first-class passengers, aware by now that the several dignitaries on the dock had come to welcome "the Sisters of Charity," deferred to them. The six sisters and Miss Caraher ranged themselves behind Mother Marianne. "Father Leonore, accompanied by his Excellency, the minister of Foreign Affairs, and the Queen's maid of honor came on board and welcomed us in the name of the Bishop, their Majesties etc."

Father Leonor presided over introductions. Mrs. Beckley curtsied. In English words correctly chosen, yet pronounced in the soft Hawaiian way, she presented the queen's aloha and her regrets.

Courtly Mr. Gibson, from his great height, bowed low over the hand of each sister as he murmured, "Aloha... Welcome to fair Hawaii." A romantic who thought, spoke, wrote, and comported himself in all the clichés of all the Victorian novels ever written, never the less so as he grew older, Gibson was smitten at sight of these "Angels of Mercy," so austere, so pure, so ethereal, so beautiful—not to mention so necessary to the realization of his great plan for improving medical care in the kingdom. And so, of course, he promptly fell in love with all of them, in the best manner of the romantic, casting himself instantly in the roles of generous host, gallant champion, elder brother, doting uncle, and concerned father, who would care for them in every tribulation and defend them against every danger—that did not jeopardize himself.

Father Leonor directed the group toward the shore. Mother Marianne, weak and unsteady still, after that journey across the unruly sea, walked down the gangway, to stand at last in the land which had called to her so irresistibly.

The attentive gentlemen escorted the ladies to the royal carriages. "In the second rode Rev. Mother Marianne with Her Majesty's maid of honor," the newspaperman in Syracuse reported. "In the third and fourth each two Sisters, and in the fifth and last, two Sisters and Miss Cassie Carrier [Caraher], the lady who accompanied them from Syracuse," Presumably, the Foreign Minister, the President of the Board of Health, the President of the Board of Education, the Lord High-Everything-Else, all by himself, in his own barouche, brought up the rear of the procession.

As was only proper, Father Leonor sat in the first royal carriage, at the head of this gallant parade.

"The procession was driven through the principal streets," its reporter informed Syracuse, "while the bells of the cathedral rang with joy."

The cavalcade took the long way home. It could have gone straight up Fort Street, which leads from the waterfront to the cathedral and to the valleys beyond. But the quick route would not have served Father Leonor's purpose. Instead, the carriages rolled first toward Waikiki, through the drying mud of Honolulu's own Embarcadero, then inland along muddy Punchbowl Street to the creased and furrowed mud of King Street. There they turned left, to drive past Iolani Palace, the Merry Monarch's newest and grandest folly, not yet a year old. The sisters could see, beyond the high stone wall that surrounded it, the confection of slender columns, airy balconies, lacy balustrades and railings fashioned of finest wrought iron, the building's white facings looking as if they had been made of spun sugar, all leading the eye up and up and up to those six mansard towers they had discerned from the ship, and the six tall flag poles from which flew the royal standard and the Cross and Stripes of Hawaii.

It was beautiful, the sisters agreed, very different and perfectly grand. Syracuse certainly had nothing like it.

By contrast, the stores and shops and livery stables along King Street, in the very heart of this city of 20,000 people, were tawdry, filmed with dust and spattered with mud. The carriages turned right, on Fort Street at last, heading for the end of the show. Like lines in an artist's illustration of perspective, countless wheel tracks in the crusted mud directed the sisters' eyes to the most welcome sight of all : the high tower and the long roof of the Cathedral of Our Lady of Peace—the second largest church in Honolulu. Its excited bells sounded louder with each turn of the carriage wheels.

As the procession drew up before the West Portal the bells ceased to send out their joy over the town. In the cathedral's central doorway stood His Lordship, the Bishop of Olba, clad in purple vestments, flanked by priests and brothers of the Congregation of the Sacred Hearts, and by boys from St. Louis College, the Brothers of Mary's school, wearing the surplices of acolytes, swinging shining censers. Great numbers of people lined the street, others stood in the church-yard beyond the wrought-iron fence. And grinning barefoot boys clung to the trunks of the young date palms growing at either side of the gateway in that delicate fence.

Father Leonor handed Mother Marianne from her coach, chosen parishioners assisted the six sisters and the two ladies from their carriages. In the expectant hush, Father Leonor led the sisters forward, presented them to His Lordship. Mother Marianne knelt in the dust, to kiss the bishop's ring. One by one, her daughters in Christ followed her example. Father Leonor, his triumph achieved, backed away, to stand among his brethren. Thereafter, the Bishop of Olba would preside over the ceremonies of Holy Church.

His Lordship blessed the kneeling sisters. Most tenderly, and most privately, for he was much moved, "he spoke to them a few words of welcome." At the moment he was done, "the grand organ within pealed forth strains of rich melody to a beautiful hymn being sung by the choir." Sister Bonaventure's letter being quoted in Syracuse noted that "Some beautiful hymns and the Te Deum were sung."

The bishop and his retinue of priests, brothers, and acolytes led the sisters into the cathedral. Along the central aisle, "carpeted from the entrance to the sanctuary," people of the faith, who filled every space on the floor of the long nave and in the galleries above, stood facing them, welcoming them, some with smiles, some with tears.

The exultant music, the sweet incense drew the sisters in. The brightness of many candles upon the high altar, the image of the crucified Christ raised above it, called them forward, into the great open space beneath the vaulted and painted ceiling. Through their tears the Sisters of St. Francis saw the tall paintings high upon the walls at either side of the altar, the one representing Christ the Redeemer offering the world His Sacred Heart, full of grace and mercy, the other representing the Blessed Virgin Mary offering Her Sacred Heart, full of love and compassion.

In their pews at the front of the congregation the Sisters of the Sacred Hearts, clad in white habits and fluted white coifs resembling pleated haloes, with pale hands clasped as if in prayer, bowed solemnly, as do the ladies of France. The girls of the Convent School stood with them. The Brothers of Mary, clad in black frock coats, smiled cheerfully, as do the young men of America. Many boys of St. Louis College stood with their teachers. In the glow of light from the Holy Table the Sisters of St. Francis beheld the Tabernacle.

They felt the presence of the Blessed Sacrament. They knew the peace of safe arrival, the joy of coming home.

For the Sisters of St. Francis the ceremony of welcome was an affirmation of the ancient and Catholic faith, no different in Honolulu than it would be in Syracuse or in Rome.

For Bishop Hermann and Father Leonor it was, quite properly, an opportunity for giving public expression to that faith—and for impressing upon their parishioners the importance of perpetuating it.

The bishop and his cortege entered the sanctuary. Ushers seated the Sisters of St. Francis in chairs placed before the sanctuary rail. Standing upon the step leading to the episcopal throne, His Lordship addressed the sisters. "Even while his Lordship was welcoming us tears streamed from his eyes." Speaking in English he said "that their coming to the islands was a great blessing to the poor inhabitants. He welcomed them in the name of the good Queen and the government, at the same time expressing his own great joy and thanks for their coming, wishing them from his inmost heart God's choicest blessing on their noble work."

Sister Leopoldina, repeating what she had heard, enlarged upon the bishop's address: ". . . when He told Mother and the Sisters do not look for prase or gratitude because you will have much to suffer and many crosses, there was dead silence broken only by the sobbs and growns of that great crowd of people."

"Then came the Benediction of the Blessed Sacrament," concluded the article in the Syracuse newspaper, "after which his Lordship addressed the crowded congregation of Portuguese and Hawaiians, in the native tongue, which, although the Sisters were unable to understand it, appeared to be very moving, judging from the weeping of the people."

NOTES on Chapter IV

1. Pilot boat off Honolulu harbor: By 1960, convent lore in Syracuse had transmuted pilot boat and canoe into "the Royal Yacht." Prandoni, 1960: *Greater Love*, p. 68.
2. Miss Caraher: Sister Bonaventure's cousin disappears from the Franciscans' account at this point. Her reasons for traveling to Hawaii and her subsequent history cannot be traced.

Chapter V

RESPITE

NEEDLESS TO SAY, all the large promises had not been fulfilled. Nothing was ready for them. Construction of the new convent had scarcely begun. Almost two more months would pass before, finally, in the first week of 1884, it would be habitable. In the interval, Father Leonor and Gibson had to arrange other accommodations for the Franciscans.

Mother Judith and the Sisters of the Sacred Hearts sheltered the newcomers for three days, in their own crowded and aging convent adjoining the Cathedral of Our Lady of Peace. The Sacred Hearts sisters, as in time Sister Leopoldina would relate, "did everything that could be done to make it pleasant for them." Nevertheless, the American sisters needed a place of their own in which to stay.

Gibson found them one in his usual grand manner: he rented, at Board of Health expense, a big house in the heart of town. The fact that it belonged either to him or to his daughter Talula, Mrs. Fred Hayselden, didn't bother him in the least. Conflicts of interest, as they are called today, never deterred Walter Murray Gibson. But the way in which he enabled his daughter to make a pretty profit, at public expense, did annoy certain of his critics. During the legislative session of 1884 they questioned several items listed among payments the Board of Health had authorized during the year just passed. Conspicuous among those items was one for "Mrs. Hayselden for two months rental of home, $225." The arrangement, the questioners said, was too familial, the profit excessive. Gibson rebutted the charge in organ tones: ". . . His Excellency," reported the *Pacific Commercial Advertiser* on June 21, 1884, "explained about the arrival of eight sisters of Charity, and there being no suitable place for their reception, and the house in question was rented at what was considered a fair rental."

Relishing every bit of his part as lord-protector to these helpless homeless females, Gibson managed their move from the Sacred Hearts Convent down to the least detail. A florid note, indited upon the Foreign Minister's official stationery, informed "the Lady Superior" that an omnibus would be sent to fetch her company and their baggage at "one quarter to 9 o'clock" on the morning of November 12.

The same dispatch also told Mother Marianne that an omnibus would call each morning, "at one quarter to 7 o'clock, to convey the Lady Superior and Sisters to Mass—and to return at about 10 minutes to 8 A.M." The sisters could have walked in ten or fifteen minutes to the cathedral, less than half a kilometer away, and undoubtedly would have enjoyed the excursion on days that were not too humid or rainy. But Gibson's gallantry could not allow them such freedom. And so, for a while, the sisters rode to Mass in style—and in happy innocence.

For this gracious courtesy, too, the Board of Health paid: "James Dodd, carriage and omnibus hire, for the Sisters of Charity . . . $245.75." Gibson's critics should have known better than to challenge him about this expense. But they did—and were demolished for their miserliness. His Excellency said, the *Advertiser's* reporter continued in his article of June 21, 1884, "these self-sacrificing Sisters of Charity, who came here voluntarily to nurse and attend to the wants of the lepers, desired to pay their daily visits to their house of worship, and, in order to do so, it was necessary that some conveyance should be provided for them, as they could not walk the distance; this had been done at an expense of $4 per day, amounting in all to $245.75. Was that too much, he asked, for the services they were rendering? (Loud and continued applause.)"

On the day after they reached Honolulu, while still they enjoyed the hospitality of the Sacred Hearts Convent, Mother Marianne and her companions were visited by the King and Queen of Hawaii. Their Majesties called in person to thank the sisters for taking up a burden that no one else would assume. The king and queen came as quietly as could be managed, in watchful, gossipy, and Protestant Honolulu. They came separately, each riding apart in a solitary carriage, without ceremony, unattended by equerries or guardian outriders. Apparently the queen arrived first, accompanied by a maid of honor. The king called later in the morning.

King David Kalakaua, in 1883 ending the forty-seventh year of his life and the ninth of his reign, was a man of middle height and portly girth, become fleshed and soft from too much easeful living. His fine eyes, wide, dark, and lustrous as are those of most Hawaiians, were set off by smooth brown skin, wavy black hair, and a full mustache falling past the mouth to meet luxuriant Burnsides. No beard covered the rounded chin or hid the pouting sensual lips.

Like Gibson, Kalakaua too was a romantic, although not so forceful a one. Whereas Gibson was canny enough to keep a careful guard over most of his deeds, whether public or private, Kalakaua was too trusting, too self-indulgent, too unworldly to protect himself. And he was too full of foolish fancies about the divine rights of kings ever to worry, as yet, about the consequences of his actions. These illusions about kingship, drawn doubly from his Hawaiian heritage as a chief of high rank and from an imperfect acquaintance with Europe's monarchs (but not with their histories), persisted in Kalakaua at a time when, in many parts of the world and even in his own isolated realm, those rights and privileges of rulers were being challenged by upstart republicans and, in some countries, had been terminated most ruthlessly. In his tiny kingdom, whose tax collectors never amassed enough money to fill its treasury, he squandered his allotted income and more in royal fashion: upon a tour of the world in 1882; upon a grand and opulent palace, completed early in 1883; and—crowning extravagance!—upon a glittering and costly coronation held in January 1883, nine full years after he had been elected sovereign over his people. All these indulgences, and many more, he achieved with Gibson's assistance, applied both in and out of the national legislature. The two happy spenders declared that, in those displays of state, they were helping native Hawaiians to gain a sense of pride in king and country. Kalakaua, Gibson, and their supporters were correct in believing that Hawaiians needed encouragement in every aspect of their lives. They had been assailed for a hundred years by ideas, things, and diseases imported from the great countries beyond the sea, and in the process they had been overwhelmed. Their indigenous society had collapsed about them, and they themselves were dying in its debris. As a consequence of this unstoppable tragedy, the survivors had become, as they said, "huikau"—"lost in the shuffle," confused, and filled with despair.

The concern of the king and his prime minister for the Hawaiian psyche was genuine—but only up to a point. Unfortunately, it was also so shallow and so diffused as to be ineffective. They shared the ignorance, and the hopes, of the age. At that time, no one anywhere, and no knowledge imported from any place in the whole world, could save the Hawaiian race from the effects of its encounter with the deadly mechanisms of Western civilization. As have the peoples of all other societies who have been exposed to the things, the thoughts, the machines, and most especially the germs of the Westerners' world, Hawaiians too had to endure the experience of assimilation through annihilation. As is always the way, when a superior culture meets an inferior one, the weaker one must succumb. Among the first things to die, in the weaker culture, are its gods and its people. Hawaii's native culture stands as a model for that sad ordeal.

Moreover, Kalakaua's concern for his people, and Gibson's, was tainted by their naive delight in public spectacle as well as by sybaritic pleasures enjoyed in private. In a land of peasants (who subsisted comfortably enough upon foods they grew on the land or caught in the sea, but who had almost no money to spend), which was governed by striving Puritans (whose taxes helped to sustain the government and paid for all of Kalakaua's pretensions), those two reckless wastrels caused scandal to businessmen and amaze in Hawaiians. In 1887 their excesses would goad the businessmen into "a bloodless revolution," which put a firm end to their conjoint folly. But in 1883 Kalakaua Rex, "the Merry Monarch," as artful sycophants and sneering critics alike called him, and Gibson, his "Master of the Revels," were still being tolerated—mostly because their disloyal opposition had not yet become sufficiently annoyed to agree upon a policy for controlling them.

Most of their adversaries were Calvinists who still kept the sense of duty, if not of loyalty, which characterized Christians in that simpler era. The fact that most of Kalakaua's severest critics either had been born in the islands to missionary parents come from New England or had been well treated after settling in the kingdom, complicated their wrath as rebels by confusing their concepts of morality. Whether or not they knew it, they thought like schoolmasters, behaved like sportsmen, observing the rules of fair play. Accordingly, prompted by gratitude and decency—"out of aloha," as they would have claimed—they deferred rebelling for yet a while and took refuge in that other Christian virtue, hope. After all, they could argue, Kalakaua was not utterly without value to the economy of the kingdom. He possessed great personal charm—which he had used to excellent effect in Washington, D.C. in 1875, when he persuaded the American government to agree to a reciprocity treaty with Hawaii. The arrangement allowed the islands' few agricultural products, among which cane sugar was the only important item, to be admitted duty-free to the United States, and in exchange the duty-free entry into Hawaii of a great number of America's goods. Hawaii's prosperity, rising gratifyingly since the treaty went into effect in September 1876, could be attributed to Kalakaua, his supporters declared. How, then, could the businessmen—those primary beneficiaries of his diplomacy—deny him a tour of the world, a fancy new palace, a coronation, a privy purse that enabled him to live in the style of a monarch who was both a father to his people and an ornament to the nation? Although the businessmen grumbled, they gave him what he wanted—and turned their rancor upon his "henchmen." Foremost among those, by nature and in zeal, was Walter Murray Gibson.

Although King Kalakaua spoke English fluently (if somewhat ungrammatically at times), his consort could not match his ease in the foreign language. As did almost every native Hawaiian, she commanded certain English words and the commoner expressions of courtesy, but in the presence of strangers she was too shy to attempt conversation. For this reason Their Majesties asked Father Leonor to speak for the queen when they visited Mother Marianne.

Unlike her plump and indolent husband, Queen Kapiolani was short, stocky, solid. Many people who stood in awe of her saw only the hard unwomanly body, the strong masculine jaw and firm mouth, the hair piled high atop her head, as if it were a crown. They did not see the traces of a woman's beauty in the noble brow or in the brooding eyes, which all too often gazed in sorrow upon the world. An aristocrat by birth, made haughty by privilege and training, she resembled an imperious sovereign much more than ever her complacent husband did. She inherited both body and rank from the Kaumualii, the noble family that once had owned the island of Kauai, before the conquering Kamehameha absorbed it into their realm. Kapiolani's rank, in fact, exceeded that of her husband. And gossips in Honolulu whispered that he had married her—"a woman much older than he" (when, in truth, she was only eleven months the elder) and a widow as well—not in love but for her lineage, because, in the manner of chiefs of old, he hoped through her to increase the mana of their children. Such gossips ignored the evidence that when Kapiolani and Kalakaua were wed, in 1863, the Kamehameha dynasty still ruled all Hawaii and he had not the slightest prospect of ever being king. Nor did they remember that, in 1863, a marriage between nobles that would increase the mana of their progeny was still as proper in Hawaii as it was in Great Britain, or in Germany, or in many another eminent nation throughout the world.

Alas! the mana of their offspring was not increased, because these two who had become Hawaii's rulers could create no children. Everywhere they went, in their royal progresses among the eight islands of Hawaii, the king and the queen exhorted the people: "Hooulu lahui," they urged, "increase the race." But these two, who should have been examples to their people, could not produce a child of their flesh. Neither could almost all other members of the great princely families of Hawaii. The Kamehameha and the Lunalilo were dead, or barren and near death. The Kalakaua were without issue, save one: only King Kalakaua's younger sister, Her Royal Highness Princess Miriam Likelike, had borne a child to her Scotch husband, Archibald Cleghorn. And in 1883 this lone child, Kaiulani, a beautiful princess upon whom the whole nation fixed its love and hope, was only eight years old, and not yet marked for early death. The last child to be granted a reigning monarch, the Prince of Hawaii, the only son of Kamehameha IV, had been born in 1858—and had died in 1862. After Kamehameha IV, sovereigns went to the grave as childless as did commoners. And, robbed even of its princes, the nation mourned, feeling that in this too it was abandoned and accursed.

Upon many occasions Queen Kapiolani could be as regal as she looked. Sister Bonaventure's first impression of the queen, quoted in the Syracuse *Evening Herald,* describes her well: "She is a fine woman, very charitable and good. She . . . was well and elegantly dressed as any lady of taste in the States." Yet, as is so often the case with Hawaiian women of her age and bearing, at other times the heart in her bosom would be soft with kindness, and the challenging eyes could shed tears. She, more than all others of the nation's dwindling number of nobles, worried about the appalling rate at which the race was dying. She was especially alarmed about the speed with which leprosy, that most ghastly of the imported plagues, was spreading among her people. Indeed, as letters of Gibson and of Bishop Hermann imply, she may well have been the questioner who first asked if "Sisters of Charity" could not be invited to serve as nurses for Hawaii's lepers.

On the day when she met Mother Marianne and her company in the parlor of the Sacred Hearts Convent, the queen's heart, as she made clear, was soft "with aloha." And she wept, with grief for her dying people, with gratitude for the compassion being shown by these women come to her land from that generous country across the sea.

Sister Leopoldina Burns, writing about forty-five years later, described the meeting as Franciscan tradition developed it. The details may be incorrect, because Sister Leopoldina herself was not present in Honolulu on that November day in 1883. But the emotions and sentiments she set down are beyond questioning:

". . . The queen could not speak english, so Mr. Gibson [sic] transolated for her, and while he was speaking great tears were streaming from her beautiful black eyes. I love you! she said You have left Your home and country to come to these far away Islands to cair for my poor afflicted children; I shall never forget you, and you are my Sisters and I shall always love you. The King was a very grand knoble looking man and while the Queen was speaking his eyes were cast down and his face showed that he felt as she did."

The queen's words were as genuine as her tears. She never forgot her country's debt of gratitude to the Sisters of St. Francis. And in the years to come, despite difficulties in communicating, differences in religion, revolutions in politics, and many sorrows of her own, she helped the sisters in every way she could.

Mother Marianne, in her work among the lepers did not hesitate to ask the queen for assistance in gaining goals that otherwise might have been delayed or eliminated by bureaucrats. The Kapiolani Home they founded in 1885, to care for healthy girl children born to leprous parents, was the most notable of their achievements. Mother Marianne's respect and affection for Her Majesty, not withheld in life, was also expressed privately: upon the back of a small and treasured photograph she wrote, "Our Mother, Queen Kapiolani."

Mother Marianne and her companions, eager though they were to begin their labors at the Branch Hospital, had to accept an enforced vacation. Although even the younger sisters would have benefited from the respite, Mother Marianne especially would have been helped by it. She admitted as much, in the brief report of these first months in Hawaii that she prepared in 1887: "they moved to a pleasant cottage to rest, till the Convent. . . would be completed."

Despite a strong will and years of firm discipline, weariness from the long journey across the American continent and from those days and nights of seasickness aboard the *Mariposa* had weakened her more than she allowed herself to admit. Age, too, was asserting its claims: in

November 1883 she was only two months away from beginning her forty-sixth year. In Honolulu, for the first and last time in her life, she was given the chance to enjoy relative ease. The plain and narrow house on Utica's Schuyler Street in which she grew up, the succession of austere convents in which she served, offered few of the comforts that Walter Gibson would have provided for them at that rented residence on King Street. He and St. Francis's Lady Poverty could never share the same abode. Mother Marianne called it only "a pleasant cottage," but some of her companions passed on to Sister Leopoldina more glamorous memories of their sojourn there. And, naturally, Sister Leopoldina made it much more sumptuous than even the prime minister, or an ordinary citizen of Honolulu, would have seen it: "... 'the place was a dream.' The little castle had all the modren improvemence... the lawn and gardon so beautifully kept and the sweet air always filled with perfume of the ever blooming flowers...."

The sisters were not left alone in this idyllic setting. "A Committee of Catholic Ladies" came to call. They included Mrs. Paul Neumann (wife of the kingdom's attorney-general) and Mrs. John F. Bowler (the woman who remembered this event thirty-five years later). Talula Hayselden, although an Episcopalian, gave advice and help, with her father's generosity.

Members of the Catholic ladies' committee would have accompanied the sisters on their shopping forays into town, as they purchased the furniture, linens, chinaware, staple foods, and other items needed for the convent being built at Kakaako.

At the cathedral, the Sacred Hearts priests and brothers spread the good news: "The Sisters of Charity have arrived from America last week," old Brother Bertrand wrote to Brother Quentin on November 13. "They number 6 plus the Superior General who has come also to get them settled. But once they're settled she will leave for America."

Father Leonor would have bustled in and out, bringing assorted advice, cheerful anecdotes, relevant bits of information about important personages in the town, and more than a word or two of instruction for the Portuguese women he had hired as servants. Walter Murray Gibson himself would have stopped by, during his busy rounds, to inquire about their comfort, to assure them that their new convent would be ready "soon, very soon," to offer them the use of his carriage if they should wish to go for a ride, and—in the hospitable Hawaiian manner—to bring gifts of flowers or of fresh fruits and vegetables.

Their expeditions into the town's shops and to the cathedral gave them opportunities to see Honolulu's healthy citizens, unspotted by leprosy and therefore unbroken in spirit. Already the congenial commingling of races for which Hawaii is noted was being displayed: Hawaiians, part-Hawaiians, Americans, Englishmen, Scotchmen, Irishmen, Chinese, Blacks, Portuguese, Micronesians, Norwegians, Germans, Swedes, even a rare Japanese, walked in Honolulu's streets or worked in its stores. The sisters, fascinated at first by this variety of complexions and features, soon became as accustomed to it as everybody else. They took a longer time to get used to the high costs of merchandise imported from their own homeland. "Dry goods are dear here," observed Sister Bonaventure in her New Year's Day letter to Mother Bernardina, "shoes particularly." But the diversity and inexpensiveness of foodstuffs grown locally compensated to some extent for the price of American goods: ". . . here it is summer & we have fresh vegetables daily. Bananas are only 5 cts a dozen, Wednesday last we had our first strawberries."

Sister Bonaventure was interested also in the natives' style of dress when they went to Mass on Christmas morning: ". . . the men [wear] white coat vest & pants & the women white dresses (some of them elegant ones) long trains & veils on their heads, no hats (there are hardly any of the women approaching the Alter here with hats, they will take them off & put on the veil) & veils of different varieties, lace, mull, dollier mull, crocheted &c. I believe most of them had on shoes, but as a general thing most of them go barefooted. . . ." Not only the high cost of shoes, but also the acute discomfort of having to wear them, made sensitive Hawaiians avoid those haole inventions on ordinary days. But Christmas, being a most special feast day, brought them out in all their torturesome finery.

Much to their relief (and, they believed, to the safety of their immortal souls), the sisters were presented with a problem in the two Portuguese women whom Father Leonor chose to attend them: ". . . they could speak no english [wrote Sister Leopoldina], and could not understand so the poor Sisters had to be their servants and wait on them. Many times the Sisters laughingly said it is good we have something to do, we can serve these poor people and they can draw the pay. They could fone [sic] for anything they were in need of, and every day a convance [sic] was sent to take the Sisters to Mass."

At that time in Honolulu's history, any parishioners whom Father Leonor might have rounded up for the duty probably spoke—and certainly heard—only the prevailing variant of pidgin English, a dialect composed of basic English and Hawaiian words, all strung together in a thoroughly original syntax and pronounced in the relaxed Polynesian manner. This practical if debased mixture of tongues, often further complicated with borrowings from Chinese and Portuguese, in deference to laborers imported from those countries to work on sugarcane plantations, was the only medium of communication shared by the people of Hawaii in 1883.

The servants' loyalty to Father Leonor, and above all to the church, would not have allowed them to pretend ignorance of English merely in order to take advantage of the sisters' innocence in local ways and speech. The malihini sisters, whose ears were not yet attuned to this dialect, did not comprehend the Portuguese women's attempts to speak in any language. They "cannot speak a word of English," Sister Bonaventure reported, "so we make signs." And, because the Franciscans had not yet learned the basic vocabulary of pidgin, they in turn could not supervise their hired help. The servants, for their part, would have been just as mystified by the crisp and rapid American speech in which these foreign women addressed them.

Later, after further acquaintance with native patients, all the Franciscan sisters became experts in the island vernacular. Sister Bonaventure, in joking about their experience, also anticipated their future: "We speak English, German, Hawaiian, Portuguese & soon I suppose will add the Chinese, as you see we are getting wise." But, unlike Catholic priests, all of whom learned to speak Hawaiian as soon as possible (and, in some instances, Portuguese and pidgin English as well), none of the Franciscans acquired a working command of the native language until they went to Molokai. Proficiency in Hawaiian was not necessary for them before then.

Sister Leopoldina's account suggests that the sisters actually enjoyed doing the housework and managing the establishment. After the rigors of convent life to which they had been trained for so many years, they would have been incapable of just sitting around the house, doing nothing. Mother Marianne's immediate imposition of the Order's Rule, during the weeks they spent in that temporary convent, would not have kept them busy enough to fend off the evils of sloth or the traps of boredom. The sisters, Mother Marianne most of all, welcomed the servant problem as being heaven-sent. A jaunty Protestant hymn of the period (which vastly amused less harried Hawaiians) promised all good Christians "Something to do in Heaven, something to do with our hands." Although Father Leonor would have blanched with horror at being associated in any way with Protestants, he, most of his fellow priests, and all the Sisters of St. Francis were just as compulsive as Calvinists about using every waking moment to worthy purpose.

They, too, had been indoctrinated with admonitions. "Idleness is the enemy of the soul," warned St. Anselm. "Always be doing something worthwhile; then the devil will find you busy," advised St. Jerome. And St. Francis himself had said, "All the friars must work hard, doing good."

Mother Marianne, as her Scrapbook shows, believed with Massillon that time is "a gift of God . . . a precious benefit of His mercy." It is not to be squandered, therefore, but must be used well here on earth, in working for the glory of God and for the reward of being with Him through all eternity.

Even though Mother Marianne and Queen Kapiolani had exchanged only the few phrases of politeness that Her Majesty could say in English, she needed no translator to express the worth of the American woman whom Father Leonor presented to her. The queen perceived the power in those steady dark eyes, the compassion in that serene and beautiful face. Great is her mana, she would have known at once. Like all Hawaiians, she could feel the mana, the spirit-power granted by the gods, that is present to some degree in each human being and in every other created thing. She herself, by birth rather than station, possessed more mana than did any other person born in Hawaii. And in Mother Marianne she met the only other woman in all Hawaii who possessed so fully the powers of the spirit. The queen felt, without need for words, how in this holy woman from America she, too, could find strength and comfort in her times of need.

The first of those times came very soon after they met. "One day the royal carriage drove to the door" of the sisters' temporary convent in the Hayseldens' "castle." Father Leonor, mounted upon his own horse, "delivered the Queen's messag," as Sister Leopoldina would write. "Her Majestie's Sister was very sick and desired to see Rev. Mother and the Sisters. so Rev. Mother and two of the Sisters answered the call." Sister Bonaventure, present in Honolulu at the time, remembered that the queen "sent two carriages for us to come and see her sister who is very sick & not expected to live."

When the king and the queen attended church, they usually went to St. Andrews', the Episcopal cathedral in Honolulu. Even so, neither

Kalakaua nor Kapiolani allowed sectarian divisiveness to rule their interests or dictate the company they kept. During their several meetings that preceded Father Leonor's departure for the United States in quest of Sisters of Charity, the queen had taken his measure too. His jolly good humor entertained her, his devotion to the assignment won her approbation, and the fluency with which he spoke Hawaiian put her at ease—despite the French accent. Sister Leopoldina confidently asserted that "he was the Queen's great favored [favorite]. She loved him and He could always console her in all her troubles." Although Sister Leopoldina may have exaggerated his influence, the queen did send him as her emissary to ask Mother Marianne to visit her ailing sister: ". . . He went ahead of the Royal carriage to the house of the Queen's sister. It was a beautiful castle and everything rich and grand, the poor lady was indeed very sick. the Queen accompanied them to the door. She lovingly took Mother's hand in both hers and placed [a] $100 bill in it and said this will not be the last. You are my Sisters. I love you and you will always be my Sisters."

Mother Marianne, accompanied by Father Leonor and two sisters, made at least one consoling visit more to the bedside of Her Royal Highness, Princess Mary Kinoike Kekaulike Piikoi. But by that time she could give the queen and her sister no more than prayers and sympathy. The princess suffered from "heart disease," as newspapers of the day called it. Death was coming for Her Royal Highness as surely as it was stalking the lowliest leper in the Branch Hospital at Kakaako.

During the second week in January 1884, at Ululani, the great mansion recently built for her on Beretania Street in the district of Makiki, near the edge of town, about two kilometers east of the palace in which her queen-sister dwelled, Princess Kekaulike died.

Chapter VI

THE BRANCH HOSPITAL AT KAKAAKO

ON ONE of those restful days in November 1883, Mr. Gibson took Mother Marianne to visit the Branch Hospital at Kakaako. Sister Bonaventure and another member of the company went with them. The Franciscans had noticed the hospital from the deck of the *Mariposa,* just before the ship entered the channel to Honolulu harbor. They would have remembered the high wooden fence, weatherbeaten and grim, and the roofs of the cottages it enclosed.

Now at last, on this fated day, Mother Marianne was going to enter within the pale, to see the place to which devotion to God and the seraphic St. Francis had brought her.

This Branch Hospital had been established in 1881, as "a receiving station" for people suspected of being lepers. Physicians and constables throughout the nation would commit suspects to Kakaako, by persuasion if possible, by force if necessary. There the suspects would be kept under observation until examining physicians agreed upon a diagnosis. A receiving hospital of this nature was necessary because in those days, before modern laboratory techniques of diagnosis were available or even imagined, competent physicians could determine whether or not a person was leprous only by studying the signs and symptoms his body exhibited. In most cases, especially among Hawaiian natives, the questionable signs and symptoms ultimately developed into those of undoubted leprosy. Yet occasionally among Hawaiians, and rather oftener among foreigners living in the islands, the signs and symptoms of other diseases might resemble those of leprosy so closely as to confuse both constables and doctors.

Thus, for example, chronic diseases of the skin and underlying tissues caused by several kinds of fungus infections, or by syphilis, tuberculosis, allergies, eczemas, certain kinds of tumors, and most especially by infestations with the tiny scabies mites, can so closely resemble those of leprosy in its earlier stages that differential diagnosis by visual inspection alone can be extremely difficult, even for an experienced physician. As a consequence of this sharing of signs, quite a few people who suffered from other diseases than leprosy were mistaken for lepers. And, of course, clever folk who feared that they might have leprosy and wanted to avoid incarceration for as long as possible, could insist that they were suffering from one of those other conditions. A number of unfortunate victims of mistaken identification had been sent to Kalawao on the island of Molokai in the years since 1866, when the Leper Settlement there received its first patients. Only a few of those pawns of ignorance were lucky enough to be released, in time, when finally a physician visiting or working at the Settlement recognized that they were not leprous. Most of those misdiagnosed people died at Kalawao, almost as quickly as if they had indeed been lepers.

Several years before 1881, then, in trying to avoid such errors in detection and disposition of patients, responsible physicians succeeded in persuading the Board of Health to set up a receiving station in Honolulu. "When a leper is seized and taken to Molokai, it is a sentence of death," acknowledged W. N. Armstrong, President of the Board of Health in 1882. "He has committed no crime. He has met with a great misfortune. He is driven out of society, that others may live. Without intending to act harshly, the government has not been careful enough of his feelings. For this reason he has often refused to give himself up, and the disease has spread. . . ."

The physicians' arguments were both compassionate and practical. Such concern was unprecedented in countries where leprosy was epidemic. At the same time, it also helped to comfort the physicians themselves. A confirmed case could be transferred from the Receiving Hospital to Molokai without arousing any guilt in the physician-judges who, by pronouncing him a leper, condemned him to the prison of Kalawao for the rest of his life. A person who suffered from some other disease than leprosy would be sent home, a free man again. His tuberculosis, or syphilis, or scabies, or ringworm might be more easily transmitted than another man's leprosy ever could be but, because people did not dread those familiar conditions nearly so much, cases of those "ordinary diseases" were set loose without restraint. The law sought out only lepers. The law banished only lepers to Kalawao, because the men who ruled Hawaii dreaded leprosy more than any of the other diseases with which mankind is affected.

A suspect whose ailment could not be identified was kept at the

Branch Hospital until, in good time, progressing in one direction or another, the tell-tale signs and symptoms appeared that would enable a committee of physicians to decide how to dispose of him. People in whom the symptoms developed slowly spent many dreary—and dangerous—months in the confines of Kakaako Hospital, waiting for the judgment.

Inasmuch as, in those days, in all countries, adequate regimens for treatment of infectious diseases were not yet available, both a patient and his physician could do nothing else but wait for time and "Nature"—or, as most preferred to think, for "Providence"—to achieve either a spontaneous remission or to terminate in death. Some physicians stayed the progress of syphilis with mercurials, and relieved the symptoms of malaria with chinchona bark. Some had learned to apply unguents containing compounds of sulfur in order to eradicate scabies mites from their burrows in infested flesh. But most physicians in Europe and America, and in Hawaii too, were as ignorant, and as helpless, in treating all infectious diseases as were the herbalists and "witch doctors" practising their arts in more primitive societies. In no country had any one found a medicine to cure leprosy.

Hawaii's Board of Health, acting from motives both humane and political, established a small receiving station in central Honolulu in an attempt to safeguard the rights of non-lepers while hoping to placate healthy citizens who demanded that all lepers be segregated, immediately. Then, as the number of lepers increased, a second makeshift institution supplemented the first. Finally, in 1881, a third one was built on the seashore at Kakaako. This one, everybody hoped, would be large enough to cope with all future needs. It opened on December 12, 1881, with forty-eight patients. Dr. George L. Fitch, a callous, opinionated, and very small-minded physician, was appointed its director.

Fitch is a prime example of the closed mind at its intractable worst. He cared nothing about the new discoveries in bacteriology that were revolutionizing medicine; he accepted nothing about Hansen's studies upon lepers in Norway; he ignored the evidence piling up around him in Hawaii. Worst of all, he entertained a very low opinion of the very people who trusted him to minister to their confined lepers. He arrived in Honolulu about 1880, and soon made up his mind about leprosy and Hawaiians, not to mention almost everything else under the sun. Altering neither his opinions nor his prejudices, he believed, and loudly proclaimed, that (as his superior, W. N. Armstrong, President of the Board of Health at the time, reported to the legislature in 1882), "leprosy is merely syphilis in its 'fourth' stage; that by constant use of medicine it may be considerably but not permanently relieved: and that it is not quickly contagious, especially among Hawaiians, whom Dr. Fitch claims are 'saturated with syphilis.'"

Fortunately for Hawaiians, whether leprous or clean, several more intelligent physicians in Honolulu gave greater attention to the clinical evidence at hand, if not to the new discoveries in Europe. They dared to disagree with the disputatious Dr. Fitch. They maintained that leprosy was a disease distinct from syphilis, and that it was contagious—most ferociously so among Hawaiians. Some of those physicians (Dr. Eduard Arning would be one of their number, after he had had time to draw his own conclusions) asserted that the incidence of syphilis was no greater in Hawaiians than it was among populations of other races and countries. But, they declared, in opposition to the annoying Dr. Fitch, the incidence of leprosy among Hawaiians was so high as to be frightening.

Another resident who did not see the evidence before him was Robert J. Creighton, compiler of *The Honolulu Almanac and Directory for 1886*. He described the Kakaako Hospital as he supposed it looked in 1885. In an effusion of meretricious prose he mentioned "about a dozen separate cottages, hospital, school, cook house, laundry, and other conveniences." These had been erected "about a mile from the business center of town." They stood upon the shore, just inside the broad and shallow reef. Until 1881 the low land they occupied had been a salt marsh, where "for centuries natives had made salt." Laborers hired by the Board of Health hauled in wagonloads of rubble and earth to fill up that end of the marsh. The area so made "had been securely fenced and laid off in walks and ornamental grounds, flowers and shade trees being planted. A good carriage drive to it along the shore line was also made."

Creighton's essay proves that he'd never gone near the Branch Hospital, not even for a fast ride along the "good carriage drive" leading to it. His tender sensibilities would have been tested to their limit had he actually looked at the place; and he was equally careful to shield the few townsfolk and the rare tourist for whom he wrote his dishonest guide book. He neglected to tell them certain ugly truths about the Hospital, preferring to make it a model institution of which Hawaii might boast to all the world.

But Sister Leopoldina, who joined Mother Marianne there in April

1885 (and who, incidentally, found it immeasurably better than the first Franciscans had discovered it in 1883), did not overlook some of the more brutal facts. For its patients the Kakaako Hospital was also a foul prison. It was surrounded by "a high close board fence and large strong locked gates. . . . A large building [sat] over those gates where the lepers were allowed to talk with their relitaves through prison bars. no one was alowed to enter without a permit from the Board of Helth."

And, moreover, once he entered that gatehouse, a clean person was not allowed to touch the inmate he had come to visit. A few days after the Franciscan sisters arrived in Honolulu they could have read in the *Pacific Commercial Advertiser* an article about the fate of one visitor who broke the law. He was a young musician, who played in King Kalakaua's military band, and he was sentenced to a term in prison for the crime of "having kissed his wife, who is a leper confined in Kakaako Hospital."

Nor did Creighton in 1885 even hint at the stupidity of the Board of Health's decision makers in 1881. In choosing the salt swamp at Kakaako for the site of their hospital, they picked one of the worst of all possible locations. For one thing, as Honolulu's nervous merchants soon complained, it still stood too close to their precious jeopardized selves. And, for another, it was much too visible to passengers aboard ships approaching the harbor. It practically advertised the presence of leprosy to tourists, those potential investors from abroad, and other important wanderers, whom the Honolulu Chamber of Commerce, founded in 1850, hoped to attract in increasing numbers to enjoy beautiful Hawaii's unparalleled and unexploited charms.

Few townsfolk, however, knew about the trials the hospital's location laid upon its inmates. At certain times of the year, when tides rose high and winds from the south blew strong, waves from the sea rolled across the reef and into the hospital compound, sweeping beneath the enclosing fence and the outermost buildings, over the walkways and the ornamental shrubbery. Deposits of salt left by the waves wrought their usual effects: grasses and weeds alike withered and died, scrawny shrubs and transplanted trees never had a chance to grow. Whitewashed stones that once marked the pathways lay scattered about like rubbish upon the bare earth, because after the second inundation no one bothered to put them back. Even when the waves did not flow into the yard, the ocean lurked beyond the edge of the shore, making its presence forever known in its ceaseless murmur, the scent of seaweeds, the spray-laden winds. Hospital walls and furnishings, blankets, mats, the patients' very bodies became sticky with salt. Crystals of seasalt clouded the window panes. Metals corroded. Nail holes ran red with rust, counterparts to lepers' sores weeping fluids stained with blood. Flakes of whitewash dropped from walls, like scurf from a leper's skin, exposing the silvered wood beneath, as lepers' ligaments and bones are revealed when the dead flesh falls away.

Once the Branch Hospital had been built, the Board of Health did little to maintain it. Always grudging, always counting pennies, it expected grateful patients to take good care of the property that the benevolent state had so generously devoted to their well-being. The Board also expected inmates to help sustain themselves by growing vegetables in Kakaako's infertile dirt. Somehow, the Board contrived to ignore the fact that the hospital yard was just as sere as the primordial salt marsh had been. Or that the patients immured in that graceless prison thanked neither gods nor men for the privilege of being there.

A catalogue of Kakaako's deficiencies would not be complete without a mention of the worst of its affronts to nose and eye. The place stank. It reeked with the stench of lepers' untended sores. Neither fresh and salty breezes from the sea nor perfumed zephyrs wafting from the land could ever disperse that nauseating smell. And no matter where he looked the desperate visitor could never find relief from the sight of lepers. The hospital, built to accommodate only about a hundred patients, had become overcrowded. In November 1883 more than two hundred patients and suspects—men, women, and children, of all ages in all stages of decrepitude—languished at Kakaako. At least as many other cases, by the Board of Health's own admission, could be found living in Honolulu—"and the number is increasing constantly." By far the majority of the people in the hospital were lepers, exhibiting symptoms so clearly defined that even the most cautious physician could recognize the condition at sight. Despairing, sullen, helpless, and embittered, they waited for the release of death in this charnel house beside the sea. Feeling that they had been unfairly rejected by men and abandoned by God, they took a peculiar revenge: they did as little as possible to help themselves.

According to law and Board of Health policy, diagnosed cases should have been sent as soon as feasible to the Leprosarium at Kalawao. The Board of Health in 1880 would have "shipped them off," as the expression was in those days, much like bags of freight consigned to Kalawao. By 1881 Dr. Fitch had persuaded his superiors in the Board to "make a permanent leper settlement" at Kakaako, "as an experiment," and to send only disobedient patients to Kalawao.

In 1883 Walter Murray Gibson had just become president of the Board and was in no great hurry to change some of its more controversial activities. And, ever sensitive to the petitions of people who might be able to return a favor someday, and more than a little soft-hearted about the plight of all lepers, Gibson continued to accept Fitch's experiment. A word from a pastor or priest, a friend or relative, sometimes even from the king or the queen, easily persuaded him—or his minions—to hold a favored patient at Kakaako for an indefinite period. Strict segregationalists, annoyed over this "weakness," even went so far as to accuse Gibson (or his minions) of accepting bribes for arranging such postponements of exile. Although the charge was never proved, it probably did apply to some of Gibson's employees if not to himself. A few reputable physicians pointed out that as long as Kakaako was so full of confirmed lepers, it could not receive the many patients still at large and spreading the contagion. As usual, Fitch scoffed; as usual Gibson paid no attention to critics or to advisers, and did nothing to alleviate the crowding at Kakaako.

Naturally, Gibson's "laxity" infuriated the self-righteous, the certitudinous, and the frightened among Honolulu's citizens. Thus, Thomas G. Thrum, printer and publisher since 1875, a dedicated if selective chronicler of most events in the islands, but also a man throughly convinced that only white Anglo-Saxon Protestant males knew how to run the world, never missed a chance to "expose" Gibson's inaction. In the "Retrospect for 1883," published in his *Hawaiian Annual for 1884,* Thrum arraigned the President of the Board of Health in lugubrious tones:

"Health matters have claimed the attention of the thoughtful minded, and no little agitation has been given the subject in the public press at the inaction of the Board of Health in all that pertains to sanitary reform, or in carrying out the laws of segregation and isolation of lepers. . . . Leprosy, that plague spot on Hawaii's fair name and fame, has been and is yet being trifled with for political ends in spite of public opinion and the condemnation of the press. 'Tis true that several loads of unfortunate lepers have been removed to Molokai, but the menacing lazaretto at Kakaako is still full. . . ."

Thrum's complaint is typical of the opinions held by Gibson's enemies. They expected instant results, an immediate end to the leprosy problem, an expunging of that "plague spot" at least from Honolulu's waterfront, if not from distant Kalawao's. And, typically, they quibbled over every cent appropriated for matters of public health, and gave Gibson no credit at all for any of the actions he did take to improve "health matters."

Thrum's "Retrospect for 1883," for example, devotes not a word to the arrival of Mother Marianne and her companions; says nothing about Dr. Arning's being invited to investigate the epidemiology of leprosy; makes no mention of the new government hospital being built at Wailuku on the island of Maui (or about the two proposed for Hilo, Hawaii and Lihue, Kauai); refers to none of the several other meritorious projects being advanced by Gibson's Board of Health, least of all those that would improve the water and sewerage systems of Honolulu itself. All these, and more, could be ignored by Gibson's critics, not only because the projects proved that he was more efficient than they liked to admit, but mostly because the proposals would cost the nation considerable sums in sacred money.

Thrum's own personal bias against Catholics, Mormons, and "Asiatics," indeed about anyone who was not both Caucasian and a Congregationalist or a Church of England man, accounts for his failure to mention the Franciscan sisters. Not once, during the fifty subsequent years in which he wrote most of the accounts published in his *Hawaiian Annual,* did he print a word about Mother Marianne, Father Damien, or any other Catholic sister, brother, bishop, or priest. For him, they were beneath notice. The prejudices he cherished against "foreign religions," "colored peoples," and "costly innovations" were shared, unfortunately, by too many of his contemporaries. In the presence of the likes of them, Bishop Hermann had good reason to feel uneasy.

Obviously, by 1883, despite the best of intentions, everything about the kingdom's program for controlling the leprosy epidemic was going wrong. Successive ministries had tried to stop the plague ever since 1864, when Dr. William Hillebrand first warned the Board of Health about the disastrous speed with which the disease was spreading among native Hawaiians. The government strove to combat this insidious importation with generosity and intelligence. Where other countries simply abandoned their lepers, casting them out from society and forcing them to care for themselves until they died, Hawaii adopted a sensible if selfish plan to isolate its lepers but to take care of them while still they lived. In 1865 the legislature passed an Act to Prevent the Spread of Leprosy, which declared the policy of segregation and arranged means for enforcing it. In 1866 a leprosarium was established in one of the most isolated places in the kingdom: at Kalawao, a corner of the tiny promontory of Kalaupapa, which juts into the sea, like the prow of a ship, from the northern coast of the island of Molokai. Kalaupapa, "the flat plain," lies at the foot of a spectacular escarpment of seacliffs. Their steep walls, rising about 675 meters above the leaf of land, deny sick lepers access to the rest of Molokai, sloping away southward from the tops of the cliffs. The surging restless sea is an unconquerable barrier on the promontory's three other sides. Kalaupapa, too, is a prison. But it is a prison made most beautiful by encompassing sea and soaring precipices and overarching blue sky. Compared with Kakaako, it was a paradise.

Cruel though it was to lepers, the plan to segregate recognized cases was the only practicable one for its time—and for almost a hundred years thereafter. Not until the 1960s, when at last effective chemotherapeutic drugs were achieving their miraculous cures, could the incidence of leprosy be checked in any other way than by separating the sick from the well. In 1883, however, the people of Hawaii could not know that their government's isolation policy would indeed help to slow the advance of leprosy among the islands' residents. Although today epidemiologists believe that other factors also were involved in halting the epidemic, they do agree that isolation of known cases at Kalaupapa did prevent the indiscriminate transmission of the leprosy organisms among susceptible children and adults, thereby saving them from the infection. But this merciful decline in the incidence of leprosy would not be attained until early in the twentieth century, only after three more generations of lepers had been banished to Molokai. Meanwhile, the cost in anguish was immense, to sick and to well alike. And the price that the successive governments of Hawaii paid in terms of money alone was greater than that paid by any other country on earth for the care of its lepers.

In 1865 the legislature gave the Board of Health responsibility for administering the program to control the spread of leprosy. Everyone who took part in preparing the plan, from King Kamehameha V down to the most thrifty legislator, agreed that patients exiled to Kalawao for the sake of the public weal should be supported with food, clothing, shelter, medical care, and a modest allowance in cash, all to be provided free of charge by the government. But, as is usual in complex programs of this nature, noble intentions were never quite realized in good effects. The number of lepers increased faster than did the appropriations to sustain them. Always the perennial vexations that characterize an untrained bureaucracy—such as unthinking clerks and martinet bursars and timorous physician-administrators—were complicated by Honolulu's distance from foreign sources of materials and Kalawao's distance from Honolulu, by bad weather and boisterous seas, and by uncooperative self-pitying lepers themselves. In consequence, the miseries of patients sent to Kalawao were increased rather than relieved. The defects of the program almost destroyed it before it had a chance to be effective. The medical profession's lack of knowledge about the disease itself—its cause, manner of transmission, treatment, and the course of its progress in a patient or through the population of a country—added to the confusion. Inasmuch as, even in 1980, these same questions have not yet been answered to the satisfaction of all epidemiologists, physicians in 1883 can hardly be blamed for their ignorance.

By 1883 almost everyone involved in the national effort to control leprosy was thoroughly discouraged. The businessmen whose taxes paid for the Board of Health's appropriations begrudged every cent spent "needlessly"—by which they meant upon programs that did not increase the country's sources of income and their own accumulations of wealth. Their families were not threatened by leprosy. In their opinion, only the dirty, the wicked, feckless, debased, and debauched native poor ever contracted leprosy. Dr. Fitch, in his usual insulting manner, gave them official endorsement for this comforting opinion: "The disease," he wrote in his report to the Legislature of 1882, "is everywhere among us, members of the police force, the soldiers, the band boys, pastors of churches, teachers, students, are all among the sufferers. (Of course it will be understood I refer only to natives)."

Primitive statistics of the time gave Fitch and businessmen the figures to make this assertion, and their own casual observations sustained them in this certitude. They did not draw the further conclusion that the poor might not have been so debased and so diseased if they had been given the opportunity to be as clean, well fed, well housed, and uncrowded as are the rich. Accordingly, Hawaii's businessmen watched jealously over appropriations made to the Board of Health. Their distrust of Gibson, after he took over as president of the Board in 1882, merely strengthened their general reluctance to "pour good money down into that cesspit." They wanted to know when all this expensive benevolence was going to show some benefits to themselves as well as to the lepers. Fitch did not help matters much when he declared, in his report of 1882, "the endeavor to enforce the law of segregation as it has been carried on here for years, has been a most complete failure. . . ."

Gibson, with all his faults, was genuinely concerned for the health and well being of all the people of Hawaii, poor or rich, native or foreign, leprous or clean. He, the natural gadfly, the asker of questions and seeker of knowledge, was not easily discouraged by the immensity of the problem or the contentions of adversaries. He, more than anyone else in Hawaii, even its esteemed physicians, had learned about the great discoveries being made by Louis Pasteur in France and Robert Koch in Germany, proving that specific bacteria are the causes of specific diseases in men and animals. Gibson knew that where mysteries persist, men must ask questions. More than any one else in Hawaii, he realized that only through the methods of what he lovingly called "scientific research" could the important questions about leprosy be asked—and, he believed, answered. Among all the men who managed the affairs of Hawaii, Gibson alone had the mind to appreciate the significance of the astonishing discoveries being made in Europe in all the sciences during that great and fruitful era. Out of his pride in Hawaii (and also, perhaps, as some people sniffed, out of vanity in himself), he decided to make Honolulu a center for scientific investigations into leprosy. At the suggestion of Dr. William Hillebrand (by that time retired to Montreux in Switzerland), Gibson invited Dr. Eduard Christian Arning to come from Germany to Honolulu, to work under the auspices of the Board of Health. Gibson chose Arning precisely because he expected the young doctor would apply his learning in the new science of bacteriology to studying the mysteries of leprosy. Recently, Hillebrand told Gibson, Dr. Armauer Hansen of Norway had demonstrated the presence of a special kind of bacterium in the diseased tissues of lepers. And Gibson wanted Arning to see if "Hansen's bacilli" could be found in Hawaii's lepers also.

Such studies, Gibson realized, would take time—perhaps even as long as two or three years. In the interval, he understood, the deplorable situation at Kakaako must be eased. Father Damien, at Kalawao, had improved conditions at the settlement most remarkably during the ten years he had lived there among the patients. But Kakaako had not been given a Damien. Kakaako was a ghastly lesion upon the conscience of the government—and upon Gibson's tender own.

Gibson asked for Bishop Hermann's help in finding Sisters of Charity. He did not expect them to end the leprosy epidemic. But he did hope that, by their presence and with their care, they could soothe the spirits as well as the bodies of imprisoned lepers. He knew enough about the horrors of the disease, and the miseries at Kakaako, to understand that only selfless, sacrificing nurse-sisters, who ministered to souls as well as to bodies, could bring surcease to the torments of the living dead.

On that pleasant sunny morning in November 1883, when Gibson first took Mother Marianne to Kakaako, at sight of the carriage approaching along the road from town, the guard swung open the gate in the prison wall. The coachman drove the prime minister's smart barouche into the hospital yard. Scores of patients, surprised by this invasion from the land beyond the fence, gathered around, to learn who dared to venture in so boldly.

And then, for the first time, the Sisters of St. Francis saw the lepers.

Gibson should have winced at the prospect before them—and groaned at thought of what he was asking these gentle women to do. Sending for them had been easy: they had been faceless, incorporeal ideals then, little more than the imagined ministering angels addressed in hymns and prayers. Greeting them in Honolulu had been satisfying—to plans, to hopes, certainly to self-esteem. Thinking of himself as their lord-protector, beginning to dote upon them as a fond father might over a flutter of daughters, had become a kind of pleasing charade. But now, after he had visited with the Franciscans several times and learned to know them as persons, each with her individual features and graces and voice, each with her strong clean hands and a heart as immaculate as the coif that framed her clear eyes and smooth unblemished cheeks and smiling lips, he must have shuddered at the hideousness of the hell into which he was about to thrust them.

He would have turned to Mother Marianne, sitting beside him in the shining carriage, to see how she responded to that amassed ugliness.

She did not shrink back. She looked full into the face of horror that day, and she did not turn away.

"They drove to the office [Sister Leopoldina would write] the Queen's white man stepped out on the veranda. he was a fine looking man, his big white [face?] and jet black hair shining in the bright sun, and his long black beard waving in the lovely morning air he reached his hand to Mr. Gibson and bowed very low. Mr. Gibson introduced him. This is Mr. Van Giesian [sic]... who has full charge of the Branch Hospital. He reached his hand and again bowed very low. I am pleased to meet you he said and will be most happy to show you around the Hospital."

The introduction to Henry Van Giesen was the only pleasant incident of the morning—and probably the happiest encounter the Franciscans ever had with "the Queen's white man." Apparently at Queen Kapiolani's intercession, the Board of Health had appointed him as superintendent of the Branch Hospital before Gibson began his regime, and Gibson saw no reason to replace him with another man. Van Giesen had married a half-Hawaiian woman. His wife, when they were wed in 1880, was eighteen-year-old Caroline Sweetman, a member of a family from Kauai. And she, or someone in her family, as Kapiolani's concern for Van Giesen's employment suggests, must have been a retainer, or even a friend, of the queen, whose ancestors had been the ruling kings of Kauai. Very soon afterward, Mrs. Van Giesen developed signs of leprosy. He chose to enter the hospital at Kakaako with her (possibly in order to gain the well-paid job as its superintendent), and, by implication, to go with her eventually to the settlement at Kalawao. The law permitted devoted mates, parents, children, or friends to accompany confirmed lepers to Kalawao—provided they agreed to stay there for the rest of their lives. Those healthy attendants were known as kokuas, the Hawaiian word for helpers.

Despite this show of loyalty to his wife, and certain other attributes of refinement as well, Van Giesen at Kakaako proved to be a man more brutal than kind. Like most foreigners who enjoyed a freedom from leprosy and so many other diseases that devastated Hawaiians—a puzzling phenomenon that was explained only by later discoveries in immunology and genetics—Van Giesen looked with scorn upon vulnerable natives. Most haoles considered the natives as members of a weak and degenerate race doomed to extinction. Moreover, like the arrogant males of the time, he manifested none of the softer sentiments for unfortunate individuals of any race. The fact that he accompanied his wife as a kokua suggests that he may have loved her, once upon a time, at least when she was unblemished and attractive. But later, as the ravagings of leprosy consumed her body and stole her beauty, he became as cruel to her as to everyone else. He performed his job as hospital superintendent according to his prejudices, running it like a prison camp or an insane asylum. The locked gates and police guards were signs of the repression within as, in his determination to maintain law and order, Van Giesen terrorized the many patients and the few employees. Under such duress, they submitted to his commands and hated him for his callousness.

He had some justification for using those methods, of course, as does the administrator of every hospital and prison. Discipline must be maintained, if chaos is to be avoided. Victims of Hawaii's plan to segregate lepers, especially native Hawaiians, did not easily adjust to being locked up in Kakaako's stockade. Not all of them had yet given up hope for rescue—by miracle, by the reprieve of a different diagnosis, by intervention of some friend in power, even by some magical medication yet to be discovered. Hope would fade only when their names appeared upon the lists of patients whom the doctors and Henry Van Giesen decided should be shipped off to Molokai. Hope would die, utterly and forever, when finally they set foot upon the stony beach at Kalawao.

At Kakaako a few patients still clung to the world of freedom beyond the high fence, to brief visits with friends and relatives in that barred room above the locked gates, to glimpses of clean people coming and going along the carriage drive that linked the hospital with the city beyond. Even though they could have escaped easily, by going over or under the fence and across the reef, or even along the beckoning carriage road, few of Kakaako's prisoners ever made the attempt. Most were too sick to try. And those few who were still strong enough to run away knew that, no matter where they went to hide from policemen, they could find no refuge from leprosy. When a rare patient did break out from Kakaako's confines, his freedom could not last. Where could he go to hide from the devourer? Relatives might take care of him, for the while, but eventually an informer or a constable would see those sores upon his body and recognize him for the danger he was. And he would be taken back again, this time in chains, to the lazar house beside the sea.

The "refinements" of hospitalization—cleanliness, decency, a degree of privacy, the therapy of useful occupation, even the minimum amount of medical care—meant nothing to Van Giesen or to most of his healthy contemporaries. Uninstructed in those forms of generosity, they were hardened in heart. Lepers, they reasoned, are destined to die soon anyway. Why bother, then, with costly attendance to prolong their miseries for a few more weeks or months? Let them care for themselves—or let them die. In Hawaii, as elsewhere, the majority of prosperous and healthy people other than native Hawaiians both feared and resented lepers. They wanted lepers kept out of sight, out of mind, and off the legislature's appropriation bills.

Lepers, for their part, did very little to ease their lot. Despairing and stricken, they raged at God for afflicting them so unfairly, and hated clean folk for treating them so harshly. Without someone to lead them by example, to show concern for them, they gave up. They sank into squalor and apathy. They, too, awaited the release of death. And, such was their condition, both physical and spiritual, death did come for them much sooner, both at Kakaako and at Kalawao, than it would have taken them had they been living at home. "No one ever dies of leprosy," as physicians have been saying for centuries. But that cheating aphorism neglects to explain that lepers do die of other superimposed infections, such as pneumonia or erysipelas or gangrene, which kill them with greater ease because of the debilitations caused by leprosy. And lepers, especially among Hawaiians in the nineteenth century, could die very easily of despair alone. A perfectly healthy Hawaiian, upon being convinced that he had committed a grievous offense against some punitive god or some vengeful man, could be so seized by despair that he would take to his bed and die within four or five days. Hawaiians who despaired because the leprosy—or any other foreign disease—had smitten them were weakened even more in both body and soul. They amazed haoles, and themselves, by the ease with which they could die: "Na kanaka kuu wale aku no i ka uhane," Hawaiians were saying as early as the 1840s, even before leprosy became an important affliction among them, "the people freely gave up their souls and died."

Insensitive though he was toward his patients, Henry Van Giesen was far from being the worst man the Board of Health might have installed as "Steward" of the Branch Hospital. And, bad as it was, the hospital at Kakaako was one of the best institutions anywhere in the world that had been established for the care of lepers. And yet Van Giesen is typical of the sort of administrator whom, time after time, the bureaucrats who run governmental agencies will choose as their lieutenants. The qualifications that most recommended Van Giesen were an imposing presence, a smooth tongue, a manly confidence, a specious show of efficiency, a pretense at obeying rules handed down by committeemen who value dollars more than souls, and, above all, the resolution to operate within the limits of an allotted budget. Gibson, who shared with Van Giesen all those attributes except the last, must have been well pleased with his man in charge at Kakaako.

In all Hawaii, before 1883, Father Damien was the only haole who showed the lepers that he cherished them as persons, rotting though their bodies might be. He proved himself by going to Kalawao to live among them, sharing their hardships, binding their wounds, consoling their spirits, and, at the last, by becoming a leper like themselves.

On their first visit to the Branch Hospital, Mother Marianne and her companions were taken on a tour of inspection by the lordly Van Giesen. Sister Leopoldina's account was drawn from Mother Marianne's remembrance of that terrible day: "A short distance from the office they entered a long narrow building made of rough boards and they were whitewashed, this is the lepers dining room he said. Our gentle Mother and the Sisters stood stairing—never in their lives had they met with such horrors, the dirt and sworms of flies that covered the long tables and benches. they were wondering if they had ever been cleaned? when they passed along a covered veranda at the end was the kitchen which was in a most frightful condission, thick with filth and flies. The slick handsome man having charge of the place was not ashamed—he seemed to think it was good enough for the lepers."

With the sure instinct of the cunning steward, Van Giesen showed them the best part first. He conducted them next to the patients' wards, long narrow cottages given roofs but no ceilings. The rough walls, once whitewashed, were as mottled as the people propped up against them. Fat bedbugs nested in the cracks. Brown stains upon walls, floors, and bedding showed where their blood-filled bodies had been crushed by desperate patients. Straw mattresses, each more or less covered by a dirty blanket, lay upon the unswept floor or, for more affluent inmates, upon planks supported by low carpenters' horses. Blankets, mattresses, clothing, and patients all supported an ineradicable population of lice. No attempt had been made to separate patients according to age, sex, or stage of illness. Men, women, adolescents, young children, the moribund as well as the quick: all were thrown together in those precincts of hell. "All looked alike young and old seemed so disponded their wards so empty and cheerless. [They had] no table chair or bed, the poor unfortunates were crouched on the floor with their knees drawn up to their chins, and in every face utter despair not a smile from one of them, most of them had thin little gowns barely enough to cover them."

The sisters looked about in disbelief. Less than a month ago they had been taking care of patients in the bright, clean, cheerful rooms of St. Joseph's Hospital in Syracuse. . . . ". . . as [the sisters] passed from those distressing sights every place meeting that dreadful picture of despair their hearts were bleeding with sympathy, Mr. Van Giesiean said, now let me show you the most interesting place and he led them to a long narrow building that extended so far out on the beach that the high tide brought the waves under part of the building. There were three rooms. This first room he said is where we keep our dying lepers and when they die we put them in this second room for the benefit of the Doctors, after the Doctors have finished their work the remains is then placed in this third room to await the coming of the cart and it is taken away to be burried."

The slick warden ushered them into the first room, saying: "We never bring a sick leper in this house until they are hopeliss and not one has ever recovered it is sure death when they are brought here. and this poor man (pointing to the poor unfortunate on the floor) will soon die."

While Mr. Gibson and Mother Marianne stood talking with Van Giesen at one side of the room, one of the sisters "bent over the dying man who was on the floor with only a dirty mat under him and that gray blanket to cover him. She tried to speak consoling words, but he did not seem able to answer her. but She never could forget those sad pleeding eyes as he looked up at her. He was a young man and how sad it was to see him so helpless and suffering without any one to cair for him, his large [muscular] arms thrown out on the bare floor and death agony in his ghastly face. There was a boy standing near and Sister asked him Where is the water? Does some one give him water to moisten his dry feverish lips?"

The boy answered, speaking in pidgin English. "No can geeve watah.—Bimebye die."

"Does somebody give him milk or something to eat?" persisted the sister.

"No can eat, s'pose come eenside dis place.—Bimebye die."

"Does someone stay with him at night?"

"A kind of sick look covered the boys face and shuddering he said, No can stop inside dis place.—Bimebye die."

"While Sister was telling Mother and Mr. Gibson what she had learned from the boy, the dying man's eyes were [fixed] on Mr. Gibson and the Sisters, a little gleem of hope appeared in his sad face Mr. Gibson's kind eyes filled he was horrofied Oh, he said, I had no idea that the sick were treated like this. Have this man removed at once to his room give him a nurse and plenty of milk and nurshment even if he should not get well, never treat any one like this again, that will be very good Mr. Van Giesiean said they have a horror of coming in this building they rebell and we always have trouble to get them to come. So the poor man was taken to his room, and with careful nursing soon recovered."

Sister Leopoldina, mercifully, did not mention the other assaults upon the senses that Mother Marianne and her companions experienced during that first visit: the ravaged mutilated bodies of patients far advanced in the disease: the blinded eyes: the parts of faces eaten away, leaving gaping holes where noses had been, rounded O's of tight scars where once lips had smiled and kissed: the lost fingers and toes: hands contracted into claws: legs ending in stumps: the open ulcers, oozing blood and serum, or encrusted with pus, or teeming with maggots: the heaped-up mounds of tumors where the flesh, in a last frenzy of exuberance, proliferated before it died and dissolved away: the mottlings, red or purple or brown or white, that dappled the skins of cases just starting down the steep path to decay and to death. . . .

And the eyes. Always the eyes. Dulled with pain. Soft with grieving. Glittering with hatred. All staring—if they could still see, if the pupils in those questioning eyes had not yet been consumed and scarred and sealed forever against the light—all staring in wonderment and envy and resentment at these *clean* people come into their filthy hell. All asking, in a harrowing silence, Why me? Why me? Why not you?—

And, above all, permeating everything—air, clothes, straw pallets, greasy blankets, even the wood of the walls and the dirt on the floors—hung the stink of lepers: the revolting stench rising from sores unwashed and uncovered, the miasma of dead and rotting flesh, in which voracious microorganisms by the billions eagerly devoured the debris from the tissues that they, and the implacable causers of leprosy, had killed in the bodies of their hapless hosts.

Mother Marianne saw, smelled, heard, felt all those horrors. Many a weak and lesser person has been exposed to these terrors only once, and has turned to flee from them, in dread, forever. Even the young Francis of Assisi did so, when first he met a lone leper standing in his path. But neither Mother Marianne nor her companion-sisters admitted that dread into their hearts. All those horrors filled them with pity. And pity strengthened the resolve that had brought them to Hawaii, into this compound of sorrows.

Sister Leopoldina, in her account of this initial day, devised one of the most amazing understatements in the history of compassion when she wrote: "Mother Marianne could easily see what good the Sisters could do there."

Father Marie Joseph Coudrin, founder of the Congregation of the Sacred Hearts of Jesus and Mary, explained in more elegant terms the insuperable power of Christian love: "Nature may shudder, but in the end grace will triumph."

NOTES on Chapter VI

Remarks of Presidents of Board of Health and Government Physicians: *Leprosy in Hawaii, Extracts from Reports,* 1886: (a) Armstrong, pp. 113–116; (b) Hillebrand warning, p. 7; (c) Fitch report, pp. 117–122; (d) Hillebrand-Gibson correspondence, pp. 154–158; (e) Gibson's account of appeal for Sisters of Charity, pp. 137–140.

Chapter VII

WORKING FOR GOD

AT LAST, during Christmas week, carpenters and painters put the final touches to the convent at Kakaako. The sisters, impatient to live near their place of work, planned to move into the new home on December 31. But Father Leonor forbade the move, "for fear the paint, if not entirely dry, would make us sick." Given an unexpected holiday, Sister Bonaventure took the chance to write a letter home to Syracuse.

At length the fresh paint dried satisfactorily, Kakaako's vagrant breezes dispersed the fumes, and Father Leonor pronounced the air safe to breathe. On Thursday, January 3, 1884, the sisters left Talula Hayselden's mansion for the austerities of their convent. The very next day Father Leonor blessed the building and placed it under the protection of St. Francis. This was the first Franciscan institution to be established in Hawaii; and Mother Marianne's was the first community of Catholic religious women founded in the United States to initiate a new foreign mission apostolate independent of affiliation with a European community of women religious.

Sister Bonaventure's New Year letter described this westernmost convent of St. Francis: "... it is a square two story house with the front door in the centre opening into a fine hall from which is an entrance to the chapel for the priest. on the right of the hall is the parlour about as large as your Community room, & back of that is a smaller room. the parlour has four windows. on the left of the hall is the refectory & back of that a large pantry. from the refectory opens a door to a covered lattice walk which leads to our kitchen, a neat little house with a large sink, water, etc. a few steps from the kitchen stands the wash house, & a bathroom (bath tub etc.). to the left of the house & near the [convent's] gates stands the portress' house (we have a native woman as portress who speaks a little English). then upstairs in our house is a large hall & on one side three rooms, on the other side one large room & one small one."

The sisters, who never asked for much in beauty or comfort, were content with this dwelling. Although it was as bare and graceless as everything else in that singularly unbeautiful hospital complex, at least it was painted, a pure dazzling white, both inside and out. It stood at the western end of the compound, with a front door (protected by a narrow covered porch) looking toward the west, beyond the entrance to Honolulu harbor, to the coastline of Oahu. Like the whole "immense place" (as Sister Bonaventure thought of the Branch Hospital), the convent too was surrounded by a fence made of closely fitted boards. This one, however, was lower, only six feet high. A narrow gate pierced this wall, and a graveled pathway linked the convent with the nearest hospital buildings. The enclosure afforded space enough for "a large garden" the sisters hoped to have someday. But in January 1884 not a tree or a bush or a blade of grass added its touch of green to the scene, either inside the fence or outside it. The fence, and the portress, offered token protection against the world's intrusions, not against contact with lepers—or any one else. Once, when the sisters locked themselves out by mistake, Mr. Van Giesen scaled the wall with the ease of a cat, and opened the gate from within.

A small chapel, also painted white, was attached to the rear of the convent. The sisters and Father Leonor agreed that it should be dedicated to St. Philomena, who was being much honored at the time by Sacred Hearts priests. The officiating priest, as well as the sisters, entered the chapel from the convent's hall. Lepers attending services came in through the chapel's front door, which opened upon the hospital compound. It was furnished with "nice pews," said Sister Bonaventure, and soon would receive the altar, "donated by a gentleman." A modest statue of St. Philomena, to be given by Father Leonor, would be placed upon a shelf above the altar. And His Majesty told Mr. Gibson that he planned to "give us a handsome picture."

One day in December, while the sisters were busy preparing the house for occupancy, the king himself called upon them, arriving "in his carriage with drivers and footmen. . . ." Sister Bonaventure told how "we were presented to him by his Lordship (dressed in his purple) who came with Father Leonor." King Kalakaua "thanked Mother very feelingly for having done them the honour of having come here to care for his sick people."

At the farther end of the hospital yard, in a prophetic opposition, stood "the two-story cottage" of Mr. and Mrs. Henry Van Giesen. A low picket fence, once whitewashed, marked off the superintendent's home from the lepers' precincts. Attached to the back of their house, just as the sisters' chapel was affixed to the convent, stood a small hut. This shack served as a makeshift laboratory for Dr. Arning, that other representative of secular power in the Kakaako compound, that other advocate of intellect rather than of compassion in mankind's war against leprosy. Within this hut Dr. Arning performed his bacteriological research into the cause of leprosy and the manner in which it is spread.

Compared with their former quarters in Syracuse, whether at St. Anthony's Convent or at St. Joseph's Hospital, the residence at Kakaako, although spacious within, was more like a prison, or an asylum for the insane. Yet Mother Marianne and her courageous companions entered into it with thanksgiving. Here at last they gained a home of their own, close to the place of their mission. Now at last they could live and work according to the discipline of the Rule and the needs of their patients. The new convent may not have been worthy of Sister Bonaventure's favorite adjective, "grand," but the paint on the walls was still fresh and clean, the metal finishings of windows and doors had not yet begun to corrode. Nor did the house always reek of lepers—although a slight shift in the wind would bring into it that reminder of corrupting flesh, as pervasive as were the others of Kakaako's scents, the aroma of seaweeds upon the reef, marsh gas from the unfilled parts of the swamp, and the ammoniacal vapors from manure heaps in nearby stables.

Nonetheless, the high fence around the whole hospital, more than anything else at Kakaako, proved to be as oppressive as it was useless. Some sisters had not cut so completely the ties binding them to this world of emotions as to be able to ignore entirely the ways in which it affected them. Sister Leopoldina, a long lifetime later, remembered her three years at Kakaako with shudderings: "They were so cut away from everybody that the loneliness of the place was so dreadful. You could see nothing [beyond the fence] and all you could hear was the continual plash of the ocean." The servants hired by the Board of Health did not stay long within those restricting walls: ". . . young people could not endure the loneliness—and it was dangerous for married people" because they might carry the contagion of leprosy home to their children.

Discontent servants could quit their jobs and go elsewhere. But the Sisters of St. Francis, like the lepers trapped within the larger walls, could not run away from Kakaako.

Each morning the sisters' day began before dawn, at 4:30 o'clock, when the sound of a hand bell rung by one of them awakened the group. They washed and dressed by candlelight, and then went in silence down the stairs to their cubicle in the chapel, to kneel in the presence of the Blessed Sacrament. The prescribed devotions—about ten minutes of community prayers, a half hour of private meditation, followed by recitation of Matins, Lauds, and the Little Hours that honor the Blessed Virgin Mary—prepared them to face the labors beyond the convent's wall. Without breaking their fast, they performed household chores or remained at prayer in the chapel until about 6:15 o'clock, when a priest arrived to say Mass. He passed through Kakaako's great gate and the convent's smaller postern in order to reach the chapel, where his little congregation of sisters and lepers awaited him.

In the beginning Father Leonor served as their priest and confessor. "These are good religious," he reported to Father Bousquet in Paris on January 15, 1884, "but at the same time it is a great increase of work for me. The hospital is a league from [the cathedral], I leave on horseback every morning at 6 o'clock [to ride to Kakaako] and go directly from there to the college [of the Brothers of Mary] on the opposite side of the city to conduct the catechism class, &c &c. I feel more and more that I am old. . . ."

Such a riding about the town placed too great a strain upon Father Leonor. By February 26 Father Clement Evrard was assisting him three days a week as the sisters' chaplain. Father Leonor continued to hear their confessions, if they wished to make them, and those of the lepers who felt in need of absolution. Only after the visiting priest had celebrated the daily sacrifice for his little congregation did the sisters partake of a light breakfast.

They ate their main meal at midday, and immediately went back to work. No interruptions broke their schedule, whether for coffee or tea or the time-wasting chatter of lay folk who have no urgent duties to perform. They heeded the injunction of Brother Giles, one of St. Francis's first disciples: "Work, work, and don't talk."

Late in the night, after a light supper, more household chores, another session of prayers, and "ablutions," they went upstairs, each to her tiny cell, for a few hours of healing sleep. Seven days a week, except on rare holy days, eighteen hours a day, they worked for God. Because the spirit commanded, and fortified, the body no longer protested the rigors of this rule. "The prudence of the flesh is death," they had learned, "but the prudence of the spirit is life and peace."

The sequence of events at the beginning of their service at Kakaako is not clear, inasmuch as no one thought them important enough to record. More than likely the sisters did not make their concerted attack upon the hospital's many problems until after they themselves were settled in the convent. Preparing that for their arrival—rounding up all the necessary furnishings and linens in Honolulu's stores, sweeping and mopping the new-made rooms, installing the furniture, setting up the routines of housekeeping—probably kept them busy during most of November and December. On the other hand, one of Sister Bonaventure's remarks in her New Year letter to Mother Bernardina indicates that by the end of December the patients at Kakaako knew the sisters well enough to respond to their presence: "these sick people are very contented & happy & pleased that we are going to take care of them, they told Mr. Gibson, these ladies did not come here for money, God sent them. . . ."

God may have sent them to Kakaako, as Mother Marianne herself believed most firmly. Then, after two months' exposure to several of Hawaii's most expert politicians, in and out of the Church, she perceived that they, not God, determined the circumstances under which her mission would labor for the Lord. But she had not yet learned the full extent of her dependence upon those maneuverers with words and rules.

On January 7, 1884, three days after the sisters entered their convent at Kakaako, Mother Marianne sent a letter to Walter Murray Gibson, as President of the Board of Health. "We are ready for work," she informed him, and proceeded to ask for a clear definition of her administrative relationship with respect to the Board of Health and its personnel at Kakaako.

Before she left Syracuse, Father Joseph Lesen had urged her, more than once, to obtain this definition—in writing—from the Hawaiian government. She did not succeed in doing so, for reasons that cannot be inferred from surviving correspondence. More than likely she did not actually insist upon it, preferring to put her trust in God and in the situation as she encountered it in Honolulu. If that is correct, she was being practical as well as trusting. How could she know what to expect of a contract with a foreign bureaucracy so far away? How could she know what details to stipulate until she could arrive on the scene and observe for herself not only the conditions under which the sisters would work but also the people who would be employing them? Moreover, to wait for detailed specifications from Hawaii, and for the inevitable slow scrutinizings that Father Lesen and his clerical counsellors would want to give every line and word in those contracts, meant interminable delays, endless correspondence, innumerable obstacles. All those complications, combined with Father Lesen's paternal concern, would pin her down in Syracuse for months, and she was in a hurry to go to work "in that large field." Weighing present freedoms against future traps, she took a chance—trusting more to God than to Father Leonor's assurances that "all would be well."

Now, on the scene in Honolulu, she saw the threatening danger—and understood at last that she could not trust the promises made by mere ordinary men.

On January 7, 1884, she wrote to Gibson: "Allow me to inform you that we are ready for work . . . before we assume the heavy responsibility of caring for the unfortunate "Lepers" we beg, for our security and protection a written and duly signed agreement in which we wish to have plainly stated what the government may expect of us, not only at the present time, but also in future. We would wish to know exactly the extent of our authority in the institutions of which we are to take charge, in what relation we shall stand to the Doctors and Stewards. (In regard to the Stewards, I beg to say that we cannot be *subject* to them, however we have no objection to work with them provided they respect our rights and will not interfere with us). Officers or Attendants should be forbidden to use profane or indecent language in our presence. . . . As far as practicable each party should have their duties assigned to them, so there may be no unpleasant misunderstanding.

"We are as yet strangers here and unacquainted with the regulations of the Institution, but at one glance we can see much that must be changed, hence we expect to have the authority to establish such regulations as we shall think proper or rather deem necessary, to carry out the object for which we were called here."

The next paragraph is significant, not so much because of its place in this declaration, but rather because it reveals the philosophy under-lying her approach to one of the major problems that distressed the Franciscans: ". . . the main cause of the terrible affliction resting upon the poor people is well known to every intelligent man, there is every reason to believe that the great immorality is calling from heaven God's punishment, therefore our first step toward improving their sad condi-tion, should be to remove as much as possible the cause of sin and immorality."

At Kakaako, if no where else, "immorality" was scandalous. Mother Marianne and her company were especially disturbed by the plight of the women patients. In determining to help those unfortu-nates, the Franciscan sisters were far in advance of the sanctions of their generation: they became champions of women's rights against the men who ruled society in America, and therefore also in Hawaii. "For us it is shocking to see how poorly the helpless females are protected, and how much they are exposed to danger. Their pitiable condition appeals strongly to our sympathy, and we *most earnestly* beg your Excel-lency and the Board of Health to make arrangements without delay to separate the sexes."

She reminded Gibson about more visible defects at the hospital, mentioning specifically "the condition of the dining room, the bathing rooms, the water closets and the gate. . . ." To repair these, she realized, "will be an expense to the government, but an expense that will be a benefit and draw God's blessing on this poor and so sadly afflicted country."

She rose to an affirmation that—because of her very presence at Kakaako—could never be read as a meaningless exercise in piety: "For us it is happiness to be able to comfort in a measure the poor exiles and we rejoice that we are the unworthy agents of our heavenly Father through whom He deigns to show His great love and mercy to the sufferers. . . ."

Then, with a realist's swoop, she brought everyone back to this earth again, giving to Gibson himself the primary responsibility for being God's steward here below: ". . . but we cannot accomplish much without the cooperation of the government and the Board of Health. We confidently hope that our first request will be cheerfully acceded to and that the points herein mentioned will be favorably considered."

Two days later, on January 9, Gibson answered Mother Mari-anne's "first request." After expressing happiness at learning that "you are ready for work," he gave her a dismaying glimpse into the mind of a wily politician and an unyielding male: ". . . when you were invited to come to the rescue of the sick poor of this Kingdom, the nature of your position or authority in relation to the sanitary care of sufferers was not then considered." He had merely appealed to the Lord Bishop of Olba to find some Sisters of Charity. For Mother Marianne's instruction in the historical background of that search, he enclosed a copy of the petition he had addressed to Bishop Hermann almost exactly a year before.

Now, for the first time, Mother Marianne saw that very pertinent document. She recognized how vague were the written instructions that had started Father Leonor upon his journey to "America and the Canadas." In Syracuse, that desperate man—interpreting this appeal to his every advantage, as he must—had assured her that she would be given "full charge" of the hospitals in which Franciscans would work. Now, in Honolulu, Gibson blandly presented her with yet another reading of those same instructions: ". . . You and the Sisters under your direction, shall have full independence in your work for the organization of the nursing of the sick at the Branch Hospital and at other hospitals or places to be designated, under the sole direction of the Board of Health."

With a cavalier flourish, Gibson consented to "instruct the steward . . . that you and your associate Sisters have unrestricted charge in the nursing care and administration of the patients. . . . You will receive instructions from the physician of the Board at the Hospital in regard to the remedies and treatment for the sick; otherwise your management of the hospital in regard to care of patients will be untrammeled."

In other words, the wily old fox was saying, you and your sisters were hired to be nurses only, to take care of the sick, and that's all I ever intended you should be. The administering of the entire big hospital is man's work. We already have a fine man on the job. We have a system that is working well, under my direction. I do not wish to change anything at the higher levels of management. Woman's work you can do, in wards and kitchens. You are welcome to all of that—"untrammeled." But don't ask for anything more.

From his point of view, in that era of overweening males, Gibson's attitude was quite understandable. Indeed, it was so universal as to be accepted without question (men thought) by every man and woman endowed with even a modicum of common sense. More than likely, too, he had not yet learned how, for several years, Mother Marianne had managed most effectively a far better hospital in Syracuse, and administered with notable efficiency a whole community of Franciscan sisters Furthermore, as a politician exquisitely attuned to the harmonies of his sphere, he was not about to turn over to a bunch of Catholic nuns the managing of an institution that was financed by a government which Protestants virtually owned, in a nation they operated for their profit. He could imagine the storms of outrage, sweeping through Honolulu, if ever he gave these Papists complete control over Kakaako. No, the sage man convinced himself, in the manner of all politicians, let well enough alone. Woman's proper place is in the kitchen and in the sick room. . . .

Thinking that, with his avuncular tone and these magnanimous concessions on lesser matters, he'd quieted her, Gibson dismissed Mother Marianne's inquiry from his list of worries. He may have instructed the Board of Health's secretary to put her requests for improvements to Kakaako's facilities on the agenda for the next session of that body. He probably talked with Henry Van Giesen (as a letter from Sister Bonaventure implied), but must have done so only in the most general and affable of terms. Most certainly, he was too good natured (or too wary) ever to be severe with Van Giesen, whom he failed to recognize as being the worst of all the problems festering at Kakaako.

Being nurses as well as women, the sisters knew exactly what to do when finally they descended upon the hospital. Mother Marianne had been planning her campaign since first she saw that foul internment camp. Six of the seven Franciscans—one Dutch, four Irish, and one strong-willed German by descent, determined Americans by exposure, and dedicated sisters by training—passed through that stockade like a divine wind. They tied back their sleeves and, with great vigor and irresistible good cheer, cleaned up the place from the convent's end of the compound to Van Giesen's picket fence at the other. Possibly (but this is by no means certain) they pressed into service the few "stewards" the Board of Health had managed to hire for assorted jobs at Kakaako. Probably the six sisters themselves did most of the work, while the government hirelings pretended to be absorbed in their usual tasks.

The seventh Franciscan, Sister Ludovica Gibbons, never went into the hospital compound. At Mother Marianne's direction, she remained in the convent, serving as cook and housekeeper. In those days many physicians thought that the contagion of leprosy entered a susceptible person by way of the mouth, in food and drink. Mother Marianne accepted this belief, and always sequestered one housekeeper-sister in the convent, free of contamination, to prepare the meals for the nurse-sisters. She also insisted that sisters must never eat foods prepared by lepers.

She also required nurse-sisters to be "prudent" at all times, by which she meant that they should observe the rudimentary precautions then being observed, such as careful washing of hands with soap and water, and wearing work-aprons over their robes. Surgeons' masks and gloves, just coming into use in the most advanced hospitals of Europe and America, were never available to the sisters in Hawaii during Mother Marianne's regime. Considering the nature of the nurse-sisters' duties, these precautions could not have protected anyone from the contagion. Nonetheless, they succeeded for the Franciscans. "You will never be a leper," Mother Marianne promised Sister Leopoldina in 1889, "nor will any Sister of our Order." Her trust—and theirs—was not misplaced: the promise and the prophecy have been fulfilled. Despite years of exposure to lepers, many in the most fulminating stages of the disease, not one Sister of St. Francis has ever contracted the infection.

This conviction held by Mother Marianne and her companions did not deny, of course, another and far more important component of protection, in which they placed absolute trust: the mercy of God. For thousands of years saints and sages and other positive thinkers the world around have demonstrated a medical fact that some modern scientists are only now beginning to recognize: strong belief in forces for good can protect the human body from sickness and other perils, just as strong belief in forces for evil can weaken the body or even destroy it.

However they did it, "the great-courage-showing Sisters," as Father Lesen had dubbed them, began with the cookhouse and the so-called dining room. With unprecedented applications of soap, water, brushes, and energy, they scoured pots, pans, dishes, cutlery, tables, benches, floors, and walls, washing away the filth piled up during three years of neglect. The swarms of startled flies flew off to other refuges, never to return in their disgusting myriads. Thereupon the sisters directed a critical appraisal upon the persons and habits of the lazy cooks and dishwashers, who had allowed all that grease and litter to accumulate. By the time they finished their raid, the kitchen staff, spectacularly slovenly until this typhoon swept down upon them, must have been driven to the point of nervous exhaustion.

Throughout the whole strenuous session the sisters received no help from the patients. Neither did the "handsome" and "clever" superintendent lift a finger to assist. Van Giesen raised eyebrows and shoulders instead, winking knowingly to the hospital's male population, thereby strengthening their disdain for this bunch of interfering haole females. From that time on he took pains to be as uncooperative as possible, hiding his deceit behind a mask of politeness, the while he found pleasure in devising ways and means to torment these threats to his dominion.

"The sisters triels were very great for the first few months," wrote Sister Leopoldina. "they had very poor food as they were at the mercy of Mr. Van Geesean they were obliged to receive their bread and meet from the bleeding hands of the lepers and most of the time not even [with] paper round it, their milk was taken from the large milk can in the dirty dishes of the lepers and it was brought to the Sisters in the sore bleeding hands of the lepers. The Sisters being straingers they hardly knew how to act . . . so they spoke to Mr. Van Geesean about it, he laughed in a mocking way [and] said you live to eat and I eat to live. . . ."

Fortunately, the dairyman who delivered the milk each day heard about the sisters' distress and arranged to take their supply to "a side gate . . . before going in the leper yard, he was a very nice man [who] often brought buttermilk and other little things to the poor Sisters, and they were grateful for they could feel that he was their friend." But still the bread and meat and vegetables, unwrapped, were brought to the convent gate clutched in the hideous hands of lepers.

After the cookhouse and dining room had been washed clean, the sisters turned their energies upon the patients' cottages. Knowing a great deal about human nature, they exacted help from no one. They simply marched into a ward, armed with brooms, mops, brushes, rags, cakes of hard soap, pails of water—and those insuperable smiles. They swept, dusted, mopped, and scrubbed, beginning the unrelenting task of routing out dirt, vermin, and mildew, throwing away stinking rags and greasy mats and noisome blankets. But they could not throw out the bodies of those pitiful lepers huddling against the walls, or lying sick upon the floors. Nor could they sweeten the air in those crowded rooms.

Nothing like this grand purification had ever happened in that lazarhouse beside the sea. And, of course, human nature being what it is, many a suspicion and scowl went out the doors, along with the dirt and the rubbish. Even the angriest of patients, those hopeless and raging ones who hated the whole world beyond the high fence and all the clean people in it, could not help but marvel at these peculiar "virgins" (as they called the sisters), who worked so hard, from morning till night, at such degrading chores that even lepers refused to perform. The hard-headed ones, intransigent males for the most part, swore and spat and stalked away, going off to grumble in other wards, or to sit with fellow complainers on the bare earth in the shade cast by the cottages. The bedridden, the blind, the helpless, having no where to go, lay where they must, and the cleaning teams moved them about as they made their progress.

The six toiling sisters happily accepted whatever help was offered by the gentler patients, and directed them as unaffectedly as if all were members of a household being subjected to its annual spring cleaning. When the scouring squad went on to work in the next ward, many patients in the one just cleaned felt as if they too had been cleansed.

Almost without saying a word, the Franciscans won their first victory. They did so in the best of all possible ways: by using the power of good example, rather than by calling upon the force of command. And they demonstrated once again what countless heathens in many foreign lands have learned since Christian missionaries first went among them: that the power of Christ's love is best shown in good deeds, not in words mouthed by preachers nor in theologies printed in books.

After that proof of concern, many of the ambulant patients took better care of themselves and of their living spaces, without waiting for the sisters to do the work for them. But after the fine start achieved by that hygienic campaign, the sisters—like able generals, or nagging wives, or watchful mothers—did not hesitate to remind a negligent patient that cleanliness came close to godliness. Whether or not they believed in God or even cared about cleanliness, few patients could stand up against these formidable haoles, with their imperious glances and fearless tongues. Never again would Kakaako's lepers live in such squalor as the sisters found when first they saw the hospital. And, as the more introspective among the patients soon realized, never again would they be free of the swift inspecting gaze, the persuasive smile, the pointing finger, even, on deserved occasion, the abrasive commentary of "a seestah," forever expecting perfection from these most imperfect of God's creatures here below. . . .

Then came the most difficult test of all: dressing the lepers' sores.

Although Dr. G. L. Fitch was the hospital's director and physician, he did not dream of dirtying his hands, or offending his nose, or risking his health, by touching a leper. He examined and diagnosed infrequently and from afar; and he collected his salary, as well as the townsfolks' respect, because of his learning, not for his ministrations. In all Hawaii, few physicians were so foolhardy as to touch a leper, or so humane as to try to soothe his sores. Many doctors lived in such fear of the disease that they shut the doors of their consultation rooms to people who appeared to be suffering from it. Many another physician, if he deigned to accept a leper as a patient, treated him from a safe distance: he would fill a jar with whatever useless salve or lotion the profession was recommending at the moment and place it upon a railing or a fence post outside his chambers. Then he would shout instructions at the unfortunate man, standing in the yard or in the street, telling him how he should apply the medicine to the affected parts of his body. The pieces of silver those fastidious physicians received in payment for such tender care they would not touch until after the coins were "purified" in fire.

However faint her heart may have been at the prospect of touching a loathsome leper, none of the sisters balked at the task. In the names of Christ and of St. Francis, each sister won this victory over herself. For at least one of them, however, the cost was far greater than her spirit was prepared to pay.

After that, everything else was easy. All the labors she performed, all the sickness and misery she saw in others or suffered in herself, during her lifetime of dedication to the care of lepers, demanded no greater sacrifice than the one she offered during that first day when she and her companions dressed the wounds of Kakaako's untouchables.

Each sister-nurse learned to wash away the scabs, the pus, the maggots, the rot from those fetid ulcers, to cut away the dead putrescent flesh at the margins of the sores, to apply soothing ointments to the raw wounds, and to bind them about with clean cloths. The treated patients, sweet-smelling for the while, went back to their wards, comforted more in spirit than in body, at this evidence that not everyone in the world of men had rejected them.

Father Damien, when first he offered this kindness to the lepers abandoned at Kalawao, forced back the vomit rising in his throat by an act of will, and overwhelmed the foul stench with tobacco fumes from the pipe he learned to smoke for that purpose. Mother Marianne and her sisters in mercy could call only upon acts of will to sustain them—and upon the message of St. Francis, sent to them across the span of seven hundred years: "When I was in sin, the sight of lepers nauseated me beyond measure, but then God himself led me into their company, and I had pity on them. When I had once become acquainted with them, what had previously nauseated me became a source of spiritual and physical consolation for me."

The sisters also earned the approbation of men in their own time. On February 5, 1884, Father Leonor concluded a brief note to Father Damien with this tribute: ". . . there are 207 lepers at Kakaako; but at present, when they have the Sisters to take care of them *it is* and it will become still more difficult to make them leave for Molokai. Only Dr. Fitch can tell you that they are doing too much, and that never will so few people be able to do so much work." And by September 23, 1884, in a letter to Father Bousquet in Paris, Father Leonor—after referring to the dangers involved in administering the sacraments to lepers at Kakaako—accorded their nurses an admiring mention: "our saintly Franciscan sisters."

The sisters' courage and devotion, offered every day, soon conquered most of Kakaako's inmates. But not all. Some still held out against the foreign women, with their "crazy ways" and determined wills.

"Rats as big as cats" still frisked about at night, scavenging for food wherever they could find it, in the kitchens and pantries especially, but also in the wards. There they nibbled at the patients trying to sleep, as well as at the packets of dried fish and jerked beef, the candies, fruits, cookies, and cakes, even the flower leis, they'd received from friends and relatives.

Van Giesen, loping about and sneering like a villain in some Victorian melodrama, became more obnoxious with each passing week, raising objections to Mother Marianne's plans for improving the hospital's services. According to hearsay reported by Sister Columba O'Keeffe (who wrote in 1923), Gibson had instructed Van Giesen to be "guided in all matters by Mother Marianne's advice, but although he sometimes asked the Sisters' advice, he rarely followed it, but continued his old system of neglecting and ill-treating the lepers." Dr. Arning did not help to relieve tensions when he told the sisters what Van Giesen thought of them: "They are only a lot of little girls. I can wind them around my finger."

Van Giesen's callousness did not spare even his wife. One day, when Mother Marianne and several Franciscans visited Mrs. Van Giesen in her home at the eastern end of the hospital yard, she "looked so sick that the Sisters pitted her, and when they tried to comfort Mr. Van Geesean, Yes he said, she is sick and will be dead a week from this [day], and she did die at the time he said she would." No one, least of all Van Giesen, ever suggested that grief over his wife's rapid decline caused him to be so cruel to everyone around him.

A number of undisciplined children, running wild, refused to submit to the sisters' authority. So also did the fallen women who, for pleasure or for gain—or, as many claimed, out of fear—had turned to whoring. The sisters guessed but could not know as yet how at night, when they themselves had withdrawn behind their fence, the hospital became one vast brothel.

The bullies in this cage, those hulking louts who flaunted their masculinity by terrorizing everyone weaker than they, respected no rules issued by anyone, even by brutal Van Giesen. They simply laughed at the regulations sent down from the Board of Health, and scorned those coming from "the virgins." "In this place there is no law," lepers had learned to snarl, whether they were exiled at Kalawao or immured at Kakaako. They made their own rules to please themselves, took without thanks whatever was good that the authorities provided, broke the regulations of those same authorities with completest freedom, and no longer heeded the code of morality that in their Christian country judges and churchmen called the law of God. After all, the lepers reasoned, what worse punishment than the disease they suffered could judges or society inflict upon them?

Van Giesen could not control the inmates of Kakaako. "He was obliged to have a Police Force of eight strong fearless lepers [wrote Sister Leopoldina], and Tom Burch was the cheaf. Tom's father was an Irish man and his Mother a Hawaiian. So Tom was a great man, with Mr. Van Geesean and Tom runing the place there was much injustice disorder and trouble all the time."

Quietly, calmly, Mother Marianne and her sisters in charity went about their work, biding their time. They "suffered great hardships during their first years in Hawaii," as Sister Columba would write. ". . . Although Mr. Gibson was extremely kind at all times and did everything in his power to make them comfortable, they had to make many sacrifices, which were, however, rendered easy to our good Sis-

ters by the example of our beloved Mother's unfailing patience, courage, and cheerfulness."

Mother Marianne herself, in the factual and laconic report she
wrote in 1887 for the Order about this mission she was establishing in
the Kingdom of Hawaii, dismissed the ordeal at Kakaako in a single
sentence: "They met with many trials and difficulties the first few
months."

Here is the authentic voice of Mother Marianne. To her, trials and
difficulties in this world, sickness and pain and disappointment, did
not matter—except as they interfered with her ability to go on working
for God.

NOTES on Chapter VII

Details of the sisters' daily schedule are taken from Constitutions and Manuals in use
in the Franciscan community at the time, and from references to times for services
mentioned in letters and reports.

Mother Marianne in 1881, when she began her second term of office as Provincial Mother of the Sisters of St. Francis of Syracuse.

Mother Bernardina Dorn, one of the co-foundresses of the Sisters of St. Francis of Philadelphia and the foundress of the Sisters of St. Francis of Syracuse.

St. Joseph's Hospital, the first hospital in Syracuse, New York, opened in 1869. Mother Marianne was in charge from 1870 to 1877, when she was elected Provincial Mother of her religious community.

Bishop Hermann Koeckemann, SS.CC., Bishop of
Honolulu, Vicar Apostolic, about 1886.

Father Joseph Lesen, Order Friars Minor
Conventuals, Minister Provincial of Franciscans
in North America, about 1883.

Walter Murray Gibson, about 1883. As president
of the Board of Health, he supported the hopes
of King Kalakaua and Queen Kapiolani to bring
sister-nurses to Hawaii. In 1883 Mother
Marianne responded to their need.

Father Leonor Fouesnel, Vice Provincial of the
SS.CC. in the Hawaii Province, in 1883. The
Hawaiian government sponsored his trip to the
United States and Canada to search for sister-
nurses.

King Kalakaua in 1886.

Queen Kapiolani in 1886.

A panoramic view of the Kalaupapa peninsula, Molokai, about 1940. The village of Kalaupapa is in the foreground; Kalawao is on the far side of the promontory.

Sisters of St. Francis who served in 1886 at the Branch Hospital for Lepers in Kakaako, Honolulu. Left to right: Sr. M. Rosalia McLaughlin, Sr. M. Martha Kaiser, Sr. M. Leopoldina Burns, Sr. M. Charles Hoffmann, Sr. M. Crescentia Eilers, and Mother Marianne Cope. At center, rear: Walter Murray Gibson, by then prime minister of the kingdom.

Patients' cottages at the Branch Hospital for Lepers in Kakaako, Honolulu, about 1886. Mother Marianne's interest in improving the grounds by planting trees and flowers is evident.

Sisters of St. Francis who served at Malulani Hospital and at St. Anthony School for Girls in Wailuku, Maui, photographed about 1895. Left to right: Sr. M. Renata Nash, Sr. M. Antonia Brown, Sr. M. Bonaventure Caraher, and Sr. M. Cyrilla Erhard. Malulani Hospital, established in 1884, was the first hospital on the island of Maui.

Father Damien DeVeuster, SS.CC., two months before his death in 1889. The flowered sling supporting his arm was given to him by Mother Marianne.

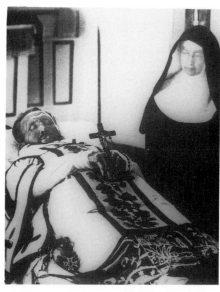

Mother Marianne Cope, in April 1889, at the bier of Father Damien DeVeuster. She was the quiet organizer of funeral arrangements for the heroic priest, fixing his coffin appropriately, and bringing with her the more able-bodied girls and women from Bishop Home as mourners. Sadly, few other patients attended his funeral.

Sr. Elizabeth Gomes, the former Olinda Gomes, who helped the sisters at the Branch Hospital for Lepers in Honolulu, with a group of young patients at Bishop Home, about 1900.

Charles R. Bishop Home for Unprotected Leper Girls and Women at Kalaupapa, Molokai, about 1900. The Convent of St. Elizabeth is at the right, and patients' cottages are ranged at the left.

Sr. M. Leopoldina Burns in 1886. She was the main "soredresser" for women patients at Bishop Home during its first years.

A leprous patient at Bishop Home during its first years.

Mother Marianne in 1918, only a few days before she died on August 9. Not all of the patients' names are known. Smiling Adelaide Bolster, standing to the far right of Mother Marianne, was a teacher at Bishop Home from May to November 1918 and became a general assistant to Sr. Benedicta after that time. The sisters are, from left to right: Sr. M. Albina Sluder, Sr. M. Benedicta Rodenmacher, and Sr. M. Leopoldina Burns.

Memorial to Mother Marianne above her grave at the Kalaupapa Settlement. The patients contributed the money to raise the monument.

Chapter VIII

TRIALS

MOTHER MARIANNE and her companions had scarcely begun upon their labors at Kakaako when further burdens were laid upon them. Gibson's program to provide each of the larger neighbor islands with a government hospital had favored Maui with the first one. In January 1884 the building stood finished—and empty, awaiting furnishings, equipment, patients, above all nurses.

Such trained assistants to physicians were very rare in Hawaii, and those few worked in Honolulu. They had come to the islands from the United States, in search of adventure, or health, or money. A few had been taught their duties by resident physicians. Doctors in other towns who needed nurses' help put their wives to work, or household servants, or, in most cases, relatives of patients instructed in simpler tasks for the occasion.

Gibson turned to Mother Marianne for help with Maui's vacant hospital. Mother Marianne was quite willing to take on this additional work eventually, but not quite as soon as Gibson, Bishop Hermann, and Father Leonor united in wishing. All four of those planners feared, as Father Leonor confided to Father Damien on November 27, 1883, "the impending arrival of the Episcopalian Sisters." Because of that threat, the Franciscan sisters, Father Leonor continued, "are putting me or rather *us* in a big kaumaha [worry], precisely because they [the influential Protestants] seemed to insist on Molokai [for the Episcopalians], giving the impression also of promising all the rest to the Englishwomen. Also Rev. Mother Provincial [Marianne] told me this: Father, the lepers do not frighten us; but such conduct is truly a little discouraging for our sisters who are counting on all the hospitals except Queen Emma's [the single private hospital in Honolulu]. That is why we have insisted especially on Wailuku and we have gotten from

Mr. Gibson that Rev. Mother would go to take possession of Hilo, Kauai, and Kalawao. . . ."

In mid-January Gibson made his request more or less official, saying that Queen Kapiolani asked Mother Marianne to open the new institution and to take charge of it thereafter. Gibson seems to have been reluctant to involve the Franciscan sisters in this additional enterprise before they had really settled all the many problems at Kakaako. He told Mother Marianne as much, in a letter dated February 26, 1884: "The work at Wailuku was altogether secondary, where patients had yet to be gathered together, but in this matter I yielded to the wish of Father Leonor.—However, there is work all over these islands for your blessed spirit of charity."

The practicability of assigning Franciscan sisters to serve on Maui—or Hawaii or Kauai—would have been the least of worries to the three men in Honolulu who disposed of their lives. But the political implications to such an arrangement would have disturbed the bishop, if not the prime minister. His Lordship, perennially aware of Calvinist feudings (and always inflating them, usually beyond their worth), would have feared that Protestants might attack this disposition as another sinister Catholic maneuver to take control of yet one more government institution. He wanted to be sure that every important Protestant in the kingdom thoroughly understood that sending the sisters to Wailuku was not the opening play in a Catholic conspiracy to seize the whole archipelago.

Father Leonor, on the other hand, would have regarded the assignment as a Heaven-sent opportunity to extend the bounds of the Catholic cause. To judge by his letters (which, to be sure, are not necessarily proofs of his convictions), he professed to live in a continual apprehension that "the heretics" (in this instance the Episcopalians) would soon be sending a whole army of nurse-nuns to the islands from England. The heretics were being driven to that ardor of competition, he felt, because already—in Father Damien on Molokai, and in Mother Marianne with her Franciscans at Kakaako—the one True Church had proved twice over, to all men everywhere, how noble was the spirit of Christian compassion it inculcated in the hearts of its religious. Who could doubt that, while Protestants merely stood around and talked about the problem of lepers, zealous Catholics leaped into action and did something about it?

The fact that he was so right, at least in Hawaii, made him smile and—as he loved to imagine—caused Calvinists to gnash their teeth.

Ever since Father Damien went to live among the lepers of Kalawao, some island Protestants regretted having missed the Great Opportunity to show what they might have done. And all island Catholics, despite admonitions to refrain from being puffed up with pride, felt very virtuous indeed, if not unbearably smug, in the knowledge that one of their priests had moved into a place which even angels seemed to shun—and where Protestant pastors definitely declined to tread.

With the advent of the Franciscan sisters, come to care for the lepers at Kakaako, Catholics scored again in this form of rivalry. Therefore, Bishop Hermann wondered if sectarian antagonisms, relatively quiet during these past few years, might not flare up again. Not over the sisters' labors at Kakaako. No, no: au contraire. . . . Even he recognized that most Protestants in town and legislature expressed both admiration for the Sisters of Charity and utmost relief because they had taken over the duties that no one else seemed willing to assume. But, His Lordship asked, would these same Calvinists, with their strange American notions about the complete separation of church and state, accept with equal complacence the delegating of Catholic sisters to operate a hospital that would not be receiving lepers as patients?

Gibson, unlike Bishop Hermann and Father Leonor, spoke with Protestants rather more often than he conversed with Catholics. He could discover no good reason why Father Leonor's wish to send Franciscan sisters to Maui would not be acceptable to Protestants in and out of the legislature. They were practical men, he knew, always interested in getting things done. Just as he was. Nor would they mind who did the work, as long as it was done well—and at the least possible expense to taxpayers. In these respects, the sisters commended themselves admirably: not only did they take care of lepers, they also worked for love of God, rather than for love of money. The salary of twenty American dollars a month each received for her labors was a mere pittance, compared with the sums that lay nurses and physicians would demand—if they could be hired.

Presumably, either one by one or in a delegation, Gibson, His Lordship, and Father Leonor spoke with Mother Marianne about all those interrelated prospects and hazards before Gibson composed his formal request to her. If she had not been acquainted with the facts of political life in the islands before those conversations, Mother Marianne most definitely learned them during the last weeks of 1883. And she understood from them how her mission could be used as a pawn in the political gambits of this contentious kingdom. Nothing of this nature, on so large a scale, had troubled her in Syracuse. She, who asked nothing more than the chance to minister to the sick and the rejected, realized now that her mission in Hawaii stood in double jeopardy.

If she said no to this untimely request for help at Wailuku from queen, prime minister, lord bishop, and father confessor, she closed a very weighty door upon the very purpose for which she had brought her company to the islands.

If she said yes, she opened another door—this one to repercussions and recriminations, interference from bureaucrats, even the possibility of harassment from Calvinists, if not actual persecution, in the event that the government's ministers should change.

Moreover, by saying yes, she would divide her weak forces and strain to the breaking point the few workers she had brought to serve in this hospice of horror at Kakaako. How could only seven women manage to care for the sick in two hospitals, when attending the lepers in one already demanded the fullest devotion of both body and spirit?

And yet how could she say no? How could she deny both her personal vocation and the larger call of the whole mission?

The dilemma could not have worried her for long—if, indeed, she considered it one at all. To her, who had heard the call so clearly, Mr. Gibson, the bishop, the nation were not overburdening her with sacrifices. They were giving her more opportunities to serve.

Besides, she could draw upon twenty years of experience, to remind herself that a woman of purpose can always find ways to manage officious priests and commanding bishops, difficult patients and sulking sisters. Kings and queens and premiers and warring legislators were creatures new to her, actors of larger dimensions posturing upon a bigger stage, but were they not also human beings who would respond to the message of Christ and St. Francis? Hope—and trust in those exemplars—promised her that she would find ways to avoid the traps that Hawaii's factions might set for her. Once again, now as before and always, she put her trust in the Lord, knowing that he would answer her needs as they arose.

"Feeling that duty called her," as Sister Columba O'Keeffe would write, Mother Marianne accepted this additional responsibility.

On January 15, while Gibson was still engaged in composing his official request to Mother Marianne, Father Leonor wrote to Father

Bousquet in Paris, treating the matter as decided: "I go next week to install the Hospital Sisters at Wailuku."

Mother Marianne agreed to sail for Maui aboard the interisland steamer *Kinau,* leaving Honolulu on Tuesday, January 22. She did not go sooner because she wished to attend a most important ceremony.

On January 21, in the presence of Queen Kapiolani and Mr. Gibson, Bishop Hermann dedicated the convent's little chapel of St. Philomena. As Mother Marianne herself informed the Order in her brief report of 1887, His Lordship was "assisted by a Jesuit Father from San Francisco and three fathers from the mission." Sister Bonaventure, in her report of 1900, identified a fifth priest, who seems to have been present as a guest rather than a participant in the rite. He was Father Damien, come to Honolulu for one of his infrequent and short visits. The worldly delights of the capital city did not draw him, nor a yearning to enjoy the company of clean people: he came because he himself needed a priest to whom he could confess his sins, from whom he could receive the absolution his spirit craved.

An article in the *Pacific Commercial Advertiser* for January 22 described the ceremonies at "the dedication of St. Philemon's." Before 9 A.M. "a crowd of lepers was assembled in the large room. There were also present Her Majesty the Queen, attended by Mrs. Iaukea [wife of the secretary of the Department of Foreign Affairs], the President of the Board of Health, and Mrs. F. H. Hayselden, the Mother Superior and Sister Theresa, of the Sisterhood of the Sacred Heart. The clergy present were the Lord Bishop of Olba, and Fathers Damien, Clement, Sylvester, Leonor, and Bouchard [the visiting Jesuit]." In his determination to list the visiting dignitaries, the reporter quite forgot to mention the Franciscan sisters.

But the Master of Ceremonies did not forget them. In his preliminary address Mr. Gibson said that the people of Hawaii, and especially the patients in this hospital at Kakaako, "had great reason to be thankful that these noble-hearted ladies had left home and duties elsewhere to come and devote themselves to the care of the sick poor of the kingdom."

Bishop, priests, and acolytes, "chanting solemn dedicatory hymns," performed the ritual that consecrated the chapel, both inside and out. Upon returning to the altar, Bishop Hermann and his assistants celebrated a pontifical high Mass. "After the kyrie and gloria had been chanted by the choir (which is chiefly composed of lepers) Bishop

Hermann . . . addressed the congregation. His Lordship was so visibly moved by the solemnity and peculiarity of the occasion that the audience was also deeply affected . . . there was hardly a dry eye to be seen—a spectacle never to be forgotten. After controlling his emotion, the Bishop proceeded with his address. 'This is a supreme moment in my life,' were his first words. . . ."

The bishop finished his sermon. "Four baptisms were then performed and the service was then concluded by the singing of the Sanctus and Agnus, from Mozart's fourth Mass." The reporter, obviously a friendly Protestant wandered into unfamiliar territory, was much impressed by "the choral part of the service [which] was unexpectedly very pleasing." Not the least interesting part of his report upon an occasion that in itself was nothing short of amazing, was this casual sentence: "Mr. Van Giesen presided at the piano."

On that day of ceremony Mother Marianne and Father Damien met for the first time. Gibson and other newspapermen had already made him famous throughout the world as "the Priest to the Lepers." But early in 1884 their disease had not yet progressed in him to the point where soon, in fascination mixed with sadness, he would be recognized as "the Leper Priest." Neither Mother Marianne nor Father Damien thought their meeting—or themselves—important enough to write about; accordingly, nothing is known about the manner in which each of these servants to lepers reacted to the other. More than likely all the notables gathered at the convent that day demanded most of Mother Marianne's attention, giving her little chance to talk with the four Sacred Hearts fathers, relegated to the background.

On the other hand, Damien—who was never shy about putting in a word for the needs of his lepers at Kalawao—may very well have greeted Mother Marianne with more than a polite bow. Ever since, almost eleven years before, he went to live at Kalawao, he had been begging two successive bishops and a sequence of father provincials for nurse-sisters to attend the ravaged exiles in the Settlement. He would have been thoroughly out of character if, on that festive morning at Kakaako, he had not impressed upon Mother Marianne his most earnest hope that soon she would assign some of her company to serve in a hospital at Kalawao.

In her brief report in 1887, Mother Marianne noted that Queen Kapiolani, still in deep mourning for her sister, "seemed much affected during the service." Her Majesty had good reason to be moved. Quite apart from the spiritual impact the ceremony might have had upon an emotional woman so recently bereaved, this visit to the convent at Kakaako could only emphasize the contrast between the beauty and the luxury in which she dwelled at Iolani Palace and the poverty in which the Sisters of St. Francis chose to live.

Their chapel, for example. Compared with the splendors of the two churches which Her Majesty attended—the Congregationalists' huge Kawaiahao Church for state occasions, and the Episcopalians' Pro-cathedral of St. Andrew for private worship—this meager little place was dreary and depressing. It was not yet completely finished, but even with all its furnishing it could never be considered impressive. Despite "the surprising zeal and activity" Henry Van Giesen "showed in the decoration and construction of the Chapel" (as Father Leonor wrote in testimony to Father Damien on March 25), it still suffered from deficiencies in materials, money and craftmanship. The ceiling, low and only slightly arched in the nave, swelled up in a timorous sort of vaulting above the sanctuary. The altar itself had been made by Sacred Hearts brothers, probably using materials purchased by the "unknown gentleman." From the surface of the relatively plain Holy Table rose a single tier of ornamented wood work in which the Tabernacle reposed. (For ordinary days, Mother Marianne used discarded medicine bottles to serve as candle holders.) A third layer of lacy crenellations, resembling a Dutch gable, ascended toward a bracket shelf affixed to the rear wall. From this lofty pedestal a painted plaster image purporting to represent St. Philomena gazed down upon the congregation.

A narrow cubicle opened at the right of the sanctuary. In this tiny room, about three meters wide and as many deep, the sisters knelt during Mass and at more private times of prayer. High on the wall, above doors at either side of the altar, hung a large framed chromolithograph. The one at the right depicted the child Jesus with Mary, His Mother. The other showed the Holy Child with St. Joseph, His foster-father. Framed chromolithographs bordered in black, each only about a foot square, representing the fourteen Stations of the Cross, graced the wall at either side. "The beautiful picture" promised by King Kalakaua may have been present at the rear of the chapel, but it is not visible in a photograph taken sometime during 1885. If, as is probable, it depicted a secular subject, the sisters would have displayed the picture in their parlor.

In front of the sanctuary rail the carpenters installed two tall wooden doors, extending from floor to ceiling. These partitions could be rolled aside, into narrow apertures, in preparation for Catholic services, or drawn forth to conceal the altar from disapproving Puritans and unbelieving pagans. The closed doors also helped to give the sisters the privacy they wanted for their community prayers and silent meditations. With this simple and unexpectedly modern contrivance, the Catholic chapel could be reduced into an even smaller box in which Protestants might meet for services offered by pastors of their sects. "Amongst the lepers," Sister Bonaventure noted, "is a minister who officiates & occasionally the Episcopalian Bishop, & Ministers of other Religions have visited them in their clerical capacity, but this is seldom." When, in 1884, an organ was purchased for the sisters, the console was set outside the sliding partitions, so that Protestants too might enjoy its music.

Sometimes a patient might play upon the flute, to accompany the hymns; or another would play the organ. In 1936 Sister Benedicta Rodenmacher (who arrived at Kakaako in 1885) would remember how the hymns, being sung in Hawaiian, were "strange to us, but very devotional."

Mother Marianne probably was responsible for these thoughtful arrangements to share the one place in the whole hospital compound where religious services might be held. She saw that the inmates needed all the consolations of religion they could possibly receive, if only because the medicines they took into their devastated bodies were so useless, but most of all because—for them, more than for other men—Death was so imminent. As Mother Provincial of the Order that opened two hospitals in Central New York to all people, regardless of race, color, sex, or creed, she could not possibly be possessive about the convent's chapel at Kakaako. In later years, on Molokai, she often repeated to the sisters words written to a benefactor during her years at St. Joseph Hospital in Syracuse: "The charity of the good knows no creed, and is confined to no one place."

Mother Marianne "left the very next day for Maui, taking with her Sisters Renata and Antonella, and leaving Sisters Bonaventure, Crescentia, Ludovica, and Rosalia in Honolulu. . . ." Even though Maui lies only about 160 kilometers southeast of Honolulu, the sisters thought of it as being a place somewhere close to the edge of the world, to be reached only after enduring untold hardships, a bourne from which travelers never return. "The parting was very sad, no one could tell how long it would be, if ever, that they would be together again." With these doleful lines Sister Leopoldina prepared her readers for an experience that (at least in her recounting of it) almost proved the sisters right.

Father Leonor accompanied the travelers to Maui, as their guardian and guide. For him it was a doubly pleasant assignment, because he would be returning to the place in the islands he claimed to like best. He had been stationed for twenty-seven years in Wailuku, as priest in charge of St. Anthony's parish, when Bishop Hermann (probably at the suggestion of Father Bousquet, their superior in Paris) chose him to go to the United States in search of teaching brothers and Sisters of Charity.

The *Kinau* sailed from Honolulu at 10 A.M. "It was a bright beautiful morning," perfect weather for most passengers, but the trade winds blowing from the northeast were fresh enough "to toss the little ship and keep her rolling all the way." Mother Marianne became seasick as soon as the vessel emerged from Honolulu's placid harbor, and kept to her bunk-shelf for the entire passage. In that respect she was luckier than most passengers, who simply sat or lay upon the deck, regardless of weather, for want of other accommodations.

Maalaea Bay, the place at which the sisters were to be landed, is nothing more than a long curve in Maui's southern coast. In 1884 neither breakwaters nor headlands protected the landing place. A short rickety pier ventured out from shore, but ships could not tie up beside it because the water there was too shallow. Smallboats rowed by sailors ferried passengers and cargoes between ship and pier.

As often happens in the narrow strait between Maui and Lanai, a storm blew up at about 5 o'clock in the afternoon, while the steamer approached its destination. Strong winds whipped up enormous waves, pelting rains tried to beat them down, both fought to delay the struggling ship. Several hours later, in the dark of night, the vessel arrived off Maalaea. Despite the gale, native sailors, not as afraid as they should have been—or, much more likely, not nearly as impressed by the storm as Sister Leopoldina imagined it—set passengers and baggage into a smallboat, lowered it into the foaming surf, and started rowing toward a shore they could not even see. For more than an hour of heroic effort, during which they were in danger of being swept out to sea or swamped by the breakers, "the brave Hawaiian boys steered her safely up and down those fearful waves." Finally, near midnight, they brought the smallboat alongside Maalaea's pier. As an incoming wave lifted the boat near the level of the wharf, two sailors tossed a passenger toward it. The passengers were fortunate, on this wild night: all of them, and their baggage, were delivered safely. The sisters and Father Leonor did not know that they were in greater danger of being swept off the pier and drowned in the surf than ever they were threatened while still aboard the smallboat.

The sailors in their lighter disappeared in the night and eventually returned to the *Kinau*. Whatever "the brave Hawaiian boys" may have thought of the storm, the passengers they deposited at Maalaea were sick, terrified, and exhausted, soaked to the skin, more dead than alive. Somehow they staggered along the length of the unprotected pier and, thanking God, gained the land.

Father Gulstan Ropert, loyal to his trust, waited there to greet his vice-provincial and the American sisters. He took them "in a big carriage" to Wailuku, "seven miles over rough bad roads, big stones, roots of old trees, many [pot]holes and mud so that the horses could not travel fast." Strong winds and heavy rains continued to beat at them for several kilometers, until the travelers came within the lee of West Maui's high mountains. Near dawn, "suffering with hunger and cold," they reached the mission in Wailuku. The storm had quieted, come to a tame end. The new day brought a fickle promise: "The fresh morning breeze was sweeping gently through the bright green leaves of the grand old trees that had been planted so many years ago by the Fathers in the early days of their mission. . . ."

After that ordeal "Sister Renata and Sister Antonella were unable to leave their beds for several days." Indeed, frail Sister Antonella Murphy never did recover from it. While still in America she had contracted pulmonary tuberculosis, which was not apparent when Mother Marianne chose her to be a member of the mission bound for Hawaii. The exposure to cold and fright during that dreadful passage to Maui, aggravated by the horrors she forced herself to endure each day at Kakaako, so weakened Sister Antonella that in Wailuku the infection flared up, never more to be controlled by her body's weak defenses. The ravaging consumption caused her to die before the year ended.

Mother Marianne, just as weary as her companions, would not allow herself any rest: "Courage kept her up. There was so much to do and all depended on her."

Wailuku was a quiet town spilling along the hillside that slopes down from the mountains of West Maui toward the isthmus connecting it with the vast bulk of Haleakala that forms East Maui. The town existed because of the government building that an earlier king than Kalakaua decided to construct there, near the island's center of population. That edifice made Wailuku the capital city of Maui.

In March 1855 Father Leonor became the first Catholic priest to settle permanently in Wailuku, in a mission earlier visiting priests had established in a sheltered hollow somewhat nearer the sea than the mountains. In the 1860s the manager of the town's first sugar plantation built its millhouse and factory almost across the wide muddy road from the Catholic mission, thereby drawing even more residents into the neighborhood. By 1873 prospering Catholic parishioners could afford to finance a fine new church in the mission yard. At the consecration of this very church to St. Anthony, on May 3, 1873, Bishop Louis Maigret chose Father Damien to be the first of his priests to live among the lepers on Molokai, "for only a few months."

The new government hospital, Gibson's gift to his constituents of Maui, was built upon land given for the purpose by Claus Spreckels, the Sugar King. It stood atop a low hill about a hundred meters to the west of St. Anthony's Church. A small two-story frame house, it resembled a rather modest home. A narrow verandah along the front of each floor allowed light and air—and people—to enter its interior. The gable ends had no windows, although several little vents high up near the eaves did permit warm air to escape from the attic. Next to this structure stood a tiny narrow bungalow, where two or three nurses might live—if and when they could be found.

Mother Marianne and her companions moved into this doll's house.

At least Wailuku's hospital was new and clean and empty, unlike the lazarhouse at Kakaako. In fact, the place was so empty that the Franciscans had to furnish it with every single article that was needed to make it "ready as soon as possible to receive the patients," as Sister Leopoldina recounted. "All the bedding and hospital clothes were to be bought and the sewing done."

Father Gulstan Ropert and his fellow priests, with support from Protestant and Mormon clergymen of the district, involved the women of the whole community in the effort. "Some of the ladies from different parts of the [district], natives and part Hawaiians, came day after day to assist Mother," Sister Leopoldina reported. "I heard her say many times that she would be forever grateful to them and that she did not know what she would have done had it not been for their help." In this respect, as in others, the people of Wailuku showed that they were better Christians than were the residents of Honolulu.

At Wailuku's hospital, moreover, the sea did not sweep in over the yard, no high fence shut the sisters in or hid the views beyond, no constables would ever stand guard over its patients. Sister Leopoldina, who visited Wailuku many years later, loved the place: "The scenery is grand from all sides. When you are on the front veranda you can see far out over the ocean and watch the steamers coming. As you turn you can see great fields of sugar cane and as you turn still there are the interesting native huts and beautiful green taro patches. There are the wonderful mountains with their tops reaching the clouds. Between the mountains is that beautiful Iao Valley."

After studying the hospital building, Mother Marianne thought it needed some minor alterations. She told Father Leonor what changes she wanted made; and he, upon returning to Honolulu, transmitted her requests to Mr. Gibson. His Excellency approved them at once, and—as he informed Mother Marianne on February 12—sent "an instruction to Board of Health agent Mr. Everett. I will support you and your Sisters in the noble work of Charity to the best of my ability . . . whatever may be the stress of public business, your wish shall be attended to. . . ."

In this same cordial letter Gibson added: "I paid a visit to our Branch Hospital on Saturday last, and I was highly pleased with the notable improvements effected in the female wards by Sister Bonaventure and her associated Sisters—"

In Wailuku, as in Honolulu, the needs of her church divided once again Mother Marianne's little company. The girls' school, Father Gulstan lost no time in telling her and Father Leonor, suffered from a lack of good teachers. In 1884, Sister Leopoldina recalled, the parish school at Wailuku numbered "about twenty or thirty little girls, taught by a native. They could neither speak nor understand English." In this particular, too, progress had not caught up with Wailuku. Resident Catholic priests, who spoke Hawaiian better than they managed English, realized as well as Honolulu's politicians did that their pupils should be learning the language of the masters of commerce in the kingdom. Native children learned Hawaiian easily enough at home or in play, and had no need for schooling presented in that language.

Nonetheless, the mission fathers also believed that, until they could offer instruction in English, a school taught in the native tongue was better than no school at all.

Mother Marianne met this demand too: she "gave Sister Antonella charge of the school, while she and Sister Renata prepared the hospital for use." Sister Antonella, still weak from the strain of the voyage to Maui, could better be used in the classroom. No one yet realized that she was mortally ill. "Dear soul," sighed Sister Leopoldina, "it was her last work in this world, but she tried to do all she could for the little girls." By mid-July she was too sick to spend a full day in the classroom. Once again Father Gulstan had to hire a native teacher for the girls' school, by that time enlarged to fifty students. On December 12, 1884, still in her twenty-eighth year, Sister Antonella Murphy died, the first of Mother Marianne's company in Hawaii "to go to her reward."

The Franciscans who followed her at Wailuku did not soon forget Sister Antonella: for them she became the perpetual reminder of awaiting death and promised reward. Sister Leopoldina noticed that memento mori: "Just back of the Sisters Convent yard, perhaps three minutes walk, is a little side hill. On it is a dear little burrying ground. There our saintly Sister Antonella's remains are resting. We can see her grave from many places, but the place I like best is from the door of the church. When the Priest is saying Mass and turns to give the blessing, he could also give the blessing to the dead for he can see their graves from the alter."

Early in March 1884, John Owen Dominis, King Kalakaua's Boston-born brother-in-law, visited Maui in his office as the island's royal governor. His wife, Princess Liliuokalani, the king's sister and heir apparent, accompanied Governor Dominis. During their brief stay in Wailuku, she called at the new hospital and inspected it with Mother Marianne as guide. Before departing, Her Royal Highness promised to assist the institution in any way she could.

A few days later, on March 11—at Prime Minister Gibson's suggestion, said Sister Leopoldina—Mother Marianne addressed a formal request to the princess, by then returned to Honolulu: "As you were the first member of the Royal family to honor the hospital with a visit [she wrote], I beg to suggest, if it please your Royal Highness, to give it a distinctive name in memory of your kind visit and to inspire the poor sufferers who may come to its sheltering arms. . . ."

The custom of asking royal personages to confer names upon children or places or institutions is not exclusively Hawaiian, but it is one that Hawaiians very often observed. The fact that Mother Marianne made the request, whether or not Gibson proposed it, indicates that she was learning the niceties of politics in the Kingdom of Hawaii. She could not foresee that, only seven years later, Liliuokalani would succeed her brother as the nation's first sovereign queen. But in 1884 both Gibson and Mother Marianne knew very well that this haughty and Protestant princess was not as well disposed toward the Roman Catholic Church and its missioners as was her sister-in-law, Queen Kapiolani. Any action they might take to win her favor was not to be overlooked.

Princess Liliuokalani gave a gracious answer. "Its name shall be Malulani," she declared, "which means 'under the protection of heaven.'" In that potent name any Hawaiian would recognize the promise it implied. Inasmuch as lani, the Hawaiian word for heaven, also means, by extension, "a child of heaven," a descendant of the great gods, such as a high chief or prince or king, the name that Liliuokalani gave the hospital offered it also the protection of the royal family. Kalakaua and Liliuokalani kept that promise during their reigns. After the monarchy ceased to exist in 1893, when Honolulu's disgruntled businessmen forced Queen Liliuokalani from her throne, a sequence of successor governments continued to support Malulani Hospital. Regardless of the nature of the government ruling from Honolulu, Franciscan sisters operated it until 1929.

Mother Marianne, Sister Renata, and the ladies of Wailuku strove to put Malulani Hospital "in working order," to use Sister Columba's phrase. Furnishing it was not easy, in that remote town in this most isolated country on earth. Wailuku's stores could provide little more than needles and thread, and perhaps a bolt or two of cotton cloth. Almost everything the hospital required had to be imported from abroad, usually from the United States, by way of Honolulu's watchful middlemen. Even if the Board of Health's clerks had anticipated Malulani's need and ordered items from the United States, the Franciscans still must wait for them to be delivered at Kahului, the tiny port nearest to Wailuku, where a steamer called not oftener than once a week. And then they had to distribute the articles when finally draymen deposited the barrels and crates in the hospital yard.

In the interval, while Wailuku's ladies sewed, Mother Marianne and Sister Renata taught a pair of employees the rudiments of hospital procedure, and laid down rules about preparing meals, personal hygiene, institutional sanitation, the keeping of reliable records, and the dozens of other details that mark an efficient organization. Probably, also, they helped Wailuku's Government Physician, Dr. Enders, to train those same two employees as surgical assistants and nurses' aides. Inevitably, because both the doctor and the sisters came from America, Malulani Hospital would be administered in the American manner. The island's few physicians would be responsible for medical and surgical treatment of patients they admitted to the institution, and Dr. Enders would be the Board of Health's agent-in-charge. The sisters and their aides would do the menial work of preparation and care, for both patients and facilities. All types of cases would be received, except for those suffering from leprosy. Malulani would not admit lepers because, by law, those unfortunates—whether confirmed or only suspect—must be sent to Kakaako for diagnosis and disposition.

Slowly, much too slowly, the supplies trickled in. Mother Marianne and Sister Renata could consider this period as almost a second vacation, compared with the unremitting strain of working at Kakaako. At the very least they were spared the sight and smell of lepers, and, during the days, the sound of pale Sister Antonella, coughing her life away in the schoolhouse for girls. Sister Renata—quiet, unassuming, yet frank when she wanted to be, as slight as an adolescent boy (and with something of a youth's sharp features and shy bearing)—did her best to relieve Mother Marianne of lesser chores, thereby freeing her to catch up with the correspondence relating to her duties as Mother-Provincial of the Order. Mother Antonia Eulenstein, assisted by Sister Delphina Mueller, managed most of the details of administration in Syracuse; but Mother Marianne, as elected head of the Order, still had to decide upon some of the larger issues, such as changes in policy recommended by general chapters and legal aspects of acquiring property or spending unusually large sums of money for extraordinary purposes. For more than twenty months, from the time she left Syracuse until the middle of 1885, she served the Order as Mother Provincial, sending advice, signatures, decisions, and documents back to Syracuse. During most of that time, certainly until the end of February 1885, she acted as if she fully expected to return to the Motherhouse. Because she was an honest woman, we must assume that, until the first months of 1885, she did intend to return to

Syracuse—in spite of a growing realization that, in Hawaii, among the needy sick and the suffering poor, especially among the despairing lepers, she had found the people who called most insistently upon her compassion.

Meanwhile, at the center of affairs in Honolulu, Father Leonor and Mr. Gibson entered into yet another conspiracy. The political stew of 1884 was heating up, in preparation for the convening of the legislature on April 26. The two planners, indifferent to reality, wanted Mother Marianne to go as soon as possible to the Leprosarium on Molokai. Father Leonor explained to her "the *real* object" of that visit in a letter written on March 3: "the great desire of the King to have the visit made before the opening of the Legislature, that he might be able to say you took possession of the leper settlement of Kalawao which is one of the most important hospitals of the archipelago, and one most likely to draw the attention of the legislative body and to prompt it to decide definitely that *all* the hospitals of the government ought to be given exclusively to the Franciscan Sisters because they have accepted the *hardest*. . . . I think it best for you to return to Honolulu on Holy Saturday, then we could go to Molokai Easter Monday and Tuesday."

If ever Mother Marianne replied to this plan—or even concurred with it—her letter is not preserved. In any event, other forces leading to a climax in Honolulu spared her the need to add yet another hospital to her burden. The two at Kakaako and Wailuku were causing difficulties enough.

Letters from Sister Bonaventure at Kakaako brought such alarming news about the rising tension between Henry Van Giesen on the one hand and the sisters and the lepers on the other, that Mother Marianne decided the time had come for her to act. On March 14, "not without hesitation," as she told him, she wrote to Bishop Hermann. "The present trouble at Kakaako causes me no little anxiety," she began. Whereupon she asked him to visit the Branch Hospital and to appraise the situation there in talks with sisters, Van Giesen, and Mr. Gibson. "Your knowledge of the parties with whom we have to deal and of the condition of things will enable you to be our protection and to secure for us the rights we should have to be able to do Justice to both the Government and to the poor entrusted to our care. . . . Your Lordship knows the conditions under which we came here. It was promised us that the Sisters direct the Hospitals, and that they were to have as many servants as they would want for work. So far neither of these two things have been done. . . . Now that there is so much dissatisfaction expressed against the steward, would it not be the time to make a change, when it can be done without offending anyone. . . . Please, your Lordship, act for us in the matter as you would do if your Sisters were concerned. . . ."

Her estimate of the several men who were weaving this tangled web of intrigue about her mission directed Mother Marianne to the only one who could help her to escape it. Bishop Hermann, plaintive though he might pretend to be in his letters, was by no means a mere helpless bystander. "Prudent," Father Lesen's favorite word, applies equally well to Bishop Hermann. The imagination, curiosity, and wit of a cultivated European did prepare him to be an aloof and amused observer of the Hawaiian *opéra bouffe* he witnessed from one of the best loges that Honolulu had to offer. But he was also a benevolent and patient administrator of his diocese, and a careful protector of his Apostolic Mission.

His Lordship, fully acquainted with Mother Marianne's worth as a person and as a symbol, and of the value of her mission not only to Hawaii but also to the Catholic Church, went forth at once to be her champion. Being wise, he visited the hospital at Kakaako and heard the sisters' side of the story. Then, armed with a set of facts, more or less indisputable, he called upon Walter Murray Gibson.

Being cautious, he wrote his reply to Mother Marianne in German, and in two instalments. The first he indited on March 16, the second—a long postscript—he added two days later. In 1884, as a year earlier, he identified exactly the primary reason for all the problems at Kakaako. "We realized very well that [in Gibson] we were dealing with a man who easily promises, but then in devious ways evades matters in order not to displease other people. Therefore, with him you may have to put your questions in a decisive manner to receive definite yes or no responses."

The arrival of the Franciscan sisters at Kakaako had introduced a few complicating factors, he conceded. "Presently, the good Sr. Bonaventura is not ready to assume certain duties or responsibilities without express permission from you. Therefore your personal presence is necessary to settle this matter."

His Lordship had called upon Gibson "and told him about our dissatisfaction. He, of course, finds an excuse . . . if things do not go right yet the reason is that the Sisters have not clearly made known their wishes." To prove his willingness "to do anything we would ask from him [Gibson] has now in my presence given his secretary the authority to smoothen out all that hinders the formal opening of the hospital by a letter to you and one to G. Everett and one to Dr. Enders. You will be able to see soon how matters stand."

After waiting two nights and a day for Gibson to act, Bishop Hermann too made a decision: "Matters have not changed much," he began his postscript. "It remains always the same story." Gibson, to be sure, had gone to visit the sisters at Kakaako on Saturday afternoon, March 15, "at which time he made many promises but he has done little." By this tactful interpolation the bishop meant that Gibson had not spoken seriously to Van Giesen, as the necessary first step toward restraining the chief steward's cruelty to the lepers and his arrogance toward the sisters. The ultimate step, the "change" that Mother Marianne most earnestly desired—the dismissal of Van Giesen—His Lordship may have implied, but did not demand, in his conversation with Gibson.

Father Gulstan, His Lordship continued, added a further complication by expressing "a strong wish that you should stay a week longer in Wailuku." And Sister Bonaventure "also believes that matters here will go on another week."

In view of all contending factors, however, Bishop Hermann agreed with Mother Marianne: "Yet, I think that after 1 or 2 weeks the wagon will go into the slump too deeply if we do let the present opportunity pass. The little man [Van Giesen] will bow and bend to hold his position whereas the larger gentlemen [Gibson] will promise everything but will do nothing for us. (I mean, he will give full power of authority) if we don't force him—and the sooner the better."

Gibson's official letters to Maui (to which Bishop Hermann referred in that cautious letter to Mother Marianne) were concerned only with arrangements for managing the hospital in Wailuku. He did nothing to prevent the troubles that were gathering at Kakaako. The bishop, fearing worse difficulties at any moment, abruptly concluded his confidential letter: "I ask you to come to Honolulu as soon as possible. We are expecting you by the end of the week."

The communication from Gibson's secretary at the Board of Health, G. W. Parker, arrived in the same mail that brought her Bishop Hermann's summons to Honolulu. While the bishop's news would have distressed her, Parker's brisk notice should have pleased. It did determine, in terms adequate for those years, the position and responsibilities of the sisters at Malulani Hospital. "The President of the Board of Health," Parker wrote, "has appointed the Lady Superior of the Franciscan Sisters, at Wailuku, either yourself or a successor, as an agent of the Board of Health. . . . Your special duties will be to take charge of the Hospital just erected, and to attend to all the internal and domestic arrangements as regards sanitation, diet of patients, dispensing of medicines ordered by the Physician etc. Dr. Enders as the Government Physician in charge of the Wailuku District will afford the necessary medical and surgical assistance; while Mr. Everett will aid you in procuring such helpers as you may require, besides overseeing all whitewashing, repair, etc."

This authorization should have been accompanied by a similar directive covering the Franciscan sisters' duties and responsibilities at Kakaako. But Gibson did not send that important document. The reasons for his failure to do so can only be conjectured. Probably he liked Van Giesen as a person or respected the queen's interest in him, and accordingly overlooked his defects as a steward. By his usual tactic of ignoring whatever he did not want to see, Gibson hoped to avoid making any decisions that would offend any one. Yet in his consideration for Van Giesen the President of the Board of Health did not realize how he exposed both the Franciscan sisters and the lepers to the oppressions of a madman.

Almost two months after they arrived in Wailuku Mother Marianne and Sister Renata still waited for some of the hospital's supplies to come in. They could not predict when it would be ready to admit its first patient, even as they prayed that the great day would come soon. They could not guess that when finally it did arrive, on April 23, Mother Marianne would not be present to help celebrate the event.

In the Branch Hospital at Kakaako, under Van Giesen's reign of terror, cruelty and viciousness were being fought with violence and murderous hate, to a degree that neither Gibson nor Bishop Hermann nor the sisters were prepared to imagine.

Bishop Hermann's letter, calling Mother Marianne to Kakaako, could not be ignored. "She dreaded to leave the two delicate Sisters alone," Sister Leopoldina remembered, "but the order came from His Lordship. . . . She had no choice. She must go."

NOTES on Chapter VIII

1. Gibson's program for government hospitals: *Speeches and Measures Proposed and Discussed by Hon. Walter Murray Gibson, Member for Lahaina in the Hawaiian Parliament of 1880, 1881:* pp. 36–37.
2. The archive in Rome of the Congregation of the Sacred Hearts contains the official correspondence exchanged between the Superior General or other members of the General Curia and the members of the Congregation or other persons. Fortunately, some personal correspondence from members of the Hawaiian Mission is available in *La Père Damien—Vie et Documents.* From this collection of documents transcripts were obtained of the Damien-Fouesnel letters as well as of other correspondence for which the originals are no longer available.
3. Appeal for "Organ for Sisters of Charity": *Pacific Commercial Advertiser,* July 1, 1884. Later mention of this organ in the chapel at Kakaako is in 1936 notes of Sr. Benedicta, now in AS.
4. Queen Liliuokalani, patroness of Malulani Hospital at Wailuku, Maui: *Leprosy in Hawaii,* 1886, Gibson's report, p. 137.

Chapter IX

RESOLUTION

MOTHER MARIANNE returned to Honolulu on March 29. Worry about the reasons behind the bishop's summons, about the problems awaiting her at the Branch Hospital, added to the miseries caused by the sea.

Sister Bonaventure, Sister Crescentia, the others at Kakaako, soon told her what had happened. Van Giesen, with the madness of a man determined to destroy himself, had bedevilled everyone in the hospital, even the sisters when at night they withdrew to the convent. "He told the sisters repeatedly that the lepers had no use for white people [Sister Leopoldina would write] and that they had many times threatened to take his life. 'yes,' he said, I am afraid of the lepers. They are a very bad lot, but I will never give up. I will conquer them or die.'" Such bragging hid a weak man's terror—but not a sadist's pleasure in reminding the sisters that they too went in peril among the lepers they wanted to help.

Thinking to protect himself, Van Giesen rigged up a signal device of a modern sort—a long wire strung from his office to a bell in the convent. The bell would ring whenever he tugged at the wire, and the sisters were supposed to run to his side. A telephone installed in his office gave him another link to security: in the event of a serious threat he could call the city's station house, asking for constables to assist his "leper police force." He actually believed that those fragile life lines would be useful to him in a real emergency. Why the lepers never bothered to rip them down is no mystery at all: they knew very well that, when the time came, they would seize the hated steward long before he could reach his life line.

Van Giesen started to express his dislike for the sisters almost as soon as Mother Marianne went off to Maui. Sister Bonaventure, imposing as she was in person, could not control this sneering man nor end his persecutions. "Mr. Van said to the Sisters, 'as there is not work for you to do, you may remain in your home. I will ring for you when I need you . . .' he continually called the Sisters for every little thing. Sometimes he would call them in the middle of the night just to tell them what he was intending to do the next day. The Sisters naturally had a dread of going through the long dark yard to Mr. Van's office in the dead hours of the night." Nevertheless, each time the alarm sounded in the convent hall they suppressed their fears and hurried to his office.

"I will conquer them or die," this fine figure of a man boasted. And yet whenever he thought a gang of lepers was planning an attack upon his precious person, or if ever he just felt like venting his scorn for people in general and for women in particular, he yanked upon that signal wire. Usually Sister Bonaventure, as Mother Marianne's deputy, would answer the call. Tall and heavy and grave, she never allowed herself to become disturbed, never lost her temper. Almost always little Sister Crescentia went with her, like a dark, fearless, unexcitable shadow. At moments like these, when Van Giesen jangled that peremptory bell, they might have regretted the absence of "stormy" Sister Dominica Cumming. With her Irish temper and tongue, she would have subdued Van Giesen at the first encounter— and finished the lesson by tearing that wire loose from its hooks. But she was not there to protect the sisters. And neither was Mother Marianne, with her low calm voice, the dark eyes that saw right into a man's heart, the quiet manner that soothed and at the same time stirred most men into doing their best. Van Giesen feared Mother Marianne most of all among those intrusive females, and therefore he hated her most of all. Especially in her absence did he hate her.

One dark night the pair of sisters responded to Van Giesen's tocsin. His prowling leper minions had brought him a woman taken in adultery. He actually mouthed the biblical phrase, actually pointed his long tainted haole finger at the captured girl, standing before his desk, guarded by a huge policeman holding her by either arm.

Van Giesen, screeching and dancing about the crowded little room, described the severe punishment he meted out to such vicious criminals: confinement to their wards. "'If they make any trouble or do not take their punishment as they should, we handcuff them, keep them in their rooms, and give them very little to eat. I want to tell you that these bad people must be punished.'"

Sister Bonaventure "remained a silent listener until he finished speaking, when she asked, 'And where are the men?' 'Oh!' he stammered, 'the man ran away. We could not find him . . .' Sister said, 'He could be found. It is unjust to punish the poor girl and let the man go.' " Sister Bonaventure's argument did not sway Van Giesen. ". . . the poor girl was punished but the man was let go."

If Van Giesen himself had been above reproach, his determination to impose continence upon the lepers might be understandable, if not justified—or, for that matter, practicable. But in all this exhibition of Virtue Outraged he was being utterly hypocritical. Everybody knew about his flagrant misbehavior, even the priests at the cathedral—and, very soon, even the sisters at Kakaako. "He no good. He worse 'n us . . .' " the lepers told them, Sister Leopoldina reported. "'He take little kanaka girl his house, make allsame wife for him. He . . . never keep rule. He do plenty bad things. . . .' " The patients' list of grievances against their faithful steward grew longer with each day. So did the sisters'. They understood how, in calling their attention to the woman taken in adultery, he wanted to debase all women—most especially the Franciscan sisters, so obviously, so infuriatingly, chaste.

Another night, about 12 o'clock, "in inky darkness . . . as silent as death," the bell clanged again. This time the sisters found Van Giesen "alone in his office . . . in a dreadful excited state, walking rapidly back and forth, swinging his arms, shaking his long beard, grating his teeth. In a low bitter voice he said, 'Something must be done. Those men are smoking opium.' " His policemen, having sniffed the sweet fumes wafted upon the midnight air, had traced them to a dark and dangerous room.

The Franciscan sisters, too, on principle, would have opposed the smoking of opium by people who were not actually ill. But the sisters, unlike Van Giesen, would have felt some sympathy for Kakaako's imprisoned lepers: they, more than most other people in Hawaii, were genuinely sick, and forever in need of every kind of solace, however it was provided. The sisters might not have condoned the lepers' resort to illicit opium, the one reliever of pain, the only bringer of bliss upon their verge of hell. But neither would the sisters have hated the lepers for yielding to their need.

On this special midnight, Sister Bonaventure and Sister Crescentia listened until Van Giesen finished his monologue. " 'We will go and see them,' Sister Crescentia said gently." At the culprits' hiding place they found a ridiculous tableau: "two policemen holding tight on the end of a rope that was fastened to the knob of the door." The sisters swept into that den of iniquity. "'Now what have you been doing?,'" Sister Crescentia asked. "'You promised me you would be good.'" Within half a minute the lepers, like schoolboys, gave her "the two little stumps of pipes with a very little opium in them." Generous even under stress, the men also offered to share their hoard with the sisters, "'s'pose you like some.'"

This sad little incident explains better than does any other the sister's method for influencing the patients. Some of those prisoners of society's fear, being filled with resentment for the clean people who had jailed them, could be as dangerous as lunatics. And yet most of them responded to loving kindness when it was offered. The opium smokers on that inky night submitted to the two gentle sisters with every sign of respect—which, they carefully specified, right then and there, did not extend to Van Giesen.

Predictably, the superintendent disdained the sisters' plea for leniency. After a mockery of a trial, he imposed a penalty that in itself was a mockery: "to remain in their rooms and hold no communication with anyone for several days." More than ever "the sisters felt so helpless. On the one hand he would call them and ask for their advice, then cast it aside as worthless."

"One very dark still night" the drama came to its climax. "The Sisters were aroused by a frightful racket . . . as if the whole place was on fire." The alarm bell did not awaken them that night, because Van Giesen did not have a chance to tug on the line he had so carefully rigged. "When the Sisters reached the great crowd of lepers [milling around the steward's office], the noise, the clamer, and the excitement were frightful. . . . They found Mr. Van in his office. He looked as though he had gone through a frightful agony. 'Well,' he said, 'they were trying to kill me. They came so silently, broke in my door, and there were nine rough lepers rushing in upon me. One took me by the beard, others by the arms, and others by my legs, and so they dragged me from my house. They said we will kill you and throw your body in the ocean. I thought it would be the last of me and likely [it] would have been were it not for you Sisters. How quickly they were quiet when you came . . . Poor Van. He looked as if he had been sick for many months. He was trembling from head to foot."

Those nine rough lepers treated him more gently than Van Giesen deserved—or else were as confused about the purpose of their raid as gangs usually are. They could have killed the villain in the instant they laid hands upon him. But they neglected to do so—and thereby allowed his leper police to rescue him. The fact that the nine angry men did not murder him suggests that they hoped to scare Van Giesen into decent behavior. They should not have been surprised to learn, during the morning's trial after that wild night, how mistaken they were in their estimate of him.

The terrible experience taught the sisters something too. They saw at last that Van Giesen could never be a decent man, and therefore could never be a reliable steward. Forebearance ended with the night. The next morning Sister Bonaventure telephoned "to His Lordship... and Mr. Gibson telling them there must be something done." Prelate and Premier hurried to Kakaako, "counciled with the Sisters, and decided to fetch Mother back to the station. Mr. Gibson decided to send the would-be murderers to the Leper Settlement, Molokai, as soon as he could get a boat that would take them. Until then they must be kept in prison. Mr. Van G. was quite determined that he should have police officers from Honolulu to protect him from the lepers, but the Sisters did not think it necessary. Sister Crecsentia had control. They would do almost anything for her."

For almost three months the sisters had been showing, with each day, how compassion works wonders that brutality can never gain. Nonetheless, Gibson and Van Giesen, products of a repressive society, insisted upon punishment as the only means for maintaining law and order at Kakaako. Van Giesen ordered his leprous constables to lock their nine fellow prisoner's into the hospital's jail—those two barred cubicles, each only 1.2 meters broad, high, and deep. They stuffed five men into one cell, four into the other. By day the criminals sweltered in the heat, by night they shivered in the chill damp winds blowing in from the sea. Sister Crescentia took them food, blankets, and the obligatory lecture: "Everyday Sister tried to teach the poor unfortunates to do right, and not bring upon themselves more suffering for their unlawful deeds." But rage against Van Giesen surpassed their aloha for Sister Crescentia. "They continued to wish to take the man's life. So they had to be sent into exile to that lonely dreaded Molokai, never again to see their dear ones in this world, the poor unfortuante creatures."

When she wrote these chronicles in the 1920s, Sister Leopoldina
had worked for thirty-five years and more in the Leper Settlement on
Molokai. Yet she never considered herself to be "a poor unfortunate
creature" because of it. Nor did she grieve because, for all those years,
she had been cut off from all contact with her own "dear ones in this
world."

The *Pacific Commercial Advertiser* for March 8, 1884, gave its
readers a rather different version of this sensation, and added details
Sister Leopoldina could not have been told. Six men, said the *Advertiser,* not nine as the steward claimed, "about 5 o'clock yesterday
morning... broke open the door of Van Giesen's house and made an
assault upon him in his bed." While several of the attackers mishan-
dled him pretty much as he described, another sprinkled kerosene
about the room, promising to set fire to the place. "An extra guard on
the premises at the time" heard Van Giesen's cries and rescued him.

"The Excitement at Kakaako," as the *Advertiser's* headlines named
it, was directed (the reporter said) not against Van Giesen personally,
but against the government's policy of segregation. Ironically, the lepers' response to the Franciscan sisters, those emissaries of charity and
exemplars of peace, helped to incite the patients to open rebellion.
Perhaps because the newspaper's reporter was not yet informed of it,
he said nothing about Van Giesen's brutality.

Several patients at Kakaako had sent letters "to members of the
Royal Family [threatening] that blood would be shed if any attempt was
made to remove any of the people from the Branch Hospital to Molokai.
They all stated that since the arrival of the Sisters of Charity all the
patients were greatly improving under their constant and unremitting
care, and they (the patients) felt better in consequence of having to
have a well ordered home, where there seemed to be a chance for their
lives, [rather than] to go into banishment to a place where there
seemed to be no chance."

The patients were deluded in their expectations of the sisters'
medical treatment. Nothing, in those days, could cure them of the
disease, although some medications could alleviate the condition, or
soothe the pain, for a while, for some cases. The psychological consequences of the sisters' "constant and unremitting care" are not to be
discounted, however; and, because of it, the lepers may have felt
better, both physically and emotionally. Sister Bonaventure herself
recognized how greatly the Franciscans had improved both hospital

and patients: "No one would know the place today," she wrote in 1887, as she compared Kakaako with the mess they had found in 1883: "... there are no ugly and disgusting sores to be seen, but happy and contented faces. . . ."

In the hope of quieting the excited lepers, Gibson called upon some of Honolulu's most potent personages. Queen Kapiolani arrived about 9 o'clock, accompanied by another of her sisters, Her Royal Highness Princess Pomaikalani. Several other influential citizens also responded to Gibson's alarm. He assembled all the patients "in front of Her Majesty who was seated on the verandah of the office of the hospital." Queen Kapiolani's sacred presence in itself ensured her subjects' best behavior.

Gibson "spoke very earnestly and feelingly to the people, expressing his heaviness of heart at the great calamity afflicting the people, and the necessary law to provide for a separation in order to save those who were well. He said that out of great evil, great blessings sometimes arise. . . ."

Here he was, caught in the middle again: damned by the haole citizenry if he did not enforce the law of segregation, and even more violently condemned by the natives if he did. This has always been the classic posture of the misfortuned government official who is responsible for administering any controversial policy, and it is especially so for the poor man who must deal with lepers. During his years as President of the Board of Health, Gibson was constantly the target of outraged taxpayers who thought themselves endangered (or overcharged) and of lepers who believed themselves persecuted (or neglected).

But he, with great patience and consummate tact, using his orator's gestures and sonorous rolling rhetoric, calmed the embittered lepers, prepared them to listen to reason. Speakers who followed him preached the same message of submission, imploring the lepers to spare the clean people of Hawaii. Her Majesty brought the proceedings to an emotional peak with "a few gracious parting remarks expressing her great love for her suffering people and urging them to be obedient to the law."

The Reverend J. Kauwa, himself a patient, "addressed Her Majesty in behalf of his fellow sufferers. He said that since the good and religious women had come (the Sisters of Charity) who were constant in their care and attention to them, their hearts had revived and many were now hopeful of health who had formerly despaired and therefore there was such a sad and painful feeling to leave this well ordered hospital and their kind and gentle Sisters who waited on them like Angels. He then lifted up his hands and read a short and impressive prayer."

Her Majesty rode away amid "vigorously repeated hurrahs." Most of the dignitaries quickly followed her through the gate. But Gibson stayed for the rest of the morning, to talk with "about fifty who had been marked for departure" on the afternoon of that same day. He divided those reluctant ones into "lots of five, and after some kindly discussion and representation, about 30 willingly assented to go to the Molokai Settlement." Later in the day, when the steamer *Mokolii* anchored beyond the reef in order to take on passengers from the hospital, thirty-nine lepers "came forward of their own accord...." Gibson's skillful handling of the crowd had won this round, too.

The *Advertiser* wrote nothing about Van Giesen's nine—or six—assailants being locked up in those two torture cells. Possibly he didn't know about Kakaako's jail, or they hadn't been confined as yet, or Sister Leopoldina's informant misremembered when, many years later, she talked about this violent event in the career of Henry Van Giesen.

Sister Leopoldina's chronicle about this period in the founding of the Franciscan mission lacks a number of details that would help to reconstruct that history. And, naturally, the skeptical reader must always question her point of view, which is both biased and naive. Even so, her anecdotes are valuable because they do capture a sense of occasion and they do suggest the atmosphere of trouble and suspense that hung over the hospital at Kakaako, like a miasma of the spirit mingling with the stink of the lepers' sores. Furthermore, her tales preserve, as she intended, the responses of the pioneer sisters to people and problems they encountered in that miserable concentration camp.

As the years passed, Sister Leopoldina's reminiscences and those of her contemporaries, including Mother Marianne, were transmitted orally to contingents of younger sisters coming to join them in Hawaii, and by means of letters and reports to members of the Order who served closer to the Motherhouse. In the course of time these accounts—invariably garbled in the retelling, yet still keeping some connection with reality—coalesced to form "the tradition" relating to the establishment of the mission in Hawaii. At the very heart of this lore, ineluctable and inspiring, are the sisters' memories of the mission's foundress. These are the memories that illumine the career of

Mother Marianne. And out of them has been created the legend that, within the Third Order of St. Francis, is accepted today as *The* Life of Mother Marianne.

The process is natural, inevitable, commendable. But the legend that has been produced in the process must be regarded with caution. So also must be the several written accounts upon which today's tradition (and this biography) are founded in part. Foremost among those accounts are Sister Leopoldina's long chronicle (by far the most extensive compilation in the Order's archives), and the several briefer ones written by other sisters who knew Mother Marianne personally. All of these may be valued more for their tone (which is always edifying) than for their "facts" (which sometimes are correct, often are beyond verifying, sometimes are demonstrably wrong). The sisters' several compositions should be recognized for what they are: the writings of admirers who actually sat down to express their regard for the Faith, for the Order, above all for Mother Marianne, the woman whom they did not hesitate to call a saint. In other words, they were amateur hagiographers, not temperate historians. Not unduly concerned with the world's influences beyond the confines of the hospitals in which they worked and the convents in which they lived, they wrote down their memories, uncomplicated by "the facts" of history (when those could be ascertained) or by the impact of other personalities (when those were known).

But who can blame them for being unprepared to write a critical biography of their heroine? Rather than criticize, we should marvel that any of the sisters, worn after a lifetime of labor for the mission, and tired after each long day's attention to the lepers, ever found the time or the strength to set down their thoughts on paper. And we must agree that their offerings, however inadequate they may be as documentation for history, are the offerings of love—and therefore are truest testimonies to the character and influence of Mother Marianne.

Nonetheless, all this gathering of memories and witnessings, which far-seeing Mother Provincials encouraged during the decade after Mother Marianne's death in 1918, presents us with a remarkable irony. During her long life, Mother Marianne considered herself unimportant as a person, as an individual. Always, she tried to avoid needless mention of herself in talk or in writing; and she broke this self-imposed rule only rarely, to instruct a young and worried member of her community, for example, or to point a moral for a nephew agonizing over the choice of a vocation, or to send home to Syracuse a morsel of information that she knew Mother Bernardina would want to hear.

Mother Marianne could never have been one of those silent penitentials, morbid and morose, who haunt some convents, observing the Rule with lowered gaze, closed lips, cold hearts, and thoughts fixed upon hope of heaven or dread of hellfire and damnation. She talked often enough, pleasantly, even amusingly, quoting an old adage to emphasize a point, or sustaining a weary sister with a kind word, or cheering a leper wincing with pain, or telling little stories to make leper children smile. But she talked for instruction and comfort of others, not for advertising her own importance. And she imposed silence upon her company just as easily, when the Rule required it, or when talk interfered with work.

Nor was she one of those swooning ecstatics who, when they are seized, hear voices, see visions, cry out prophecies and revelations. In all her fifty-six years as a religious she was surrounded by sisters who would have observed any such evidence of an ecstatic's behavior. But not one of them ever did so. She may have been a silent mystic, of course, who kept to herself those transcendent moments of communion with God attained in the solitude of her cell. Certainly her communion with the Lord was the source of her strength. But all testimony indicates that she was too practical a person, too busy *doing* things. And that therefore, by her very nature, she would not have been subject to the divine seizures of the true ecstatic.

In choosing this approach to quiet service, she was being both a product of her practical country and century and a true Franciscan. Had not Brother Giles, the humblest of disciples, said: ". . . he who wishes to learn much must work much and bow his head low"? Had not the seraphic saint himself said: "More than all grace and all the gifts of the Holy Ghost, which Christ vouchsafed to his friends, is the conquering of yourself and the willing endurance of suffering, injustice, contempt, and harshness. For of the other gifts of God, we cannot take any credit to ourselves, for they are not our own but come from God. . . . But of trials and sufferings and crosses we can take the credit to ourselves . . ."?

In her relationships with the sisters of the mission, she must have been a generous and cheerful companion, as well as a thoughtful mother superior, else they would not have worked for her as devotedly as they did. Nor would they have admired her so wholeheartedly. She held the group together, gave it courage as well as meaning. Although we may find this difficult to believe, she and they were happy in their work among the lepers. They may not have remembered St. Francis's dictum, but they exemplified it: "For what else are the servants of God than his singers, whose duty it is to lift up the hearts of men and move them to spiritual joy?"

Wisdom and simplicity made her unaffected and humane. To her companions she was not a commander, but a leader.

Because of these same extraordinary virtues, however, she kept an important part of herself hidden, in deep reserve. In both conversation and correspondence she clung to privacy with the determination of an eccentric and all the humility of a recluse. Privacy, with its boons of inner peace and serenity: this is the greatest need she felt as a person, and the most insistent fact to be learned from the letters she wrote and the conversations her companions recorded. And humility, with its connotations of pure spirit, simplified, stripped of all falseness and all pretense, forgetting self in the work she did for God: this is the message of her whole life.

In that need for privacy she did not destroy correspondence pertaining to herself, as some recluses and eccentrics have insisted upon doing. She destroyed her ego instead. She did not push herself into personal letters and speech, as did those egotists Walter Murray Gibson and Father Leonor. She was incapable of considering herself as the center of the world, because she had yielded that place to Someone else.

And yet, when she had finished her lifetime of service to Him, she became the helpless victim of dozens of memorialists, journalists, columnists, and writers of books, all intent upon preserving every incident, letter, scrap of paper, photograph, piece of furniture, length of fabric, worn keepsake, or artifact that had any association with her whatsoever.

None of those diligent collectors ever thought to respect her passion for privacy, quite probably because, after her death, they thought it was no longer necessary. A few sentences from her letters (many of which were saved by their recipients), together with the snippets of articles, pious homilies, and hortatory poems she cut from newspapers and magazines to paste in a scrapbook during her years in Syracuse, tell us more about her private thoughts than do the commentaries written by all the people who knew her. She is better known by her deeds than by her words. This very self-effacement is a virtue to be lauded and imitated.

Try as she might, she could not prevent associates and visitors from seeing her as a person, or even worse, as a personage—as a figure in the foreground of a landscape, so to speak. And that is the kind of image they have transmitted to us. They show us a figure garbed in the habit of a Franciscan sister, doing good deeds in convents and hospital wards, traveling from one country to another, even suffering, most humanly, from seasickness, from bloody hemorrhagings of the lungs, from a weakening heart as she neared the time to die and a remorseless dropsy swelled the aging body she had never taught to rest. They show us the face, coiffed, beautiful, serene—but revealing so little of her private self. Pain, sickness, grief, and worry she knew in fullest measure. But she learned to hide them from her companions as from the world. So did she also with her innermost thoughts: over those she put a veritable mask.

But, as Yeats has written, "there is always a living face behind the mask." Almost never do Mother Marianne's observers show us the face behind that mask, the woman within that black and white habit: they do not reveal what she is thinking, in that mind behind the countenance with its hint of a smile, or what she is feeling, in that heart beneath the wide white collar and the heavy crucifix.

The Mother Marianne all those determined anthologists present to us, whatever their purpose or persuasion, is only a doll dressed up in a sister's habit. She herself has eluded them—as she will elude everyone else who attempts to "analyze" her. And that faint smile, barely detected in photographs, is a bodhisattva's smile. We cannot know what it means, this smile. It is modest, maddening, dismaying, fascinating, knowing, promising, inscrutable—and, at the last, comforting. It epitomizes the mystery of this quiet woman, who gave her self to the service of that higher Self.

Sister Leopoldina Burns is the Franciscans' prime example of the heroine-worshipper. Although her chronicle is always enjoyable, it is not always a reliable history either of her own life and times or of Mother Marianne's. It is too full of gaps in continuity to be completely trustworthy, and of fallacies in logic as well. And, for the important period before she herself arrived in Hawaii in April 1885, it is based upon hearsay. Yet, despite these faults, it does give the perceptive reader hints, clues, feelings about people and places she did know. Hers is the best picture we have about Mother Marianne's career in Hawaii. But it is suspect because it was offered out of a love that approached adulation.

Truly Irish, and therefore unabashedly romantic, Sister Leopoldina could be sentimental, even gushing, when she wrote about scenery, fellow religious, and most especially about Mother Marianne. She could be very dramatic when she described events involving "unfortunate lepers" and nature's excesses, such as storms at sea or devastations at Kalaupapa. On the other hand, and in significant contrast, she never indulged in flights of fancy when she mentioned matters of policy. In her innocence, then, she reduced many a problem to its essence (as seen from her point of view). In doing so, she made most problems appear to be much simpler than in fact Mother Marianne found them, or wanted others to find them. This naivety makes the pattern of events much easier to follow, but it also obscures the complex reasons behind them.

As many quotations from her chronicle will demonstrate, Sister Leopoldina's political innocence allowed her to compose some dazzling understatements—all of which delight, because they surprise, and some of which annoy, because they slide over details that historians would dearly love to know. One of the grandest of her simplifications concerns the settling of the crisis at Kakaako: "When our gentle Mother came back to the Station, instead of being discouraged, she grabbed the difficult task with an iron hand. She told Mr. Gibson that the lepers would not be managed while Mr. Van G. remained there."

When Mother Marianne returned from Maui to the troubled scene at Kakaako, she faced the greatest crisis in her entire career. The mission she had brought to Hawaii stood in jeopardy. Her own private vocation, the call to work in this large field, was in peril. Her competence as a missioner, a leader, an organizer, a mother superior was being put to the test. The welfare of hundreds of lepers was being ignored. Between her and the realization of her mission stood three obstructive males: a maniacal steward; a preening politician; and a bishop who pondered and discoursed—but had not yet found an effective way to help her weak company.

The time had come, she saw, when she must fight a decisive battle in this war she waged for the lepers. Among thousands of pages of letters, histories, minutes, memorials, and observations concerned with events in Hawaii at that time, those two swift summary sentences of Sister Leopoldina give us the only information yet found that helps to explain how Mother Marianne fought this climactic battle.

She asked Bishop Hermann to arrange a meeting with Mr. Gibson and herself. His Lordship, happy to give his support, did so.

Judging by the results of that confrontation (which are documented), it is not difficult to imagine what happened when Mother Marianne met with Mr. Gibson in the presence of Bishop Hermann. Those complacent gentlemen learned at last that she had more than a gentle voice, a sweet smile, and an almost incomprehensible compassion for suffering lepers. Behind that serene countenance with its bodhisattva smile she hid a will of tempered steel, infinitely harder than a hand of mere iron, even one stripped of a lady's velvet glove. Now she turned that adamantine will upon the man who in his endeavors to please everyone pleased none.

Calmly, politely, but with a firmness that she had not displayed in earlier meetings with those powers in her life, Mother Marianne informed both bishop and prime minister that she and her sisters would not stay in Hawaii unless certain conditions were met. The first of those conditions, mentioned often before, she stipulated again—and for the last time: the promises that Father Leonor had made to her in Syracuse, in the name of the government, must be honored. And honored at once, not at some vague time in the future. The second condition was something new, added because of very recent developments: Mr. Van Giesen must be removed immediately from any connection whatsoever with the hospital at Kakaako.

If these conditions were not met, she would have said, then she would be forced to believe that the Hawaiian government was neither honest nor serious about its vaunted concern for lepers. This being so, she and her companion sisters must conclude that they were wasting their lives and labor in Hawaii. Therefore, she finished her quiet ultimatum, all the Franciscan sisters would return to America, where work aplenty awaited them.

Naturally, she deployed that "low, sweet voice" during this session with her superiors. She was no stormy thrower of tantrums, no weeping weakling with tears in the eyes and sobs in the throat. She was a woman most reasonable, always definitely in control of emotions as well as thoughts, a veritable queen in grace and courtesy. But she was also a Mother Superior aroused, defending her daughters and their mission. The time had come, she implied (but did not say), for putting an end to this shifting game in which Gibson, if not the bishop, pushed the sisters around as if they were lowliest pawns.

She could afford to speak softly to the Lord Bishop and the Lord Pooh Bah: she knew very well that, upon the checkered board at which those politicians played, each Franciscan sister was not a pawn but a crownéd queen. After three months of ministering to Kakaako's prisoners, the sisters had proved their worth beyond all question, and in doing so had increased their spiritual power beyond all measuring. The whole hospital offered testimony to their worth. Witness the elevated morale among the patients, the noticeable improvement in the very sight and smell of them. Witness the cleanliness and good order in the hospital's kitchen, dining room, and wards, rid now of flies and litter and stench. Witness the sisters' plans, presented in discussions and in writing, to raise the moral and spiritual tone from the degrading level in which those "poor sufferers," especially the girls and women, had lived since the day the policemen delivered them into that sink of misery.

Both Gibson and Bishop Hermann knew that neither they nor the lepers could afford to lose the sisters. To allow them to go home now would be a disaster in every sense of the word. Lepers would rebel at being deprived of their nurses, the only solacers they had ever known. Honolulu's merchants and legislators would rise up to ask why now, after so much good money had been spent upon bringing those nuns here to Honolulu, they should get up and go home again—at public expense. Protestant bigots—and Honolulu's simpler wits—would take huge and odious delight in Catholic withdrawal from a field they had claimed, so complacently, for their very own. The whole world would laugh at yet another exhibition of ministerial bungling in a Lilliput already renowned for its comic opera plots and characters.

Mother Marianne did not need to remind Bishop Hermann or Premier Gibson of a truth most obvious: no one else in all Hawaii wanted either the work or the responsibility which the Franciscans had assumed so cheerfully. The Franciscans could have them by default. Mother Marianne could take them by choice—or, as she would have thought, in accordance with God's plan.

Bishop and Knight knew they were checked.

His Lordship would not have missed his chance: both by position and in faith he was destined to support Mother Marianne. Perhaps before this time, out of a sense of delicacy in matters of church politics, he had been overscrupulous in refraining from taking the Franciscan sisters under his full protection. Immediately after this meeting, however, he made arrangements with Father Joseph Lesen in Syracuse, whereby he, a prelate belonging to the Congregation of the Sacred Hearts, included the Franciscan sisters in the administrative structure of his diocese as well as in the benefactions of his regard.

Gibson argued a bit, thrashed about, hemmed and hawed, not out of pride in position but simply because he found himself entangled in another of his webs of conceits. He did not want to offend anybody, least of all the Calvinist opposition. He did not wish to commit himself irrevocably to any one decision. And, possibly most important of all, he did not want to hurt Van Giesen's tender feelings, or chance for future employment, or need for income, or some such sportsmanlike concern. Gibson, this singular man, could be loyal to his friends in spite of the most damning of evidence mounted against them. Therefore, in this showdown with Mother Marianne he did not yield at once—much as he may have wanted to make "the Lady Superior" happy. So he tried his usual trick of arranging at least one compromise in his hope to please everybody.

Mother Marianne would not consider any compromises. She refused to continue "the status quo," as Bishop Hermann's acute priests at the cathedral referred to the situation. Gibson capitulated, no doubt with his usual grace. On April 7 he sent Mother Marianne the letter which served as the contract she had requested in January.

She accorded her triumph for the mission the last of three brief sentences in the laconic report prepared for the Motherhouse in 1887: "... April 2, 1884, Sisters were given full charge of the Leper Hospital and the Superintendent who was there before them, and who caused the sisters much trouble, was removed." The reference to April 2 suggests that her meeting with Gibson and Bishop Hermann was held on that date.

Mother Marianne had rid Kakaako of Van Giesen, but she did not rescue the lepers on Molokai from the attentions of that baneful man. Nor did her compact with Gibson save Van Giesen from the lepers he abhorred. Sister Leopoldina mentioned Gibson's new arrangement without a gasp of surprise: "Mr. Gibson was very kind to poor Mr. Van and gave him another position in the Leper Settlement Molokai (which the poor man could hold only a short time)."

The mind reels at the insensitivity of both those megalomaniacs.

Much as Gibson may have liked the man or hated to wound his feelings or deprive him of a job, he must have known that by sending Van Giesen to Kalawao he would be thrusting him into a place far more dangerous than Kakaako had been. Van Giesen's bravado is nothing less than foolhardy: he must have known that he was delivering himself into the hands of scores of lepers who hated him, and of at least six men who had already threatened to kill him at Kakaako.

Nonetheless, with the confidence that only a mad white man can command, he went to Kalawao, as overseer to a work crew sent from Honolulu to construct new buildings in the Leper Settlement. Father Albert Montiton, one of Bishop Hermann's priests visiting in Honolulu (and himself being driven to the verge of madness by an intractable affliction of the skin that itched intolerably) hastened to warn Father Damien of impending troubles. His letter, written in French on April 7, is doubly significant because it presents the only known statement explaining Mother Marianne's refusal to submit to what Father Albert called, so airily, "le statu quo": ". . . As I have already announced to you Van Giesen is going to betake himself to Molokai, to begin the work projects. But above all watch out that he does not have charge of the administration. Ambrose is worth infinitely more. Try to see Mr. Meyer and beg him to keep Ambrose. This thing is of the utmost importance."

Ambrose Hutchison, a half-Hawaiian leper, both able and respected, served as the resident superintendent of the Settlement at Kalawao. Rudolph Meyer, a rancher on Molokai, and not leprous, was the Board of Health's official agent in charge of the Settlement, and Hutchison's immediate superior. Because of the Settlement's location at the foot of a precipice about 675 meters high, Meyer visited it only occasionally, and conducted most of his supervisory business by mail.

"Van Giesen," Father Albert continued his letter to Damien, "is too violent, too rough [muddle headed] and above all too corrupt to be superintendent at Molokai. At his return from Kalawao, he has again roused new troubles at Kakaako where he has had very many Kanakas imprisoned against the will of the Sisters and all that probably to be more free to make [in] the night the Kolohe [mischief] with three girls whom he is keeping at his home. Mr. Meyer who wishes peace above all in the leprosarium cannot at any price accept this libertine even when Minister Gibson would offer him to him for he has made too many enemies for himself among the lepers of Kakaako and of

Molokai. . . . The hospital Sisters are very unhappy about this and they would have gone back to America if the Minister had desired to maintain the status quo. . . ."

Father Albert's estimate of Henry Van Giesen just about closes the thin file on that strange, unhappy man. Little more of any importance is known about him. Apparently, as Sister Leopoldina said, he stayed "only a short time" at the Settlement. His enemies there did not murder him, or even attempt to do so. Had they turned upon him, Honolulu's newspapers would have reported the event in detail. Possibly their antipathy, expressed in more subtle ways, prevented "the poor man" from staying long at Kalawao. Probably, however, by the time he strode, booted and spurred and arrogant, into that larger lazaretto, the lepers there had found or imagined a dozen other troubles to engage their interests. They might not have forgotten or forgiven Van Giesen his cruelties, but in that new and nobler setting they may have understood that vengeance was not theirs to claim.

The *Pacific Commercial Advertiser* could not allow Van Giesen to fade unnoticed into oblivion. On June 4, 1884, in a news article devoted to "Dr. Fitch's Report," it printed this informative paragraph, in which the sarcasm seems to be directed more upon the physician than the steward. But the scorn is heaped upon Van Giesen:

"The services of the Sisters of Charity are duly recognized by Dr. Fitch. The services of Mr. Van Giesen, before their arrival, were exceedingly numerous and diversified according to this report. He did the entire nursing (?), provided for and watched over this extensive hospital, superintended (we presume, as the language is ambiguous): the construction of buildings and filling in of the yard, the compounding of drugs and taking photographs, as well as keeping the books and records. The doctor wonders how he ever accomplished the work and well might he wonder. From recent revelations it would appear that the late steward did 'many things he ought not to have done, and left undone many things he ought to have done.'"

"After the removal of Mr. Van," Sister Leopoldina resumed her account of events at Kakaako, "the lepers were easily managed they were willing to obeay all the Sisters and thankful that the Sisters should have charge. Our gentle Mother's low, sweet voice was *law* and everyone seemed delighted to obeay her."

In town and legislature no one opposed Gibson's decision to give the Branch Hospital into Mother Marianne's keeping. As a matter of fact, few people ever heard about this tempest in a pest house. In a nation of provincials, who scarcely knew what was happening anywhere, either in their own country or in the world abroad, hardly anyone ever paid any attention to the Board of Health's purposes or its policies other than the one of segregating lepers. Those who did hear about Gibson's concession to Mother Marianne, whether they were Protestants, Catholics, or unbelievers, accepted the sisters' sacrifice with something like the satisfaction of a city merchant who has just turned a pretty profit in a deal with a country bumpkin.

Although Mother Marianne's victory went unnoticed in the kingdom's larger history, it was extremely important both to her and to the Franciscan mission. Her determination saved the mission in its time of greatest peril, when it was threatened not by religious fanatics, or political adversaries, or budgetary limitations, or even by tyrannical Henry Van Giesen. She identified her threat as Gibson himself, assisted by those most insidious of bureaucracy's henchmen: innate inertia, creeping apathy, and chronic indifference. She knew that if she did not stop Gibson at once, he and his bureaucrats would smother her mission in neglect. In correcting Gibson, she won a war, not a mere battle: upon the firm foundation thus established with the Board of Health in 1884, she and her successors were able to continue their mission for many more years, and eventually to enlarge it in response to needs for other services.

Never again, after this settlement of 1884, not even in times of turmoil and change—as when, in 1887, the Protestant merchants broke Kalakaua and drove Gibson into exile; as when in 1893 they deposed Queen Liliuokalani and for five years thereafter ruled the land as a republic; as when, at length, in 1898, the United States accepted for their own these proffered isles—did anyone question the right of Mother Marianne and her company to minister to Hawaii's lepers.

Challenging Gibson would not have called for much courage. Even though he held the office of prime minister and half a dozen other positions as well, including that of her employer, Mother Marianne would have studied him well enough by then to know that all those titles and responsibilities did not make him a fearsome ogre. Quite the contrary: he was so kind, so fatherly, to the sisters that she had to overcome a reluctance to hurt his feelings. Resolution, then, not courage; simplicity, not a loyalty divided, accompanied her to the council table. With such considerate participants, the negotiations could not have been unfriendly.

Her success in arranging this contract with Gibson also rescued Mother Marianne personally from an embarrassing predicament of exactly the kind that Father Lesen, at home in Syracuse, had warned her to avoid. Although she would not have been worried much by fear of embarrassment and censure, her priestly superiors in New York, Father Provincial Lesen and the Bishop in Albany, most certainly would have reprimanded her if the mission failed because she had neglected to safeguard it.

The weapon with which she won her war reveals the secret of her strength, not only then but during all the years she devoted to the lepers in Hawaii. She may not have known the power of that strength when she went to the islands. But she must have been filled with it when she confronted Gibson and the Bishop: those weeks of attending the lepers at Kakaako had perfected it. Because this weapon is so simple, it is a power beyond resisting, the strongest that a man or a woman can employ. St. Francis, who knew how it affected popes and cardinals, princes and friars, called it "humility, patience, perfect simplicity."

Her power grew out of her wish to work for God alone, not for mere men like premiers, or bishops, or kings. By putting behind her all interests in the vanities and illusions of this world—the allures of political maneuverings, sectarian vauntings, financial profit, the praise of society, the pleasure of position, the body's ease, and all other such temptations which gratify the ego and suborn the spirit—she freed herself to listen to the call from God. In hearing Him, she dedicated herself to working only for Him. In working only for Him, she did not diminish her power. She enhanced it. She became an insuperable force—purest consuming compassion.

Gibson, the king and his queen, Bishop Hermann, the lepers at Kakaako, the many others who met her in Honolulu soon after she arrived, felt her quiet purposefulness, her dedication to a cause. "Great is her mana," the Hawaiians sensed and said. And all of those people saw how it grew, this spirit power, to become an awesome force, as day after day she and the companion sisters brought solace to the lepers, those most sadly afflicted of God's creatures, from whom the rest of mankind shrank in fear and revulsion. Each day, seven days a week, she and the company she led gave selfish humankind yet more examples of selflessness. In the presence of such charity, the most rabid bigot, the most liberated freethinker, even the most ambitious of politicians, must be humbled. As Robert Louis Stevenson would testify only five years later, after he had seen Mother Marianne and the sisters attending the lepers at Molokai, in their presence "even a fool is silent and adores."

All dedicated religious and laity, whatever their creed or congregation, possess this power to some degree. It is not exclusively a Catholic attribute, nor is it limited only to Christians. In Mother Marianne's own Franciscan company, grave Sister Bonaventure had much of this virtue, as did imperturbable Sister Crescentia, beautiful and guileless Sister Leopoldina, and the others in their courageous band. No one can deny them that recognition. Compared with the multitudes who, models of selfishness, remain in the world and withhold compassion even from their neighbors, everyone of the Franciscan sisters who labored for the lepers was a saint.

But when we compare them with Mother Marianne, they rather fade into the background. We see them arranged at either side of her central self, much as in paintings troops of disciples are arrayed at either side of great teachers, or lieutenants are gathered around famous generals. In every respect the sisters of St. Francis were indeed Mother Marianne's disciples and lieutenants. And in every respect she was their unquestioned leader because she possessed virtues and attributes to a degree that they lacked.

Leaders attract attention, just as tall trees, cathedral spires, and mountain peaks draw lightning from the skies. Her attributes, whether she received them through heritage or refined them by training, helped to make Mother Marianne the leader of a whole community of Franciscan sisters in America. They raised her to the position of Mother Provincial, from which, when the moment came, she could arrange to be the leader of the mission to Hawaii. Yet a dispassionate appraiser of Mother Marianne's career must concede that, until late in the spring of 1883, when Father Leonor Fouesnel's letter of inquiry reached her desk in Syracuse, several other sisters of the Order, who were endowed with administrative abilities, could have served successfully as the community's Mother Provincial.

But the dispassionate observer also must conclude that no other Franciscan sister of Mother Marianne's generation was ready to listen to Father Leonor's plea when it came—or to hear, beyond it, that Other Voice calling to her.

Perhaps it was a mystical experience after all, the hearing of that call in the solitude of her office in Syracuse. Perhaps it was only a thought welling up from her own zeal to serve. However it came, it chose her—as lightning chooses a tall tree to strike. And, in striking, it transformed her.

It readied her for the sacrifice.

NOTES on Chapter IX

1. Montiton-Damien letters and the Fouesnel-Damien letter of November 27, 1883 are found in *La Père Damien—Vie et Documents*.
2. Reference is made to the Bishop of Albany because the Diocese of Syracuse was not established by the Holy See until November 20, 1886.

Chapter X

THE SACRIFICE

UPON RECEIVING Gibson's appointment—"to be an Agent of the Board of Health and, in this capacity to take charge of the Branch Hospital," as G. W. Parker wrote—Mother Marianne assumed administrative command of the receiving station at Kakaako.

At her request, Gibson's assistants drew up a set of "Rules of the Branch Hospital, Kakaako," which were published over his name on April 12. Regulations were needed, to be sure, but unfortunately the language in which they were cast employed the usual peremptory style of bureaucrats everywhere. The rules instructed everyone, in or out of the compound, how the place and its inmates would be governed "under the general superintendence of the Mother Superior of the Order of Franciscan Sisters." Eleven brief articles stipulated controls over visitors, nightly curfew at 9 o'clock, gifts of food from patients' friends or relatives, disposition of such gifts once they'd been admitted, "games of chance for money," indulging in "profane, or indecent language or songs." The last of those hopeful decrees forbade "men to visit the women's departments, and women that of men." Rather surprisingly, they said nothing about drinking alcoholic beverages, the fire hazards associated with smoking tobacco, or the crime of taking opium in any form.

Mother Marianne, much more tactfully, assigned duties and responsibilities to everyone in the compound, stewards and patients alike, and added her endorsement of the published rules of conduct. Only the pre-eminent Dr. Fitch stood beyond her control, but inasmuch as that busy man—who was "Physician and Surgeon to the Dispensary, to the Branch Hospital, and to the Leper Settlement at Kalawao [as the *Advertiser* noted] and probably . . . indulged in a little private practice as well"—sauntered most mornings into the hospital only to hand down opinions concerning the diagnosis of suspect cases and to decide upon medications for all, he was not much of a hindrance. Dr. Arning, the Board of Health's visiting investigator, busied himself with research in his laboratory, not with the patients. And physicians from the city, like Dr. George Trousseau or Dr. John McKibbin, who might visit the compound to treat more affluent patients or as consultants to Dr. Fitch, did not establish more than a nodding relationship with the Franciscan sisters. Everyone else in the hospital, trapped within its high walls, accepted with relief Mother Marianne's quiet efficiency after Van Giesen's demented regime. Kakaako's inmates settled down, for the time being, to a peaceful routine. The only persisting difficulties were those caused by lack of help: she never had enough workers to run the hospital properly.

Her company at Kakaako, already overburdened after Sister Renata and Sister Antonella went off to Maui, was reduced in numbers twice again. Knowing that Sister Renata by herself could not possibly do all the work at Malulani Hospital, Mother Marianne sent Sister Bonaventure to take charge of that facility and to be superior of the little Convent of St. Anthony next to it. Sister Bonaventure (escorted by Father Leonor) reached Wailuku on April 22, and officially opened the hospital on the following day.

At Kakaako, during that trying spring of 1884, Sister Rosalia McLaughlin fell ill. She was the merry-eyed, wide-mouthed Irish lass in a Franciscan habit who—judging by a letter Gibson wrote a couple of years later—was something of a tease. The old man's happy relationship with all the Franciscans, and especially with Sister Rosalia, is revealed in a letter he sent to Sister Bonaventure on November 8, 1886. Sister Rosalia, feeling relatively well at the time, had been sent to Maui for a short vacation. "Tell dear Sister Rosalia," Gibson wrote in a style that seems to be continuing the affectionate banter those two carried on in Honolulu, "that her father Walter is very anxious on her account since he heard of her scanty accomodations at the Convent of St. Anthony.—He hopes his daughter will return to St. Francis at Kakaako without any serious hurt. 'Father Walter' sends his aloha nui to her, and to Sisters Benedicta, Renata, and Ludovica."

Pert and pretty she might be, but Sister Rosalia was confined to her bed throughout most of 1884. The nature of her illness is beyond identifying. In view of her later history of mental instability, a sickness of psychogenic origin can be suspected. But, admittedly, that diagnosis is so facile as to be unfair to Sister Rosalia, who may have been troubled with a disease not at all caused by her responses to the horrors at Kakaako. Fortunately, during those intervals when she did seem to regain her health, she was able to help around the convent, if not always in the hospital. In 1884, however, her condition was so serious that Mother Marianne had to burden Sister Ludovica Gibbons, already the convent's housekeeper, with additional duties of being nurse to Sister Rosalia.

Those domestic arrangements left only Mother Marianne and Sister Crescentia to care for Kakaako's two hundred lepers. "It was indeed a trying time," to borrow another line from Sister Leopoldina. Mother Marianne's division of labor put her "in charge of the Office and Dispensary, as well as supervising generally, while Sr. Crescentia gathered many of the lepers around her to dress their sores and to encourage them to keep themselves clean and to take better care of their health and appearance." Whenever she could find the time, Mother Marianne too dressed the lepers' sores, attending to the blind and the bedridden ones who could not walk to Sister Crescentia's clinic. The two sisters who labored in the hospital, the one who slaved in the convent, worked to the edge of exhaustion each day. But not once did any of them utter a word of complaint. They did not need the little reminders about humility and self-abnegation that Father Lesen would be addressing to them later in the year.

Mother Marianne cleaned up the mess that Van Giesen had left in the office and in the dispensary adjoining it. She had to do now all those things he ought to have done and left undone. The patients' records and the steward's account books bore no resemblance to the actual hospital census or to the bills strewn over his desk. And the dispensary was almost as nauseating as a lepers' ward had been before the sisters arrived. Dirt, mildew, cobwebs, and fly specks adorned every surface. And flies, banished from most other rooms in the compound, found a home here, drawn to the sticky syrup that Van Giesen had spilled all over the dispensary.

Dr. Fitch's primary remedy for lepers, which he freely prescribed but never himself administered, was sodium salicylate dispensed in syrup. "Mr. Van mixted it in a large keg... [the syrup] splashed on the outside... drew sworms of flies. Mother quietly changed that by mixing the medicine in a clean container and putting it in large clean bottles, carefully avoiding leaving anything around that would draw the flies." She may not have been "the professional druggist" that some admirers credited her with being, but she certainly knew how to organize a dispensary and liked things anywhere to be neat, clean, orderly, and available in the moment of need. In a very short time she had scrubbed and swept and arranged everything in that dispensary, until it gleamed from ceiling to floor. When next the delivery man from town arrived with medical supplies, he could not believe his eyes. "'Well, Madam!' he exclaimed. 'Where are the flies? There used to be sworms of them. I always had a *deadly dread* of coming here, but now I don't. . . . It is so different!'"

Shy Sister Crescentia, with her crooked mouth and averted gaze, assumed the heaviest burden of all. "She prepared a box with sore dressing materials and started out" for the wards. One day, on the path from the dispensary, imperturbable Sister Crescentia met unimpassioned Dr. Arning, the scientist who performed an autopsy on the corpse of every leper who died in the hospital but who never lifted a hand to treat a living patient. Sister Leopoldina described this meeting in an unconscious parody of the nursery rhyme: "'Where are you going?' he said. 'I am going to look for sores,' she said. . . . His face turned pale and with a little sad smile he passed on. . . .'"

Every day, for several weeks, Sister Crescentia went "from ward to ward, cleaning and dressing the lepers sores. . . . They would gather around her and she would work for hours sometimes in their wards, but most of the time on the veranda." The air was not so foul there, and in the light of the sun Sister Crescentia could see more clearly the ravening ulcers over which she worked for ten hours a day. "Finely Mother succeeded in having the cottage where the lepers were put to die and fixed it up nicely for a sore dressing room." She remembered that grim cottage all too well: in one of its rooms, on her first visit to the hospital, she had found a young man lying on the floor, left there to die, abandoned and in despair. She and her companion sisters had saved his life by opposing that heartless neglect. With food and water and the comfort gained from a steward's care, the man had not died, as Van Giesen said he would. The man had recovered, to live yet a while longer. Life is precious even to a leper, that nameless man had taught all other men. And now, by her inspired choice of that same lonely cell, from which many a soul had been hurried into death, Mother Marianne declared to all the inmates of Kakaako's hell that the Sisters of St. Francis cared enough about them to want to hold death at bay.

Sister Crescentia also taught the lepers many ways in which they could help to care for themselves. In doing so, the practical little woman also found a helper for herself. "She trained one of the boys to assist her. After that it was much easier."

Those months of lonely labor, bending over the wounds of lepers, could never have been easy. Even lepers can scarcely endure the sight and smell of their sores. Mother Marianne, who knew well what Sister Crescentia was enduring, gave her both praise and gratitude. Years later, in an undated letter, Mother wrote: "Some day she may be canonized. If not she will be on the list of uncanonized saints."

Slowly, with unceasing devotion, the two sisters gradually restored peace to the hospital compound, if not respite from all suffering for the lepers or a standard of morality that good Christians might approve. Each evening, when Mother Marianne and Sister Crescentia returned to the hush of the convent, they could feel that they had made some little progress toward their goal.

Then, once again, a selfish male rose up, intending to elevate himself at the expense of all others. Tom Burch, the half-Irish, half-Hawaiian patient whom Henry Van Giesen had appointed the chief of his eight-man leper police force, thought to fill the social and political vacancy left by the superintendent's removal. Sister Leopoldina's account of this little drama of conflict, much too typical of life among the lepers to be doubted, presents Mother Marianne in yet another of her many roles.

"Tom Burch was a tall muskler man. In fact before he contracted leprosy, he might have been a handsome man . . . he was a little dark with big black eyes and thick black curlie hair . . . he could speak english well was polite and graceful to Mother and the Sisters he was not well liked by the natives on account of his loud boasting overbaring manner." In other words, here was a half-Hawaiian version of Van Giesen, two-faced, double-dealing, small-minded, and vain, just waiting for the chance to take over as cock of the Kakaako walk.

His underlings among the hospital police recognized the danger and sent a delegation one night to talk with Mother Marianne. "We don't want Tom Burch for our chief. He is going around telling everybody that he is the great boss of this hospital. He is a bad man." But she, "always slow to believe the bad reports until she would be sure"—and knowing, too, how underlings can misrepresent the actions of superiors—upheld Burch's authority and advised the men to be patient.

Burch soon heard about both the delegation and Mother Marianne's trusting reply. Assuming that his time had come to prevail over this weak woman and all other inmates in that seaside coop, he posted notices on trees and walls, proclaiming himself "the great boss and manager of the Branch Hospital." Because the notices were written "in native," the sisters could make nothing of them except for Tom Burch's name inscribed in large letters. When Mother learned what the posters actually announced, she told Tom himself to take them down. "he was very angry but he obeayed and still held his possession as Chief."

A few nights later the furtive delegation went again to see Mother Marianne, with a complaint that revealed more than they intended. "He is no good. He break rule all the time and we can do nothing. But suppose we do little bad, break little rule, he come after us like one big boss." Tyrants never learn from the mistakes of predecessors: Tom Burch had made the same accusation against Van Giesen, in his day. Once again, still hoping that Tom would grow up to be a responsible assistant, Mother quieted the aggrieved policemen.

Her trust, and Tom's reach for autarchy, soon came to an end. One dark night, a policeman, lantern in hand, arrived at the convent door, with a whispered message: Tom Burch, at that very moment, was seducing Julia, a beautiful sixteen-year-old Hawaiian-Chinese girl, still in the early stages of leprosy. The sisters had become very fond of Julia, "a quiet well-behaved child . . . graceful in her ways and loved by everyone." The policeman led Mother Marianne and Sister Crescentia through the hospital yard, to the door of a small room at the rear of one of the women's wards.

"Mother tried the door. It was locked. Not a sound came from inside. So she said in her natural gentle voice, 'Open the door please.' Still not a sound. Then she said in a loud commanding voice, 'Tom Burch, open this door at once.'

"he bounded to the door through it open and stood towering above her like a wild tiger he was in a frightful fit of anger. Sister said that she could never forget his looks when the light of the lantren rested on his ghastly face. and the large vains and musils on his large throat were swollen and his eyes were blazing.

"'Tom Burch,' Mother said in a cool commanding voice, 'You can be a policeman no longer. Give me the keys.'

"He stamped and raged like a demon. 'You shall never have the keys! he said and with a mighty sweep of his strong arm through the keys far out in the sea, then turned and walked slowly to his department. Mother took poor little Julia by the hand and led her to her ward. it was so sad that that big beastly man should take the advantage of a poor [innocent] child. she looked so like a child when Mother told her 'Now Julia you must not do this anymore. Are you not ashamed?' "

Julia's innocence, at her advanced age and in that lawless place, is arguable. But Julia, knowing what was expected of her, hung her head in shame and asked for pardon, which Mother "willingly granted."

The next morning a gang of men and boys from the hospital spent hours on the reef, "searching for the keys, but they were never found." Mr. Gibson, true to form, talked earnestly with Tom, threatening to ship him off to Molokai if ever he was "unruly" again. So, like Julia, Tom hung his head in shame and promised to be good. "As they all had a dreadful horrow of Molokai everything apparantly were going smoothly for a time" at Kakaako. The policemen fared best in this realignment of social forces. They "told Mother they only wanted Mother to be their chief. They would report to her and obeay all her orders. After that Tom remained most of the time in his room."

This was not the last occasion in which the sisters had to rush to rescue one or more of their "innocent girls" from the attentions of eager males, either at Kakaako or at Kalaupapa. The sisters would make many a midnight sortie out of the convent for the sake of virtue threatened, in the wards or in the woods, and often against men far more dangerous than Tom Burch had been. And always the sisters charged heroically to the rescue—just as always, at least in those mass confrontations, they won their battles against rampant sin. The quieter close encounters between consenting adults that went on in the dark of night, the sisters tried not to know anything about.

Mother Marianne was not so naive as to think that, after Burch's fall, her loyal leper police force ran the Branch Hospital with equal justice for all, or that they put a stop to all the night-crawling that enlivened the nocturnal scene. Mindful of the need to raise the level of morality among her charges, she talked with Mr. Gibson about certain changes she wanted made in the hospital compound.

"By degrees matters improved"—this time the phrase is Sister Columba O'Keeffe's—both in the Branch Hospital and in the sisters' official relationships with Bishop Hermann. As a person he had always been friendly and interested in their welfare, since the day they arrived in Honolulu. But as a bishop and Vicar Apostolic he had not accorded the Franciscans the legal protection and administrative supervision of his office as soon as he might have. While still at home in Syracuse, Mother Marianne had insisted to Father Lesen that, unless circumstances changed drastically, she and her missioners to Hawaii wanted to remain under his jurisdiction in spiritual matters of importance regarding the Franciscan rule and customs. Now, however, after observing the circumstances in Hawaii, she recognized that her greatest need was an active ecclesiastical authority on the scene, who would advise the Franciscans and direct their relationships with the civil government—always subject to approval from Syracuse. From the beginning she must have expected this degree of assistance from the Bishop of Olba inasmuch as the government's appeal for sisters had been made through his office.

Following this belief, she had appealed to Bishop Hermann from Maui, on March 14, asking him to protect them in their mounting difficulties with Van Giesen, and to obtain for the Franciscans the rights of supervision over the hospital which Father Leonor had promised them. "Please, your Lordship, act for us in this matter, as you would do if your own Sisters were concerned," she had written. "Consider us as your children and be to us a Father and Protector," she asked, using these dutiful formulas of address with more than mere politeness.

On March 29, the very day of Mother Marianne's return to Honolulu from Wailuku, and in direct consequence of their morning's conference, Bishop Hermann wrote to Father Lesen. His letter is not preserved. Apparently, he made suitable (and understandable) excuses for not having done anything earlier to establish the Franciscans in their rightful position with respect to both church and government. His reason for "prudence," as always, would have been the delicate balance in the relationship between the Protestant government and the Apostolic Mission. Nonetheless, in that letter he seems to have accepted his role as father protector to the Franciscans, and offered proposals for regularizing their position with respect to his episcopal authority.

In Syracuse, Father Lesen was heartened by Bishop Hermann's letter. Not entirely aware of the personalities or the circumstances involved in Honolulu, he seems to have believed that a written agreement, properly signed and sealed, establishing the position of the sisters in the islands, would be obtained as soon as Bishop Hermann, in his prudence, decided to ask for it. He, too, like Bishop Hermann, knew from experience that in the area of politics no one is less certain of tenure than a minister of state, and no one has a shorter memory than a legislator. And, of course, both shared the fear that bigotry, latent perhaps in 1884, could rise to hurt the Catholic cause at any time in the future.

A copy of Father Lesen's cordial reply to Bishop Hermann is available. "God be praised," he wrote on April 16, "and your zeal also for the encouraging progress of the good Sisters." He fully understood the bishop's "prudence" in having deferred taking the sisters under his protection, approved his assumption of partial authority over them, and accepted his proposals for easing some of the Order's regulations that added needless trials to their already difficult life. "I have no objection that they should be dispensed from fasting . . . even from abstinence." Yet, characteristically, Father Lesen did not countenance a complete relaxation of the regimen: "They may make compensation by greater faithfulness in keeping other rules. . . ." The one thing he asked, Lesen concluded, is this above all else: the sisters must "keep up the spirit of the Order, that is the spirit of poverty, of penance and humility, and St. Francis' blessing will then enable them to conserve their usefulness to the Mission."

The crisis at Kakaako disappointed the Catholics' plan for Mother Marianne to take over the Leper Settlement on Molokai before the legislature convened. But the king made certain to mention the Franciscan sisters when he addressed the initial session of the legislature on April 26. His Majesty, following tradition, touched upon many subjects: the renewal of the favorable Reciprocity Treaty with the United States (in exchange for rights to use Pearl Harbor as "a coaling station"); the encouraging posture of foreign affairs; the need for more immigrants to supplement the waning native population; a silver coinage; the health of the nation being only the most prominent among them.

About midway in his message, King Kalakaua paid public tribute to the President of the Board of Health and to the Sisters of St. Francis:

"I regret to speak of a national affliction of what is deemed a disease of a contagious nature, but the measures taken by the Health Authorities in carrying out the law of segregation have placed the evil under better sanitary control than ever before, and I am very hopeful of increased health in My Kingdom, and an improved sanitary condition of the country, owing in part to the ministrations of the Sisters of Charity, who have come to the help of My people with their devotion of spirit and faithful nursing skill, so that I trust that the disease will not only be held in check, but controlled to the point to which charity and human skill can attain."

People who heard or read this address could not know that all those grand claims and high hopes for immediate benefits in public health were premature, to say the least. For many years yet, not all its rules and bureaucrats, but the Sisters of St. Francis, with their devotion and their nursing skill, would be the only effective weapons the government of Hawaii would be able to direct against the scourge of leprosy.

And yet, with an unflagging resolution that must be praised, the Hawaiian government—persuaded by Gibson and his "Health Authorities"—strove mightily to combat "a calamity of widespread disease that would baffle the resources of private benevolence." In the biennium ending March 31, 1884, Gibson reported to the legislature convened on April 26, the Board of Health had spent $238,508 upon matters of public health, primarily upon the care and treatment of lepers. "This is a large sum to be expended by the Government of about 75,000 people," Gibson observed, "for the care of the health of the community; the amount is about 10 per cent of the whole revenue of this Kingdom." In Hawaii, he continued, "the Government undertakes the whole charge of the hospital treatment of the sick poor of the Nation." At least two per cent of the entire population, he estimated, was "being attacked by a fearful . . . malady that demands separation and isolation." Hawaii "is laboring under a state of suffering that calls for all the energies and resources of the State, and I am warranted in saying that Hawaii has faced her great calamity bravely, and has made a provision for her suffering people that will compare favorably with the efforts made by any other State to meet a similar exigency."

Even so, he concluded, generous as the nation was being with its concern for lepers, more money was desperately needed. The legislature's appropriations in 1882 had been insufficient to meet the Board of Health's expenditures. The reason was clear—and frightening. The number of lepers was increasing: "the appropriation [of 1882] was based upon an estimated average of about 700 patients in charge; whereas there have been treated at the settlement . . . on Molokai and at the Branch Hospital, an average of about 1,000 patients for some time past." During the biennium of 1882–1884, "the report of the

Marshall of the Kingdom shows that . . . 777 lepers and suspected lepers have, in accordance with orders from the Board of Health, been arrested and taken from their homes."

Queen Kapiolani, the Franciscans' very good friend, also helped in her prestigious way. In Honolulu, during the last week in June, she gave a garden party; sponsored an entertainment at the Music Hall; and a ball at the Hawaiian Hotel, "all for the benefit of lepers," the *Advertiser* announced.

On July 21, she bravely visited the Leper Settlement at Kalawao. During a stay of two days, she went to "every home in the Settlement" to hear the opinions of the patients.

The third year of Mother Marianne's second term as her community's Provincial would end on July 14, 1884, and, under the terms of the Constitutions of that time, another Provincial must be elected. Realizing that to leave her overworked companions in Honolulu would be endangering the mission at a delicate stage in its development, she asked Father Lesen to excuse her from attending the general chapter.

As kind as ever, he answered her on July 9. He had heard enough from Bishop Hermann and Father Leonor to be relieved about the progress of the mission, weak though it might be: "I can but praise your work and the spirit of sacrifice that informs you. I praise God for the success that has crowned your labors, and firmly hope to see the Mission solidly established under your cares, to God's glory and many souls' salvation."

He agreed with her request that more sisters be sent to Hawaii: "You are too few in your labors and need help. By an effort this could be had. Several Sisters are ready to go." Inasmuch as the Franciscan community could not afford to pay for the costs of traveling, the Hawaiian government must arrange to do so: "See whether and how means can be obtained. No time should be lost. . . ."

He excused her from the duty of attending the general chapter, summoned for mid-August: "Do not be disturbed about your long remaining in the Islands. I see the impossibility of your leaving at this stage of the enterprise. Surely I shall not allow you to remain forever. But prudence requires your longer staying. . . ."

Bishop Hermann, Father Leonor, perhaps Mr. Gibson as well, had already guided him toward that notion of prudence, by maintaining that the future of her mission was still uncertain. The reasons for their apprehension are not fully known. Perhaps they imagined stronger opposition than actually existed at the time. People in Honolulu were always talking about "getting rid of Gibson," because of the way he "squandered" public money. And "the change of government" that would happen with Gibson's downfall would affect very directly his successors' attitudes toward Mother Marianne's mission, if not toward the whole Catholic establishment. For month after month Bishop Hermann anguished over this possibility—and some of his worry he must have conveyed to Father Lesen in far-off Syracuse.

Perhaps real opposition did flare up, as grudging merchants muttered about Gibson's spending tax moneys upon something so unprofitable as nurses for lepers, and as glowering Calvinists and sleek Episcopalians sought ways to rout the Papists and replace them with Sisters of Charity from a more acceptable Protestant denomination. The Right Reverend Alfred Willis, Anglican Bishop of Honolulu, was actively trying at the time to arrange for a group of nurse-sisters from England to be assigned to duty in his diocese; but a close reading of newspaper accounts indicates that Willis expected those English nuns to serve at the Queen's Hospital in Honolulu, which admitted patients sick with ailments other than leprosy. The Anglicans may well have intended to show that they, too, could care for the sick poor of Hawaii, but Bishop Willis's statement, as presented in Honolulu's newspapers, most certainly did not lay any public claim upon the hospitals for lepers at Kakaako and Kalawao.

Probably Bishop Hermann, Father Leonor, and Gibson did not fear the Protestants nearly as much as they worried about the possible collapse of Mother Marianne's mission if ever she went home to Syracuse. By this time they realized that only Mother Marianne, with her strengths of spirit and of personality, could influence the people with whom she worked, both in and out of the Branch hospital, without antagonizing them. As Henry Van Giesen and Tom Burch had so clearly demonstrated, villains within the pale of Kakaako could be just as dangerous to the security of the mission as were shopkeepers in Honolulu, grumbling about high taxes and wastrels in high places.

Whatever their reasoning, bishop, priest, and premier convinced themselves (and her) that Mother Marianne's position as the Provincial of her Order was a weighty factor that must be employed to support her mission. They were by no means incapable of presuming that Mother Marianne's high rank in the Franciscan Order put her in a powerful position for persuading the Motherhouse to send more nurse-sisters to Hawaii. Gibson and his fellow conspirators may even have comprehended, by then, that the five functioning sisters in the islands were dreadfully overworked, and could not possibly survive the intolerable strain unless their number was increased, very soon. And the thought of losing Mother Marianne revealed another weakness: although other sisters might be devoted to the cause, not one of them could command the mission as effectively as she did.

In every sense, then, Mother Marianne was indispensable to the security and continuation of her mission.

Father Lesen accepted the conclusions of the strategists in Honolulu—for the immediate future. "I cannot call you back now," he finished his letter of July 9, "nor can I call for a new election in the community... because if your authority of Provincial Mother should cease in your present position towards the government of the Islands, maybe [that would] make a [bad] impression and create difficulties. I therefore put off the election of the Mother Provincial for one year, and confirm you in your office till next year." Her able deputies in Syracuse, Mother Antonia Eulenstein and Sister Delphina Mueller, assured him that "no extraordinary difficulties" required her immediate return. Everyone would understand, they said, why she should "remain away some months yet." And, the implication is clear, everyone in Syracuse wanted her to return just as strongly as the claimants in Honolulu wanted her to stay.

At a meeting held in the Motherhouse on August 15, 1884, Father Lesen told the assembled sisters that he had "confirmed" Mother Marianne in her position as the community's Provincial for yet another year. A circular letter sent to all houses of the Order informed them of this fact, and postponed the General Chapter "to the following year."

In Honolulu, on July 15, Gibson wrote to Mother Marianne, making the official commitment that, during the previous week, Father Lesen in Syracuse had directed her to obtain: "... having been informed by Father Leonor" that she was intending to "communicate by this mail with your Order in respect to the condition of our hospital," Gibson asked her "to invoke other Sisters... to come and assist you in your blessed work.... Their Majesties and His Majesty's Government," he declared, "highly appreciate the invaluable service rendered by your Sisterhood of Charity to the people of this Kingdom." The Board of Health would welcome eight more sisters "at present" and would pay for their "travelling expenses and establishment here."

Father Lesen and Mother Antonia, sympathizing with Mother Marianne's need for more help, hoped to send a second group of sisters soon, even though the community could never find members enough to staff its schools and hospitals in America. Fortunately, prospects for the future were encouraging: during the fall of 1883, twenty aspirants had entered upon the novitiate. Mother Antonia expected that in the spring of 1885 she could spare a few of the professed sisters, even before those novices took their final vows. She and Father Lesen asked for volunteers during the meeting in August.

To their surprise they met with considerable reluctance, even outspoken opposition. Little more than a year before, when Father Leonor spoke to them about Hawaii's desperate need, almost all the professed sisters and many of the novices had gladly responded to his appeal. Now, in 1884, almost no one wanted to go. Rumor, gossip, and active imaginations, all excited by lack of information, had set loose some very strange fancies among the residents of the Motherhouse. We can suspect—without proof—that morbid letters from Sister Rosalia, periodically sick in Honolulu, started those apprehensions in the minds of her friends in Syracuse. America's newspapers, too, undoubtedly helped to stir up alarms and second thoughts in Franciscans both male and female. "A Revolution Feared," warned the Syracuse *Evening Herald* on January 5, 1884. "Kalakaua's Crown in Danger," blared the *Sunday Courier* on January 6. America's editorialists, alerted by Washington's, were relaying in predictable fashion the outrage of Honolulu's tax payers over the latest of King Kalakaua's "Extravagant Bills." And, as Father Lesen's letters to Mother Marianne imply, hints dropped by Franciscan priests who opposed his support of the mission to Hawaii may have stirred the gossips even more. One of the more active of those opponents would have been Father Francis Neubauer, Vice-Provincial, who would succeed Father Lesen in the high office in 1889.

Father Lesen expressed his reaction to the sisters' distress in a letter to Mother Marianne, begun on August 15. "The news that the Sisters, contrary to the formal declaration of Father Leonor, are now attending to the lepers, has made no good impression upon many . . . some even want to know, that the Sisters are already dissatisfied, and in a short time the Mission itself will be a failure. They also say that the government wants to send the Sisters to the lepers' Island. Explain then all the particulars of the condition of the Mission and the Sisters, that I be satisfied of the untruth of the rumors, and may correct them when necessary. This rumor may be a drawback for some Sisters that would come, and I hope that the gloomy news are unfounded."

At first glance, this letter arouses a certain bewilderment in a reader already confused by conflicting claims and attitudes. Father Lesen appears to be saying that he and the sisters in Syracuse are dismayed to learn, at this late date, that the sisters in Honolulu are actually being nurses to lepers. A closer study of the letter, however, which makes allowances for Father Lesen's Latinist's approach to etymology, explains his intention easily enough. The important word is "attending." For him, "attending to the lepers" meant the physical labor involved in actually washing and salving the lepers' sores, making their beds, feeding the blind and crippled, doing the daily drudgery that untrained servants should have been hired to do. He and the Franciscans in Syracuse defined "nursing" in more elevated terms, similar to the service the sisters performed at St. Joseph's Hospital, where they were intermediaries between physicians on the one hand and hired aides on the other. The people in Syracuse, unacquainted with details about the situation at Kakaako (and undoubtedly agitated by Sister Rosalia's vivid descriptions) were shocked to learn how revolting—and how dangerous—was the nursing care the missioners were giving to lepers in Honolulu. Father Lesen, with good reason, wanted to know why the Hawaiian government had not hired all those helpful servants whom Father Leonor and Walter Murray Gibson had promised to Mother Marianne.

Father Lesen's question about the government's intention to send the sisters to "the lepers' Island" also needs explanation. Here he is afraid that the government will force them to go to Molokai, whether or not they wish to serve there. His fear, although legitimate, was unfounded. Neither the government nor Mother Marianne ever intended to force a sister to work on Molokai. But he, and the sisters in Syracuse, needed to be reassured on that point.

At that juncture a report came from Mother Marianne, giving the facts he needed and—with Gibson's request for eight more sisters— allaying his fears that the Hawaiian government was not supporting her work. On August 19 Father Lesen finished the letter he had begun four days earlier. He expressed satisfaction over the government's attitude, but doubted the community's ability to send eight more helpers because of both the lack of qualified nurses and "a cooling up of fervor amongst many Sisters, attributable, I believe, to the news of the Islands." He stated his cautious philosophy: "I believe not prudent to send any Sister that does not want to go by herself. Great trouble could arise from dissatisfied Sisters. . . ." Needless to say, Mother Marianne concurred heartily with that point of view.

He interposed a solicitous inquiry, and gave advice that Mother Marianne would never heed: "How is your health? Be not too disregardful of yourself, for it would bring too great difficulties. Better to let undone what is over your strength."

He told his dutiful daughter in Christ how, in a letter written earlier to Bishop Hermann, he agreed "to modify your Rules according to circumstances and prudence, especially in regard of fasts." Always the Franciscan, he reminded her of observances in which she needed no instruction: "I recommend to all to keep up the spirit of the Order in all points, especially in what regards poverty, humility, obedience, and self-abnegation. The work you have on hand is a hard one, and requires a great fund of virtues to perform it well to God's glory and your own merit. As you have done so much, do also that little which God expects yet of you, that is, those little sacrifices which we have to make daily, in order to live according to our vocation. They will bring God daily nearer and nearer to you and His presence will be your strength and happiness. Yes, I hope that being so far away from your other Sisters, you will feel the need of watching closer on yourselves and striving harder to the fulfillment of all religious duties."

Father Lesen, as his letters consistently show, was a good man and a considerate superior. But, as this short quotation indicates, he was also a man as unacquainted with the facts of Mother Marianne's work among the lepers as were the sheltered sisters in Syracuse. His earnest advice to Mother Marianne is so pietistic as to draw snorts of impatience from realists. Had he been able to see and hear and touch and smell the lepers at Kakaako, just for a minute; had he known the conditions under which Mother Marianne and Sister Crescentia offered up daily the sacrifice of themselves for the greater glory of God, he would never have mentioned "self-abnegation" and "those little sacrifices." Because he did not know, he must be forgiven his insistence upon penances more appropriate to cenobites in convents than to nurses in lazarhouses.

Five days later, on August 24, conscience seems to have touched him. He took up his pen again—not to lighten the burdens of the Rule but to apologize for having been impatient with Mother Marianne and

Gibson. Apparently in a letter written earlier in the month, before he received Mother Marianne's report of August 1, he had fretted over Gibson's inability to make up his mind about the future of the mission. Now, with the arrival of Gibson's promise to support eight more sisters, Lesen makes generous amends: "I appreciate you as [much]as a Sister can ever be appreciated, I praise you for your heroical devotedness to your hard task, I must admire your prudent tact in the establishment and direction of the Mission. . . . The praises I give You for the noble work You are doing to God's glory, and neighbors charity I extend to all Sisters under your charge. I am proud of you and them all. May God pour on you all his full blessing. . . . May St. Francis obtain to you a continual increase of the self-sacrificing spirit so needed to you. . . . I give You and to all others my blessing. . . ."

During that busy summer of 1884 Mother Marianne made some significant changes in arrangements at Kakaako hospital. A team of laborers, with drays and draught horses, picked up the whole convent building and moved it to a new site, a few meters away, where drainage was better. In the process they removed the low fence that had stood between the sisters and their patients. The useless wall was not put up again. In its stead carpenters raised another and higher fence that divided the hospital compound into two parts. Into the wards on the nearer side of the partition, sharing the same area as the convent, Mother Marianne transferred all the female lepers. On the farther side she housed the males. The rampart was something more than just a symbol signifying that Christian morality had come to stay at Kakaako: in general, it served its purpose of protecting genuinely help-less females from the unwanted attentions of males.

At this time of rearrangings, too, the patients' cottages were refur-bished: painters applied fresh coats of whitewash to walls, and dressed the verandah floors, posts, and railings in a contrasting gray. And once again, in the areas safe from the reach of the sea, another attempt was made to bring a touch of beauty into that dismal yard. Someone— probably the less disabled patients, not gardeners from the town— planted grass in the patches of bare earth, set flowering shrubs and young trees into the hard-packed ground, restored the disordered pathways. Mother Marianne supervised this landscaping at Kakaako, just as, later, she managed the landscaping of the new convent and hospital at Kalaupapa. She was interested in plants, in green growing things, both for their beauty's sake and for the practical yield of their fruits and flowers. And she knew how the sight of them could lift up the spirits of sickened people. Under her direction, during the summer of 1884, the depressing bare buildings and grounds at Kakaako were transformed. Sister Leopoldina noticed these improvements as soon as she arrived in April of 1885. And these touches of verdure gave journalist Robert J. Creighton the idea that the Branch Hospital had always looked so attractive, ever since it opened in 1881.

In the midst of those alterations at Kakaako, a package arrived from Syracuse, reminding Mother Marianne that some things do not change. Mother Bernardina had sent her spiritual daughter a letter and "a pretty little book" to mark her nameday, the Feast of St. Ann. On August 31 Mother Marianne found a few minutes in which to thank her revered teacher and sponsor for being so thoughtful. Keeping to her private rule, she said almost nothing about herself, and made merely a glancing reference to her work, simply to give credit to other agencies: "Only want of time is the cause of silence. . . . We have almost constantly 200 sick here afflicted with a horrible disease; in a strange country among strange people, and are responsible to a Government for our transactions, from this you may judge that we have our hands full and our heads, too. Sometimes our duties are very trying but God is good and helps us out of all difficulties. I think it is all owing to the good prayers of our dear ones at home."

The children of Hawaii, she explained—having been told this pleasing fact by one of the Sacred Hearts priests—honor St. Ann more than do the children in the United States. "In our little out of the way Chapel the Feast was grandly celebrated with high Mass and Benediction by Rev. Father Leonor, of course. You know we are *his Sisters*." In a lingering conclusion, as if she were beginning to sense that the need for her in Hawaii was greater than the one at home, and that she must prepare herself as well as the hierarchy in Syracuse for an eventual decision to stay, she asked about sisters and laity at St. Joseph's Hospital. Wanting to assure Mother Bernardina that she had not forgotten her (or the hospital's problems), she said, "I deeply sympathize with you in your many trials and difficulties" and declared her belief that everyone, including Mother Bernardina and herself, must submit to God's will. She allowed only one sentence in the whole letter to refer directly to herself: "I am painfully disappointed not to be able to return home but must submit to this as the holy will of God."

She slipped into the envelope the only kind of gift she could send from Hawaii—a frond of lacy fern, pressed and dried, which she had plucked during her stay on the island of Maui.

Early in October 1884 the sisters at Kakaako gained at last a servant who was willing to join them in their endangered household. Father Leonor found this prize—a seventeen-year-old Portuguese girl, still aboard the ship that had brought her to Honolulu, along with father, stepmother, five younger brothers and sisters, and about 600 other contract laborers and their families recruited in the Madeira Islands to work on Hawaii's sugarcane plantations. Because he spoke a kind of Portuguese, Father Leonor boarded the *City of Bordeaux* soon after she docked on October 2, taking pastoral comforts to the immigrants along with advice about landing procedures and life in these islands of Hawaii. As he talked with the newcomers he asked if any of the women were willing to help the Franciscan sisters. Olinda Gomes answered that she would like to go. With her parents' consent, she left the ship for the convent on October 4. She went to work at once, in the kitchen helping Sister Ludovica with the endless round of preparing meals, washing dishes, scrubbing floors, and taking care of Sister Rosalia, too often sick abed upstairs.

About that time, too, good news came from Syracuse: Father Lesen and Mother Antonia promised to send more sisters to Hawaii, not eight as requested, but four volunteers who said they did not fear to take care of lepers. Other letters from home said who these four helpers would be: Sister M. Benedicta Rodenmacher; Sister M. Placida Tierney; Sister M. Carolina Hoffmann; and Sister M. Leopoldina Burns. Mother Antonia planned for them to leave Syracuse late in March or early in April of 1885. Mother Marianne and her two weary companions rejoiced that relief would be coming so soon.

No one knows when Mother Marianne decided that she must remain in Hawaii. Arguments persuading her to that conclusion had been facing her since the moment she first entered the hospital yard at Kakaako. She may have known in her heart, ever since that terrible day, that the lepers needed her much more than did the sisters in Syracuse or even the patients at St. Joseph Hospital. The conscious resolve to stay in Hawaii seems to have come much later, however, else she certainly would have discussed it with Father Lesen sooner than she did.

By February 1885 her sense of responsibility to the Order, political circumstances in Honolulu, inquiries from Father Lesen, and, more than likely, her own wishes all convinced her that the time had come to settle this important matter. God's Will had called her to Hawaii, in accordance with His purpose. Now God's Will must determine whether or not she should remain in Hawaii, to fulfill His purpose.

On February 28 she wrote to Father Lesen. Because her letter has been lost, we cannot know the manner in which she presented the issue. In all likelihood, she managed the problem with her usual attention to the protocol expected of a subordinate addressing a superior: she reported upon the state of the mission, in general and in particular; weighed the several factors affecting its future (not the least of which would have been an estimate of the character of the woman who must lead it); and then asked for advice. She may even have stated what she preferred to do but, with the necessary humility and obedience, left to her Provincial Minister the formality of making the decision. Nonetheless, she also submitted opinions from other people, to help him make up his mind.

With her letter she enclosed one from Gibson, addressed to herself, written on February 19. A copy of this letter survives. The President of the Board of Health looked with dismay upon the possibility of her returning to America. Speaking for Their Majesties, and for himself, he begged to say that "I would regard your leaving us as a great misfortune to the suffering people of this country, therefore I pray that you remain to continue in charge of your Mission of Mercy in these Islands."

A week earlier, on February 12, Bishop Hermann had sent his own memorial to Father Lesen, discussing at greater length, and with more persuasive detail, the subject of Mother Marianne and the Franciscan mission. "I cannot enough praise their self sacrificing labor of charity. . . . Public opinion is most decidedly in their favor, nobody darest say the first word of blame against them. Still for the reason that this favorable impression reflects a great credit to the catholic religion, we cannot be surprised, that heretical jelousy is continually working under hand, trying to undermine their influence. Queen Kapiolani seems to be entirely devoted to the good Sisters; King Kalakoua and his Minister Mr. Gibbons are greatly pleased with their work, but guided by political ones, out of fear for some powerfull heretics, seem to avid to much public show in favor of a Catholic institution. Therefore notwithstanding their good intention and best promises, certain measures are not always so well realised as we expected. . . ."

In this roundabout way Bishop Hermann is delivering the same old warning about perfidious heretics that he and Father Leonor never failed to sound. The Franciscan mission, he is telling Father Lesen, is still in peril. And Mother Marianne is the only one who can save it: "I hear that you are occupied with the question, wether the Rev. Moth. Marianna shall remain here or return home. You will pardon me the liberty I take to tell you most decidedly, that we consider the presence of Mother Marianna quite necessary for the success of your colony in these Islands. Besides her many excellent qualifications certainly fully known to you, she has learned by personal experience how to deal with persons and circumstances in her rather complicated position, and she enjoys the highest esteem and full confidence of all she has to deal with. Sister Bonaventure is doing well where she is at present at Wailuku, but she was not able to do full justice to her position at Honolulu during the abscence of Mother Marianna." In other words, Sister Bonaventure—whom Mother probably had intended to take over as head of the Hawaiian mission when she went back to Syracuse—had not measured up to the need.

Father Lesen might dismiss Gibson's plea as being merely pressure from a politician. But he could not ignore Bishop Hermann's opinion.

He knew, now at last, that he must allow her to stay in the islands. He gave his permission in curiously indirect language—and in two separate letters, both written on March 21. The device reveals the mind of an experienced diplomat trying to cope with distant adversaries he does not know, in a country so foreign as to be a cause for suspicion.

The first letter, as he told her in the second, "I wrote separately . . . to enable you to show it to the minister and to the King or Queen." Quite clearly, it is intended for others to read: in it Father Lesen is playing the part of the powerful Provincial Minister, expressing regard for the mission in Hawaii and concern about its future. "You know how interested I have always been in your Mission . . . although I was much opposed by the opinion and advises of almost everybody. I looked upon it as a great act of charity toward a people in need, who therefore, no matter of what country or religion had a right to your work. I disregarded opposition, I submitted the Community to hardship for loosing Sisters necessary at home." Skillfully, he sweetened Hawaiian tempers with compliments: "My leading thought was the full confidence I had in the honor of the Hawaiian government, and above all, in their royal Majesties. Facts confirmed and justified my expectation and Hon. Gibson's letter has the same effect."

Nevertheless, he warns, her mission is still not established safely. Among Franciscans in Syracuse, apparently in both male and female contingents, "the talk is, that the Mission will, anyhow, be a failure: an eventual change of government can easy make the position of the Sisters untenable and oblige them to leave the Islands. Some one goes so far as to expect the Sisters home after two, three years."

He seeks to arouse a proprietary interest in the Hawaiian hierarchy: "I combat such ideas. Their Majesties will never allow any one to interfere with the noble work they have founded. Yet, you understand, such kind of talk must produce anxiety in the mind of many, and be a great drawback to the vocation of many a Sister for the Islands."

Looking back, into the history of ventures that have foundered, trying to peer ahead, into the unknown—for he, too, understands far too well how ministers and even kings do come and go—he suggests a plan that might safeguard her mission: "To stop then, effectually, idle talk, and reassure timid ones would it not be proper to have some governmental enactment, by which the position of the Sisters in the Islands be put in such a state, that any future government be obliged to recognize it as an accomplished fact? They have already seen your work and appreciate it thouroughly. I should then suppose that no difficulty will they find in doing, what, after all is almost necessary to the future prosperity of the Mission."

Sounding like a parent reasoning with a feckless child, he even raises the ultimate threat: "I shall not be always superior, and my successor could see things in a different light. Of course I make only a suggestion, but I expect you to give it a serious consideration."

In the second letter, written only for Mother Marianne to see, the wise old diplomat shares his more private thoughts. She is instructed to show the first letter to Mr. Gibson and Their Majesties. It "corresponds to the true state of affairs here and should make some impression upon the government to throw off the too fine politics, and to do what should have been done long ago. Words and promises and even facts is all very well. But a Community cannot live on that. It needs an unshaken basis to rest [upon], and that is only a governmental act recognizing and establishing the Sisters. Political changes [occur in] every nation, and bigotism now latent in the Islands, may easy come to power and ruin in one day the work of centuries, not to say of years."

In Syracuse, he concedes, he cannot "appreciate all the circumstances" that commit the Hawaiian government to the policies it follows. Even so, he is becoming tired of hearing promises from others that are never fulfilled, and he is especially weary of the procrastination of Gibson and the prudence of Bishop Hermann. "But determined governments find always ways to do what they absolutely want, despite of opposition. They know that opposition to a measure of public welfare is restricted, and brakes down soon before the general opinion of common sense people."

Father Lesen, it is evident, thought and acted in much the same autarchic terms as did Walter Murray Gibson. Lesen's summation of politics, in the church or in the world, is a fair accounting of the manner in which Gibson ran the Hawaiian government. But, as Lesen foresaw, it also presaged the end that always comes to parties in power. Fearing the worst, Father Lesen repeated to Mother Marianne the primary message he had written in his public letter: the Hawaiian government "should show energy, and do without delay, what, as I noted, the prosperity of the work they protect, requires."

He returned to the opposition he is receiving from Franciscans at home: "Here I am almost generally condemned for having sent the Sisters to the Islands. What then if one of my adversaries comes to power, as, most probably could soon be?"

He is beleaguered, but unconquered. So also must she be, he urges: "Be not timid . . . and be neither discouraged nor silenced by a first repulse." With this he comes to the very heart of his secret communication: "Think that this is what the Community expects of You, and that this is one of the reasons that I leave you in the Islands. Till an act of the government for the Sisters is a fact, our action here toward you must always be dishearted and distrustfull. Give then your whole energy to the matter."

Lesen concludes this private letter with the usual formula of the times: he "appreciates" her prayers, asks her to "assure all Sisters that they are dear to me, and [I] shall always be a father to them."

He could be matter of fact by then, because in ending the public letter he had already bade her a moving farewell. In every sense it is a valediction, written with grace and dignity: "My wish was always to see you home as soon as possible. Yet I see myself, that, under the circumstances, your presence is necessary in the Island. Moreover I would not contradict His Majesty's and his government's wish. I bid [you] then to remain longer and to attend with renewed courage to your work. God will accept and bless your sacrifice."

NOTES on Chapter X

1. Rules of Branch Hospital, Kakaako: *Leprosy in Hawaii,* 1886, Gibson's report. pp. 184–85.
2. Description of Mother Marianne as a "professional druggist": *Report of the Special Committee to Visit the Kakaako Leper Settlement to the Legislature of 1888,* p. 2.
3. Expenses of Board of Health for biennium ending March 1884: *Leprosy in Hawaii,* 1886, Gibson, pp. 130–36.
4. Queen Kapiolani's visit to Molokai: Mouritz, 1916: *Path of the Destroyer,* pp. 295–312.
5. Bishop Willis sought Anglican nurse-sisters from England: (a) *Pacific Commercial Advertiser,* November 23, 1883; (b) *Leprosy in Hawaii,* 1886, Gibson, p. 138.
6. Letters relating to the establishment and business in the Hawaiian Mission: Mother Marianne preserved the original letters that she received from Father Lesen and other priest officials of the Franciscan Order, as well as copies of some important letters written by herself or others to authorities in Syracuse. A thorough search in the several archives of the Franciscan priests for these letters written by Mother Marianne or others to those same authorities has been unproductive. However, the certified copy of the Charter of Incorporation, and the correspondence relating to it, sent to Father Lesen by Gibson and Mother Marianne in February 1887, are preserved in AS. It is probable that the Provincial Minister preserved nothing more.
7. Trials and difficulties at St. Joseph's Hospital: a newspaper clipping of the time (1884) indicates that some changes in hospital policy being advocated by a physician could have been troublesome to Mother Bernardina. No doubt Mother Marianne also was concerned about the details of the building program that she had helped to initiate.
8. Facts about Olinda Gomes (later known as Sister Elizabeth): (a) *Record of Postulate in Hawaii;* (b) *Reminiscences from Sr. Elizabeth* as told to Sr. M. Sebastian Hensler, Commissary General in H. I., 1935–1946.
9. The letter of Bishop Koeckemann to Father Lesen dated, February 12, 1885, would not be available except that Mother M. Delphine Mueller made a copy of it for the archive of the Franciscan Sisters. Errors in spelling in the copy have been retained in the text.

Chapter XI

CHANGES

THE FIRST company of reinforcements for the Franciscan mission reached Honolulu on April 22, 1885. Three of its number, chosen months before, came according to plan: Sister Benedicta Rodenmacher; Sister Carolina Hoffmann (whom her companions called Sister Charles); and Sister Leopoldina Burns. God's will had kept Sister Placida Tierney in Syracuse, and sent Sister M. Martha Kaiser in her stead.

The four newcomers brought sad news: Mother Antonia Eulenstein was dead. She had caught a cold while traveling to Albany in order to arrange for Sister Martha to take Sister Placida's place. The cold developed into double pneumonia and—"cut down by the cruel frosts of . . . winter," as the Syracuse *Evening Herald* reported—she died at eleven o'clock in the night of Easter Sunday, April 5. And, the newcomers added, poor Sister Placida, who had been dying for several weeks, was not expected to live much longer.

Father Joseph Lesen, himself ailing at the time of Mother Antonia's sickness, had appointed Sister M. Delphina Mueller to be Acting Provincial—or, as he wrote on April 6 in a general letter sent to all of the Order's convents, as "the representant of the Provincial Mother till the celebration of the Provincial Chapter." This careful phrasing indicated that, even though sixteen days earlier he had authorized Mother Marianne to stay in Hawaii, she was still regarded as the Mother Provincial according to the terms of the Order's constitutions, and would remain so until a chapter properly convened could elect her successor.

Father Joseph and Sister Delphina, in conference late on that sorrowful Easter night, agreed that Sister Leopoldina and Sister Charles should follow the itinerary that Mother Antonia had arranged for them. Sister Benedicta and Sister Martha had already started upon their westward journey, having been given permission to make a farewell visit with the Kaiser family in Kentucky.

Sister Leopoldina, who had nursed Mother Antonia during her last illness and was both weary and grief stricken, rose in the cold dawn of April 6 and said a sad farewell to Sister Placida, closer to death than anyone guessed. (She would die at 3 o'clock in the afternoon of April 7.) And then, weeping still, Sister Leopoldina and Sister Charles slipped quietly away, in time to catch the 7 o'clock express train to Chicago. "The house was so full of sadness," Sister Leopoldina remembered, "that they paid little attention to Sister Charles and I." Nor did the weather cheer them: "it was a dark unpleasant morning, the air was filled with fine snow and the cold frosty wind mournfully howling and whirling the snow wildly against everything." Sister Leopoldina could not know that thirty-three years would pass before she would see snowflakes whirling through the air or feel an icy wind touching her cheeks. Or rejoice in the coming of spring.

In Honolulu, on April 22, the bright Hawaiian sun shone down upon the four sisters as the steamer *Alameda* moved slowly into her berth. Father Leonor and Mr. Gibson waited on the dock to greet them. From the ship's rail Sister Leopoldina, looking out upon the crowd gathered on the pier, searched for Mother Marianne—and worried: "Is she sick? If she were not she would come to see us."

Sister Leopoldina remembered Father Leonor, from the time he visited the Motherhouse in Syracuse. How could she fail to recognize that, had God not sent him to Syracuse, only two years ago, as an agent in His Divine Plan, none of the Franciscan sisters would be serving Him today in this distant and foreign land? Father Leonor and Mr. Gibson—"a kind looking old gentleman with drooping shoulders and a long white beard"—led the four sisters from the ship's side through the staring throng. "It was the strangest crowd I ever could imagine nearly all were in bare feet loos close some gay loud colors others dirty and ragad jumping on each others shoulders to get a peep at us. We followed our brave leader. a little way from the wharf there were two of the grand royal carriages waiting for us. When Mr. Gibson opened the door of the first royal carriage out sprang our Mother."

Now at last we arrive at the time when we are presented to Mother Marianne in person, as something more than a shadowy imagined presence implied from the testimony of letters she has written and a few aging photographs. The loving gaze—and the rapturous voice—of Sister Leopoldina describe a living woman, and give a very good idea of the effect Mother Marianne had upon people who knew her: "She was always beautiful in my eyes but I can never forget how lovely she was that day, her sweet pale face a little flushed and her full chery lips with sweet smiles of welcome but loveliest of all are her wonderful eyes what a welth of love and tenderness were in those angelic eyes. Oh from the depths of those wonderful eyes was the reflection of loving charity."

The language is a bit fervent, Sister Leopoldina having been as schoolgirlish when she wrote this description during the 1920s as ever she was in 1880 when, as a young girl from Mother Marianne's own home town of Utica, she entered the novitiate in Syracuse and first saw her heroine. But her love for Mother Marianne is evident in this outpouring of age, as it is in the many other descriptions she entered in her long chronicle about the Franciscan mission. Her accounts of Mother Marianne, as well as those written by other witnesses, all depict a woman beautiful in face and, at the very least, engaging in manner. The combination of personal beauty, spiritual power, efficacy in deeds, and quiet authority was extraordinarily impressive. Beyond any doubt it was charismatic, in the overused praise of today. And this charisma, this gift of God's own grace, potent and immanent, conquered not only Sister Leopoldina.

For this arrival of Catholic workers for the Lord, Father Leonor did not arrange a grand parade through the city, or even a joyful Te Deum at the cathedral. The event certainly warranted advertisement and celebration, from every Catholic point of view. But, possibly at Mother Marianne's request, the sisters rode off quietly in the queen's handsome equipages. "Sister Benedicta and Sister Martha went with Mother in the first royal carriage and Sister Charles and I in the next."

Her first view of the kingdom's capital city disappointed Sister Leopoldina: "Why it is not even as nice as one of our little towns at home." But the Branch Hospital made up for the town's lack of glamor: "When the big gates were opened by two of the lepers and the royal carriages rolled in we were surprised how pretty and pleasant it looked with the many whitewashed cottages large verandahs painted gray the grass and young trees so beautifully green we drove to the office in the lepers back yard the back door of the office opened into the Sisters yard and we passed through the Sisters yard to our little convent home. It was a neat little two story cottage all painted white inside and out, how good it seemed to be home with our good Mother and Sisters."

Thus simply did Sister Leopoldina give herself, and fifty-seven years of her life, to the mission.

Sister Leopoldina herself appears now, too, as a real person, not merely as a writer of quaint reminiscences, who hadn't quite learned how to spell or to punctuate her compositions. The sight of Sister Leopoldina in person would draw an appreciating eye in any setting. But to find her slaving away in the pest-house at Kakaako is cause for shocked dismay. Photographs of the Franciscan company at Kakaako, taken on January 20, 1886, about three months after her thirty-first birthday, and after she had been confined within the walls of Kakaako for nine long months, show Sister Leopoldina still keeping the untroubled countenance and the clear innocent eyes of a young girl. She is tall, slender, lissom, altogether beautiful. She is, in fact, one of the most beautiful women ever to walk upon this tainted earth.

Small wonder, then, that strong men paled when they heard that she and her companions were going to Hawaii to serve as nurses to lepers. Sister Leopoldina told how the officers of the S.S. *Alameda* expressed disbelief and despair, in words and actions, when the four sisters boarded the ship in San Francisco. And Sister Leopoldina recalled, also, how more than once the fatherly captain, during the eight-day voyage to Honolulu, tried earnestly to dissuade her from throwing her life away upon such a dreadful mission. He shared the fear of leprosy that most people harbored in those days, and he could not bear to think that those sisters would be risking their lives in such dangerous circumstances.

Mr. Gibson, too, responded to the new sisters with concern and fondness—and, inevitably, with a stab of guilt. Ever since Mother Marianne and her companions went to work at the Branch Hospital, he had tried to ease their poverty by sending them gifts of food, flowers, and other material proofs of attention and appreciation—such as a carriage with full harness, purchased (at Gibson's suggestion) by Claus Spreckels, the millionaire sugar king from California who was extending his empire to Hawaii. To sybaritic Gibson the sisters' vows of poverty meant nothing; and he would have dismissed impatiently Father Lesen's frequent adjurations to them to keep their trust with St. Francis by practicing all those little acts of mortification and self-sacrifice that chasten the flesh and purify the spirit.

At first, Mother Marianne must have protested Gibson's generosity. But soon, finding that he paid no heed to her remonstrations, and recognizing that his gifts were but signs of concern for the sisters and appreciation for their work, she accepted them. The foodstuffs were welcome additions to their limited fare, and the more permanent pieces of bric-a-brac added permissible color to their parlor. She insisted upon only one criterion: such gifts must be shared by all the sisters, because all of them shared a common poverty and therefore an equal need.

On this festive day of arrival, April 22, 1885—which happened to be Sister Martha's thirtieth birthday—after parting from the Franciscans at the wharf, Gibson went to his office, to conduct whatever business of state awaited his attention. But he could not forget the sisters.

During the afternoon he sent Mother Marianne a note that epitomizes his fatherly attitude toward the Franciscans, and his love for Hawaii: "It is the custom of the Hawaiian People, when a high chief or chiefess, or any highly esteemed... stranger comes to visit them, that they make an offering (hookupu)... of some product or creatures of the land or water, and of some article of food:—and I conforming to this custom of the land of my adoption offer for the acceptance of the noble ladies of your sisterhood just arrived, who have come to the help of a poor and suffering people, a few flowers from my garden, a turkey from my ranch... and some light cakes baked this afternoon by my cook. The hookupu is regarded by Hawaiians as a small heart offering to the noble and most welcome stranger. In this spirit I hasten to make my humble offering."

The *Alameda* brought also Father Lesen's letter of April 8, in which he informed Mother Marianne how death had taken Mother Antonia and Sister Placida. The loss of Mother Antonia, so sudden, especially affected him: "... Oh! a sad day for us all, a sad day for the Community that has been left orphan, You being absent, and Mother Antonia gone." Later in this epistle, after the obligatory moralizing about the need to accept God's will in this as in all matters, he added: "I have already appointed Sr. M. Delphina to act as Provincial Mother. I see that I cannot call you back, and see no one else fit for the office."

In this too God's will helped Father Lesen to choose wisely. Sister Delphina Mueller, who had assisted Mother Antonia in administering the community, just as Sister Mary Ann in her day had assisted Mother Bernardina, was well prepared to serve as Acting Mother

Provincial. Mother Marianne, while still in Syracuse, had recognized
the young sister's abilities and transferred her from Albany to St.
Anthony's Convent, to be novice-mistress there.

She became a worthy successor to Mother Marianne and to
Mother Antonia and Mother Bernardina, those eminent founders of
the Sisters of the Third Order of St. Francis. At the Fifth Provincial
Chapter, held in the Motherhouse on August 13, 1885, the assembled
electors voted for Mother Delphina to be their third Mother Provincial. Whereupon, as the minutes of the chapter related, "Ven. Mother
Delphina was canonically announced to the whole Community called
together by the sound of the bells, the seal handed to Provincial
Mother elect, thanks given to God and obedience to the Mother Provincial."

Mother Delphina Mueller proved to be so excellent a Provincial
Superior that she was "successively reelected" at the end of each
three-year term "until 1907, serving the Community in this capacity
for 22 years."

At that important chapter of August 1885, Mother Marianne Cope
was still identified as "Provincial Superior" and marked as being "absent." But neither the assembled sisters nor Father Lesen forgot to
arrange a position for her. They presented a special resolution propos-
ing her election as "Commissary Provincial of the Sandwich Islands"
and recording their wish that "thanks should be rendered to her for her
faithful administration as Provincial Mother and sacrifices made as
Superioress of the Sandwich Islands." The chapter minutes stated
that "all votes were given in her favor."

The title of Commissary Provincial for the distant province of the
Sandwich Islands seems to have been a new one in the Order, especially created for Mother Marianne. Father Lesen's sagacity would
have thought of this distinctive name, for the sake of her prestige in
Hawaii. The title gave her the power to manage directly her mission's
lesser affairs without having to refer every decision to the Superior
General in Syracuse. It also placed her in a position of some rank from
which she could treat with Bishop Hermann, Prime Minister Gibson,
their successors, and officials in the kingdom's bureaucracy.

On the other hand, the Franciscan administration in Syracuse, by
recognizing Mother Marianne's physical separation from the center of
the Order's affairs, also set her apart with that new title. They reduced the power that once she held, limiting it to the narrow stage of

the mission in Hawaii. In larger matters of the Rule and of canonical regulation, she and her mission would still be controlled from Syracuse. Compared with the greater authority she would have exercised had she returned to her position as Mother Provincial, the office of Commissary Provincial was a minor one indeed.

She did not regret the loss of power. She had renounced it long before, when she chose a different country in which to live, another field in which to labor. Her empire, which once had covered several American states and embraced a score of schools, hospitals, and convents, shrank now to two tiny convents, a minuscule school for girls, and two hospitals, one of which was so appalling that few healthy people ever set foot in it. Yet the will of God was sending her an endless supply of lepers to take care of. In bringing them succor she would find both purpose and contentment.

Before she assigned the newcomers to duty, Mother Marianne granted them a period of eight days in which to recover from the fatigue of the journey and to adjust to the heat and humidity of Honolulu. Those days of grace also helped them to recover from the shock of seeing their first lepers, in the compound beyond the fence.

The customs of society also took up some of the interval. The day after they arrived, Sister Leopoldina remembered, "the King and Queen called with Rev. Father Leonore." The priest interpreted for Her Majesty, who wept as she thanked them for coming to take care of "my poor afflicted people." The King, almost as moved, said very little, but showed by his expression that he too was grateful for the sisters' help. On the following day Bishop Hermann came to greet the newcomers and to give them his blessing. No doubt several of the town's Catholic ladies came to call on other days, helping to assure the four sisters that not everyone in Hawaii was leprous—and that beyond the hospital's high fence the world they had forsworn still continued upon its way.

Mother Marianne kept all the newcomers at the Branch Hospital. She put Sister Leopoldina in charge of about twenty leprous girls and women, and presumably gave Sister Benedicta, Sister Martha, and Sister Charles the same responsibilities. Later, in November, she would send Sister Benedicta to Wailuku, to take charge of the girls' school that Sister Antonella's sickness and death had deprived of an English-speaking teacher about a year before. At some time during the spring of 1885, probably in May, Sister Crescentia, exhausted by the demands of her daily clinic for dressing the patients' sores, went to Wailuku for a brief vacation.

Mother Marianne did not accord herself the same kind of rest. She had so much to do—and never enough time or help in which to do everything. Those social interruptions, when people from town came to call, gave her at the least a few minutes of respite from the daily routines with patients and stewards.

Sister Leopoldina found her twenty charges "so interesting that I became very fond of them. There were few who could speak English and the native [language] seemed such a gibberish little did I think I could ever learn it and it was three years before I could speak it."

It was gibberish, in fact, not the pure and mellifluous Hawaiian language, but the same sort of practical pidgin English that confused the Franciscans when they first lived in Honolulu. Fortunately for everyone, a few patients spoke both English and Hawaiian, not to mention the pidgin variants, and were able to translate messages and instructions. Sister Leopoldina found such a one among her twenty: "a tall half white girl she looked like a Irish girl she would do anything for the Sisters she could speak english and she was a great help with the little ones."

Often enough those little ones managed to be just as troublesome to the sisters as were the older patients. All the children were undisciplined, noisy, foul in both body and mind, utterly amoral. Most, having no models of good behavior to follow, were unmitigatedly bad. A few were not even lepers. Both at Kakaako and at Kalawao a number of healthy children lived with their leprous parents or, after those had died, with any adult who would bother to take nominal responsibility for them. As the children grew older (if they lived that long) they took care of themselves, running in packs like feral dogs, stealing or begging food and clothing, preying upon adult patients—just as, in their turn, many elders preyed upon them as soon as they reached a certain age. Father Damien, seeing all this at Kalawao, worried about these wild children, and tried to provide a home in which some of them might have the chance to live decently. At Kakaako, where relatively few such juvenile delinquents were caged, the Franciscans did their best to correct or protect the children, without much success.

Such a little demon was Ellen Davis, a half-Hawaiian girl ten or twelve years old who appeared to be half that age to Sister Leopoldina. Ellen was encrusted with dirt from head to foot, a running mess of rags, vermin, and tangled hair, "a horrod child in every kind of mischief." Sister Crescentia, one day soon after arriving at Kakaako, scrubbed Ellen down to her skin and uncovered a pretty child. She was so much paler than anyone had dreamed that Mother Marianne called her "Snowdrop." But Snowdrop, alas, refused to keep herself clean and soon acquired a fresh coating of dirt, although she insisted upon being called by that fancy new name, because she liked the sound of it without knowing what it meant. Sister Crescentia, busy at dressing patients' sores, could not give the child any more cleansing baths. Neither did any of the women patients who might have helped the girl. And so Snowdrop accreted more layers of filth, along with lice, itchings, sores, and scabs, until once again she was indistinguishable from an idiot child.

Mother Marianne gave this odious creature to Sister Leopoldina, as a kind of challenge. She, undaunted, scrubbed away the accumulated dirt, from crown to sole, clothed the sanitized Snowdrop in a pretty green dress Sister herself had fashioned from a cast-away gown "some lady sent in." The loving attention, the resplendent green dress, and—how could even a fiend resist it?—the angelic beauty of Sister Leopoldina herself, transformed Ellen, inside and out: "her little round dark brown face so soft and smooth like velvet and her features so very perfect, thin red lips even white teeth, and that dirty blue black niggery wool was changed to black silky ringlets around her interesting little face and her lovely black eyes were dancing."

As sometimes happens, in real life as well as in films and story books, generous applications of loving kindness will convert hellions into—well, not angels, perhaps, but at least into tolerable human beings. From that day forth, when Snowdrop emerged transfigured from her bath, she became a different girl, almost—but not quite—reformed. Instantaneous conversion requires a miracle, and Ellen-Snowdrop had not been so deeply touched. Nonetheless, she tried—and by her own efforts made commendable progress along the path to decency. She "gave up telling lies and was seldom known to steal, being a clever child she spent some of her time around the office," where Mother Marianne gave her little chores to do, or taught her to sew and to crochet. "She loved Mother so much she was happy if she was only near her." Sister Leopoldina's faithful pursuit and daily inspection, supported by Mother Marianne's high expectations, actually kept Snowdrop from backsliding into darkest pollution.

Ellen Davis's story is one of the very few with a happy ending to come out of Kakaako. Sister Leopoldina and Mother Marianne, able now to see her unblemished body, clean in both senses of the word, presented her for examination to the diagnosing physicians. They pronounced Ellen free of leprosy and soon released her from Kakaako into the care of healthy relatives in Honolulu.

Snowdrop was fortunate: she could be saved only because the sisters saw her in time. but the plight of other healthy children at Kalawao disturbed Mother Marianne.

Father Damien, too, at Kalawao recognized the problem and tried to find a remedy for it. By mid-1885 he was taking care of forty-two "orphans," as he called them. His "orphanage," supported by the Catholic mission, not by the government, fed, clothed, and housed—in separate dwellings—thirty boys and twelve girls. Most were leprous, a few were clean. Without Damien's care, all would have been "friendless." Dr. Arthur Mouritz, the Settlement's resident physician from 1884 to 1888, considered Damien's orphanage "one of the finest works that this priest undertook and carried out."

Many other healthy children, however, still lived with parents or relatives. Some received loving care. Others were kept as servants, or abused as little better than slaves. All were continually exposed to the chance of infection with leprosy; and all, at any age but especially as they neared puberty, were in constant danger from the attentions of older boys and the men. Moreover, no proper schooling could be given any of Kalawao's children, whether leprous or clean. This neglect of the mind distressed Gibson and Mother Marianne almost as much as did the danger to their morals.

Dr. Arning told Mother Marianne about the healthy children of Kalawao after he returned from a visit there sometime in 1884. Arning, that new kind of man, that paradigm of scientific dispassion and Germanic thoroughness—who worked day and night at trying to cultivate Hansen's bacillus upon laboratory substrates; who did not hesitate to inoculate Keanu, a condemned Hawaiian murderer, with tissues taken from a leper, in an attempt to transmit the disease to him; who terrified Sister Leopoldina by raging at her when she tried to withhold from his autopsy table the body of a young girl just dead of the disease; who, in his determination to be "scientifically honest," soon entered into a long feud with Gibson that ultimately led to his being fired summarily from the Board of Health's employ—Arning, that man of coldest intellect, also felt a tug of concern for the health of the clean children at Kalawao. He spoke to Mother Marianne about "the poor helpless children who are not lepers [left] in the sore bleeding hands of their leper parents," wrote Sister Leopoldina, using again one of her favorite and goriest expressions. "He was quite sure he said if those children could be taken care of by well people they would never have leprosy." Mother Marianne, who had not yet visited the Leprosarium on Molokai, reacted as Arning expected and, as Sister Leopoldina described, in language more her own than Mother's: "oh! what a pity and horror to leave the poor innocence there in that frightful sink of sin and filth."

Mother Marianne resolved to rescue those children—or at least the girls among them. The boys, she decided, being less vulnerable, would have to wait until later. Early in 1884, even while she and Sister Crescentia were all but overwhelmed with patients at Kakaako, she talked with Mr. Gibson about saving those girls in peril. He, according to Sister Leopoldina, agreed with her in principle, but asked "how can you think of starting anything new with so few Sisters? Each one has more than she can do." Mother Marianne "pleaded if we had a home for the little girls in the Convent yard, we could see that they would not be in any way connected with the lepers, and it would be very easy to get a woman to take charge of them, and we could help to take cair of them."

Gibson had good reason to protest her taking on any more burdens. But, as he was learning, Heaven hath no power like a woman dedicated. Once Mother Marianne thought of a way to help "the poor and the afflicted" (among whom she did not include either herself or her sisters), she never gave up until she had realized her plan. Gibson, allowing himself to be persuaded, asked the Legislature of 1884 for an appropriation of $15,000, to be used in building such a home. The legislators, allowing Gibson to persuade them, approved the appropriation but, as he explained later in the address he delivered at the ceremonies dedicating the home, "the amount was not immediately available."

At that juncture King Kalakaua and Queen Kapiolani joined Gibson in appealing to the community for funds. All members of the royal family, together with many other residents of Honolulu, subscribed $6,575 for Mother Marianne's new project. "With this means in hand," Gibson said, the home was constructed. Because of the queen's interest in the welfare of her "unfortunate people," said Sister Leopoldina, "Our Mother expressed a wish that the home should have her sweet Name." Accordingly, this worthy institution was called "The Kapiolani Home for Girls, the Offspring of Leper Parents."

The Home, a rather large two-story wooden structure, was built about fifty or sixty feet west of the Franciscans' convent and within the same enclosure. Broad verandahs, twelve feet wide, around three sides of each story, gave the girls lots of room for playing on rainy days. Heavy columns supported the upper floor, and low railings kept the girls from falling off the porches at both levels. "Large windows and glass doors," wrote Sister Leopoldina, "gave sufficient light and air. a large school room, store room kitchen and dining room on the first floor On the uper story were two large dormitorys and a room for the Matron. In each of the dormitorys were from fifteen to twenty neat little iron bedsteads new matresses white spreds large soft pillows, and by the side of each bed was a strong wooden chair. a few steps from the house was a neat little hous for their toilets and bating, the children were to have plenty of fresh milk and the best of plain food."

The whole building, Sister Leopoldina noted, was painted "a cheerful gray outside and white inside." Photographs of the newly finished Home, set down in a muddy yard not yet green with grass or shrubs, make it look institutional and cheerless by today's standards. Yet, for its time it was very modern, and much better than many a cold and stony orphanage in the United States or Europe. At least it had those wide lanais, and the ocean's edge beyond them, and the cooling breezes from the sea or from the mountains. And the sisters, to prove that somebody cared. Most certainly it provided the girls who lived there with a better home than anything they could have known in Kalawao.

In his opening address, Gibson explained that the Home was designed and "fitted to lodge conveniently, with a view to their health and comfort, about fifty girls. Here, although tabued from the general society of other children, they may enjoy all the advantages that may be obtained by healthy girls in a well ordered boarding school establishment."

By November 1, 1885, the Kapiolani Home was functioning, with an initial census of ten girls sent from the Leper Settlement on Molokai. Although the Home was supposed to accept only healthy girls, apparently a few of its first inmates were suspects, not yet clearly demonstrating diagnostic signs of leprosy. "Annie was the baby only five years old ... and the oldest ... was [Lilia] a stout healthy looking girl of almost sixteen."

Even though the girls' parents or guardians at Kalawao readily consented to their coming when the plan was explained to them, on the day of parting, October 29, as Sister Leopoldina wrote, they "changed their minds and were very angry and rebellious." Two enraged male patients objected so violently to being separated from their shared foster-daughter that they stabbed three leper constables who were escorting the group of girls to the waiting smallboat. Two constables died soon after being attacked, the third recovered eventually. The assailants were arrested, deported to Lahaina, tried, convicted, and sentenced to ten years in prison—in jail-less Kalawao. As the patients said so often; "Worse than death itself is life as a leper at Kalaupapa, Land of the Given Grave."

Only one thing went wrong in Mother Marianne's planning for the Home: "When everything was ready Mr. Gibson advertised for a Matron either white lady or Hawaiian but not one in the Kingdom would take charge of those children of leper parents. So our good Mother appointed Sister Martha to take charge of the Home. Sister was a beautiful tall thin graceful Sister but not strong her [disposition] was so angelic that she was loved and respected by everyone, but she was especially loved by children. Poor gentle Sister Martha what she had to suffer from the little wild cats of Molokai, but her love and patience were rewarded I know."

So began one of mankind's most intelligent programs to care for "the afflicted orphans" who are the healthy children of leprosy patients. Dr. Arning thought of the program, Gibson promoted it, the people of Hawaii supported it, and Mother Marianne's determination achieved it. No other country in the world at that time even conceived of such a plan, and today few nations make any effort to separate leprous parents from their healthy children. In Hawaii the policy of separating at birth all children from their leprous mothers or fathers, adopted in 1894, was maintained until very recently. Today, fortunately, it is no longer necessary, both because the incidence of new cases of leprosy has fallen almost to zero and because drugs for the treatment of newly reported patients are so effective that the danger of their transmitting the infection is negligible.

Until these new chemotherapeutic drugs became available, the need to separate children from parents was cruel, of course, because it denied infants the comfort of parental love and parents the pleasures of their children's company. In consequence, one of the saddest things about the Leper Settlement at Kalaupapa after the policy went into effect was the complete absence of healthy children. Even clean employees of the Department of Health were forbidden to bring their children even to visit the Settlement before they reached the age of fifteen. Nonetheless, if ever the epidemic of leprosy in Hawaii was to be stopped, the government had to enforce the policy of segregation for people of all ages. Dr. Arning was right: with a prescience founded upon intuition rather than upon data, he guessed a truth that epidemiologists have confirmed since his time. In most instances, infection with leprosy organisms seems to be contracted early in life by infants and children who are in constant and intimate contact with active cases of leprosy. The only way to reduce the opportunity for transmitting the infection, and therefore to decrease the number of cases in a population, is to reduce the opportunity for exposure of susceptible children to known sources of contagion. Until the mid-1960s, when at last effective medications could successfully arrest the disease itself in recognized cases, and thereby make them non-infectious, the only feasible way to prevent the spread of leprosy was to separate vulnerable children from diseased adults, adolescents, and playmates.

In Hawaii, beginning in 1894, the separation was made at birth with children of either sex born to leprous mothers. As soon as a child was born in the Settlement, it was taken away from its mother, first to a house of isolation at Kalaupapa, and later it was sent to Honolulu, to be raised by Sisters of St. Francis or by relatives who wished to claim the infant. Kapiolani Home served this purpose for girl children until 1938, when, happily, it was closed for lack of babies born to lepers. Since that year infants born to the few leprous mothers have been raised in foster homes or by relatives. During the fifty-three years in which Kapiolani Home did function, only very few of its wards developed leprosy. Accounts differ: one says two girls, another five, a third six girls became lepers; but, even so, the number has been small.

During that same period, the number of lepers isolated on Molokai decreased dramatically, from 641 in 1885 to 93 in 1938. Today, the number of new cases detected annually ranges between none and four, and almost all of these are found among immigrants rather than among people born in the islands. Obviously, in terms of epidemiology, the two interdependent policies of segregating known cases of leprosy on Molokai and of separating newborn children from their leprous parents have been successful in the period before effective chemotherapy was available.

"The prophets for evil predicted grave disaster," Dr. Arthur Mouritz observed sarcastically in 1916, "pointing to the fact that the Kapiolani Home was baptized in blood [with the slaughter of two constables at Kalaupapa], therefore its aims and mission would be brought to naught. This has not been realized, the prophets have long since been gathered to their fathers, the home flourishes and accomplishes well the work it was intended to do."

Of the four people most involved in founding the Home in 1885, Mother Marianne and Dr. Arning (who died in 1936) lived long enough to see the statistical evidence proving that their efforts to prevent the spread of leprosy among Hawaii's people had been rewarded.

Mr. Gibson arranged to dedicate the Kapiolani Home with a colorful ceremony, to which all dignitaries in Honolulu were invited, on November 9, 1885—two years and a day after the Franciscans arrived to take up their mission.

At the end of the ceremony, as a reporter observed, "King Kalakaua stepped forward and inviting the Reverend Lady to a seat nearer his person, decorated her with the Order of Kapiolani, . . . established by His Majesty chiefly to reward acts of benevolence in behalf of his people. So quietly and unobtrusively was this done that few of the general audience were aware of the fact. Through Mr. Gibson the Mother Superior, who was taken by surprise, thanked His Majesty for the honor conferred."

She had been outwitted. For once in her life she received the recognition she deserved and the public attention she disliked. Gibson and the sisters understood her well enough to know exactly how to manage her—at least for that one occasion.

She had received the insigne awarded to "a Lady Companion" of the Order, and was one of nine eminent women in Honolulu upon whom the honor was bestowed during the year 1885. King Kalakaua founded the Order on August 30, 1880, as a means "of commemorating the deeds of Our Ancestors, KAPIOLANI THE GREAT, and of manifesting Our appreciation of services rendered to those who have labored to save the Hawaiian race. . . ." The decoration was conferred "for services in the cause of humanity, science, art and services rendered to the state or sovereign."

If the honors she received and the distinguished people she met are to be taken as measures of success in this world, then November 9, 1885, must be considered as being the zenith in Mother Marianne's career. After that day she began upon the long slow descent into the anonymity she preferred, toward the death she did not fear.

She herself would not have given much importance to either the honors or the dignitaries who ventured, that once, amid the dangers of Kakaako. She did not mention the decoration in letters sent to Syracuse, and neither did any of her companions at Kakaako write about it, not even Sister Leopoldina.

Mother Marianne knew that honors received from kings and potentates are of no significance, are but empty things, as false as the coating of gilt upon an iron housekey. She knew that only God's judgment has meaning. Of the trappings of ceremony presented to her during that morning, she valued only the keys to the Home. They soon lost their pretentious gilt, as she and her companions used them to lock and unlock doors in that Home filled with hope. They endured for many years, performing their service faithfully until, eventually, long after she was gone, the aged and decrepit Home was razed. The keys, no longer wanted, were kept for a while but now cannot be found.

The red velvet cushion survives, upon which the keys were presented to Her Majesty—who thereupon opened the symbolic door and gave the keys into Mother Marianne's keeping. She kept the cushion, as she did the keys, because those things belonged to the Home. Protected now within an envelope of clear plastic film, the cushion, still richly crimson and gold, is preserved at the Motherhouse in Syracuse. So also is the Letter-Patent, signed by Kalakaua Rex, in testimony of the presentation of the Royal Order of Kapiolani.

But the insigne of the Order, the elegant bauble given to herself alone, has vanished.

NOTES on Chapter XI

1. Details of the double funeral rites for Mother Antonia Eulenstein and Sister Placida Tierney: *The Evening Herald*, Syracuse, N.Y., April 9, 1885.
2. Mother Delphine Mueller: (a) recognition of abilities by Mother Marianne: bio-

graphical sketch of Mother Delphine in her personal file; (b) "capacity" for service: Prandoni, 1960: *Greater Love*. p. 33.

3. Father Damien's "orphanage" at Kalawao: Mouritz, 1916, *Path of the Destroyer*. pp. 76–79.

4. Details about Kapiolani Home: *Dedication of the Kapiolani Home*. 1885: (a) appropriations, p. 14; (b) Gibson's address, pp. 8–16.

5. Royal Order of Kapiolani: (a) decoration of Mother Marianne with the Order of Kapiolani: *Dedication of Kapiolani Home, 1885*, p. 17; (b) *Hawaiian Royal Orders* by Gordon Medcalf, pp. 24–30; (c) *Statutes of the Royal Order of Kapiolani*.

Chapter XII

"THIS PURE AND EXALTED FRIENDSHIP"

DURING 1886 and the first half of 1887 King Kalakaua and Gibson, either individually or in concert, committed a number of errors in judgment and perpetrated such a variety of political follies that Hawaii's businessmen and sugar planters decided to tolerate them no longer. The "most foolish scheme" of all was a plan to invite the chiefs of Samoa and assorted other specks of land in the South Pacific that had not yet been claimed by Britain, France, or Germany to join a "confederation" of small independent Polynesian states, over which Kalakaua and Gibson would preside. The "most irresponsible" plan, to Hawaii's businessmen, considered borrowing $2,000,000 from bankers in London, with which to maintain the government (and its Merry Monarch) at a level of extravagance that few taxpayers thought they could afford. The "most immoral act" was a bill brought before the Legislature of 1886 to license the sale of opium, profits from the traffic in which would help to fill the nation's depleted treasury.

King Kalakaua's zest for living on a grand scale, and his readiness to empty that treasury faster than it could be filled, did little to soothe the feelings of merchants who believed in balanced budgets for all and in tidy profits for themselves. Not incidentally, it also caused Gibson himself many anxious hours, as he tried to find the money the king had already planned to spend. Many other "affronts" to common sense or Christian morality also provoked haole horror and agitated their conversations. The most unforgivable of those interests was Kalakaua's "revival" of interest in the dances, chants, religious rituals, and medical practices of his people, all of which Protestant missionaries from New England had been trying to suppress ever since their first representatives arrived in 1820.

Gibson was responsible for having proposed only some of those

228

insults to haole intelligence. Nonetheless, as Kalakaua's prime minister and preeminent counsellor, he was blamed for all of them—and for everything else that people didn't like, whether or not he had anything at all to do with starting it. He, the insidious, sinister, duplicitous, diabolical corrupter, drew the opposition's hate. Kalakaua, the buffoon and dupe, drew its malice and its scorn.

Their opponents, who for years had been protesting by all legitimate means "the extravagance" of the court and "the excesses" of the prime minister, agreed that they'd had enough of both. Loyal no longer, opponents met to organize systems for achieving changes in government—by force, if necessary. Organization took a number of courses. Some were entirely legal, ethical, and public. Others were seditious and secret. Most opponents of the regime hoped to gain the desired reforms by peaceful means rather than by violence. They did not wish to depose the king, but sought only to limit his constitutional powers and, most especially, to reduce the sums of money spent upon his follies. But those practical men did want most intensely to rout Gibson from the government and to deny him any position from which he could influence king, legislators, and enfranchised voters.

Gibson's enemies, whether avowed or hidden, strengthened their several political parties in membership and programs; increased the pace and virulence of their attacks in articles and editorials published in newspapers they controlled and in debates during sessions of the legislature; and established "drill teams," ostensibly for exercise and recreation, for which they smuggled in arms and ammunition against the time when their "Sunday soldiers" might be used to support a coup d'etat.

Less principled adversaries also resorted to psychological warfare. Anonymous poetasters wrote scurrilous ditties, ribald skits, and sneering essays about "the puppet king" and "Nosbig," his "Minister of Everything" who pulled the strings. Whispering campaigns passed along hints about scandalous goings-on at court or in trysting places around the town. And some especially ingenious types got the bright idea of trapping bachelor Gibson in a breach of promise suit brought by Mrs. Flora Howard St. Clair, "an attractive widow" newly arrived in town.

Mrs. St. Clair and her sister came to Honolulu from San Francisco in February 1886, selling (of all things!) "art books." Apparently Gibson purchased some of her wares, but how much he bought and how extensively no one was ever able to say. On March 9, 1887, a gossip columnist in the *Hawaiian Gazette* reported that Gibson "meditated taking unto himself a wife soon," and a week later bet "six to four on the widow." By that time Gibson himself, whatever sentiments he may have entertained earlier for Flora St. Clair, could no longer abide the sight of her. "Torment of *that* woman," he wrote in his diary on April 19. "Impossible to recognize her in any way—a miserable intrusion."

She, cut to the heart, of course, wounded nigh unto madness, beseeched him tearfully and publicly in his office—and with cold calculation in letters delivered to his home. Those letters read as if a committee of lawyers composed them, not the grieving brain in her own pretty head. In those missives she threatened to take him to court for having "broken his solemn word." And he, thrashing about in a net woven of gossip and legal feints, insisted that this was one proposal he most certainly had never made. Whereupon she, less to save her good name than to blacken his, filed her breach of promise suit. A bailiff served him with the summons on Saturday May 21, 1887—just as Gibson's whole palace of cards was about to collapse in the grand debacle that ended his political career. Anyone with any sense at all recognized that Flora St. Clair's case against the poor man was contrived, that her suit was nothing more than blackmail, impure and simple. But no one lifted a hand to help him, no one intervened to stay the majestic process of the Law.

Until those campaigns of attrition began to mount in 1886, Gibson was rather good humored in his attitude toward opposition. Possibly because he won often enough to enjoy being magnanimous, he parried opponents with wit and legislative maneuverings, never with vicious devisings of the sort his enemies directed against him. But by mid-1886, harried from all sides, he began to break under the strain. His body failed him. Age, worry, lack of rest hastened the course of his tuberculosis, which seems to have been more or less arrested until about then. Sickness gnawed away now at body and spirit. He suffered from progressive weakness, unrelieved fatigue, periods of gastric distress (which may have been caused by ulcers), bowel complaints, and frequent bouts of depression—or "melancholia," as he liked to call it. His diary for 1886 and 1887 (the only surviving part of a record that he kept for several years) holds almost as many complaints about his health as it contains comments about social or political events in his busy calendar. These signs of preoccupation with health indicate that he was feeling the effects of his adversaries' attacks, both physically and emotionally—and far more intensively than most of his friends or enemies realized. Yet he did not give up any of his posts in the government or alter in the slightest the policies by which he drew upon himself the rancor of those antagonists. Nor did he admit to himself the suspicion that he would never be well again.

As the victim of assailants both internal and external, he needed, as all men do, solace for the spirit. He found much comfort in the company of his children and grandchildren, Talula Hayselden's three sons and two daughters. And he found a haven from stress in his association with the Sisters of St. Francis. The sisters had enchanted him since the day they arrived. As the passing months gave him the opportunity to know them better, he grew fonder of them as persons, more paternal, more determined to thank them for the care they gave to the patients at Kakaako. Of all the gifts he had presented to the people of Hawaii, he liked to think, the sisters were the best—and to him, the most rewarding. In their company he could relax and forget the cares that awaited him at the legislature, in the palace, in his several scattered offices, even at the soirees and grand balls and feasts he so loved to attend.

At Kakaako Sister Rosalia—when she felt well enough to emerge from her sickroom—delighted him with her Irish wit, the sauciness with which she dubbed him "Father Walter." Sister Leopoldina's fresh beauty, her sweet solicitude, touched his heart. Olinda Gomes's cups of tea and sugary cookies fortified his wasted body, perpetually hungry yet never fattened. And Mother Marianne's cool common sense about everything, her directness and efficiency, her invincible cheerfulness and endless patience with the needs of every one, from moppets like Snowdrop to personages like the prime minister himself, he laid like a balm unto his smarting ego. At the hospital office or, for special treats, in the convent's quiet parlor, he found the only medicaments Honolulu could offer his decaying body and lacerated spirit.

The Franciscans' poverty made Gibson want to ease the austerity in which they had chosen to live. Many times he arrived at Kakaako bearing things to be enjoyed by all the sisters—a bouquet of flowers, a basketful of fresh vegetables or a box holding cakes or pies prepared by his cook.

On very special days he would bring something extraordinary and costly. Thus, on Saturday, January 23, 1886—which, by no strange coincidence, was Mother Marianne's forty-eighth birthday—he presented a plated silver tea service to the "Convent of St. Francis"—as the engraving on two of the pieces specified.

He thought of improvements and comforts he might introduce into the compound at Kakaako. On February 15, 1886, he instructed carpenters to enclose "a small space with wire netting for a new fernery." Nine days later he decided the fernery would not be adequate for growing enough plants to fill the hospital's wards with greenery, and so he "ordered Mayhew to construct a small conservatory or glass house for plants, to be attached to the Convent of St. Francis—a present to the Sisters." In July 1886, probably because she was ill again and confined in her room, he "took Sr. Rosalia a small bird in a cage." And on St. Patrick's Day, 1887, he "Ordered a pound cake at Horn's [Honolulu's foremost confectionery] tastefully ornamented with 'St Patrick,' a † and 'Sr R' in sugared letters on the icing. Sent as a compliment to Sr Rosalia." He commissioned photographers to take pictures of Kapiolani Home and its girls, of the sisters—and of himself, standing ghostly beyond them. This sense of history, his instinct for preserving the facts of an event in photographs, publications, mementoes, his diary, is another of Gibson's virtues unappreciated by his contemporaries. Without those photographs taken on January 20, 1886, we today would not know how each of the sisters looked, nor even how Kapiolani Home appeared to them.

The self-indulgent sybarite could not abide the thought that the sisters were supposed to practice abnegation. Always the flood of delicacies poured in. The giving gave him pleasure, and he was a man accustomed to pleasing himself. He was wealthy beyond his needs, quixotic, paternal, and lonely. This combination of attributes is dangerous to any man. It is especially inflammable in an aging egotist.

The sisters' responses to his "kindnesses" pleasured him. He liked to be thanked so sweetly, either in person or with little notes sent by the returning coachman. Most of all, he liked to be noticed, needed to be the center of attention. With those gifts he purchased access to the sisters' company, he bought their attention. He had never known anyone like these Franciscans, and he never wearied of their company. Each time he came to call he renewed his love for all the saintly sisters. He, the most complex and theatrical man in all Hawaii, doted upon them, those models of purity and simplicity, those ministering angels abiding in a state of grace. "A happy hour at Kakaako," he wrote many times in his diary. On Saturday, June 5, 1886, he explained why he felt so happy there: "the kindly sweet courteous ways of all the Sisters."

In their company he discovered and refurbished his soul. The sisters, so full of unshakable faith in the powers of God, evoked in him a yearning to share it with them. He may have professed faith of a sort in his youth, probably Anglican in its alliance, possibly Roman Catholic. Bishop Hermann, writing to Superior General Father Bousquet on February 13, 1885, about important Catholic laymen in the Kingdom of Hawaii, stated that Gibson "is Catholic by baptism, perhaps a sort of defrocked seminarian. He seems to have a trace of faith without an open avowal and without practice. . . ." Only Gibson could have provided the bishop with that sort of information about his past. But Gibson was also quite capable of inventing such a history and adapting truth to suit his purposes.

On December 12, 1887, as Gibson lay ill in St. Mary's Hospital, maintained in San Francisco by the Sisters of Mercy, he wrote in his diary a tribute that showed how deeply he had been impressed by "the Sisters of Charity" he had met: "What a glorious company of sweet good women they are. The Catholic religious woman is a true woman and the best of women—blessed I sincerely feel. How I love and reverence my Franciscans, and these Sisters of Mercy."

Lapsed Catholic or no, in 1885 Gibson certainly was a renegade Mormon, and probably had been for many years a skeptic who attended no church at all. By 1886 the sisters of St. Francis had softened both his doubting mind and his hardened heart. He went several times to Mass at the Cathedral of Our Lady of Peace, or to attend the funerals of friends, or for occasions of state, such as "a Grand Requiem Mass for the repose of the soul of the late Alfonso XIII, King of Spain."

The date upon which Gibson was received into the Catholic Church is not known; he did not record it in his diary. Probably everything was managed with discretion, in order to avoid giving his more bigoted critics yet another reason for reviling him. Sister Leopoldina, who should have been well informed about the matter, remembered how "during lent [of 1886] Mr. Gibson returned to his religion and after receiving the Sacraments he was very happy much happier he said than he had been for many years." Thereafter, as his diary notes, he went often to Sunday Mass at the cathedral, and without secrecy.

Members of the Sacred Hearts mission of the cathedral, too, kept a watchful eye upon this most conspicuous of parishioners. Brother Victorian Bertrand, writing to a priest-friend on May 25, 1887, was able to report: "Mr. Gibson . . . surprised us and at the same time edified us to see him make his Easter duty during Holy Week by approaching the Holy Table with a great deal of fervor. Father Raymond was his confessor. . . ."

The public, even his severest critics, seem not to have minded his church going at all—quite possibly because none among them could be convinced that this new devotion would be any more permanent than the ones that preceded it. Yet he proved himself a better convert to the Roman faith than to the Mormon. And "he died a Catholic," as Bishop Hermann declared at the Grand Requiem Mass for Gibson dead.

While Gibson regarded all the younger Franciscans at Kakaako with a paternal affection, he gave his heart to Mother Marianne. His was a worshipful form of love, the kind that Victorian novelists liked to call "platonic." However pure such a love may be in intent and in fact, it does not prevent some men from being dependent upon the need to affirm it. Gibson was no diffident languishing poet, no mystic saint, sublimating earthly love into good deeds or great art. Gibson, the egotist, the center of his universe, insisted upon expressing his love— and upon gaining some response to it. The entries in his diary, all too brief—and frequently all too ambiguous—reveal that his need to win Mother Marianne's attention progressed from respectful to demanding to possessive to despairing to resigned—until, at the end, the poor mixed up old man was less consoled than distressed by his frustrating kind of love.

The story is there, complete for everyone to see, in his diary: it portrays not the heroic passion of a tempestuous lover, nor yet the anguish of a rejected suitor, but rather the sentimentality of a man suffering from an obsession with an idea. Like all egotists, he is in love with himself more than with any one else. He is addicted to the kind of attention that the Franciscans give him at Kakaako. And most especially does he demand the attention of their leader, in abilities and responsibilities the obvious counterpart in her little domain to himself in the larger realm.

Not for a moment did Mother Marianne feel herself endangered by either Gibson's gifts or his presence. She recognized, from the frequency of his visits and the trend of his conversation, that he was, as he said, "a lonely old man." She understood that he needed some one like her to talk to, to confide in, to relax with, and, alas, to brag to. And so she felt sorry for him. She had always felt sorry for people nobody else wanted to be bothered with, like alcoholic priests and hospital patients down on their luck in Syracuse, like querulous lepers in the lazarhouse at Kakaako. And always, as Sister Crescentia would bear witness many years later, Mother Marianne treated those misfortuned folk with cheerfulness, humor, encouragement, and endless patience, as if she had all the time in the world to devote to each one of them alone.

Sister Crescentia, who served with Mother Marianne at St. Joseph Hospital before accompanying her to Hawaii, told Sister M. Helena Haas in 1927 that some of those alcoholic priests thought Mother Marianne should be canonized just for her acts of charity toward them. "Several times it happened," said Sister Crescentia, "that a poor unfortunate priest was brought in and, by the advice of the doctor, it was requested that he should be discharged on account of his bad conduct—but Mother insisted that he should be given special care. Through her patience and kindness, he turned over a new leaf and became a very exemplary man, which he showed through his change of life, especially by the letters which were written to Mother whilst in the Islands." Sister Crescentia added a perceptive comment: "Mother had much to suffer on account of such acts of charity."

In that same important statement Sister Crescentia also told how "I often saw Rev. Mother M. Marianne going around visiting the sick at night, ministering to them especially the poor, and doing many little kind acts which were not seen by any of the inmates." The lepers of Hawaii, too, both at Kakaako and on Molokai, received from her that same attention: "She would never allow any of the lepers to be sent away if they requested . . . to speak to her no matter how busy she was. She always had a kind word to say to them and they always went away happy and contented. During the first years on . . . Molokai, the inmates were very unruly, but by her kindness and charity she won them and made it easy for the rest of the Sisters."

Gibson, in a very real sense, was simply another needy and dependent old man to whom she wanted to be kind. But, in addition, he was also something much more than an ordinary tiresome demanding old man. After all, as President of the Board of Health, he was her employer. As prime minister he was the most important man in the kingdom. She would have been exceedingly irresponsible to her mission if she had refused to see him when he appeared at Kakaako. The opinions of too many contemporaries save her from the suspicion that she was being opportunistic in this respect: she was too generous and too kind to be merely calculating. But she was also wise enough to be sensible about problems over which she could impose some control. In this case, she did not wish to hurt the feelings of the prime minister, however boring she may have thought his company.

In her secret heart (if she permitted herself such a refuge), she may have thought his visits a botheration, his chatter a claim upon her precious time. Even though the arrival of Sister Leopoldina's group had lightened their burdens to some degree, she and all her companions were still very busy with hospital duties. Nor was she so healthy in body and in spirit that she did not feel the strain of having to do something that she really did not want to do. In the summer of 1886, for example, Gibson—with a jealous man's satisfaction, perhaps— recorded in his diary that she was "completely wearied out with Father Damien's talk—will be content when he returns to Molokai."

Gibson, to be sure, would have been easier to listen to than Damien. Courtly in manner, a gallant and cultivated man of many interests, Gibson had a personality and a way with words that made him pleasanter company by far than the monomaniacal Damien could be. He knew when to lighten a conversation, how to fetch a laugh. Rarely does such a man allow himself to be a bore. Mother Marianne and the sisters who sat with her when Gibson called might wish that they could be doing other things, but they could not have complained often of being bored.

So she put up with him, out of charity, if for no other motive, but probably out of policy as well. She who could feel compassion for lepers could spare some for him also. He, too, was sickened and beleaguered by enemies within and without. Accordingly, suppressing her wish to be left alone to do God's work, she greeted Gibson cheerfully—most of the time—when he appeared at Kakaako.

At least two other strong motives may have helped her to accept Gibson's visits. The first dealt with the things that must be rendered unto Caesar. Although no documents exist to prove this assertion, we can hardly believe that Bishop Hermann and Father Leonor did not thoroughly approve of the hospitality that Mother Marianne and her sister companions extended to the premier of the realm.

A strong second motive would have been Catholic concern for the welfare of Gibson's immortal soul. All of them, bishop, priest, and sisters alike, must have hoped that someday, given the right company and the proper exemplars, the premier would be gathered into the fold of Holy Catholic Church. The Franciscans, if Sister Leopoldina's statements can be taken as indications of their feelings, were both zealous and sincere about doing everything they could to bring to salvation all heretics and backsliders among their patients. Helping Gibson to attain that end would have appealed to them. Bishop Hermann and Father Leonor, while conceding the spiritual point, would also have considered his conversion a welcome safeguard for the Catholic mission if not a political triumph.

Yielding to mingled feelings of compassion, duty, concern, loyalty, and intelligent self interest, Mother Marianne received Gibson as an honored guest. Happily for her, as the months passed and she learned to appreciate his virtues, she seems to have developed an affection for him—the chaste affection of a nun for a generous and interesting layman.

As a number of entries in Gibson's diary indicate, she did not hesitate to direct to purposes of her own their conversations during some of those visits. She discussed plans to alter the arrangments at Kakaako, measures for elevating the morals of the patients, the founding and maintenance of Kapiolani Home, the disciplinary problems that cropped up among inmates of both hospital and Home, a request that he ask Dr. Arning "to make a professional visit to Sr Rosalia." Once, she even put him to work at "flogging" some of the Home's very naughty orphan girls, whose behavior disturbed everyone in the compound. Neither Gibson nor Mother Marianne enjoyed that experience, but the treatment was effective—as the sisters' teachings, threats, and entreaties had not been.

And, not always, but often enough to prevent him from forgetting, she reminded him that he must yet find some way to ensure the security of her mission in the islands.

She could not have seen in Gibson any threat to her virtue. She perceived that in this ancient ailing Don Quixote, somewhat mad perhaps but not at all frightening, she was presented with a man of illusions, full of dreams and delicate sensibilities, full of needs, of course, but not full of passion. Always he suffered, in the most exquisite fashion, from a "dainty spirit of melancholia." And ultimately he recognized the cause for his delectable misery: "Too sentimental for my years."

Being a prudent woman, and knowing the viciousness of gossip, Mother Marianne took care to safeguard the reputation of herself and the sisters: visits were brief when any lay person called at the convent, whether for social purposes or for business. And never did she receive visitors unless another sister was present with her. And always at least one sister accompanied Mother when she left Kakaako, to go into town upon shopping expeditions or for social purposes, such as calls upon the Episcopalian sisters who taught girls at St. Andrews Priory, or upon fern-gathering picnics with Mr. Gibson for guide and host.

Kind and considerate Mother Marianne might be toward Gibson, but she also demonstrated, gently but firmly, that she did not intend to be at his beck and call at all times. On many occasions she did not appear, but sent word that she was busy with patients, or indisposed, or at prayer, or otherwise preempted. In her stead younger sisters would receive him. At other times Gibson thought her moody and abrupt, if not actually unfriendly. Then he would go home "disappointed" or "dissatisfied" and, sulking like a spoiled child, would complain to his diary. Thus, on March 6, 1886, he wrote: "At Br H by 11 A.M. hoping for a happier mood—but not so. Kind interest of Sr Leopoldina." On October 23, 1886, an "Annoying event at Kakaako" upset him. "I am afraid I am becoming tiresome." Two days later he rejoiced: "all happy again. My misunderstanding." December 28 plunged him into gloom once more: "With M. a while this morning— occupied with her charges. I have but a secondary place."

He saw the truth that morning, as he must have guessed it during many another visit, but he fought against accepting so unwelcome a lesson. As with all egocentric people, the very fact that he could not satisfy his yearning—whatever *that* was—made him yearn all the more to gratify it. On Saturday January 8, 1887, he expressed clearly the nature of his craving at that stage in his game: "At Kakaako this P.M. M. the same tender friend as ever, who receives me affectionately— yet I need a companionship she cannot give me. But a strong and constant love binds me to her. What a pure, true, and noble character." Naturally, he being forever the romantic, he could not accept the truth: his hopes for the kind of "companionship" he envisioned rose and fell, much as do the lunar tides in response to the encircling moon. Some days he was "happy" and "delighted" to be with "my little girl." On others, as on February 19, 1887, he crept home dejected: "I lose hope of any close loving companionship. Will be appreciated only as a useful old friend."

What did he want of her? The answer to that question he himself did not discover at once. Apparently, in the beginning he aspired to the second-best kind of relationship: a chaste and virtuous companionship, a pure and platonic friendship, in which they would spend countless blissful hours together, in a meeting of souls. He seems to have clung to this impossible dream, or an approximation of it, for many months. And then, gradually, as he finally got around to facing some of the facts in her life, he fell back to the next practicable relationship he could imagine: that of the fond Victorian pater familias being doted upon by a houseful of daughters—of whom the most dutiful, attentive, affectionate, and beautiful was, of course, the eldest. The scenario he contrived for that fantasy would have enchanted a Louisa May Alcott!

At the last, when even this bubble was punctured—by the self-same eldest daughter, so determined to be her natural self—he retreated to the lowest level of all: the comfort of being just a friend of the family, a favorite one to be sure, fondly greeted, affectionately regarded, pleasantly entertained—but, alas, nothing more than "a useful old friend." Whatever he wanted, he did not get. Whatever life he dreamed of, to him it was both heaven and hell.

Much to his distress, the useful old friend continued to be intensely jealous of his beloved daughter to the very end. "Carried letters this P.M. to Convent," he noted on Sunday, March 20, 1887, just after the S. S. *Zealandia* brought in the latest shipment of mail from the United States. "One from Rev. J. Tuohy—name outside. Anxious to hear about him. M. did not wish to communicate particulars of his letter. Regret this. Had reason to believe that there was a peculiar interest between the two." Four days later the mystery still upset him: "The Tuohy letter sticks in my mind. I ought to ask her to explain all about it." But, of course, he did not ask for an explanation because he knew very well that he had no right to do so. And she, respecter of her patient's privacy, said not a word to relieve Gibson of his distress.

Gibson's nose for intrigue was half right in this case. A Father Tuohey, as records at St. Joseph's Hospital indicate (and spell), was one of those alcoholic priests whom Mother Marianne had befriended in Syracuse. He was admitted for treatment for "nervous fever," a euphemism in those days for the delirium tremens of chronic alcoholics. Apparently Mother Marianne helped to save Father Tuohey from his addiction, and the grateful man wrote to her long after she left Syracuse—thereby, quite unwittingly, thrusting yet another thorn into Gibson's sensitive flesh.

Fortunately, Gibson's sense of his own dignity, and Mother Marianne's generally cheerful courtesy, saved him from making a fool of himself in public. He confessed his weakness only to that accommodating diary—although quite likely in Mother Marianne's company his beseeching glances and tender tones hinted at sentiments too noble (or too painful) ever to be uttered in mere words.

Mother Marianne, unworldly as she may have been, must have received more than one clue that he, whether acting the part of the sighing suitor or that of Victorian patriarch (complete with judgments and exactions), sought from her concessions that she would not give. How did she respond to him, then, how did she handle him, this demanding smitten man?

Neither she nor any of the sisters left any direct words that would help to answer these questions. Gibson's diary, which tells only his side of the story, must be our primary source of information. But the portrait he presents of her there is detailed enough. She solved the problems and she managed him by being her natural sensible self. At first she gave him no more time than she could afford, no more attention than he warranted. Yet, gradually, in her too a change of attitude seems to have taken place: out of respect for the premier and compassion for the ailing aging man, grew a liking for Gibson as a person in himself. "I have never in all my life met a man like him," she said in a tribute to him after he was dead; and her opinion was shared by all the Franciscans at Kakaako and Wailuku.

She gave Gibson what time she could spare from more demanding occupations, the attentions of thoughtfulness and speech that he gratefully accepted and called "tender" or "affectionate" or, on two visits, "a cherry." By this term he meant, in the slang of his youth, an occasion both entertaining and delightful. Although at times he thought her moody and withdrawn, she was not insensitive to his dependence upon her. When she knew that he was depressed, because of illness or political setbacks or "misunderstandings" with herself, she called him on the telephone, to give him a few words of cheer. She invited him to lunch at the convent, not too often, but frequently enough to please him. Once in a while he took tea there on a quiet afternoon. She commented upon his appearance, when the caprine beard and those poetical locks needed trimming, or the long rumpled frock coat required cleaning and pressing. She, together with all the sisters, responded with exclamations of admiration whenever he showed up in full court uniform, bedecked with gold braid, flourishing a plumed tricorn, to display his splendors like the vainest of peacocks.

If, indeed, he was a lapsed Catholic, Mother Marianne must have conversed earnestly with him about the perils threatening his immortal soul if he did not forfend them by returning to the Church. Sometimes she helped to relieve the more superficial of his body's ailments. One day she and Sister Crescentia "syringed out" an ear canal that had given him much pain during the weekend. And she, or one of the younger sisters, often sent a cheerful little note to thank him for a gift delivered at the convent, or wishing him well on a birthday, congratulating a social success, commiserating in times of political loss. Unlike him, she showed no signs of jealousy—and that annoyed him too. Early in 1886, whether in desperation or in friendliness, she encouraged him to write to Mary Tanner of London, a woman he had met in Paris in 1854, and with whom he still corresponded sporadically. "I do not like it," he said flatly of her recommendation that he should write to that friend from out of his past.

Mother Marianne and her companions were good to him, just as a flock of daughters will be good to an affectionate father they do not fear. In moments of clarity, he told his diary that he knew he would never be anything more.

And he, content to count those blessings toward the last, accepted at last the role of honorary father to this bevy of engaging daughters. Including the special one, the eldest, with whom, for a while, he thought he'd been in love.

Toward the end, on March 12, 1887, this man of fantasies presented his "beloved daughter" with an extraordinary gift: a heavy gold ring. The wide band was engraved on both the outer surface and the inner in large letters deeply incised, according to the fashion of the time. Half of the outer inscription was suitably cryptic: Ruth-I-16, 17. The other half was much too obvious: a heart between the initials W and M. The inner inscription recorded a memorable date: March 12, 1885.

Gibson's diary for March 12, 1887—and the reference to the verses in the Book of Ruth—help to explain his reasons for giving Mother Marianne such an unwanted object: "The anniversary of my union with M.—our first cherry. Went to Kakaako in the afternoon. Took a ring as memento of the day." Here he wrote the inscriptions, even to the Valentine heart. "Fond commemoration of the day. So happy in this pure and exalted friendship."

Apparently he was celebrating the day, two years before, when she told him of her decision to remain with the mission in Hawaii, rather than return to Syracuse. The conversation in which she declared her decision he transmuted into a veritable union of souls. That first serious conversation, in which he and she probably talked freely for the first time about their hopes and plans for the mission, and about their need to cooperate in making it a success, had given him cause for joy and delight—to celebrate "a cherry" as he termed it.

A Catholic Commentary on Holy Scriptures confirms the relationship between "Ruth's decision" (the rubric for the entry) and the verses to which Gibson referred—and, characteristically, twisted to his own uses: "Entreat me not to leave thee, or to return from following after thee: for whither thou goest, I will go; and where thou lodgest, I will lodge: thy people shall be my people, and thy God my God. Where thou diest, will I die, and there will I be buried: the Lord do so to me, and more also, if aught but death part thee and me."

Alas for promises: his destiny would allow him to keep only one of those vows.

Of all the gifts Gibson brought to Kakaako, this ring might well have been the most embarrassing to Mother Marianne. It was personal, for her alone, not something to be shared by all the sisters, as were the baskets of food and the silver-plated tea service. It was much too worldly for a religious to wear, too costly for one who had taken the vow of poverty. Worst of all, it was the symbol of a marriage between a man and a woman. She must have gazed down upon it in amazement. Did he not know that she was a Bride of Christ—even though she wore no ring to proclaim that bond and covenant?

She could have refused the ring. But she did not. Thinking of the giver, not the gift, she would have thanked him quietly, professing a pleasure she did not feel, and accepting the ring, out of compassion, just to please him. Perhaps she wore it briefly, during that commemorative visit. Probably she did no more than look at it, lying in its velvet nest, the while she explained, gravely and honestly, how their Rule did not permit Franciscan sisters to wear such ornaments.

Needless to say, she never wore the ring at any other time: it has remained in its box ever since March 12, 1887. Two jewelers who examined it in 1978 stated that the golden band is still as clean and unscratched as it was on the day it left the goldsmith's hands. Later, when Gibson was dead, she could have thrown it away, or sold it, or given it to some one else, such as a leper bride in Kalaupapa. But she kept it, without embarrassment or guilt, in memory of the giver. Today it rests in the Archives of the Motherhouse in Syracuse, along with the few other objects that friends and admirers gave her during a long lifetime: a silver thimble, few holy cards endorsed by friends, a pair of small religious pictures for her tiny desk, and a miniature bronze Pieta set upon an alabaster base. Those were her personal possessions, after a passage of eighty years in this world of vanities and illusions.

Gibson's diary presents a virtual graph of the poor man's foolish hopes and utter disappointment. Depending upon their humors, people who read it may feel sorry for the old man, or surprised, or caustic, possibly even scornful. But anyone who reads it cannot fail to realize that, from beginning to end, it is a witness to the virtue of Mother Marianne, the woman Gibson loved but did not win.

His regard for her introduces the supremest irony of all into her history. She who destroyed or suppressed or avoided all mention of herself as a person, who fled from journalists, disliked being photographed, and wanted only to be "unnoticed and unknown" so that she would be free to "do good," became the helpless victim of Gibson's delight in attention, in show, in publicity, and in sentimentality. Yet, if Gibson, with only one eye fastened upon history, had not brought reporters and photographers to Kapiolani Home, we today would know nothing about the appearance of the place or of the sisters who served there. And if Gibson had not kept his little diary, we would know nothing at all about the unexpected part Mother Marianne played in the life and imagination of that complex man, that other and most powerful instrument of God's will in her life.

NOTES on Chapter XII

1. *The Diaries of Walter Murray Gibson, 1886, 1887,* edited by Gwynn Barrett and Jacob Adler, which were published in 1973, "are the only surviving part of a record that he kept for several years." Mrs. Kathleen D. Mellen, author of *An Island Kingdom Passes* and other works, told Mr. Barrett that Gibson's granddaughter, Mrs. Rachel Wescoatt (who had loaned her all the diaries) came to her home and destroyed four of the diary books (presumably those covering 1882–1885) by burning them in Mrs. Mellen's fireplace.

2. The service, consisting of a teapot, a sugar bowl, and a water pitcher, is preserved at the Motherhouse in Syracuse. The faces of the teapot and sugarbowl are engraved with graceful designs featuring Hawaiian fern fronds, delicate flowers, a cross, and the legend "Convent of St. Francis." Although the water pitcher does not match the tea set in either design or engraving, it was made by the same company.

3. Gibson "died a Catholic": (a) "Last Days," Editors of *The Diaries of Walter Murray Gibson, 1886, 1887,* p. 181; (b) *Pacific Commercial Advertiser,* "The Last Sad

Rites," February 20, 1888; (c) *Daily Bulletin*, "The Late W. M. Gibson," February 20, 1888.

4. Father J. Tuohy: (a) Register of St. Joseph's Hospital, Syracuse, New York, Entry No. 410. Residence is given as "transient" and age as "34." Dates of hospitalization were August 15, 1871 to September 22, 1871. Although his surname is spelled Tuohey in the hospital register, that is no doubt an error. Later references to him in *Diaries of Walter Murray Gibson, 1886, 1887*, and in Mother Marianne's Journal of 1900 have the spelling as Tuohy. (None of the very few references to him in Mother Marianne's Journal gives any more information than the date of receiving or sending a letter). (b) Sadlier's *Catholic Directory* 1876, listed Rev. Jas. Tuohy at St. Paul's Church, Macomb, Ill.; (c) According to *The Historical Sketch of St. Paul's Parish* 1854–1954, Father James Tuohy was appointed pastor in 1875. "He was transferred to Lincoln, Ill., in 1877 and remained there till his death. He built the rectory and school at St. Patrick's, Lincoln, and took care of the out-mission at Elkhart."

Chapter XIII

"ADVANCE ON THE ROAD OF PERFECTION"

GIBSON WAS NOT the only visitor who came to inspect the Branch Hospital or to be entertained in the Convent of St. Francis. A few Calvinist ladies, prompted by conscience or husbands or pastors or curiosity, came to call. Most wanted only to be sociable, having allowed a profound respect for the Franciscans to displace earlier prejudices toward benighted Papists. A few arrived under the illusion that they might offer their services as assistants in caring for the lepers. The social calls, confined to tea and conversation in the parlor, and perhaps including a tour of Kapiolani Home, were more successful. A short excursion through the hospital yard, a single viewing of those hundreds of lepers, scared every prospective volunteer out of her wits and out the gate, forever. Sister Leopoldina was rather amused by their weakness. So was Mother Marianne, "Maybe it will do some good." she told Sister Leopoldina, with more than a hint of humor. "Perhaps they can convert our gamblers. . . ." Except for Olinda Gomes and her younger sister Leopoldina (who helped with the housekeeping for a while), not one lay person, whether Catholic, Protestant, Mormon, or pagan, ever volunteered to assist the sisters in their work.

According to Sister Leopoldina, some of those same ladies who, during visits to the convent would "so friendly express so much love and admiration for what she was doing," would not recognize Mother Marianne if they happened to meet in town, "but pass her with high heads, and turned up nose." Certain other women among Honolulu's social leaders, who never went near Kakaako, scolded Gibson for allowing the sisters "to go around through Honolulu and [said] they should not be allowed to go in the stores. Although I never could blame anyone for feeling that way, yet I pitted poor Mother."

In this section of her chronicle, Sister Leopoldina presents Gibson in yet another role: as the sisters' champion against attackers they themselves could never meet. He "tried in every way to atone for their ignorance and he did everything that could be done to make life pleasant for us, although he knew it added greatly to the rage and bitterness of his enemies. . . . There were many narrow minded bigots in Honolulu at that time not that Mother had to suffer much from them but poor Mr. Gibson it seemed all their malice must rest on him." Nonetheless, honest Sister Leopoldina added, "there were also many very broad minded people who were Mother's friends to the end, even among the protestant missionaries their were some of them who were very kind to us."

Inquisitive naval officers from warships visiting Honolulu strolled through the compound, to see people afflicted with this ghastly disease. Sometimes the officers wished merely to satisfy morbid curiosity. Others, surgeons aboard ships from the United States, European countries, or Japan, were interested in learning something about leprosy and the ways in which the Kingdom of Hawaii took care of its victims. In general, the physicians managed to survive the exposure without mishap. Most of the other officers turned and fled. They, too, gave Sister Leopoldina some quiet amusement. She rather enjoyed conducting visitors through the hospital. They compensated, in a way, for the lack of holidays: in three years in Honolulu, she left the hospital at Kakaako only three times. And she never realized that, to visitors, her own young beauty, in that charnel-house, moving amid those very metaphors for corruption and death, made the contrast too terrible for ordinary men and women to bear.

Bishop Alfred Willis of the Episcopal Church, or one of his vicars, held an occasional service for their communicants in the shared church. Presumably Anglican prelates, Catholic priests, and Mormon elders not only preached in the chapel but also entered the hospital wards when called, if only to take the last rites to dying patients. Congregationalist pastors did not have to do so, at least in 1885 and most of 1886: Reverend J. Kauwa, one of their native converts and ordained ministers, was an inmate, always on call.

Bishop Hermann seldom visited Kakaako. If he needed to communicate with Mother Marianne by means other than the telephone (which kept no secrets from other listeners on the common line), he sent messages with Father Leonor or Father Evrard. For conferences about important problems, Mother Marianne waited upon him in the chancery adjoining the cathedral on Fort Street. Once, however, he sought her out at Kakaako, to talk about a matter of great concern.

Every now and then the king, or the queen, or both Their Majesties together, drove into the hospital yard, asking to speak to their afflicted people. Always the queen shed tears, the king looked sad. And always they spoke bravely to the patients, and gave their aloha and mahalo, love and thanks, to the sisters.

In general, however, clean people stayed away from Kakaako. Their dread of leprosy seemed to invest the whole neighborhood with a sense of danger, of lurking evil, all the more malignant because its cause was unseen.

The Franciscans, therefore, lived most of the time in a social emptiness, in an isolation that needed no high fence to mark its boundaries. Their patients kept them from feeling lonely, their work did not allow them time to be bored. Nonetheless, the difference to every sense between this new setting in which they served and the old ones in which they had grown up must have weighed heavily upon their spirits. Certainly, during their first years in Hawaii they must have suffered from the conditions that psychologists of this century have termed "culture shock." Some, like Sister Charles, never got over being homesick. Even Mother Marianne, in letters to Mother Bernardina, spoke of "the problems of being away from home."

Into that forlorn place at Kakaako Gibson's coach would enter, like that of Cinderella's godmother, bringing gifts from him to brighten the hospital or the convent. Often it carried him as well, ostensibly to discuss Board of Health business, actually to refresh his spirit as he chatted with Mother Marianne and her companions. In Gibson's visits the sisters would have found almost the only intellectual stimulation that Honolulu could offer them—and that their Rule and Constitutions could permit. At home in America, in any convent to which they might have been assigned, no Mother Superior would ever have allowed such worldly intrusions as Gibson represented. But in Honolulu Provincial Commissionary Mother Marianne felt that circumstances warranted her relaxing the Rule to some extent: she understood how much her companions needed some innocent relief from the mortifications of flesh and spirit that awaited them without end, in the palisaded prison they shared with lepers.

For a few days in the summer of 1886 the sisters took care of a most special guest. Father Damien arrived from Molokai on July 11, and they put him up in two large rooms adjoining the gatehouse—on the lepers' side of the fence.

Since 1882 he had been noticing premonitory signs of the disease in himself. Even earlier he had guessed that the infection was taking hold of the body he neglected to safeguard in any way. In January 1885, when the Priest to the Lepers made one of his hurried trips to Honolulu, Dr. George Trousseau and Dr. Eduard Arning confirmed Damien's suspicion. Their tests showed that the peroneal nerve in Damien's left leg and foot had been destroyed by the leprosy.

Father Leonor, as Vice Provincial, exiled the Leper Priest to Kalawao, and forbade him ever again to leave the Settlement. Bishop Hermann, remembering the provisions of the law, agreed with Father Leonor's decree.

Despite his superiors' strong opposition, in July 1886 Father Damien came again to Honolulu. Through the intercession of Dr. Arthur Mouritz, physician at Kalawao, he had gained Bishop Hermann's permission to visit the Branch Hospital. Damien wanted to try "the Goto treatment," a new kind of therapy that Gibson had arranged to introduce from Japan. He wanted to see how it worked, Damien declared, both for the possible relief of his own symptoms and to learn if the treatment might help his hundreds of fellow lepers at Kalawao. Damien was not such a fool as to throw away his life needlessly, if proper treatment could save it for further years of dedication to his people.

The Franciscan sisters too were very much interested in the possible benefits of Dr. Masanao Goto's treatment. It "increases our work," Mother Marianne wrote about this time to Mother Bernardina, "but we do it cheerfully when we see such a good effect. Several patients are so much improved that the Doctor thinks of discharging them soon— which is something quite unheard of in the history of leprosy."

Mother Marianne herself and another sister prepared the rooms for Damien, making him, as she promised, "more comfortable here than he has been for the last [thirteen] years" at Kalawao. One room served as his oratory, where he could say Mass every morning; the other, Sister Leopoldina remembered, they furnished "nicely, cheerful rugs, a nice white bed, and new [mosquito] netting, a center table. One of the Sisters served his meals in a room attached to the office. It was very sad to see the young Priest so disfigured his hands neck and face a deep purplish red, his ears so red and enlarged that they were hanging nearly to his shoulder and his nose twice its natural size and great leper lumps on his lips and face, his eyes were heavy and red but he was cheerful and happy. . . . Of course he did not come to the girls home nor to the Convent."

Gibson, almost as irritated as Father Leonor, fretted about Damien's having broken the law—and about much else besides. In his diary for July 11, the day Damien arrived at Kakaako, Gibson wrote: "He is a confirmed leper—was advised not to come—but was determined to visit the Sisters. I begin to doubt the genuineness of his religious devotion." This criticism comes strangely from the very man who had praised Damien's religious devotion in 1873, when first he went to live at Kalawao, and in doing so had drawn the world's attention to the brave young priest. The sneer reveals the depth of Gibson's jealousy of the holy man who drew Mother Marianne's attention away from his possessive self.

He would not have been well pleased when he telephoned to Mother Marianne, to complain about Damien's insistence upon visiting Honolulu. According to testimony from Olinda Gomes, taken in 1938 (by when she had been Sister Mary Elizabeth for forty-seven years), Mother Marianne told Mr. Gibson: "Send him here. We will take care of him. Do not do anything that can hurt his feelings. He has suffered more than anyone can imagine."

Despite such exemplary Christian charity, Gibson's jealousy mounted with each new day. Early the next morning he dashed down to Kakaako. "S. M. and Sisters touched by the misfortunes of the 'noble priest'—are deeply moved. I doubt not the genuineness of the charity of S M^s noble heart."

These fierce contenders for Mother Marianne's time and sympathy saw each other on Tuesday, the thirteenth—not, by any means, for the first time in their lives. "I sent Father Damien some wine & many things for his use and comfort." Fondness for Damien had nothing to do with that act of coldest charity. "S. M. rewarded me with tender thanks. I called on Father D.—and still have some misgivings—he talks too much."

In the opinion of some people, the Leper Priest had always been bumptious, garrulous, and opinionated. "Dirty" and "bigoted" too, certain Calvinists said. Not to mention high-handed and pugnacious, whenever a problem aroused his disregard for tender temperaments, such as martinet Vice Provincials possessed, or slothful bureaucrats at the Board of Health, even Vicars Apostolic and ministers of state. In 1886, not yet felled by his sickness, and quite possibly highly excited in his belief that God had blessed him with the boon of leprosy, Damien seems to have been more talkative than ever. Gibson (whose own skills of tongue should have taught him better) and others (who could not have known better) blamed Damien's floods of talk upon his self-esteem, inflated beyond decency by the adulation that Britons and Americans had been offering him ever since they learned that he had contracted leprosy. Perhaps he did suffer from such immodesty, but people who knew him well, including several physicians, never accused him of that fault. A more likely explanation can be found in his simple pleasure at being among people he could talk to about things and plans with which leprosy patients could never be acquainted. He, too, was human; and even twenty-two years after having left Belgium he still suffered from homesickness, loneliness, and culture shock. The Franciscan sisters must have been the first white women of education and sensibility with whom he could talk freely since he left his parents' home near Tremeloo, to enter the Sacred Hearts Seminary in Louvain.

And he had so much to tell the sisters! So much information to pass on to them, in his growing conviction that so much must yet be done for his beloved lepers in the short time that was left to him, in his growing certainty that these gentle sisters must be the ones to take his place at Kalawao when he was gone.

Gibson, Hawaii's other champion talker, couldn't get a word in edgewise. He sulked. And Mother Marianne found herself, as Gibson noted with considerable satisfaction, "completely wearied out with Father Damien's talk." If, indeed, she said it, this is the closest thing to an unkind remark that can be found in all the records about her.

On the other hand, Sister Leopoldina was profoundly moved by her very brief visit with Damien in his hospital room: "The first words he said, were Sister you are coming to Molokai you will soon be there. I dropped on my knees to receive his blessing and then I rushed away I could not trust myself for the minuet I looked at that young Priest in such a frightful condition the tears rushed to my eyes and . . . were beyond my control. and I was ashamed to have him see me cry, so I rushed to the chapel my place of consolation for there I could place all my treasures in the bleeding Heart of our loving Saviour. . . ."

Fortunately for Gibson, if not for the sisters, Father Damien decided to return to Kalawao much sooner than anyone expected—and far too soon to have gained any benefit from the Goto treatment. This typically Japanese regimen required a patient to steep himself twice a day for at least an hour each time, and for at least thirty successive days, in a tub filled with a very hot infusion of certain herbs and mineral salts. In addition, he had to swallow what Damien called "one dram of small pills" after each meal. Physicians of the Goto family had been employing this method in Japan for several generations, and claimed that a significant number of their leprous patients had been cured of the disease or, at worst, relieved of its more distressing symptoms for considerable periods of time. Father Damien would not submit to this slow therapy, this long detention at Kakaako. Although, as he wrote later to Father Bousquet in Paris, Damien saw in the Goto regimen "the dawn of hope for the poor exiled lepers of Molokai," after five days at Kakaako he'd had enough of its immobilizing and declared that he must "go home to Kalawao, where I belong." He left the Branch Hospital on the night of Friday, July 16.

Gibson's schedule sent him to Kalawao aboard the same little steamer. He went as President of the Board of Health, as well as a minister of the Crown, to inspect the Settlement and to talk with its inmates. A legislative committee of five members, appointed "to look into conditions at Molokai," sailed aboard the same ship. Gibson anticipated many complaints from the patients. Therefore, "the King by my request called on Father Damien" at Kakaako that Friday morning.

During the public hearing at Kalawao, the patients confirmed Gibson's worst expectations and presented a great number of complaints. He invoked the sacred names of the only two men the lepers respected: "Yesterday His Majesty the King called on Father Damien," he informed those aroused constituents. "This was not only a mark of His Majesty's respect for the man who has given his life for you, but also shows His Majesty's deep interest in your welfare." Neither the information nor the logic impressed the patients. They wanted deeds, not more promises. "An unsatisfactory reception by lepers," the President of the Board of Health admitted to his diary on July 17. An explanation for their intransigence came easily to mind: "—I feel that they have been prompted by the Opposition from Honolulu."

The subjects of Damien's conversations with Mother Marianne in Honolulu are not known. According to Sister Leopoldina, Mother Marianne talked often with him "during the week." Probably he dwelled upon two of his greatest worries: the need for someone to take care of "the orphan children" at Kalawao, and his hope that she would send a few Franciscan sisters to the Settlement, to serve as nurses to the blind, the bed-ridden, the mad, and the dying.

For thirteen years he alone had been doing all this—and more. He attended the sick in their beds and dressed the sores of those who could walk to his dispensary. He buried the dead in coffins made with his own hands, lowered into graves his strong arms had dug. He was priest, confessor, consoler, and counsellor to hundreds of patients, not only to those of his faith. He was the conscience of the Settlement, its powerful persuader and unofficial mayor, its most famous citizen and its foremost forfeit. He knew now that, with the mark of Molokai imprinted into his flesh, death would come soon to claim him, long before his work was done. He did not fear death. He worried only about what the neglect of bureaucrats, the indifference of the clean people of this world, might do to his beloved lepers.

And so he talked at Mother Marianne, endlessly, harrowingly, exhaustingly, trying to tell her, with all the words that only he and she shared, how much remained for her to do, how much the lepers of Kalawao would need the sisters' care when he was gone.

He wearied her mind, perhaps. But she heard his message.

On November 8, 1886, three years to the day since the Franciscans arrived in Honolulu, Gibson delivered to Mother Marianne the document that they believed would ensure her mission's security in the islands. Why he waited three full years before he did so is a question that adds another mystery to the enigma of Gibson. Possibly he just liked to remember anniversaries with grand gestures. He may have felt that he must wait for the right moment in the kingdom's political affairs. He may have needed time to think of a reliable procedure. Or he may have guessed that his years of political power were nearing their end: as the kingdom's shrewdest politician he could see that soon his adversaries would win a majority of seats in the legislature and the king would be required to appoint a new cabinet agreeable to the victors.

Gibson might be philosophical about being forced out of office: endings, like beginnings, are the very essence of politics. He looked forward to an honorable retirement, he told himself. He could convince himself, at times, that he welcomed the leisure to enjoy good books, good foods, and choice company. His own weariness of spirit and ailing body warned him that the time was near when he should depart gracefully from office. In the hectic pace his many interests imposed upon him, he did not realize how sick he was, nor guess how little time remained to him. His diary indicates that he felt ill almost without relief, not only with the nagging weakness attributable to chronic tuberculosis, but also with lesser ailments which, being more acute, drew more of his attention. An earache, an inflamed eye, a succession of sore throats, disturbances of the bowels, colds, headaches: one after the other, sometimes one atop the others, they plagued him, interfering with work and pleasure, adding to his gloom about shifty politicians, ungrateful lepers, criticizing citizens, countless obstacles in managing the affairs of the kingdom, a naive king, a scheming female blackmailer, and, above all, an independent, uncapturable Mother Marianne. His ailments, varied as they were, seem to have been genuine, not imagined, although of course psychic distresses may have helped to prepare his body for those assorted infections. That gaunt and ravaged body was failing him fast. In 1886 he looked much older than his sixty-three years warranted. In his plans for the future the one possibility he did not contemplate was death come too soon.

Despite sicknesses persistent enough to break lesser men, he did not betray his promise to protect the Franciscan mission. As part of the strategy, he drew up a petition for Mother Marianne to submit to the Minister of the Interior. She signed and presented the memorial on November 5, 1886. A short document, it identified herself as "the Mother Superior of the Third Franciscan Order at Honolulu . . . created for benevolent and charitable purposes and especially for the care of indigent sick." The petition requested a charter of incorporation to enable the Order "to acquire . . . real property in its corporate name . . . and to accept . . . gifts and bequests" that would "assist said order in its work of charity." The usual rights, privileges, powers, and immunities of an eleemosynary institution are requested, and the promise is made to act only in accordance with the laws of the kingdom.

The next day the Minister of the Interior (a Gibson man) presented both the petition and a Proposed Charter of Incorporation to the weekly meeting of the King's Privy Council. Gibson's diary recorded the event: "my anxiety to have considered a charter for my Sisters of Charity. Passed the Council." He hurried to Mother Marianne with the good news: "a happy hour at Kakaako."

Monday, November 8, brought another "very happy day . . . got the charter for the Franciscan Sisters all completed. Took it to Kakaako—a delightful afternoon. Commemoration of the 'Landing of the Sisters.'" Earlier on that memorable day he paid the Chief Clerk of the Department of the Interior the ten-dollar fee for the charter, and found the time to write to Sister Bonaventure in Wailuku, hailing the anniversary of the arrival of "that precious pioneer band of Charity—and the precious volunteers who followed them—God bless them all. I love and honor them with my whole soul. [Today] I accomplished a long desired purpose in behalf of your Sisters. . . . You are now a corporate institution of benevolence."

With this charter in hand, Mother Marianne felt safer. So also did Bishop Hermann and—when, ultimately, they heard about it in Syracuse—Father Provincial Lesen and Mother Provincial Delphina.

Their trust in such a document—and in the integrity of governments and the continuity of the law—although naive was not misplaced. The time had not yet arrived when "civilized" men could tear up such scraps of paper, and governments could reject at will the commitments of their precursors. The charter to "the Third Order of St. Francis" issued in 1886 by King Kalakaua's Privy Council was honored by subsequent rulers of the islands, even by those of Gibson's adversaries who drove him from power.

All Hawaii celebrated King Kalakaua's fiftieth birthday on November 16, 1886, and for many days before and after that special date.

Mother Marianne, knowing that the Franciscans must express their respect for a ruler they liked as a person, sent the only gift she could afford—a letter. She composed it herself, and wrote it out in her own hand. After invoking God's blessing upon the king, she concluded: "We bring no gift to present to Your Majesty except our service in behalf of your suffering People whose infirmity we bear in our hearts, and we pray our Divine Lord, Who healed the lepers while on earth, that health and life will prevail among the Hawaiian People to the honor and glory of Your Majesty's reign."

The King, alas, would celebrate no more birthdays in such grand style. Almost all the other gifts he received in the ceremonies of hookupu would be consumed, given away, or, after the monarchy came to an end, were sold, stolen, appropriated, or otherwise dispersed. By 1900 not one of them was to be found in Iolani Palace. But a copy survives of the fragile letter Mother Marianne sent to him. And so do the fruits of her labors in behalf of his suffering people whose infirmity the Franciscans bore in their hearts.

Two more sisters came to join the mission on November 17, 1886. Sister Cyrilla Erhard and Sister Irene Schorp went from the German Church in Lyons, France, to the novitiate in Syracuse, New York. The German Church's director, a missionary priest who admired the work the Franciscans were doing in Hawaii, encouraged the two young women to go to Mother Marianne's assistance. She kept both newcomers at Kakaako while they adjusted to Hawaiian weather and ways. Two years later she assigned Sister Cyrilla to help Sister Bonaventure at Malulani Hospital on Maui. Sister Irene stayed in Honolulu at the Receiving Station, as "a general helper."

Mother Marianne wrote to Mother Delphina about the charter sometime during the month of November 1886, and expressed the hope that it would "satisfy good Father Provincial as he was anxious that something should be done on the part of the Government to give us a more solid basis here. . . ." But, surprisingly, she did not send official notice to Father Lesen himself until more than three months later. Her letter of February 16, 1887, implies the reason for that unusual delay: apparently Gibson suggested that she wait until she learned from Syracuse whether Lesen had been replaced as Provincial Minister. When, finally, word came that he had been reelected to that office, Mother Marianne wrote to tell him how "we all uttered a fervent thanks be to God . . . that you . . . were again chosen to guide and direct the little ship of the Order . . . even good Mr. Gibson joined us; he, poor man, was, if possible, even more troubled and anxious than we were. his great fear was that, if you would retire . . . we would surely be called home. this thought made him suffer, and he was really miserable."

A study of Gibson's diary for the month of January alone shows that he was indeed most miserable with a variety of ailments, ranging from sleeplessness to prolonged attacks of coughing caused by the "catarrh" in his chest. And, as a kind of groundnote to those sicknesses more or less defined, he fretted about Mother Marianne: her moods and humors, the amount of attention she accorded him, the demands that other people made upon her time, and, most troubling of all, her own state of health. She, too, suffered from severe bouts of sickness, which so prostrated her at times that she could not leave her room. In truth, if Sister Leopoldina can be believed, Mother Marianne—"so fragile and delicate, suffering most of the time"—was ailing as much as Gibson, and as were several of her companions, notably Sister Charles and Sister Rosalia. Gibson's well-being can be correlated with variations in the warmth of his reception at Kakaako. But always he returned to the hospital compound, like a faithful dog to his home, with high hopes for "a happy hour with M," and bearing parcels of wine or fruits or expensive comestibles for all the sisters to enjoy.

"I cannot begin to tell you all he does for us," Mother Marianne informed Father Lesen, "if we were his own children he could not do more; to have us firmly established here, seems the one aim of his life." With this by way of introduction, she told Father Lesen about the charter of incorporation, a copy of which Gibson had sent to him "by the last mail," on February 12.

In his letter accompanying the copy of the charter, Gibson assured Father Lesen that "the King and Queen and all classes rejoice in the establishment of these ladies in the country as a blessing to the Hawaiian people." For himself, he added, "I am proud to have had a part in bringing them here, and I shall deem it one of the most important duties of my life, and the most exalted of its pleasures, to continue to assist in the establishment and comfortable settlement of the Franciscan Sisterhood in the Kingdom."

Mother Marianne, in her letter, went on to tell Father Lesen about some of Gibson's grand plans for the Franciscans and, in doing so, disclosed her own concerns about the mission's future in the islands: "he is working hard to found a Home for the Order in Honolulu, and as he is a man of means and of great influence he will succeed if God spare his life. Please pray for him, that he may realize the one wish of his heart, to erect a Convent, Chapel, and General Hospital in the latter he hopes to spend his last days and to be cared for by the Sisters."

Gibson had broached this "long cherished purpose" to Bishop Hermann, Father Leonor, and Father Clement Evrard when they made their New Year's call upon him. He talked about it with Mother Marianne the next day, certainly not for the first time, when he saw her at Kakaako. The chapel, he declared, would be dedicated to St. Lucy, "in memory of my Mother." Gibson noted that Bishop Hermann approved the plan and "spoke enthusiastically" about it to Mother Marianne and Sister Crescentia when they called upon His Lordship on January 3. "He evidently understands that the Sisters are to cooperate in the matter. That is my fondest hope—to cooperate with M."

"He is 63 years of age," Mother Marianne warned Father Lesen, "and has been troubled for more than ten years with an ugly cough and some bronchial effection." (Princess Liliuokalani, who saw Gibson at the great birthday party held for him on January 17, 1887, wrote in her diary: "he looks all of 78. Poor Gibson, why should they put all the blame upon him only?")

"Now," continued Mother Marianne, "he only prayes that God in His Mercy will let him live to carry out his plans for us, he wishes to see us firmly established and have ample means provided for our future support, so we may stand independent of the government in case of a change of Administration."

Nonetheless, after thirty-seven months of service at Kakaako she no longer worried about the fickleness of politicians: "the people here are just as devoted to the Sisters as they are in America, I mean the foreign Population, and as for the poor natives, they love the Sisters too well, to ever cause them any trouble. I hope and trust that all I have written will go to show that all the fears entertained about the Mission are without ground. I will repeat again what I have often said before—If we, with the help of God, do our duty and work for His honor and Glory no one will interfere with us."

In the next paragraph of this confident letter she reported upon the state of her mission. The burdens in Honolulu actually had been lightened: whereas in 1883 the sisters took care of 200 or more lepers at Kakaako, in February 1887 they ministered to only about a hundred patients. The Kapiolani Home housed only thirteen healthy girls, far less than the number it had been built to accommodate. And now, with the arrival of Sister Cyrilla and Sister Irene four months earlier, she had more workers than she really needed for the patients at Kakaako.

Toward the middle of this long communication she told Father Lesen about the next phase in her plans: ". . . You will remember that from the first it was expected that some of us would sooner or later go to Molokai to care for the suffering people there. . . . The Board of Health hesitated to ask us to go because our number was too small, but lately it has become a serious question whether we should go. And on the 9th of Feb. His Lordship the Good Bishop called here, to speak about this Serious question, and to ascertain how we felt about going. To Him it would be a great consolation to have the Sisters there, for the sake of our holy Religion, though he would not press us to go, but simply asked how we felt about going to so isolated a place. I told him exactly how the Sisters felt, that they, or rather *we,* were not only willing, but *anxious* to go and care for the poor outcasts."

The Good Bishop, the Kind Mr. Gibson, and the Worrying Provincial Minister in Syracuse: neither singly nor together could they stay this determined woman from her destined goal. From the very beginning, when first she heard Father Leonor speak about the plight of Hawaii's lepers, she had hoped in her heart that, someday, she would minister to the outcasts of Molokai. But not until this day, February 16, 1887, did she state her purpose so clearly for Father Lesen to see.

After their meeting Bishop Hermann "left with a light heart, and has since then held Council with Mr. Gibson." In his diary for Monday, February 14, Gibson revealed His Lordship's motives: "—he fears that certain English protestant Sisters will come to care for lepers at Molokai Settlement. So he wants Mother Marianne and her Sisters to go at once and occupy the field."

For suffering Gibson, the wound dealt to his very core by the bishop was hurtful enough. But then, all unwittingly, Mother Marianne heaped salt upon the bleeding heart: "The Mother said to me today that she was ready and cheerful to go to Molokai. This expression annoyed me—that she was cheerful to go—but I suppose a mere expression of willingness." The poor deluded egotist! Only five days earlier he had written: "a happy hour with M. this forenoon. . . . Talking about establishment of Sisters at Kalawao— ready—but *we will never be separated.*" The italics are his: he made that promise to himself because he wanted her to be near, always, to comfort him with daughterly affection, to dwell in the new convent he would provide, to pray for him in the Chapel of St. Lucy he would endow, above all, to care for him as he lay dying in the hospital he would build. . . .

The day after he made that vow, on February 10, Gibson began transforming the yard of the prospective new convent: he set a man "at making some ornamental figures with corals and sods in the grounds of my Queen St. house. Where I hope to establish Mother Marianne and her Sisters in a Home of their own—"

Mother Marianne realized that she herself should not go to Molokai before Gibson's great plans were achieved in Honolulu. "Now assignments are being made for four Sisters to go to [Molokai]," she told Father Lesen. "It may be two or three Months before things will be ready, as a home will have to be built and other arrangements made for the Sisters' comfort before Mr. Gibson will allow them to go. . . . You may rest assured that nothing will be left undone to make them feel satisfied. Not in any one of our houses in America are the Sisters so well cared for as here. The Board of Health supplies us with the best of food, and our house is furnished with everything that even the most exacting can wish for. We want for nothing but the Grace of God to perform our duties well, and to advance on the road of perfection according to the Spirit of our Order, and the Just Will of our Superiors in America. . . ."

About this time, too, she wrote to Mother Bernardina. In one paragraph of this letter, apparently intended to cheer her revered patroness, she also revealed a bit of her human self: "I too, sometimes look at the dark side, not long, however. I think life is all too short to spend any part of it in worry and anxiety. My heart is sad when I think of the great distance that separates us, how much I would enjoy to see you all again. In thought I make you a call every day. I wish I could make my presence felt each time. . . ."

In Syracuse Father Lesen thought he could relax at last. He wrote to Gibson on April 1, 1887, to express "my sincere thanks. . . . I am really delighted of being satisfied, by what you have done, and by [what] good Moth. Marianne writes, that our Sisters in the Islands are under the paternal care of an influencial, cleaver and self sacrificing man, who will throw all his power for the establishement of the Sisters in a condition as to be above any possible contingency."

NOTES on Chapter XIII

1. Interdenominational services in Chapel at Kakaako: *Board of Health Report*, 1886, pp. 9–10.
2. Facts about Father Damien's leprosy: (a) diagnosis and treatment: Mouritz, 1916: *Path of the Destroyer*, p. 379, and Mouritz, 1943: *A Brief World History of Leprosy*, p. 85; (b) received as patient at Kakaako by Mother Marianne: Testimony of Sister Elizabeth Gomes, 1938, in *Beatificationis et Canonizationis Servi Dei Damiani De Veuster*, pp. 74–75.
3. Petition for Charter of Incorporation for Third Franciscan Order at Honolulu: Archives of Hawaii at Honolulu (AH).
4. Details of coming of two sisters to Hawaii in 1886: (a) *Record of Professed Sisters 1860–1918*, pp. 238–39; (b) editors of *The Diaries of Walter Murray Gibson, 1886, 1887*, p. 86.
5. The letter written to Syracuse by Mother Marianne in November 1886 regarding the Charter of Incorporation has no salutation, but internal evidence suggests that it is sent to the head of the community, Mother Delphine.
6. It is possible that Mother Marianne waited for Gibson in his official capacity as Minister of Foreign Affairs to obtain "a true copy of the Charter of Incorporation of 'Third Franciscan Order'" and send it to Father Lesen before she herself notified him that she had received the original. The copy, which bears an official seal, was certified by L. Aholo, Minister of the Interior, on February 5, 1887. It lies in AS, along with Gibson's letter which accompanied it.
7. Diary of Queen Liliuokalani: January 16, 1887, Archives of Hawaii.

Chapter XIV

"A PICTURE OF THE NOTHINGNESS OF THIS WORLD."

THE END TO Gibson's career came with a rush, sooner than anyone expected. And it brought with it the very contingency that Father Lesen thought he need fear no longer.

The crowning affront to businessmen's patience and probity was dealt in May 1887 when—unknown to Gibson, apparently—either King Kalakaua himself or a bungling agent promised the license to import opium to two competing Chinese bidders, and accepted huge bribes from both. This duplicity in all directions gave the honorable opposition the immediate cause they had been awaiting. Honolulu's Puritans—who, to begin with, strongly opposed the sale of opium by any one under any circumstances—rose in righteous wrath against "corrupt" Kalakaua and his government. Firing words rather than bullets, "The Committee of Thirteen," leaders of the rebels, threatened Kalakaua with armed violence if he did not "reform" both himself and his ministries. Kalakaua, no hero, and helpless in any case, made concessions: on June 28 he dismissed his entire cabinet, including Gibson, the man the rebels most wanted to eliminate. But the king did not appoint a new cabinet, nor did he dismiss Gibson from other offices he held.

While the businessmen-lawyers dictated to the king, the mob took care of Gibson, the prime villain and sole object of their fury. The mob's ringleaders forgot Gibson's many good deeds in their rage over his foolish mistakes; and they chose not to remember his tolerance and good humor when now they could unloose upon him their spite.

The Old Fox anticipated what was about to happen, hoping all the while that he was being too imaginative. First in his thoughts, after his own safety, were the Sisters of St. Francis. During the four weeks in which the crisis boiled to its climax, he managed to visit the hospital several times, "to relieve [the sisters'] alarm in respect to the state of the community," as he put it. On Thursday, June 30, "threats of violence" were being delivered to him at his home, and he heard "rumors of armed mob, purpose to lynch me." He requested a detachment of guards from the Committee of Thirteen. The guards appeared—but were withdrawn a few hours later. Thereafter he remained alone in his silent house, threatened with being "shot down if I attempt to leave." A journalist from America, "faithful" Dan Lyons, guarded him during that dark night. The presence of "the mob around my house," beyond loyal and alert Dan Lyons, gave him an "anxious night."

On the morning of the last day in June, fearing the worst, he went to Kakaako to say farewell to the Franciscans. Sister Leopoldina described the sad event: ". . . when the doorbell rang one morning I was surprised that it should be Mr. Gibson as he always drives to the office in the leper yard, I can ever see him as he was standing when I opened the door, his bowed white head drooping shoulders and long snow white beard, when he came in he said in his usual kind manner, I have come to say good by! I had heard so little about his trouble that I had scarcely given it a thought, so I said quite indiferntly are you going away? No he said, my enemies are now about to carry out their threats of the last three years so many times they have threatened me but now they tell me this is my last day. What are they going to do? I cannot tell you Sister but I know they will not spare me they are so furious. what can it all be about I said if you were in the States they would at least give you a trial. They can not give me a trial he said, as they havent any thing to bring against me. they only want to get rid of me. Many times they ordered me to resigne and I would have resigned but the King gave me the office and he will not alow me to resigine. I do not mind much only it was my great desire to see the Sisters well established in all the Islands and especially the Bishop Home in Molokai but I leave it all in the hands of God I only crave His mercy. . . .

"I hurried away to call Mother and the Sisters. In a few minuets we were all gathered around him and we were grieved as he had been so kind and fatherly to us, His words were not many but very kind, You need not fear he said, I do not think they will be unkind to the Sisters it is only me they are after. And Mother, he said, if they are in any way offensive take your Sisters home do not remain to be illtreated by them. After saying good by he left us, and that was the last time he came to see us."

The mob came for him at his home at about 10 o'clock in the

morning of July 1. His son-in-law, Fred Hayselden, happened to be
there, so they took him along as well. Gibson, in the finest tradition of
heroes imperiled, chewed and swallowed a note of encouragement he'd
just received from Mother Marianne.

The vigilantes, younger and more hot-tempered rebels than were
the Committee of Thirteen, slung a hangman's noose around the neck
of each captive and dragged the pair through the streets to a hot and
dusty warehouse near the waterfront. As they went they urged bystand-
ers to come and see the criminals hanged. Possibly the ruffians were
only pretending, in order to scare Gibson into agreeing to leave the
islands, possibly they meant what they said. Subsequent interpretations of that morning's events differ.

Sister Leopoldina's chronicle presents Mother Marianne's recounting of the day's developments as told to her by an eye-witness,
"the Lady in the bakery:" "Oh Mother she said in a sad voice and her
eyes filling with tears . . . to see the good old gentleman draged and
pushed along through the dusty streets his hands tide behind him and
his drooping shoulders and bowed white head in the blazing
sun . . . they reached the warehouses down at the whorf where they
had prepared a gallous, dangeling over a highbeam was a stout new
rope under the rope was an old soap box he was nearly fainting
they . . . ordered him to sit there on that box until evening and if he
was ready to surrender they would save his life and send him away on a
sailing vessel, and if he would not surrender he must die there was the
rope and he knew what would happen . . . of course the poor man could
not acknowledge a crime he was not guilty of. What a picture of the
nothingness of this world Mr. Gibson who had been an honored friend
of the King and Queen, whose company Royal ladies craved, was now
forsed to remain sitting on a soap box from morning til night in the
heavy unclean air of the warehouse expecting and knowing that wicket
men were longing to take his life. . . ."

During the terrifying day Gibson prayed: "he called on that ever
loving heart [for] what consolation peace and strength and courage he
received." Perhaps, as Mother Marianne would write to Mother Bernardina on May 5, 1888, all these trials were being visited upon him
"to purify his heart for heaven." Sister Leopoldina even found for him
a Veronica, a young Calvinist woman who dared to comfort him: "a
daughter of one of his enemies came to him in tears with delightful
refreshments she expressed great grief that her father should have

anything to do with such shameful and cruel worke she begged him not to tell that she had been there."

Fortunately for Gibson and Hayselden, the Committee of Thirteen wanted no lynchings upon their consciences, and intervened in time. So, also, did "foreign representatives," members of the diplomatic corps who knew a better Gibson than the vigilantes imagined. The diplomats advised Kalakaua to comply with all the rebels' demands. These included the forming of a new cabinet composed of trustworthy members under an acceptable premier, and the removal of Walter Murray Gibson from all positions whatsoever. The king yielded, the rebellion triumphed. Without firing a shot or drawing a knife, the dissidents achieved what thereafter they liked to call "the Bloodless Revolution of 1887." Kalakaua and his supporters, however, remembering those rifles smuggled in by the Hawaiian League, preferred to call it "the Bayonet Revolution of 1887."

Gibson and Hayselden, reprieved by orders from above, were "marched back to the house." Within a few hours soldiers reappeared, to arrest them on charges of embezzlement. "Marched to the police station. Allowed to return home and remain there under guard."

With that entry, scrawled in his diary after a harrowing day, Gibson ended his account of the revolution. But his tribulations were not yet ended. On July 5 the town seethed with rumors that he and Kalakaua planned a coup. A detail of guardsmen whisked Gibson and Hayselden off to Oahu Prison, at the western edge of town. There they remained for six days, while auditors examined the accounts of the ministries and boards which Gibson had headed, as well as his private books and papers, looking for proof that the pair had misused or stolen public funds. "they were shamless enough to come to the leper Receiving Station," Sister Leopoldina remembered, "and asked Mother where and how she got our hourse and carriage and the harness and even inquired about the hay the hourse had eat." Horse, carriage and harness, Mother Marianne proved in copies of letters of thanks she herself had written, were gifts from Mr. Claus Spreckels. Although the Committee of Thirteen may have hated the Robber Baron from California almost as much as they hated Gibson, they were forced to acknowledge that Board of Health funds had not been misappropriated to buy a conveyance—or hay—for the Franciscan sisters.

To the accusers' surprise and chagrin, no proof of embezzlement could be found. On the evening of July 11 the Reform Government's attorney-general dropped the charges against Gibson and Hayselden. Rather sheepishly, the rebels freed the fallen premier and his son-in-law.

Nevertheless, the reformers could not feel safe as long as Gibson remained in Hawaii. They did not realize how sick he was, else they might have allowed him to stay in the islands, banished to his ranch on Lanai, or under house arrest in Honolulu. Taking no chances, they made him leave, "for the sake of his health." They could afford to ignore Fred Hayselden: to them he had always been nothing more than Gibson's "flunkey."

Their own flunkeys arranged passage for Gibson aboard the first available vessel, the barkentine *J. D. Spreckels,* sailing for San Francisco on July 12—the very next day.

The entry in his diary for that day, the last he would write in Hawaii, is sensible, restrained, mercifully free of sentimentality. He could face reality when he must. "A good night's rest. The dear Mother and Sr. Crescentia came before breakfast. Gift of prayer book and a comforter, and the assurance of faithful, pure affection." No sobs of anguish, no lamentations of woe, found their way into this day's entry. He seems to have recognized that, for him, and for his "beloved daughter" too, an era had come to an end.

Later in the morning Talula and Fred Hayselden, with their children, came to say goodbye. So also did a very few true friends, daring the disapproval of the new regime. Neither the king nor the queen was among those few: not yet could they do what their hearts bade them feel.

At 12:15 a carriage not his own came to fetch him. Accompanied only by a single friend, Paul Neumann—the kingdom's attorney-general when he had been its prime minister and the lawyer he had asked to defend him against the charges of embezzlement—he was driven to the pier. "Found the *J. D. Spreckels* ready to sail—got on board. The moorings cast loose—and the barkentine with sails all set sped on her way. . . ."

The *Spreckels* delivered Gibson to San Francisco on August 6, a chill and foggy day. He caught a cold almost immediately, and by the following Wednesday felt so miserable that he left his room in the Occidental Hotel and asked to be admitted to St. Mary's Hospital. Not by accident, it was the same institution at which Mother Marianne and three sisters stayed in October 1883, on their journey to Honolulu from Syracuse. The Sisters of Mercy installed him in a private room on a corner of the third floor. Its windows gave him a grand view of South Beach, parts of the city stretching to the east, and the great beautiful bay beyond. Although he recovered from the cold in a week or so, his chronic pulmonary complaint made him want to stay longer in that pleasant place. He liked the Sisters of Mercy, the doctors, the comforts, the view, and apparently everyone there liked him. Later, the Mother Superior would say that she had never met "a more estimable man nor one so well informed on every subject."

And there he stayed, more as the hospital's star guest, at first, than as a patient. He received visitors from San Francisco and from Hawaii when they came to the Bay City. Since the day he arrived reporters sought him out for interviews, asking especially for his opinions about the new regime in Hawaii. An article in the San Francisco *Chronicle* for August 7, 1887, reported that "he thought the constitution [of 1887] was a good one in the main." He even found nice things to say about the members of the new cabinet: they were "all gentlemen for whom he had the highest respect and esteem. They all called upon him while he was under arrest and were most polite and kind. . . . They are safe, conservative men and he thinks the kingdom will prosper under their guidance." By December, however, he changed his mind, calling the reformers "plunderers," and hinting broadly that, before long, the king would call him back to Honolulu, to manage the government as before.

He wrote numerous letters to loved ones left behind in Honolulu, and eagerly awaited communications they sent him. King Kalakaua, still being watched, corresponded with him in secret, entrusting his letters to couriers such as a physician serving aboard one of the Spreckels line's passenger ships. And Mother Marianne, as Gibson's diary indicates, wrote to him about once a month, giving him good cheer for a few days after each letter arrived.

When he felt well, and the weather was pleasant, he went for walks through the streets near the hospital, rode the cars on Market Street, or hired a carriage to drive him to the Presidio, or Golden Gate Park, or the Sutro Gardens. In the city's fine stores he bought gifts for children and grandchildren in Honolulu, for good friends anywhere, even for the Novitiate of the Sisters of Mercy in San Francisco. Apparently unworried about money, he continued his habit of finding ways to please the friends he remembered with affection or new acquaintances being discovered in the hospital. Interested in everything, he never had time to be bored or lonesome.

He soon knew the Sisters of Mercy as friends, to tease the young ones and revere the older. They confirmed the opinions he had gained earlier, in Honolulu, with the Franciscan sisters, that Catholic religious women are the best of all women. He went to Mass regularly, attended "the most impressive ceremony" when two novices professed their vows, visited "the Novitiate parlor, and the Home for aged and infirm females," because he was "very much interested in seeing and talking with the curious old characters" in that institution. He, looking into his own mirror, never saw himself as old or infirm, and certainly not as a curious old character. He drove to East Oakland, to visit the Convent of Our Lady of Lourdes. "Beautiful Sister M. Nolasco—in charge," he noted, slipping easily into his habit of admiring women both beautiful and unattainable. In those visits to convents, those conversations with sisters clad in a different habit, those gifts to professed nuns and novices, he was establishing again the pattern of his days in Honolulu—and finding comfort in it, although not to the same degree that he had discovered in the convent at Kakaako.

Something was lacking in San Francisco—and the lack seems to have been in himself, not in the Sisters of Mercy. The entries in his diary are sober, matter of fact, simply and dully factual. The anguish, the need, the fire has gone out of the man: he is sick now, tired, old, and "sensible" at last.

In the hospital room, on November 17, he received "news of the verdict against me in the breach of promise suit. . . . It only rouses me up—stiffens me—and does not depress me." In Honolulu a jury very sympathetic to Mrs. St. Clair awarded her damages of $10,000. When Gibson's attorney threatened to appeal the verdict, the aggrieved widow's lawyer hastened to settle the case out of court for $8,000. The editors of Gibson's journal added a sardonic footnote to his entry for November 17: "It is highly doubtful, in the political climate of the time, that the case was fairly tried. No [native] Hawaiians served on the jury, and some jurymen were members of the Hawaiian league!"

The mail from Hawaii brought something very much more pleasing on November 18: "a sweet, noble, inspiring letter from M. It has made me feel very happy."

No doubt it did, for a day or two. And yet, and yet. . . . The old romantic, the uncorrectible poseur, was proving once again the universal truth: "out of sight, out of mind." Except when her infrequent letters arrived, he never mentions Mother Marianne in his diary. He has not forgotten her, but he has forgotten the need he felt for her while he lived in Honolulu. Gone are the sighings, the yearnings, all the tender sentiments about his "beloved child" that studded the diary while he wrote in Honolulu. In San Francisco he has found other interests, new attractions—and, rising now, as in a crescendo, the most insistent of all distractions, pain and suffering.

Death was closing in. Even so, he refused to believe that he was not going to win this contesting, that he would not be returning to the Hawaii he loved. On the last day of 1887, after suffering through most of December from several complicating ailments, he wrote the final entry in his diary: "The improvement in my health continues. Very cold."

During the first week of 1888 he actually did seem to be improving. He decided to go off to a photographer's studio, to have his portrait taken. Despite the fog and the low temperatures, he did not wear an overcoat during part of that venture out of the warm hospital and, in consequence, caught a cold.

Pneumonia and pleurisy affected the lungs already rotted by tuberculosis. He died suddenly at 4:30 P.M. on Saturday, January 21. Two friends from the islands who were with him said that "the last intelligible word" he spoke was "Hawaii."

NOTES on Chapter XIV

1. Details of the Hawaiian Revolution: (a) *Diaries of Walter Murray Gibson 1886, 1887*, pp. 160–64; (b) *Pacific Commercial Advertiser*, "Nolle Prosequi," July 13, 1887.
2. Gibson in San Francisco: *Diaries of Walter Murray Gibson 1886, 1887*, pp. 164–77.
3. Details in breach of promise suit: (a) *Pacific Commercial Advertiser*, "Breach of Promise Suit," May 23, 1887; (b) *Daily Bulletin*, St. Clair vs. Gibson, October 28 and 29; (c) *Pacific Commercial Advertiser*, "$10,000 Damages for Breach of Promise," October 28, 1887; (d) *Hawaiian Gazette*, "Verdict in Breach of Promise Suit," November 1, 1887.
4. Description of "Last Days" of Gibson: editors of *Diaries . . . 1886, 1887*, pp. 178–82; *Pacific Commercial Advertiser*, "W. M. Gibson Talks," January 11, 1888, an interview about matters in Hawaii.

Chapter XV

"SO ISOLATED A PLACE"

WITH GIBSON'S downfall and departure went all his grandiose plans for endowing the Franciscan sisters in Honolulu with property of their own. Nothing ever came of that dream: the Chapel of St. Lucy, the hospital in which he would spend his last years, were never built. The house on Queen Street, with the sod and coral decorations in its front yard, was never given to the Franciscans. Once again, the man of many promisings failed to keep his word. Political adversaries might have predicted as much, but not the sisters at Kakaako.

No one can say now why he did not keep his promises to Mother Marianne. He could have arranged by mail the legal business of transferring his Queen Street property to the sisters, but he did not do so. Perhaps he wanted to lie low for a while, lest the Reform Government seize his possessions. Possibly Talula and her husband in Honolulu opposed so generous a disposition of land and a home that they thought he should bequeath to them. Possibly he was forced to sell or mortgage the place in order to pay $8,000 to the Widow St. Clair, who had won her breach of promise suit. He may have been overwhelmed by debts: although at his death Honolulu's newspapers referred to him as "a millionaire," and he certainly lived like one during the months he spent at St. Mary's Hospital, in fact he had mortgaged most of his holdings, including the ranch on Lanai, to William G. Irwin, a partner of Claus Spreckels. Payment upon those notes fell due in April 1887—and they too undoubtedly added to his load of anxieties and exacerbations during the critical months before his fall. Then, too, Mother Marianne may have told him, in letters sent to San Francisco, that the Franciscans did not need the property as yet and that he should keep it until his own future was clear. Probably the best reason of all for postponing any action lay in his insuperable optimism: he expected to return to Honolulu in good health, and with ample time for fulfilling his promises—and claiming their rewards. As it does for so many dreamers, Death took him by surprise.

In any event, with Gibson's death the Franciscan sisters were left without the "ample means" that would have made them, as Mother Marianne had assured Father Lesen, "independent of government."

Despite this disappointment, Mother Marianne offered Gibson a generous eulogy. On May 5, 1888, in a letter to Mother Bernardina, she wrote: "—indeed, our loss is great—he was to us like a kind loving mother. It seemed that nothing gave him pleasure but to serve and wait on us. I have never in all my life met a man like him. We miss him. He had great plans laid out what all he was going to do for us if God spared his life. God alone knows the *why* of all the great trials and mean persecutions He allowed to come over this poor man, perhaps to purify his heart for Heaven—With a bleeding heart, I must say God's will be done in all things."

The Franciscans were much troubled by the revolution. The fall of their employer and protector, and "the change in government" others had worried over in theory, had come in hard fact, sooner and more ruthlessly than anyone had considered possible. After the "Puritans" seized power the Franciscan mission faced the worst contingency that Father Lesen could ever have imagined. Bishop Hermann, conferring with Father Leonor, watched and waited. What purges would those dour Calvinists order throughout the kingdom? Which employees in the country's expensive bureaucracy would they dismiss? Would they send the Franciscans back to America? Or, even more shamefully, would the heretics replace the Papists they were supposed to despise with the Episcopalian nuns from England they were thought to favor? As they waited and wondered, fearing the worst, the Franciscans at Kakaako remembered Gibson's last words to Mother Marianne, uttered on the morning of his sad farewell: "if they are in any way offensive, take your sisters home."

In truth, the revolution did not endanger the sisters at all. Either the Calvinists were not as antagonistic to Catholics as Bishop Hermann and Father Leonor imagined or the reformers knew very well how indispensable were the treasures they had been given in the Franciscans. Even the most bigoted heretic muttered not a word about "shipping those Catholic nuns back to America." Mother Marianne's faith in the security of her mission, so recently expressed in her letter to Father Lesen, was sustained. "To our surprise," wrote Sister Leopoldina in her narrative, "Mr. Gibson's enemies were very nice to us, and seemed ready and willing to help Mother all they could, at least they did not show any bitterness or hard feeling toward us, and they seemed to appreciate all Mother's work."

The Reform Government appointed Dr. Nathaniel B. Emerson to replace Gibson as president of the Board of Health. Dr. Emerson, born in the islands, a son of American Congregationalist missionaries and a graduate of schools in New England, was as thoroughbred a Calvinist as were most of the revolutionaries of 1887. But he was also a man both gentle and sensible. He conveyed to Mother Marianne the Board of Health's respects, and the request that the sisters continue their work as before.

Interested in economizing though they might be, the new men in power could not simply ignore the enormous problems caused by leprosy. They slashed many appropriations of which they did not approve, the King's Privy Purse most brutally of all (from $50,000 a biennium to $5,000); but, to their credit, they did not reduce the budget that Gibson's administration had gained for the Board of Health. The new rulers did adopt a more determined attitude toward combatting the disease and segregating its victims: they resolved to identify as soon as possible every leper in the kingdom and to isolate all cases at the Settlement on Molokai. As part of their program to enforce segregation they discussed the feasibility of closing the Branch Hospital at Kakaako and of moving all its inmates to Kalawao. Doing so, the thrifty pointed out, would cost the government a huge sum. But, the civic-minded argued, doing so would rid them of that fetid place, so close to the city, a blot upon the landscape, a danger to all clean citizens.

The Board of Health's attitude toward leprosy was expressed very clearly in a letter of reprimand its secretary addressed to Father Conrardy, an itinerant (and uninvited) Catholic priest who had gone to help Father Damien at the Leper Settlement in the spring of 1888. Father Conrardy, even more outspoken than Father Damien had ever been, had written a sensational letter to a friend in America, in which he accused the Hawaiian government of not doing enough to take care of its unfortunate lepers. That helpful correspondent turned the letter over to a newspaper reporter—and the subsequent publicity touched the fretting sensibilities of the Reform Government. Father Conrardy must be scolded, they said, and so delegated the task to W. G. Ashley, secretary to the new Board of Health. "Leprosy is our bane, the nation's ulcer," pronounced Ashley, on September 10, 1888, "and good taste at least demands that it should not be needlessly exposed to the gaze of the world."

The project of accommodating all those lepers, both recognized and anticipated, called for the construction of new facilities at Kalawao. And, moreover, separating the females from the males—for Calvinists and Catholics agreed upon observing the rules of Christian morality as they agreed upon nothing else—would complicate arrangements and add to the costs. Even though some of Kakaako's cottages could be dismantled and shipped across the channel to Molokai, they would not provide enough shelter for all patients. The Board of Health's *Report for 1890,* for example, estimated that in 1889 at least 644 lepers still lived "at large" with families or friends. In that same year 1,213 segregated lepers lived as wards of the government—"the maximum number reached" in all the years since the Settlement was founded in 1865. The Reform Government meant business: no one ever accused its employees of laxity toward transporting lepers, or of accepting bribes to delay their banishment to Molokai.

As a matter of fact, as Father Leonor wrote to Father Damien on October 17, 1887, "The manner in which they treat the lepers and the Sisters at Kakaako is not encouraging. . . . These gentlemen of the new Board of Health . . . seem to want to get rid of all the sick as soon as possible . . . Without saying a word to the Mother, [Dr. Trousseau] arrives at the gates, calls the lepers by name, makes them set out and leave; as summarily as that I am told; and if anyone utters a word of complaint they will be happy to have worried us and will try to do yet more of this. . . ." In short, Calvinist efficiency did not allow much opportunity for introducing sweetness and light into their relationships with either lepers or Franciscans.

A month later, writing to Father Bousquet on November 17, Bishop Hermann said: ". . . The situation of the Franciscan Sisters grows more and more painful because they seem to be a thorn in the eye of the new regime because of the hatred which the new regime bears for Mr. Gibson and the Catholic religion." Nonetheless, he concedes, the sisters have "many admirers, even among the Protestants, but no one bears them even the sympathy or courage to avenge them against the Calvinist hate made victorious after the revolution. This clique prefers to leave the poor sick in their misery rather than have them cared for by the Catholic Sisters called for by Mr. Gibson.

As they seem not to have a word to say against the Sisters they pretend to ignore them. We cannot tell what they are going to do next in their regard. . . ."

The reformers, pondering the expense of all those new facilities and the emptiness of the nation's treasury, solved their fiscal problem in a typically American way: they persuaded the wealthiest man in the kingdom to donate funds with which to construct a new facility. The philanthropist-select was Charles R. Bishop, a banker in Honolulu, and widower of Princess Bernice Pauahi, the last member of the Kamehameda dynasty, who died in 1884. On April 18, 1888 the Board of Health accepted Bishop's offer of $5,000 "to erect a home or houses . . . for women and girls" in the Leper Settlement. In return for this gift, the Board eventually attached his name to the new institution, calling it "the Bishop Home."

In her reminiscences, Sister Leopoldina wrote of the Home for Women and Girls as if Walter Murray Gibson had been the agent who convinced Charles Reed Bishop to contribute funds for its construction. But surely Sister Leopoldina's memory failed her in this accrediting of yet another good deed to her honored friend. Evidence does indicate that Gibson was planning to enlarge the facilities at Kalawao, including building a convent for the Franciscan sisters to be assigned there. But his relationships with Bishop, that quintessential banker and most glacial of Calvinists, were not so cordial that Gibson could have convinced him to part with a single American cent for any plan that he recommended. As prime minister and President of the Board of Health, Gibson simply added the costs of new construction to the budget proposed for the Leprosarium, and trusted to legislators to find the money to pay for them.

Much as he hated the very thought of sending any of his "daughters" to labor in that hell hole in Kalawao, Gibson reluctantly accepted the prospect that he must do so, eventually. On February 14, 1887, he actually sent Fred Hayselden over to the Settlement, to select a site for the Franciscans' convent. Sister Leopoldina described Hayselden's report to his father-in-law, somewhat as Gibson himself must have relayed it to the sisters: "he was silent and seemed sad and did not want to speak of the place. His face went white and he said with a dreadful shudder Father that is no place to send them ladies! I wish you would never allow them to go there. I did not select any place for their home, nor I never would. I consider it a crime to allow those

Sisters to live in that filthy place. I shall never take part in it. It is not too late father. You can stop it if you will."

Gibson could only sigh, saying that "the king wishes the sisters to go and the sisters wish to go. It was for that he had the Sisters come to Hawaii. I would prevent it if I could, but what can I do?" When he told Mother Marianne what Hayselden had said "and his own feelings regarding the Sisters being buried in the leper Settlement Mother smiled and told him, We are not afraid. Please go ahead with the work and pay no attention to what anyone may say." Her cheerfulness about going to that "filthy place" only dismayed him all the more.

Bishop Hermann, too, did not like the thought of the Franciscans' going to Molokai—despite the fact that Father Damien had been crying for their help. In good time, His Lordship cautioned Damien on February 5, 1887, all in good time. The sisters were not sent to Molokai in the first place, he reminded the Leper Priest, simply because "there were not enough of them for such an undertaking. Besides they weren't called exclusively for the lepers. The official letter addressed to me and the one given to Father Leonor by the King speak only of caring for the diseased subjects who are (by implication) curable."

His Lordship continued: "The government has done everything without formally consulting me." Clearly he is referring to the government's presiding genius, Walter Murray Gibson. "Perhaps they should not have," conceded the bishop. "Since the government (the Board of Health) must incure all the expenses . . . and since the Sisters are there for them I remained cautious." He did not object, he said, to seeing the sisters assigned to Malulani Hospital on Maui and to Kapiolani Home for Girls at Kakaako. Then, he added, with a hint of pique, "They had new Sisters come to do something. Does the Government know what? I don't. If they want to send a certain number of them (Sisters) to Molokai I will not object to it provided the arrangements are made regularly and with the consent of the Mother Superior. By no means do I doubt that there is a lot of good to be done at your place. But it isn't so clear that this is feasible under the circumstances . . . the government will have to make very extensive arrangements with a lot of expenses. The Sisters are doing rather well in Kakaako chiefly by regularity and separation of the sexes. How to do this on Molokai without considerable changes in everything?"

His reluctance notwithstanding, Bishop Hermann told Father Damien that he would "speak about it to Mr. Gibson and to Mother

Marianne to see if there is something that can be done." The spur
behind this decision had come from Father Damien himself, in the
letter that the bishop is answering at such length. In response to
Damien's own impatient accusations that neither state nor church in
Hawaii was doing enough to take care of his lepers—charges that
infuriated Gibson and appalled the bishop—Father Damien reported to
his superior that Britain's Episcopalians were supposed to be marshal-
ling their sympathies and offering to send English nuns to care for the
lepers at Kalawao. That distant and rumored threat reinforced Bishop
Hermann's own sense of duty to his Apostolic Mission. He and Father
Leonor went to confer with Mother Marianne on February 9—and, as
Gibson's diary shows, provoked in the prime minister a fit of annoyance over Mother's cheerful reply to their inquiry.

Bishop Hermann, as he told Father Bousquet on February 15,
found Mother Marianne "very well disposed to send a colony of three
Sisters to Molokai to commence a small part of the work." She, His
Lordship, and Mr. Gibson soon "reached an agreement . . . which was
quite to the taste of the Minister." Nevertheless, Bishop Hermann
confided to his superior, he thought that the Settlement was too large a
place, with too many patients spread over too great an area, to gain
much benefit from only three Franciscans.

All those conversations, preliminary explorations, and exchanges
of letters came to naught with Gibson's fall, probably because he hoped
to put off the sisters' move as long as possible. The Bloodless Revolution imposed further delays. For almost a year after the coup the new
Board of Health pondered over the interrelated problems of Kakaako
and Kalawao. It dealt in typical fashion with a petition signed by more
than 300 inmates at Kalawao, asking that the Sisters of St. Francis be
permitted to come to the Settlement. The Board thought that it recognized Father Damien as the organizing force behind the petition, and
felt as disinclined to listen to him as had all its predecessors. It merely
referred the petition to R. W. Meyer, its resident agent on Molokai.
And Meyer simply dismissed the petition, telling the patients that the
Board was looking for male nurses, for "men who can be expected to
stand the hardships of the place." Meyer did not take refuge in a lie:
the Board of Health actually was exploring that possibility, by looking
for male nurses among residents of Honolulu. On December 16, 1887,
Dr. Emerson talked with Father Leonor about requesting Catholic lay
brothers from Europe, to serve as nurses at Kalawao. The gentlemen of

the Board shared with Bishop Hermann a strong dislike for the very idea of sending women of any provenance as nurses to lepers in that terrible place.

Meyer also felt very strongly that no women nurses should ever be assigned to the Leprosarium. "It is better that men go there," he reproved Damien in a letter written on December 10, 1887, probably in partial answer to that ill-fated petition. "I fear that you have rarely ever reflected on the position in which the poor Sisters of Kakaako would be placed if they really have to come to Kalawao." Nonetheless, he added, "if the Sisters greatly desire to go there I do not think that anyone would wish to oppose their coming. . . ." Father Leonor, Meyer admitted, did not oppose their wish, "but his tender heart makes him feel the isolation in which they would find themselves. . . ."

Mother Marianne herself made some stipulations. "The Mother Superior and the Sisters (who are not yet here in sufficient number) are very willing to accept the charge under acceptable conditions," Bishop Hermann wrote to Father Damien on April 28, 1888. "She says also that she will not write to Syracuse before receiving an official request from the authorities responsible. I think she has reason to be prudent because compliments are not a sufficient guarantee on the part of those personages who do not love the Catholic religion. I will not be surprised to see the Protestant women preferred or impossible conditions imposed on the Sisters. God is patient and we have to have patience and act with prudence in the camp of the enemy. . . ."

Finally, in the camp of the enemy, on June 15, 1888, the Board of Health reached a fateful decision: it would support "only one place of treatment," and that would be the settlement on Molokai. It would keep only "a receiving and shipping station in Honolulu." This would be established at Kalihi, a desolate, hot, and inconspicuous area west of Honolulu, far from the roving eyes of tourists and the disapproving gaze of townsfolk. "The buildings at Kakaako should be entirely removed."

In order to push the Board to this conclusion, Lorrin A. Thurston, Minister of the Interior and ex officio a member of the Board of Health, had engaged in some preliminary investigations of his own. Brilliant, aggressive, and ruthless, Thurston was the rebel most implacably antagonistic to both Gibson (whom he hated) and King Kalakaua (whom he despised). Of all the Calvinists in power, he was the one whom Catholics had the most reason to fear. On May 21, 1888, almost a year after his Committee of Thirteen had overthrown

Gibson, Thurston wrote to Mother Marianne—probably after he or someone he trusted had held exploratory conversations with a representative from Bishop Hermann's chancery.

Thurston's letter to Mother Marianne is direct and efficient, as might be expected from such a clear-thinking man, yet it is also very solicitous. Moreover, with one authoritative stroke it ended not only Mother Marianne's uncertainty but also Bishop Hermann's gloomiest surmisings. Its preamble suggests that Thurston knew very well how Mother Marianne felt about the need for sending some of her Franciscans to Molokai: "The fact is no doubt well known to you, that one of the greatest hardships at the . . . Leper Settlement, has been the lack of a proper separate residence for single women and girls." The home to be provided by Mr. Charles R. Bishop's generosity, he continued, will resolve part of the difficulty, but "will not accomplish its end unless it is well ordered and governed. From the self sacrificing example of yourself and the other sisters of your order who are now ministering to the lepers, the Government has been led to hope that others of your order might be willing to assume the charge of such a Home."

Like all the other men who made decisions affecting the lepers, Thurston too shared the misgivings about the role of women at Kalawao: "The duties to be discharged are of such a nature that I do not feel that I have the right to urge the matter upon you, or even to ask that any woman should devote herself to such work." Nonetheless, he presented her with facts that might help to push her toward a conclusion he rather anticipated: the number of women and girls needing care ("between 100 and 150"); the time when the Home would be ready for occupancy ("three or four months from now"); and his estimate ("which you are more competent to decide than I am") that six or eight sisters "would perhaps be the proper number."

He closed his "inquiry" with the promise that if any sisters of her order or of other orders "would be willing to undertake the charge of the proposed Home the Hawaiian Government will thankfully accept of their assistance, and will do all in its power to aid and assist them, and in every possible way ameliorate the discomforts and difficulties of their position."

"I will communicate the contents of Your Excellency's letter," Mother Marianne replied to Thurston on May 25, "to the Rt. Rev. Bishop who is our Superior in this country, and to the Superior of our Order in America, as we cannot without their respective consent and approval extend our work to Molokai." In saying this she was expressing the spirit of obedience, of course. But she was also being wary. The Revolution of 1887 had made her—and Bishop Hermann—extremely cautious about dealing with reformers. And Father Lesen's long silence, unbroken since she had written him about the charter on February 16, 1887, disturbed her.

Yet, characteristically, she did express her personal feelings to Thurston: "With regard to the Sisters, now here, the largest number, including myself, are cheerfully willing to undertake the work, and I am confident that other Sisters of our Order will cheerfully volunteer to come and join us." In the meantime, she finished, while awaiting the decision of her superiors "we will earnestly pray for the good God to inspire them to decide in favor of the poor unfortunate lepers."

Like Thurston, she planned ahead. Within that same week she wrote to Sister Bonaventure in Wailuku, instructing the sisters there to write to her their reactions to the possibility of being assigned to work on "the Leper Island." Only Sister Bonaventure, needed at Wailuku, was exempt from this order.

Each sister said she was willing to go—although some did not find the prospect attractive. Sister Benedicta, teaching the girls at St. Anthony's School, answered frankly: "I would like to fulfill your wishes and go. . . . I am very honest with you. I am afraid, I have heard so much about those poor people. I heard also that there are no rules and regulations. That everyone does as he pleases, but I trust in the good Lord. . . . So God's Will be done. It doesn't really matter to me if I remain here or go to Molokai. Please forgive me because I said so much."

Sister Ludovica, who had been stationed in Wailuku since 1885, wrote: "I leave myself in your hands if you send me I know it will be God's Will, but to say I want to go or to decide for myself I would be afraid. . . ." She feared that Molokai was not her vocation, and that—having just then recovered from an infection of the face—she "might be more apt to take the disease." Nevertheless, she ended, "what strength God has given me, I wish to use only in the plan and in the way He wants. These are my feelings, and my fears you know I will put aside at the thought of obedience."

Sister Renata opposed the mission to Molokai: "I am not in favor of the Sisters going there neither do I discourage those who are aspiring to go. If it is not a suitable place for any woman how can it be for the Sisters. Under the circumstances I feel sorry for you. The harvest is great and the laborers are few." But Sister Renata did not reject outright the possibility of going to Molokai, if Mother commanded her to do so.

Sister Cyrilla, in Wailuku since July 1887, said she had always wanted "to nurse the poor lepers. . . . Therefore, dear Mother, I am ready to go with God's grace whenever you call me."

Knowing that she could ask the opinions of the sisters at Kakaako whenever she needed to do so, Mother did not speak to them in May about the possible move to Molokai.

Putting together odd bits of conversation, snippets of correspondence, and observations upon the strange behavior of bureaucrats, all held together by generous infusions of hope, gossips in Honolulu and Kalaupapa came up with something pretty close to the truth. On May 17, 1888—eleven days before Lorrin Thurston addressed his inquiry to Mother Marianne, and months after Rudolph Meyer had told the inmates of Kalawao to forget their foolish petition to the Board of Health—Father Damien wrote to Father Daniel E. Hudson, a helpful colleague at the University of Notre Dame in Indiana, saying that the Franciscan sisters would be coming soon to Kalawao: "the location of their house will be selected in a few days by our kind agent Mr. R. W. Meyer and the work on the buildings at once begins."

Bureaucratic stirrings in Honolulu, after months of inactivity, encouraged him: "The Governement is making great improvements [at the Leper Settlement] such as — large water pipe" (to replace the inadequate line, only one inch in diameter, that Damien himself had installed several years before), "putting up new cottages—and for the 85 orphan boys under my guardianship y just recd lumber etc for a second large dormitory. . . ."

And Brother Joseph Dutton—a Catholic layman from America and "a repentant sinner" who simply arrived at Kalawao on July 29, 1886, uninvited and unannounced, saying that he'd come to help Father Damien—reported further developments. On July 11, 1888, he too wrote to Father Hudson, telling him that Meyer was supervising construction of "a series of houses . . . for the women and children—to be under the charge of the band of Franciscan sisters now at Kakaako . . . which is to be broken up and all sent here . . . though a portion may be retained there for a temporary 'receiving station.'"

Father Lesen and Bishop Hermann had not yet given their permission for the sisters to move to Molokai. The Board of Health did not decide officially to "abolish" the Branch Hospital at Kakaako until July

24. And yet, early in July carpenters were building the Bishop Home at Kalaupapa—and already the lepers "knew" that the Sisters of St. Francis were coming to live in that home. Everything was in motion—most especially the lepers' system of communication—but nothing really had been settled with respect to the Franciscans.

Mother Marianne, trying to anticipate the fate of her mission, whether at Kakaako or on Molokai, waited and waited to hear from Father Lesen. "You cannot imagine how keenly I feel this," she admitted to Mother Bernardina on May 5, 1888 (in the same letter in which she likened Gibson to "a kind, loving mother"). "I wonder he does do [this]. As Provincial of the Order he ought to take an interest in this mission and the Sisters working. We all came with a will to do good, and to work for God's honor and glory, which is sometimes hard. Pray for us please. I do the same for you."

She had worries enough at home, in the Convent of St. Francis at Kakaako. She herself was delicate in health "most of the time," as Sister Leopoldina noticed, although seldom allowing herself to remain in bed. Sister Rosalia—because either her body or her mind was ailing—could not always be counted upon to bear her share of the work. Sister Martha grew thinner and more wan with each passing month. And Sister Charles was failing rapidly and visibly. "The islands did not agree with her," Sister Leopoldina recalled, "and she was always pining for home." One day, while the King's Band, come to serenade the patients at Kakaako, was playing "Home, Sweet Home," Sister Leopoldina turned to Sister Charles, "to say isent that lovely? And to my surprise there was agony in her pale thin face, and tears were streaming from her lovely brown eyes. I do not think she would feel being away from home so much if she were strong and well but her health was continually failing and she was longing to return home."

Mother Marianne, out of compassion, decided to send her home and in July delegated Sister Bonaventure to accompany Sister Charles to Syracuse. She also appointed Sister Bonaventure to represent her at the triennial General Chapter to be held at the Motherhouse in August.

The General Chapter, the second to be convoked since Mother Marianne departed from Syracuse, met on August 16, with Father Lesen presiding. Toward the end of the day's session, Sister Bonaventure presented her report: "Everything is all right; the rules are all kept well, there is charity among the Sisters; they are healthy and respected by everyone. No intimacy with seculars and all the Sisters are satisfied to be in the Islands except one. The work is sometimes dangerous but if the Sisters are prudent and obedient to the Superior there will be no danger whatever."

The next morning's votations chose several officers of the community. Once again Mother Marianne was "canonically elected" the Commissary Provincial of the Sandwich Islands. On August 19 Father Lesen sent her formal notification of this reelection—but not a word else.

At Sister Bonaventure's request, the chapter discussed the matter of sending sisters to the Leprosarium on Molokai. "The question remains undecided," the minutes record. Sister Bonaventure (and through her Mother Marianne) was instructed "to write down all the points and to investigate from the government the conditions; if the conditions are favorable, that Island where the lepers are might be taken, if the conditions are not favorable, it is not to be accepted." Here sounds the voice of Father Lesen, serving also as recording secretary—and, as always, the vigilant protector of his charges. Gibson's fall, the Revolution of 1887, the rise of Hawaii's Calvinists to power, aroused again all his fears and all his instincts for prudence.

Despite so much uncertainty in Syracuse about the safety of the Franciscan venture in Hawaii, Sister Bonaventure brought two volunteers with her when she returned to Honolulu on October 28: Sister M. Antonia Brown and Sister M. Vincentia McCormick.

During the summer of 1888 Lorrin A. Thurston and his Board of Health resolved their remaining uncertainties about the future of the Franciscan sisters. They authorized construction of the Home for Women and Girls at Kalaupapa, considered a proposal from Honolulu's Episcopalian Bishop Alfred Willis "regarding nurses for lepers," and answered him that his "kind offer would be borne in mind for the future" inasmuch as "arrangements had been partially made . . . for a supply of nurses. . . ." The Board also gave great attention on August 20 to a letter from the Lord Bishop of Olba who asked "what the Board's intentions were, regarding the number and location of the Franciscan Sisters." Father Leonor represented His Lordship at that meeting of August 20, as he informed Father Damien later in the day. "Before the Sisters go to Molokai," he explained, "it is necessary that everything be written."

Both Bishop Hermann and Mother Marianne needed very much to learn what the Reform Government proposed to do about the Franciscan mission—for now, as never before, it seemed to be perched upon the brink of dismissal. Although the Board of Health may have reached its decisions, Mother Marianne and the bishop had no means of knowing what the reformers were thinking or intending. In this time of uncertainty Bishop Hermann bravely pushed for an answer.

After "sundry discussion," the Board decided that it "would want a Mother and at least 3 Sisters at the Leper Settlement for the present . . . 4 sisters at the Kapiolani Home and 3 Sisters at the Malulani Hospital in Wailuku. A total of 11, to be supplemented as cases may arise in the future. The Board providing suitable houses, board, and monthly allowance of $20 to each and every sister for private expenses. All necessities to be provided, as done in the past, at the hospitals."

Although the Board's secretary, W. G. Ashley, did not get around to conveying all this information in writing to Bishop Hermann until September 10, he—or someone else in authority—must have told His Lordship the details long before then. The bishop and Mother Marianne, assured at last of her mission's future, laid their plans accordingly. On September 10 Ashley also issued a permit to "Father Leonor and Sr. Marianne to land at the leper settlement and to depart therefrom."

In that important letter of September 10, Ashley presented in detail the conclusions that the Board of Health had reached on August 20. His tone is pleasant and generous. He attempts to cover all contingencies, even for defraying travel expenses of sisters coming to Hawaii in the future or returning to the United States. He reveals the Board's attitude in a sentence that mere official business did not require: "Recognizing and appreciating the self sacrifice made by the Sisters, in going to the Settlement, every effort will be made by the Board, to alleviate the situation." So generous a communication allayed immediately Catholic fears.

His Lordship replied soon afterwards: ". . . the terms and conditions proposed . . . are as a whole perfectly acceptable." He was "confident that the Sisters will be able to accept the care of the Home, without going against the conditions imposed by the founder." He was certain, too, that any questions that might crop up in the future—such as, for example, the number of sisters to be assigned to each establishment, or the appointment of a priest responsible for their spiritual direction in the Leprosarium "will find an easy solution by the good will of all concerned. . . ."

"Having fullest confidence in the honesty of the Board of Health,"

Bishop Hermann concluded, he would "recommend their request to the authorities (in America) on whom we depend for the supply of the necessary personnel; and I shall always be happy to cooperate with the said Board, whenever it may be desired."

Mother Marianne, after considering Ashley's letter of September 10, informed Bishop Hermann on September 15 that she was "satisfied with the terms and conditions and nothing remains for us to request in regard to temporal matters. I thank your Lordship sincerely for insisting upon having them given in writing." Her only needs now, she added, were "our spiritual wants . . . we stand in need of a prudent Priest (one free from leprosy) to guide and direct us and to Strengthen our Souls with the Holy Sacraments. I cannot accept the Mission until I have the assurance from Your Lordship that you will kindly supply this want, as you alone can."

Earlier in the year, as Bishop Hermann explained to Father Bousquet on July 29, Mother Marianne had "fully expressed to me her objections to having [Father Conrardy] for confessor for the Sisters." His Lordship could sympathize with her in that disinclination. Father Conrardy, an independent—and "imprudent"—Belgian priest (who did not belong to the Congregation of the Sacred Hearts) had come uninvited to Hawaii from the American Northwest. And now, Bishop Hermann groaned, he was exactly like "a fifth wheel on the wagon."

On Thursday, September 20, Mother Marianne made her first visit to the Leper Settlement. She went to see for herself the place about which so many terrible tales were told. She went to see if she should send any of her sister-companions into that hell hole, into that land of the living dead.

When she applied to the Board of Health for permission to visit the Leprosarium—and, just as important, for "permission to depart therefrom"—Dr. Nathaniel Emerson, the Board's president, responded with a gallantry that Gibson would have applauded. The account of Emerson's reply, and of the visit to the Leper Settlement, is presented in Sister Leopoldina's very colorful style, but her purpose is clear: she had a warm regard for Dr. Emerson. "He "was very kind and, said Mother you are indeed a brave woman to go there, but I shall not allow you to go alone I shall go with you."

He insisted upon accompanying her even though he suffered from two notable weaknesses. He got just as seasick as did Mother Marianne. And he lived in perpetual dread of leprosy. For a very short time, impelled by Christian dedication, he had served as physician in residence to the lepers at Kalawao. But he could not endure that experience, that *exposure* to unmitigated horror and insidious infection. He was so mortally afraid of catching the contagion that he would not go near the patients the government employed him to attend. Like other members of his profession who showed the same fear, he listened to patients' complaints from a distance, and filled jars with ointments for their sores or packets with pills for their pains, and set the medicines atop fence posts before his house, where the lepers could pick them up with their "sore bleeding hands." He and Father Damien represented the extremes of adaptation to the lepers that clean people made. But, as philosophers and psychiatrists understand, every extreme becomes a disease in itself. Damien, in time, became a leper. Emerson, in shorter time, became so morbid about the sickness that he fled from the very people who most needed his help. Almost all the patients at Kalawao either laughed at him for his cowardice or scorned him for his "hypocrisy." A few lepers liked him, Sister Leopoldina said, because he was "a true gentleman." That quality, the gentleness of a good man, served neither them nor him at Kalawao, but some lepers were kind because they saw themselves as he must have seen them.

On another "gray unpleasant evening," Mother Marianne, Olinda Gomes, and Dr. Emerson boarded "the dirty little steamer Lehua." Olinda Gomes—or Louisa, as the sisters had taken to calling her—accompanied Mother because no one else could be spared from duties at Kakaako. Apparently Dr. Emerson's presence spared Father Leonor the need to go. The weather was as foul as it could be, with strong winds and boisterous seas. Mother Marianne, who "was always seasick even before she would go on board any vessel," and Dr. Emerson succumbed before the *Lehua* emerged from the harbor. Dr. Emerson crept into a "little shelf bunk," one of the several moldy refuges that lined each side of "the dining room," and drew the sticky curtains across its front. Fortunately for Mother, the kind captain invited her to use his little cabin, the only comfortable and private place on the ship. Olinda-Louisa, "a prim little lady all in pink and white being such a brave sailer," took care of Mother during the overnight passage along Oahu's southeastern coast and across the channel to Kalaupapa.

At daybreak the *Lehua's* engine fell silent, and she rolled gently in the off-shore swells. The passengers hastened on deck, eager to leave. And from the deck, by the early light slanting in from the east, Mother Marianne saw for the first time the high towering cliffs of Molokai.

And the tiny little bit of earth lying at their feet, the flat plain, the leaf of land, that Hawaiians named Kalaupapa.

Cliffs rise above Kalaupapa like a prison wall, Here they are 675 meters high or more, and almost vertical, a rampart of black rock, pocked with caverns large and small, wherever they are not decked with gray lichens, and green grasses, ferns, and low wind-bent shrubs. At the westernmost end of Molokai, the part nearest Oahu, the cliffs sink into sandy beaches and the blue ocean. From there they extend for sixty-four kilometers toward the east, toward Maui, steadily increasing in height, forming a tremendous escarpment rising straight from the sea—except for the interruption of Kalaupapa—until at their easternmost end they stand 1,200 meters above the waves crashing against their feet.

The line of seacliffs is broken in a few places by deep narrow valleys and is scored in thousands of places by the courses of waterfalls. The cascades plunge straight down into the sea during times when the winds are gentle, but when the winds are strong the falling waters are blown about, like veils of filmy lace, against the faces of the high green precipices. To an unhappy leper, thinking of Kalaupapa as the prison in which he must die, those fluted palisades can be far more formidable than the walls of any jail. To a poet, whether leprous or clean, they are among the most beautiful things he will ever see in this world.

Kalaupapa is a tiny promontory, shaped like a tapered leaf or an arrowhead. The base of this triangular peninsula, at the foot of the cliffs, is about 4.8 kilometers long. Each of its sides, bounded by the sea—this prison's other barrier—is about as long as the base. The promontory was made eons ago, by flows of lava erupting from a small volcanic crater that bubbled up out of the sea at the foot of the cliffs after the long slender body of Molokai had been made. This miniature crater lies near the center of the promontory. From a ship off shore, or from the edges of Kalaupapa itself, the crater is a low mound rising to about 133 meters above sea level. The molten lava, when it drained for the last time from this firepit, left a sunken crater at its heart, about 0.4 kilometer in diameter and 137 meters deep. Spring water and seepage from the ocean have created a lake in its bottom. Although the mound looks more like a navel, Hawaiians recognized the part it played in forming the flat plain and called it Kauhako, "the dropped large intestine," or, in less poetical terms, the anal vent. Because they often buried the bodies of their dead in the waters of that cold pit, they also called it Makanalua, "the Given Grave." Lepers extended that grim name to the whole Settlement—in which, they felt, they were buried alive and against their will.

In 1865 the government of Hawaii chose this leaf of land to be the site of its experiment in segregation. It was ideal for the Board of Health's purposes, being extensive enough to accommodate thousands of lepers, and isolated enough, by mountain cliffs and fringing sea, to prevent their escaping. In the Given Grave no fence need be built, no guards must be employed.

Unfortunately, the Board of Health's agents, after the swiftest of inspections and the most fleeting of thoughts, made an error in judgment when they chose to establish the Settlement along the promontory's eastern shore, "on the Maui side," where the peninsula curves in to meet the looming cliffs. Hawaiians called this section Kalawao, "the mountain area." To be sure, the agents saw that Kalawao was more generously supplied with stream water and with springs. But at Kalawao's bay the sea is deep, the jagged cliffs bounding the flat promontory itself rise ten meters or more above the ocean waves rolling in from far Alaska. And the long curved shore is covered not with sand but with stones, grinding back and forth in the wash of the surf, forever rumbling and groaning, sounding like spirits of the dead lamenting in the netherworld. Kalawao's beach is one of the most treacherous and dangerous landing places in all Hawaii.

No wharf could ever be built there. Steamers lay safely offshore, and sent in passengers and freight in small boats when the weather permitted, or afloat on the waves when it did not. All too frequently small boats dared not venture near the rock-strewn shore. At such times the efficient sailors tossed passengers and freight into the waves, trusting to luck that eventually they would gain the land. All too often both freight and lepers would be severely damaged, or lost. No one minded overmuch the drowning of a leper, but the loss of foods, medicines, and mail seriously affected the Settlement's inmates. In the worst of weather, when huge breakers crashed against the whole sweep of the bay, captains simply turned their ships aside and took passengers and cargoes back to Honolulu or on to some other port, there to await a safer day.

At the western corner of the peninsula, "on the Oahu side," lies the district called Kalaupapa. Here the land slopes gently into the sea. Although here too rocks and boulders stud the shoreline, and a river draining a valley at the rear of the peninsula has dumped quantities of mud upon the reef, usually the promontory itself protects this area from the waves being pushed in by winds from the north or northeast. Small boats can enter this cove more easily, and can unload both freight and passengers with greater safety.

In 1885 a number of non-leprous Hawaiians still lived at Kalaupapa, farming and fishing as their ancestors had done for many generations. By that time Gibson's Board of Health finally realized that the Kalaupapa side of the promontory was far more suitable for the Leprosarium. In 1886 the government started to buy those last pieces of private property and to move the healthy residents to other locations "topside," as Molokai's residents refer to the parts of their island that lie above the peninsula of Kalaupapa. But some healthy residents did not want to leave, and the last of these was not evicted until 1895. After 1887 the Reform Government's Board of Health began the process of moving the Leper Settlement's facilities to the western side of the promontory. For one reason or another, more than forty years would pass before the transfer was completed, but at least it was underway in 1888, when Mother Marianne and her sisters arrived.

The *Lehua* hove to off the Kalaupapa landing. Dr. Emerson expected to spend the whole day there, but the *Lehua's* captain, with an eye upon the weather, allowed them only three hours for their tour of inspection. Still queasy from the trip, "they went down the rope ladder into the little boat. the clever native sailers guided them safely among the many rocks to the landing. . . ." There they found "many lepers waiting to welcome Mother with tears of joy."

Mother Marianne and Olinda, her pink dress rather soiled from contact with the *Lehua's* decks, rode in Father Damien's "little wagon," drawn by William, his listless horse. Dr. Emerson rode a tractable steed, borrowed from Dr. S. B. Swift, who had succeeded Dr. Mouritz as resident physician. "Many lepers followed the wagon . . . to be closer to Mother." The slow procession started across the base of the peninsula to Kalawao, where Mother wanted to visit Father Damien and inspect his home for orphan boys. On the way they met Damien, who guided them at once to Dr. Swift's cottage, where they had been invited to take breakfast. Dr. Swift, a cheerful Irishman, and his wife lived in the physician's official residence, "a neat little cottage not far from the beach a large well kept yard with sturdy shrubs and flowers, and perhaps half a mile from any of the leper cottages on the main road." While the clean ones partook of the Swifts' hospitality inside the cottage, Father Damien and his fellow lepers waited outside the fence.

At the Leper Priest's home for boys, "our kind Mother could see how sorely in need the poor children were of Mothers cair." Father Damien was trying also "to keep a few young girls until Mother could open a home for them a poor native woman had charge of them they looked so sad and despondent the house was dark and dirty. . . ."

The visitors hurried back to Kalaupapa, to look at the Bishop Home for Women and Girls, still being constructed. Several months before, Father Damien and Rudolph Meyer had chosen the site for this new facility. Sister Leopoldina, who would live in it for almost forty years, believed that they "selected the most beautiful spot for our home, on the top of a little hill that slopes down to the Damean Road" (as later generations of residents would name the cart track to Kalawao). The Home, Sister Leopoldina continued, "is about five minuets walk from the church which is very near the" Kalaupapa landing. "from our veranda we have a grand view of the lower part of the place and far out on the ocean, it is especially grand and interesting when the ocean is very rough. how I love to watch those great high waves, each one telling us of the Mighty power of our great and Merciful God as they come rolling in dashing against the big rocks they brake and in white fowming sprayes fly forty and fifty feet in the air, and they cause the whole Settlement to tremble so that it makes the windows and blinds rattle. . . ."

But those impressions would come later, after the sisters had lived at Kalaupapa long enough to know every mood and feature of the place. On Mother Marianne's first hurried visit to the Home she "found our little Convent nicely furnished the carpenters were still at work on the cottages for our patients. Mother was pleased with the neat little Convent. . . ."

The Bishop Home for Unprotected Leper Girls and Women consisted of four cottages arranged in double file at one side of the sisters' convent. Sister Leopoldina described it in detail after she had lived in it for many years:

"The convent was a neat little one story house painted white [with] green blinds standing well back in a large field on the top of a little hill. a six foot veranda run the whole length of the house. a narrow hall went through the house. a large parlor, two sleeping rooms and a bath room open from the right side of the hall, from the left side a small reception room, two sleeping rooms, and a small storeroom from the little reception room a door opened in to a neat little dining room. a door opened from the dining room on to a pleasant back veranda. at the end of this veranda was our poor little kitchen in the kitchen was a little rusty stove with only two holes her name was Flora we had fun with her she made us cry she was such a smoker. at the opposite side of the parlor was a small room we were to use for a chaple

"There were four small cottages (built for our lepers) of wide rough boards and they were whitewashed one to serve as a kitchen and storeroom one for a dining room and the other two were to be their sleeping rooms. . . ."

The whole assemblage turned its back upon grim Kalawao and the range of precipices extending toward the east. The new and open prospect looked down the windswept slope toward Kalaupapa's cove and the sea, toward beckoning Oahu in the west.

But at Kalaupapa no high fence surrounded the Home, the sisters would never feel that they were cut off from the sights and sounds of the world beyond their yard. Mother Marianne was pleased with what she saw.

A blast from the *Lehua's* whistle summoned the visitors back to the landing. By then the winds had shifted, and with them the surf. Huge breakers tumbled in, the rocks were "covered with boiling waves." Olinda moaned in fright, but Mother calmed her, saying "in her low gentle voice. . . . 'We have nothing to fear.'"

Oarsman and passengers were showered with spray immediately the smallboat left shore. Then Dr. Emerson "did a very grand act, that will live forever in our memory. Difficult as it was to stand, he braced his feet and stood in front of Mother and Louisa with his arms stretched high holding his large rubber rain coat to protect them from the heavy spray of the wild ocean waves . . . while he allowed himself to be drenching wet."

Aboard the bounding *Lehua* Mother Marianne and Dr. Emerson felt every roll and plunge as the little steamer fought its way along Molokai's northern coast. Dr. Emerson escaped at the first port of call, to await in relative tranquillity the arrival of a ship bound for Honolulu. Mother Marianne and Louisa stayed with the *Lehua* until she reached Maui. Once again Mother landed at Maalaea Bay, this time by moonlight, in a sea almost as rough as it had been when first she went there, with Sister Renata and Sister Antonella. Once again she rode those bumpy miles to Wailuku. After visiting for three days with the sisters at the Convent of St. Anthony, she and Louisa returned to Honolulu.

Having been informed by Bishop Hermann of developments in Honolulu, Father Lesen finally ended his long silence on October 8, 1888. He had kept Mother Marianne in suspense—and worse, in a puzzled uncertainty about his attitude with respect to her mission—since February 1887. But when at last he did write he set her mind at rest: the fatherly concern was still there, and the gentle apology with which he began was also highest praise: "True, I let you wait long time for an answer: yet, be sure I never lost my old esteem and affection for you. . . . My silence came chiefly from the uncertain state of the Sisters in regard of the governement." Moreover, Bishop Hermann had not written him for many months, because he too was studying political changes in Honolulu and their effect upon the sisters. Both Lesen and Koeckemann had feared that, because of religious differences, the Franciscans would be placed in a precarious position. And their worst fears would have been realized, "as the Bishop now hints, if your work had not taken root in the affection of the people. For this we have to thank God: but you must recognize that my silence came in fact from my affection for you all. It was directed to steer You up, that You should work to procure security, if possible." The old diplomat may have been devious, even deliberately cruel, in the interval, but he was not dishonest in the end. He knew his daughter in Christ sufficiently well to believe that she could be trusted to manage her own affairs. He did not seem to have realized that he could have set her mind at rest by telling her so.

He and Bishop Hermann had corresponded about the need to obtain safeguards for the Franciscan mission from the Reform Government. "I am now glad that the principal ones are satisfied . . . especially am glad that the government admits to the freedom of the Sisters to leave the Settlement, and promises to pay the travelling expenses. I sent them the telegram, and send you herewith the special power to arrange with the government. You may know many things unknown to me. Have then your eyes open to the future also, and try to do your best, that the document . . . be such, as to give satisfaction to the Community. That is necessary if you want to get Sisters when needed."

He closed this benign letter with news about the community in Syracuse—"Mother Delphina is an excellent Mother, and in general the Sisters have very good spirit"—with a strain of paternal advice proving that he can never really stop worrying about his "greatly daring band" in Hawaii: "How are You in health, and your Sisters? Now I lay on your conscience that, when once in Molokai neither You, nor the other Sisters should ever unnecessarily expose themselves, and every precaution be taken against contagion." How little he understands about their incessant exposure to contagion! And how impossible to heed would any of the sisters have found his command, as each day in her life she dressed the lepers' wounds—or, as Sister Leopoldina did more than once, cuddled in her arms a weeping unhappy leprous child, crying for home and mother. "I expect this of You, and that You be severe in regard of others," adjured Father Lesen in Syracuse.

Two days later he wrote to Mother Marianne again, to say that he had just "received the proposition of the Hawaiian Governement in regard to transferring the Sisters... to Molokai. I was very pleased... because they are the first ones ever made by the [Reform] Governement. They seem fair, although perhaps you may better judge, whether something else be required for the well being of the Sisters.... I therefore, by this letter, give you the power, under the Rt. Rev. Bishop of Olba, to accept said propositions of the Governement. In order, however, to avoyd any future misunderstanding," she must be sure to obtain this arrangement in writing, with promises "that it will not be disturbed by any future eventual change of Governement. I believe this most necessary for the peace of the Community, and the prosperity of the Mission."

As the time for the sisters' departure drew near, Father Leonor gave them a long and generous testimonial in a letter written on October 15, 1888, to Father Marcellin Bousquet: "These excellent daughters of St. Francis at the first appeal which was made to them, knew in advance what kind of occupation they would have here, [and] with an uncommon heroism accepted immediately the disgusting and dangerous task of washing and dressing the repulsive sores of the poor lepers. From morning until night, this is their work. Without ostentation, unknown in the world, in all humility, they make themselves the servants of these unfortunates, who are destined to see their bodies fall into shreds, their feet and hands disappear by pieces, bone by bone.... [The lepers] have welcomed with gladness these angels of charity whom they call their *Mothers;* and do they not merit the name in truth?"

Turning to other subjects, Father Leonor informed their Superior

General that, because Father Damien was a leper he would not be permitted to "minister to the spiritual needs of these holy daughters, whose devotion is without limits. Therefore a priest who is not sick must be sent to Molokai, and several have offered to go."

On the day before All Hallows' Eve Bishop Hermann informed the secretary of the Board of Health that "competent authorities in America" having approved the move, "the good Sisters are ready to go over to Molokai as soon as you are ready to install them according to the conditions proposed by the Hon. Board...." Ashley appointed Monday, November 12, as the day of departure. Later, however, because of a sudden flood at Kalawao, which washed out the Settlement's new water reservoir and about 230 meters of pipeline, the departure was postponed for a day, until November 13.

Mother Marianne had been considering all along the disposition of her company. She already knew how the sisters at Wailuku felt about going to Molokai. After Bishop Hermann informed her that the sailing date had been determined, she spoke separately with each sister at Kakaako. Sister Leopoldina's account tells of Mother's approach to this difficult problem, and of the sisters' responses.

"Mother informed Sister Vincent that on 14th of November she would be one of the Sisters for the work on Molokai. Sister Vincent was very beautiful so tall and graceful I used to love to watch her she was so Queenly. Yes Mother she said, I am ready at any time to go. But when Mother informed Sister Rosalia she would be one of the workers in the Leper Settlement," she received a very different answer. "'No indeed I'll not go to Molokai,' she said. As our kind gentle Mother would never forse anyone Sister Rosalia never even visited Molokai."

And what of Sister Leopoldina herself? "I had never expressed a wish to go to Molokai and was quite indifferent, my only wish being to do God's Holy Will. November 10th 1888 Our Saintly Mother asked me can you be ready to go to Molokai next week? Yes Mother I can," said Sister Leopoldina.

Sister Antonia Brown (also "young and beautiful" to Sister Leopoldina, who rarely said an unkind word about anyone, even villains) was assigned to take charge of St. Anthony's School for Girls in Wailuku, and "made it a grand success." She replaced Sister Benedicta, whom Mother Marianne, in a wise move, brought back from Wailuku to run the whole establishment at Kakaako.

Sister Martha, in failing health, continued to take care of the clean girls in Kapiolani Home. Olinda-Louisa Gomes served as housekeeper

at the convent in Kakaako. Sister Rosalia, not only disinclined to serve
on Molokai, but also edging closer to the madness that would disable
her in a few more years, remained at the Kakaako Hospital, as did
Sister Crescentia and Sister Irene.

Mother had given tough tireless Sister Crescentia the duty of
taking care of the many sick men at Kakaako. Among the lepers nearest
to death in November 1888 was Reverend Father Gregory Archambaux,
a Sacred Hearts priest like Damien, who had spent forty years as a
missionary in the Hawaiian Kingdom. During his life of hardship in
the remotest country districts, and as a result of inevitable contacts
with lepers known or unrecognized, he too caught leprosy. Father
Damien was by no means the only Sacred Hearts priest in Hawaii to
contract the disease: at least three others became lepers during the
nineteenth century alone. But none of them gained the recognition
that Damien received, in part because he was the first to be diagnosed
as a leper, but mostly because he was the first priest, among many who
offered to go, actually to live among the outcasts at Kalawao.

Early in 1888, after having spent a few months at Kalawao as both
patient and priest, Father Gregory became too ill to continue his religious duties. Father Leonor arranged for him to go to Kakaako to die in
comfort. Sister Crescentia, full of respect for the dying priest, took
Sister Leopoldina to his room after Mass on Sunday November 11, to
receive his blessing. The ravaged old missionary, once tall and handsome and strong, now seventy years old and lying upon his deathbed,
could not believe her when Sister Crescentia told him why she asked
his blessing for Sister Leopoldina. "'Going to Molokai!' he said in that
deep solemn voice raising his head he opened those death dimmed eyes,
and raised that almost lifeless hand, and his whole soul seemed to be
in that wonderful blessing... [it] has remained with me a priceless
treasure."

Father Gregory died the next day. The following morning Sister
Leopoldina, together with her companions, attended the requiem Mass
for the repose of his soul offered by Father Leonor in the Chapel of St.
Philomena.

Sister Leopoldina would always remember November 13, the day
of leaving. It "was indeed a very sad day Mother was so sick she could
not walk without stagering. I cannot forget the dreadful fright I had. I
was standing in the hall watching her as she tried to come down stairs
she caught on to the railing and sat on the top step while her face went
deathly pale. Oh God! I cried in the silence of my poor helpless heart,

Save her! for Thy Mercy sake, how can we go on with this work You have called us to do? You know she is our leader, Save her oh Lord! Save her! In a few minutes she stood up and stagered back to her room, and when she came from her room again she seemed a little better and She had a little color in her lips, but I know she was suffering yet she bravely faught against it."

Without Sister Leopoldina's testimony no one today would ever know that Mother Marianne too was ill during most of her time in Hawaii. This one incident, so graphically described so late in Mother Marianne's history, gives meaning at last to the very first and wonderful paragraph with which Sister Leopoldina began her long chronicle: "To me our dear Mother always seemed like a beautiful white lily so fragile and delicate suffering most of the time, yet as bright and cheerfull as the morning sun, and so strong and enduring, to write about our dear Mother's virtues, strength and perseverance is as far above my ability as the sun is above the earth. Yet as I have received the order to write about the Sisters coming to Hawaii I must do the best I can With the help of God."

The cause of Mother Marianne's chronic sickness cannot be identified at this time. Probably she too suffered from "the White Plague," chronic pulmonary tuberculosis, as did so many of her contemporaries both in and out of the Order. Sister Leopoldina relates how, in 1899, Mother almost died from severe pulmonary hemorrhaging when, during a single night and the following morning, she coughed up several basinsful of blood—and, characteristically, out of concern for her overworked companions, did not call for their help during the ordeal. But in 1888, or earlier, as well as later, she may have been suffering from other debilitating conditions as well. Of these the most likely are severe physical exhaustion and malnutrition—both the common lot of religious.

With God's help, Mother Marianne summoned the strength to finish packing all those barrels and crates and steamer trunks lying about the halls and parlor of the convent, and to go aboard "the dirty little Lehua" late that afternoon, in time to sail at five o'clock. Of all her company she took with her only Sister Leopoldina and Sister Vincent. Three Franciscans, to live among a thousand lepers. She left five sisters at Kakaako, to attend about a hundred patients and a handful of girls at Kapiolani Home.

Several reasons caused her to make that decision, not the least of which would have been consideration and caution. She wanted to see how her missioners would adjust to the loneliness, the isolation, the amassed horrors at Kalaupapa. And she respected the reactions, whether conscious or subconscious, of the sisters who did not offer themselves cheerfully for service on "the Leper Island." As Sister Leopoldina said, she would not force anyone to make that sacrifice of body and spirit. In Sister Leopoldina and Sister Vincent, she thought, she had two helpmeets who were both cheerful and healthy. And, she suspected—correctly—in time the others would follow them willingly to Kalaupapa, when the three pioneers had shown that Franciscans could live there as well as at Kakaako, and perhaps even more pleasantly— once they adjusted to the place. In the meantime, she limited her mission to caring for the inmates of the Bishop Home. That is what the Board of Health requested her to do for the present. Other duties might come later, she foresaw—when Father Damien would be called to his reward.

The three Franciscans and Father Corneille Limburg, a Sacred Hearts priest whom Bishop Hermann loaned them for two weeks, were the only passengers to board the *Lehua* in Honolulu harbor. Bishop Hermann and several priests of his mission came to the pier to bid them farewell and "were speaking with Mother when Doctor Emerson came on board." After saying goodbye to Mother Marianne he turned to Sister Vincent and Sister Leopoldina. "I have never forgoten his kind voice as he held my hand. May God bless you. he said and turned quickly away." More than any other person in Hawaii, in the whole world, he grieved for them.

"About 40 lepers more or less," as G. W. Ashley instructed the agent on Molokai, also departed aboard the *Lehua* that day. Twenty of those were women and children. "But they were not allowed to go through the city," Sister Leopoldina noticed. The little ship, once outside the harbor, stopped off Kakaako Hospital to receive the patients, brought out in small boats. Those rejects of society, no longer considered human or among the living, "were put in the cattles place," a barricaded pen in the well of the maindeck, "with no shelter and no bed poor creatures if they were sick and there was not much attention paid to them as there would be to the sick cattle." Hawaii's concern for "its poor afflicted lepers" did not grant them such amenities as clean people enjoyed when they traveled.

Mother Marianne and her companions enjoyed the *Lehua's* best accommodations. Rather than try to sleep on the shelves in the stuffy dining salon, they sat on the open deck in camp chairs placed beside the clammy rail. The sea was rough, as usual, and all three sisters were sick. "The purser offered his cabon but Mother would not except it as there would not be room for three."

Sister Leopoldina remembered every detail about that dismal journey, despite her "sick dizzie head" and the need "to go often to the railing to feed the fish," as she had learned to say. "There was no moon and the stars were very dim. Yet it was not so very dark, about eleven o'clock it was chilly the air was filled with fine rain, every where was dead silence the only sound was the sad mouning and howling of the strong wind as it swept the fine chilly rain around us, on the unprotected deck. Mother was so quiet with her arms on the railing and her head resting on her arm. I think she was dozing. . . ."

The purser came often to "ask so kindly could he do anything?" Sister Leopoldina, worrying about the leper children in the cattle pen, asked to see how they fared. "In a few minuets he came back laughing they are all fast asleep do not worry about them youngsters he said."

The "long and dreary night . . . became a little more interesting as the rain . . . ceased and our little steamer was rolling and plowing through the raging waves in the dark shadows of the great high Mountains of Molokai as we passed along it seemed we were near enough to touch them."

The purser pointed out the beacon fire blazing on the point of Kalaupapa. Soon "the darkness of the night disappeared and how we welcomed the dawn of that lovely morning, when the ship cast anchor the ocean was as smoothe as a river bed. we went down the rope ladder just at day brake, and our little boat glided over the smooth surface of the ocean as if it was glad to cast us into the valley of death."

Father Damien, "our great hero," only recently recovered from an attack of fever, awaited them at the landing, as did "many of the poor unfortunates" from the Settlement. To the sisters' surprise, the twenty women and girls who had made the trip on the *Lehua* were already safely ashore. ". . . they were as happy as if they were going to a pic-nic they gathered around Mother as close as they could. Yet not one of them would tuch her. Mother's lovely face was beaming with smiles she looked so perfectly happy that it made us all feel at home."

They went with Damien to celebrate Mass with him at the little church nearby—as gaudy as "a Chinese shop," Sister Leopoldina thought it, "neetly done, but the oddest thing [that] could be imagined for a church"—because "the Saintly old Father" [not Father Damien, but one of his transient colleagues there] . . . thought he would please his people by painting it with all the gay colors he could find."

Father Corneille (more generally known as Father Matthias) de-

scribed Damien with clinical dispassion, when he wrote to Father
Bousquet on December 1, 1888: "His face is swollen, his ears long and
inflamed, one ear broken open, his voice husky, his eyes also a little
attacked, in a word, we saw clearly it was the face of a leper. However,
he is still strong, has a good appetite since he no longer has a fever and
can still last and work for many years, to judge from his exterior. . . ."

"After Mass we went home," Sister Leopoldina recounted. "Our
Convent was nice and comfortable." The furniture had been installed.
Here, too, the walls still glistened, fresh and unmarked. But the broken pipeline bringing water to Kalaupapa had not yet been repaired,
and the convent's only source of water—rain caught in barrels as it
drained from the newly shingled roof—was "as brown as coffee" and
tasted of paint and wood. The crates and barrels of foodstuffs being
brought ashore from the *Lehua* would not arrive for several hours. "We
had no proper food neither for the Sisters nor our people. for us we
made the best of it we had cand goods and hard tack." Weeks would
pass before they were really comfortable in that hardship house. Years
would go by before, eventually, the shrubs and trees they would plant
crowned that bleak knoll with beauty and sheltered it against storms.

Nonetheless, their supreme comfort was there: "Rev. Father
Matthias said Mass in our little chapel so we could have our Blessed
Lord in the Sacrament of His great love with us always."

Good Bishop Hermann, having loaned Father Matthias to them for
two weeks, was striving mightily to send them the clean priest he had
found who was willing to live at Kalaupapa. Father Damien, his body
blighted now with open sores, rapidly failing in strength, could not be
permitted to touch the holy wafers the sisters would receive at communion, nor the chalice holding the consecrated wine.

His Lordship and Mr. Ashley, despite all their suave avowals of
continued cooperation and mutual respect, were locked in a Byzantine
sort of combat, exactly as Europe's bishops and kings so often engaged
in, over the paramount question of policy: who had the right to appoint
this priest, the church or the state?

On December 8 Mother Marianne wrote her first letter home to
Syracuse from the new station at Kalaupapa. She addressed that message to Mother Bernardina. "Here I am at the Leper Settlement on the
Island of Molokai, to which place we . . . came on the 14th of Nov. and
here it was that I spent the *19th*, the twenty-fifth anniversary of my
profession. On that day the house we live in was blessed and placed

under the patronage and protection of St. Elizabeth. I was happy to do something in honor of the dear Saint on whose feast 25 years ago I have received so many and great graces."

Gratitude wells up, as she remembers the part Mother Bernardina played in helping her to answer her vocation. We have seen these thoughtful lines before: "Accept, dear Mother, my heartfelt thanks for all you have done for me—many, many years ago—I believe only for your kind influence I would not have been received into the order, So if I have done a little good during those years, that have passed, into eternity, you share the reward of it. . . ."

NOTES on Chapter XV

1. The official communication of the Board of Health is in the Archives of the State of Hawaii at Honolulu. Three main sources were used for reconstructing of the sequence of events: (a) Board of Health Letterbooks (BHLB) for copies of correspondence from its President or Secretary to Mother Marianne (and others); (b) Board of Health Minutes (BHM) for actions taken at meetings; (c) Hansen's Disease Records (HDR) for the correspondence of Mother Marianne (and others).

2. The manuscripts in *Le Père Damien—Vie et Documents* (*V et D*) were used for copies of letters not found in the microfilm collection: (a) Father Leonor to Father Damien, October 17, 1887; (b) Bishop Koeckemann to Father Damien, February 5, 1887, and April 28, 1888; (c) Bishop Koeckemann to Père Bousquet, February 15, 1887.

3. The patients' petition to the Board of Health, asking for sisters at the Leper Settlement, apparently has been lost or destroyed. References to it are in BHM, November 26, 1887; Meyer to Emerson, December 16, 1887; and Ambrose Hutchison, HDR. Meyer's letter to Father Damien of December 10, 1887, a possible reference to it, is in *V et D*.

4. Sister Charles was the first of Mother Marianne's group to be sent home for reasons of health. "My dear companion," Sister Leopoldina mourned, "never regained her health," and died on March 15, 1892.

5. Facts about the General Chapter held in Syracuse in August 1888 are given in the *Book of General Chapters,* pp. 93–114.

6. "our spiritual wants": The original of Mother Marianne's letter to Bishop Koeckemann, in which she defines terms of acceptance of her mission to Molokai, is preserved in the Roman Catholic Chancery Archive, Honolulu.

7. The order to write—which was really a suggestion—came from Sister Flaviana Engel—who was appointed Commissary General in 1918, and who later served as Mother Superior at Kalaupapa from 1929 to 1935.

8. The chapel at Kalaupapa: Father Albert Montiton claimed responsibility for its "odd combinations of color. . . ." Charles Warren Stoddard, 1885, *The Lepers of Molokai,* p. 55.

Chapter XVI

"MY YOKE IS SWEET AND MY BURDEN LIGHT"

SHE HAD reached her goal. She had come home. The rest of her life would be a time of fulfillment, of complete dedication to the call she had heard that day in Syracuse when first Father Leonor told her of the lepers' need. If the time of fulfillment also brought many trials and sorrows, a sacrifice of the body and a long testing of the spirit, she did not think the exaction too great a price to pay for the glory of her God.

As a reward given in this world in return for the sacrifice, her God, perhaps through the intercession of the Seraphic St. Francis, granted her, eventually, a time of peace. This peace was not gained at once, or easily. Each day that followed her arrival at Kalaupapa, all the succeeding weeks and years, brought no interruptions in the work undertaken for the God of Mercy. They brought much anguish of body and very few distractions. But in Kalaupapa the wide field she had envisioned in Syracuse was narrowed, until ultimately it encompassed little more than the Bishop Home and the yard around it. Yet, from that limited domain she would exert the full power of her influence, and there she would achieve her greatest effects—until, now, the whole world has been included in that field.

In one of history's pleasanter paradoxes, Hawaii's efficient Calvinists helped her to gain the victory that Catholic champions, from Father Lesen to Walter Murray Gibson, had tried so hard to withhold.

"St. Francis will not be displeased with us today," Sister Leopoldina said to Sister Vincent as, for the first time, they rode in Father Damien's "broken down old cart" across the peninsula to visit the boys' home he maintained in Kalawao. In truth, St. Francis could not have been displeased with them on any day of the year. For their courage in the presence of his Sister Death, the Settlement's only permanent resident, for their easing of the lepers' pain and loneliness and dread, he should have showered them with blessings.

He did not do so immediately. In the beginning everything about Kalaupapa was strange, difficult, cheerless, even frightening, much more so than Kakaako had ever been. "Hardships and painful trials" abounded, seemingly without end. In this lawless place, they worried about what lawless men might do to them. The sisters, as God and St. Francis knew, did not ask for comforts. Yet Sister Leopoldina, despite herself, cried out for the solaces to the spirit that beauty brings. She could find beauty in the proud cliffs, when she had time to lift up her eyes to those looming mountains. She could rejoice in the plumes of spray the enormous waves sent up as they crashed against Kalaupapa's prow, when she looked up for a moment from the stinking sores she was dressing upon the rotting body of a girl. But closer to herself, closer to the eye which informs the spirit, she found nothing to tell her of beauty. Or to lift the pall of desolation that hung over Kalaupapa, like a cloud heavy with rain impaled forever upon the mountains' peaks.

"One could never imagine what a lonely barren place it was," she recalled forty years later, at a time when loneliness and fear had long since faded, and the Bishop Home, as well as most of the peninsula's other houses, were all but smothered in vegetation. "Not a tree nor a shrub in the whole Settlement only in the church yard there were a few poor little trees that were so bent and yellow by the continued sweep of the birning wind it would make one sad to look at them."

For Sister Leopoldina and Sister Vincent, in November 1888, the whole settlement was depressing, the very picture of squalor and hopelessness: "as we jolted slowly along [on the track to Kalawao] it was the most sad and dreary place one could ever imagine. Now and then we came to poor little shanties some of them partly broken down. Many of them with broken windoes and steps partly gone, and every one of these shanties looked as if they were deserted. Yet we knew they were the homes of lepers." Most of the hovels, sagging and unkempt, looked as leprous as the sick people who hid within them. In those days, when lepers sent to Kalawao could expect to live there for four years at the most, and in the majority of cases for less than six months, few patients found either the energy or the inclination to improve the appearance of the homes they occupied.

Among all the people of Kalawao and Kalaupapa, the thousand and more prisoners trapped upon that flat plain, Sister Leopoldina saw no beauty. Some might possess goodness of heart and beauty of spirit, as she would learn in time, but their bodies showed only the ravagings of the disease that condemned them to live and die in this Given Grave. "How long Oh Lord," she cried out one day to her troubled self, "must I see only those that are sick and covered with leprosy?"

And lo! St. Francis—or perhaps the good Lord Himself—arranged a sight most pleasing to her, a little proof that her prayers were not being ignored: "a well and handsome young Irishman, in his hunting suit" appeared at the convent porch with "a shining rifle in his hands and a beautiful bunch of birds." At first she thought he was an angel, gleaming so bright and clean. And so wonderful to look upon! When she came back again to reality, she decided he must be an Irishman, a sterling specimen of that most favored of all races, and recognized him for one of the "engineers" come from Honolulu to repair the washed-out dam at the reservoir and the broken pipeline.

But this dazzling apparition also had his dark and mournful counterpart, sent to her by the same God who tested Job. Because the feathers on those birds were "so beautiful" and would make "lovely trimings for the girls hats," Sister Leopoldina went out to the convent's back yard, intending to pin the wings to a clothesline, where they might dry properly. There she "was startled by a silent black figure kneeling in the bed of fresh dug ground with the face close to the wall. . . that is the back of the chapel. Poor Father Damien was on his sore swollen knees. . . adoring our Blessed Lord in the Sacrament of His Love, there was only a thin board wall between him and the alter and as there was no entrance to the chapel [except] through the house, and he would not do that. . . . It seemed to me there was something so sad and pitiful about it I could not keep the tears back." For the second time Father Damien was causing her to weep. She turned and ran. A few seconds later, as he was leaving, Father Damien saw her on the far side of the convent and noticed that she had been crying. "did someone hurt your feelings?," he asked. ". . . his kind words and sadly disfigured face only opened the flud gates of those horrid tears, so that I had to be very much ashamed of myself. he did not know the cause of those tears, but he knows now, and no doubt he thinks Poor thoughtless Sister! she could not see then that it was the Holy Will of Almighty God that it should be so."

Father Damien gave her a happier memory to keep, on that first morning when she and Sister Vincent went to see him at Kalawao. He stood at his "little garden gate," waiting to greet them. "how thin and

sick he looked his face so ashy and yet he was cheerful and happy . . . he stretched his poor disfigured hands to heaven thanking our
Divine Lord that help had come. I knew I could not last long he said
and many years I have been begging our dear Lord to send someone to
fill my place, and now see how He has answered my prayer. 'prase,
glory, and thanks be to our great and Mighty God.'"

With unconcealed pride he showed them the big new Church of
St. Philomena that he and his "leper boys," directed by an Irish stone
mason, were hurrying to complete before Damien died. Made of stones
and cement, it was about 27 meters long and 10 meters high at the
ridge beam, by far the biggest and most solid structure in the whole
peninsula. Damien and his crew had attached it most ingeniously, at
right angles, to the tiny wooden chapel he found there when he arrived
in 1873. In this way, both structures could be used, either simultane-
ously or one at a time, depending upon the size of the congregation and
the occasion.

Sister Leopoldina and Sister Vincent saw also Damien's own little
house, standing in the churchyard amid the graves of the many lepers
he had buried there. "I wanted my children with me dead and alive,"
he said with a laugh. "They never do any harm." ("Oh, horrors,"
thought Sister Leopoldina, shuddering as much at his humor as over
the graveyard in which he chose to dwell.)

At last he took them to see the boys' home, a cluster of cottages
next to the cemetery. "We went with him through the five
wards. . . . I will not try to describe the sad condition of the place. Poor
Father with over a hundred boys, and sick as he was what could he
do?"

Sister Leopoldina did not see, on that depressing morning, the only
beauty that Kalawao could offer: the grand prospect of the whole
coastline of high cliffs rising straight from the sea, the waterfalls
flowing down their sides, and, lying at their feet, seeming to float like
green leafbuds upon the dark blue waters, the two conical islets of
Okala and Mokapu.

If ever she wrote them, no letters from Mother Marianne survive
to indicate how she responded to the new environment at Kalaupapa,
or to present her opinions about the problems she encountered during
the first few months there. A letter from Bishop Hermann, dated
February 4, 1889, implies that other correspondents have been keeping
him informed, even if she has not: "Since your departure from Ho-

nolulu you have had a great deal of troubles and difficulties. As you have never complained I have not been able to make an official application to the Board of Health for your relievement. In the meanwhile we have always tried to do our best for your assistance. . . ."

Faithful Sister Leopoldina, however, remembered something that Mother Marianne said many years later: "In the beginning of all institutions there are many hardships, but I think there are few places where they have so little help as we have had not only in the beginning but for many years. Blessed be God in all his ways."

In Mother Marianne's private thoughts, the beginning of her stay at Kalaupapa was filled with quiet joy. The "hard trials" lay in the future, expected undoubtedly, but not yet defined. Yet for the moment she was happy. Responding to the new challenges and promises, she began to keep a journal, something she had never had time to do at Kakaako. One of the first entries in that journal (which Father Matthias labelled "Record of St. Elizabeth's Convent") reveals her happiness:

Nov. 19—Monday—What a beautiful bright morning after four days of rain and wind. The beautiful moon throwing soft light over the sleeping settlement—Exhortation Holy Mass and Communion, how I yearned to feel tender devotion on the day the twenty-fifth of my Profession After breakfast the good Father blessed the Chapel and house and placed it under the protection of St. Elizabeth—I spent the day quietly performing my usual work. During the afternoon I read the congratulatory letters the dear Sisters sent me. Their loving wishes and the pretty little mementoes moved me to shed tears. How soothing to a tired soul is the sisterly affection of the absent ones. . . ."

This serenity could not last. Even in the isolation of Kalaupapa the world and its troubles would find their way to her door.

Her companions did not share Mother Marianne's happiness. Sister Vincent, unable to speak of her fear, betrayed it in other ways. Sister Leopoldina remembered that Sister Vincent experienced "a nervous jerking of her muscles all the way to the Settlement." Soon after they moved into the convent, Mother Marianne wrote of her concern about Sister Vincent, saying that she was not acting rightly, and was sulking for no apparent reason. The entry in Mother's journal for November 24 is only one of many that would describe Sister Vincent's responses to the Settlement: "Sr V looks bad is either sick or sulky I do not know how to treat her as I do not understand her changeable disposition." Probably because she sensed Sister Vincent's horror of the lepers, Mother thought to lighten her fears by putting her in charge of the convent's housekeeping. In that position she would have no contact at all with the patients, and might be able to settle down in time.

In spite of her determination and cheerfulness, Sister Leopoldina too did not adjust easily to an underlying dread, not of the place but of the disease it harbored everywhere. Seeing all those hundreds of doomed lepers around her, too well aware of the risk she ran each day as she dressed the sores of the women and girls in Bishop Home, she could not help but worry about her own future in that tainted place. The cases of Father Damien and Father Gregory told her that even consecrated priests were not safe from the disease. How, then, could she hope to escape it?

One day Dr. Swift brought her fears to the surface. She sat in the sore-dressing room, bending over a patient's wounds, when the doctor rushed in, making one of his infrequent calls. "For God's sake Sister [he cried] what are you doing to have this crowd around you for hours? It is frightful, it must be stopped." She explained that this seemed to be a better arrangement than attending the patients as they sat outside "in the blazing hot sun." He would not accept this reasoning. "Sister . . . you are sure to be a leper, you can not keep on like this, if you do before ten years have passed you are sure to be a leper remember what I tell you. . . ." With this comforting thought he rushed off again, in his usual hurry. He moved about so swiftly, and so erratically—and probably also so noisily—that the patients called him "Makani," meaning "wind." He had not the slightest idea how thoroughly he had upset Sister Leopoldina. "Of course being a Doctor I believed him yet I knew as God has called us His Divine Providence would protect me."

Nevertheless, "the words of the kind Doctor were echoing in my mind." And the specters of dead Father Gregory, of disfigured and dying Father Damien, rose to taunt her. They, too, had been called by Divine Providence. . . .

"When my work was finished and returning to the house how restful it was to look in Mother's sweet peaceful face. Mother I asked, what will you do with me if I become a leper? thean I told her of my experience that morning and of what the Doctor said. You will never be a leper, I know she said, we are all exposed but God has called us for this work. if we are prudent and do our duty He will protect us, do not alow it to trouble you and when the thought comes to you drive it from your mind and remember you will never be a leper, nor will any Sister of our order."

Sister Leopoldina understood the effect of this good counsel upon herself: "It was wonderful what power there was in Mother's words to banash every fear, and when the thought would come to me of ever becoming a leper I could drive it from my mind with the thought, No! Mother could not be so positive if there was any doubt, I shall never be a leper nor any member of our order. Our wonderful Mother always had a way of putting ones mind at perfect ease. be as careful as you can She would say but never neglect your duty, and never forget that Charity is the greatest of all virtues."

Mother Marianne's prophecy has been fulfilled: not one of the scores of Franciscan sisters who have attended lepers in Hawaii has contracted leprosy. For this powerful protection Sister Leopoldina would not be at all surprised.

Sister Antonia Brown, herself a helper or teacher at Kalaupapa from 1905 until 1917, felt that Mother was certain that Divine Providence would protect her companions "because she had asked this favor from God, and has not her request been heard?"

Mother Marianne herself never had the slightest fear of leprosy, nor any doubt at all about why she and her mission labored at Kalaupapa. "Mother would say," Sister Antonia remembered, "the caring for lepers, the part that the world admires, is the least part of our job." Such a statement can only mean that Mother regarded the duties she and her companions performed for the lepers not as a drudgery, nor as a mortification of body and spirit, but as an offering willingly and cheerfully given, during each second of each day, to the honor and glory of her God and in memory of the blessed St. Francis. "All are to preach by their example," he told the brothers who followed his Rule. And Mother Marianne knew the meaning of that injunction. Bending over the foul wounds of lepers meant nothing to her. Bowing before the Will of God, in each thought and deed, in the sore-dressing room and in the wards, in the office and in the chapel, meant everything to her. She did not ask Him for rewards for services rendered. She accepted everything and anything He sent her, to do or to suffer. His Will was her law. God was the center of her life, as He was the whole universe around her.

In good time the strangeness of the place, the isolation, and—for the two younger Franciscans—even a lingering dread of the disease gave way before the demands of work. As habit took over, familiarity and ease moved in. Little "pleasures," too, brightened "the dark days." In that sequestered promontory, even a slight departure from the daily routines in convent and wards could be elevated into an event. With only about fifty women and girls to care for at first, few of whom were confined to beds, the sisters were not as overwhelmed at Kalaupapa as they had been at Kakaako.

While Sister Vincent toiled in the convent, Sister Leopoldina established her daily routine: she dressed the sores of the patients; supervised them in the performance of their domestic duties, from the making of beds and sweeping of floors to washing clothes and dishes; organized simple entertainments; arranged expeditions to the nearest stream for laundering clothes and filling pails with water to drink; and, at all times, tried to fend off the blandishments of prowling males. Mother Marianne took care of all the details of running the institution; of planning proper housing facilities for patients expected in the future; of ordering supplies, keeping records, and reporting to the Board of Health in Honolulu.

Except for themselves the Franciscans regularly saw only one healthy person at Kalaupapa: Father Wendelin Moellers, who had volunteered to be their chaplain. He arrived on November 20, thereby freeing Father Matthias to return to his parish on Oahu. Father Wendelin came to the convent once or twice a week, generally on Saturdays, sometimes on Tuesdays as well, to say Mass in the tiny chapel, to hear their confessions once a week, and to administer Holy Communion. On Sundays, and the other days of the week, the sisters went to Mass in the gaudy parish church near Kalaupapa landing. Father Wendelin also served as priest to Catholic patients who lived in the Kalaupapa parish of the peninsula. Once in a while Father Conrardy came from Kalawao to see them. Erratic as the winds, Dr. Swift, that comical Irishman, rode over when summoned or whenever he felt like doing so, to suggest some kind of treatment for a patient suffering from an ailment other than leprosy. (Genial he might be, but Sister Leopoldina knew that he was also "nearly a nervous wreck" from morphine he took to quiet his fears and lighten his moods.) And at least four times during a year unless special problems required his presence, Mr. R. W. Meyer would hike down the cliff trail to be certain that his leprous deputies ran the Settlement in conformity with the Board of Health's regulations, rather than according to their changeable inclinations or the persuasions of friends. On those official visits, which usually kept him in the Settlement for several days, Meyer would stop at Bishop Home to discuss Mother Marianne's needs and wishes.

Now that she had actually moved in, despite his misgivings about the place of women in the Settlement, Meyer accepted her with respect and courtesy. Whatever she wanted done or needed he provided—as soon as possible. By April 1889 he achieved a number of improvements she had requested for the Home: strengthening the supports and roofs of several cottages against windstorms of the kind they had experienced in February; constructing "a Cookhouse and covered walk . . . Servants house for them, extensions of a fence around the building," and—at long last—installation of the pipeline bringing clean sweet water from the valley reservoir. No longer did they have to catch rain from the roofs, or fetch pails full of water from the stream so far away.

Almost all the other residents in the Settlement were lepers, and more than 95 percent of those were native Hawaiians. A few healthy persons, called kokua in Hawaiian, helpers in English, lived there also, as mates, lovers, servants, or children of lepers. But the sisters seldom saw kokuas, and probably would not have been able to distinguish them at sight from patients who were not yet far advanced in "the Separation Sickness."

Father Damien, too clearly a victim of the disease, went a few times to see them at the convent, for a month or so after they moved into it. In spite of the precautionary regulations published by the Board of Health, Mother would invite the Leper Priest into the parlor, out of respect for him and pity for his condition. "No, it is forbidden," he would say, peering up at her from the foot of the stairs. "I am unclean." He would not enter the convent, although once, detained late at night upon a visit to a dying patient, he slept for a few hours on the porch floor. The sisters did not know he was there until morning.

Damien did not leave Kalawao after February 20, 1889. "He was failing," Sister Leopoldina remembered the last time she saw him alive, standing in the convent yard, "and one could see death in his face." Father Matthias had been wrong, when he guessed that Damien would live and work for many more years.

At Kakaako the sisters seldom had the time to enjoy a real vacation. Mother Marianne gave them a day off now and then, when she could spare two at a time from their duties. To help them recover from illness, she sent Sister Crescentia and Sister Rosalia for brief visits to Maui. Sister Leopoldina recalled that she enjoyed three holidays during the three years she spent in Honolulu. Both the Rule of Penance and the work they must do permitted them no more leisure. The annual retreat offered the Franciscans the nearest thing to a change of pace, but even that had to be so arranged as not to interfere with their nurses' duties in the wards.

The responsibilities at Kalaupapa—and the isolation—would allow the sisters no vacations at all, unless they went away from the Settlement. Sister Leopoldina, for example, worked there for twelve years before, finally, in 1901, she was granted a vacation of two months— which she spent working at Kapiolani Home in Honolulu. Mother Marianne had no time for any vacation at all.

Nonetheless, after they'd finished a day's housekeeping and nursing chores the sisters did have time to spare—not for mere rest and lolling about, but for recreation of a sort. ". . . There were no eight hour sessions for work," Sister Antonia observed in 1929, a softer age. "All the day long they were on duty and far into the night. One o'clock in the morning sometimes found Mother writing her letters."

Even so, in Kalaupapa they begin a different and pleasanter way of living. On bright sunny days Sister Leopoldina and the ambulant girls and women, lugging baskets full of soiled clothing and bedding, walked about a kilometer and a half to the nearest stream, to do the laundry in the flowing water. While the clean clothes, draped over bushes or laid upon the grass, dried in the sun, the girls frolicked in the stream or explored the countryside. When they did not make such excursions and stayed at home, Mother Marianne and Sister Leopoldina sewed clothes for the younger girls or instructed older ones in the domestic arts. On chill rainy days they baked bread and cakes in the patients' cookhouse, and made "surprises" for the girls. Sister Antonia, who with Sister Cyrilla came from Wailuku for "a working vacation" during the summer of 1889, gave a charming description of Sister Leopoldina: "how busy she was then. . . . In the kitchen making doughnuts with the girls all around the yard looking after the sick going up the valley with them to wash clothes She was young and never seemed to tire."

"Mother Marianne was a real artist," Sister Antonia reported. "Whatever she touched, tying a bow to trim a hat or make a dress to everything she gave an artistic touch. She was an expert in blending colors... many a lesson I learned from her. She took great pride in making dresses for the girls." When Sister Antonia joined the group at Kalaupapa in 1905, eighty girls lived in the Bishop Home, and Mother "had them all dressed in a uniform wine colored cloth. In this way the girls were made happy."

Government appropriations of $10 a year for each patient to spend upon clothes could not be used to pay for the materials that provided those extra touches and "pretty things" for the girls. Mother Marianne bought those luxuries, and many others, with the money the sisters received from the government for their services. From 1883 until 1917 each sister received an unvarying salary of $20 a month. This income went into a common treasury, to be spent upon themselves, as needed, and upon patients in the Settlement, especially the inmates of Bishop Home. In 1917 Governor Charles J. McCarthy, appalled at the inadequacy of the sisters' pay and aware of the increased costs of living caused by World War I, insisted upon doubling their monthly salaries. Mother Marianne did not request this increase, as Sister Antonia explained: [she] "never sought for the esteem of the world. She always said we loose all the reward when we seek the praises of the world. God loves the silent worker who does not let his left hand know what his right one does.... Mother Marianne did all her work for the love of God and never cared for earthly praise or rewards. She never thought of money... a great part [of] the sisters' wages [she] spent for the lepers buying books Christmas presents etc.... Mother did not work for thanks from men."

On pleasant afternoons the sisters and the girls actually got out into the spacious yard, into the fresh clean air and the golden sunshine. They met Denis the Pig there, a huge and scruffy boar, lazy and very tame, who lay about wherever he pleased, in mud or in lairs in the tall grass, and entertained everybody with his amiable indifference— until one day a leper girl "insulted him" by prodding his back with a stick. Whereupon he got up and stalked away, never to return. (He probably ambled right into the trap—and the earth-oven—of some hungry patients, who served him up as the main dish at one of their consolatory feasts.)

Sometimes, on bright warm afternoons, Sister Leopoldina accompanied the girls to a nearby beach and watched over them while they went swimming and body surfing—after removing their outer clothing. In the beginning Sister Leopoldina envied them their sport and wished she could join them. But decorum kept her on the shore, worried and alert. Only once did she feel the rush of the sea: a big wave caught her by surprise, and soaked her, habit, underskirt, and all, up to the knees. But then "the blazing sun and the heavy smell of the sea water made me so very seasick that I never had the desire to ride on the waves again."

Another time—mercifully this happened only once—she and everyone with her looked on helplessly, praying desperately, while the undertow carried "young and beautiful Camilla" away from shore. Fortunately, a leper who was fishing from a canoe not far away sped to Camilla's rescue—and saved her to live for a few more years. No one guessed then that they would be years of misery and shame that a quick death by drowning would have spared her.

Sister Leopoldina and her girls, sometimes accompanied by Mother Marianne or Sister Vincent—went for longer walks upon the grassy plain to watch the waves dashing upon the peninsula's cliffs, or up the slope of the little crater to peer into the "unfathomed depths" of the lake at its bottom, or into the two narrow valleys at the rear of the Settlement. They picked wild guavas and mountain apples in their seasons, gathered such delicate ferns and pretty leaves and infrequent flowers as they might find along the way. But always, in this "Land without Sunsets," they must be sure to come home by midafternoon, because by then the high cliffs would cut off the light of the sinking sun and the cool shadows of a long evening fell over the flat plain.

Some even climbed the steep trail up the face of the cliff standing between them and the world of clean people. Sister Leopoldina and the girls reached its very top, wanting to see how their prison looked from that vantage. Sister Vincent, badly frightened by the narrow winding path and those dizzying heights, never reached the top. The younger girls and Sister Leopoldina "went up the pali" several times. "I think in all my life I never enjoyed anything more than I did that pleasant afternoon," she wrote about her first hike up the cliff trail, "having such a desire to go up the mountain and than the pleasant surprise of finding the new trail and the lovely cool weather it was all God's own pure gift. . . ." Even this simple pleasure was taken away one day when Mr. Meyer's sons (at their father's direction, Sister Leopoldina hinted) and a pack of baying dogs chased the girls down again, as the boys shouted that lepers were not supposed to climb the trail. Meyer himself, in a note that managed to be both polite and officious, drew Mother Marianne's attention to "the laws and rules of the Board, of which you undoubtedly were not aware, that Lepers are not permitted to come up the pali under penalty of punishment." Not until twelve years later (by when Meyer was dead) did John D. McVeigh, a new and more generous superintendent, give the girls permission to climb the pali if they wished. But by then Sister Leopoldina was too old and too rheumatic to join a new generation of her charges in such an expedition.

Mother Marianne sometimes went along on those explorations. Usually, however, she stayed at the Home, to watch over the sicker patients, who could not leave their beds. Staying at home also gave her a chance to catch up with reports, plans, the paper work of administration, an overdue letter.

Nonetheless, for her too the burdens she had borne so willingly in Honolulu were lightened at Kalaupapa. During the intervals of relative quiet, when she was home alone, she refreshed her spirit by indulging her love for plants. If she had not done so in Utica and Syracuse, in Hawaii she discovered the pleasures of gardening. She liked to grow potted ferns and parlor plants. In Honolulu Mr. Gibson noticed this interest and built—"as a present to the Sisters"—a small glassed conservatory beside the convent at Kakaako. She continued the hobby in Kalaupapa, growing kitchen vegetables, ornamental plants, and useful trees in the Bishop Home's grounds. Characteristically, the only recreation she permitted herself was practical, something that did not waste precious time. Vegetables and fruits went to the two kitchens of Home and convent. Flowers and ferns went to the wards, the convent's parlor, and, above all, to the chapel. She herself kept the chapel clean, and "dressed the alter" with flowers, or ferns, or just arrangements of leaves when nothing else could be found.

Sister Leopoldina credited Mother with having begun a landscaping program a few days after they reached the Settlement. In time it would add beauty and windbreaks to Kalaupapa's slopes, as well as edible fruits and vegetables for its residents. "She would say the wind would not have so much force when they grow."

Old residents and Mr. Meyer offered little encouragement. "What is the use of your wasting your time they will never amount to anything there is no water and these strong hot winds will dry them up." the pessimists warned. "But Mother could never be discouraged, her only answer to all they said was a pleasant smile." She set out many plants in the Home's big yard, when they were sturdy enough to withstand winds and dry spells. Often enough Mother herself did the actual digging of garden beds or of holes for young trees, although usually the heavier labor was performed under her direction by the succession of men the Board of Health employed to serve the sisters as stableman, driver, and general helper. In lighter chores, such as weeding flower beds or gathering vegetables, the girls of Bishop Home assisted her.

Mother Marianne lost many plants to browsing cattle, wild pigs, or thieving patients. But always she followed a generous plan. "When the lepers . . . noticed how well Mother's plants were doing they came to her asking for plants, and that was just what Mother was wishing for, to get them interested in planting and She never refused anyone of course. She had thousands and was glad to give them. . . ."

In time she transformed the grassy knoll upon which the Bishop Home sat, making it embowered and almost invisible to passersby on the roads below. "Many years we have enjoyed and are still enjoying the work that our good Mother begone the whole Settlement is shaded with lovely trees and shrubs, and the frightful wind has lost its power."

Their Home, high on its windy hill, was still exposed to the fury of all the elements when the sisters experienced the first of the devastating storms that descend periodically upon the Settlement. "The devil-winds of Pelekunu," Hawaiians called them, because often people at Kalaupapa could see those local cyclones whirling toward the peninsula from the direction of Pelekunu Valley, a few kilometers farther east along the coast. The devil-winds, which come about every ten years or so (the patients say), howl and rage as they cross the promontory, flattening shrubs, uprooting trees, tearing roofs from houses, lifting flimsy cottages from their foundations, pushing whole churches into the sea. Fortunately, the residents of Bishop Home survived those storms without much hurt to themselves.

Their very first devil-wind took the sisters by surprise when it hit in February 1889. It ripped off the verandah roof from one of the cottages. The flying debris sped perilously close to Sister Leopoldina and slightly injured a leper girl. The gale blew Mother Marianne halfway across the yard, but she "landed in the arms of a big strong leper" who was coming to help them. The Mormon Chapel, near the Kalaupapa landing, simply disappeared without trace. But the gaudy painted Catholic church just across the street stood unscathed.

Far more dangerous than the devil-winds, and much more frequent, were the attentions of the youths and men who gathered at night outside the low fence surrounding the Home. Separating nubile girls and lonely women from the males of Kalawao was easier talked about than done. In a place that for so many years had known no law, either of God or man, the Christian standard of morality was nothing more than a joke—or an annoyance—to most patients. In the manner of people who face certain death, not immediately perhaps but within a few years at best, the lepers at Kalawao reacted in predictable fashion. A few became exceedingly virtuous, wanting to achieve salvation in the next world by being very good in this one. The greater number, both men and women, cast virtue away at the shoreline, if they had not already abandoned it at Kakaako. They wanted to enjoy to the full, and for as long as their disintegrating bodies would allow, the few comforts that exile in the Settlement could offer them. Pleasures of belly and bed became their primal preoccupations. Drunkenness, gluttony, "licentiousness" of every kind and degree threatened the peace of the Settlement, and often the lives of its inmates, every day in the week, year after year.

Father Damien, with continual scoldings and frequent bursts of anger, tried for more than fifteen years to temper the wilder indulgences of those animal instincts. He succeeded rather well in taming some of the people at Kalawao. But, as always, the more brutish patients laughed at his preachings and continued to behave exactly as they pleased. So, also, did a great number of those who pretended to obey Damien's strictures and the Board of Health's regulations. They merely became more circumspect, and hid their misdeeds from his sight. For them an important element in the perennial game was the excitement of breaking the rules without being caught. Everybody in Hawaii who was old enough to know about the Leper Settlement knew also about the "lawlessness" of its inhabitants. Sister Renata and Sister Benedicta, when they sent their letters of response from Wailuku to Mother Marianne, had ample reason to fear for the safety of any woman who set foot in that terrible place. And, after five years at Kakaako, Mother Marianne realized better than the members of her mission the dangers to which the sisters would be exposed when they went to take charge of the Bishop Home.

Naturally, the bevy of females assembled in the Home, of all ages, sizes, degrees of pulchritude, and stages of dissolution, immediately attracted the attention of all questing males in the Settlement who were not tethered by a possessive mate or crippled by the sickness. From the day they arrived at Kalaupapa the residents of Bishop Home lived under a permanent siege. And, of course, from the moment they stepped upon Kalaupapa's shore Mother Marianne and her two companions tried to guard their charges, day and night, from being harmed in any way.

Many a willing girl, forgetting the sisters' admonitions, eluded their watch and slipped out into the night, to an assignation with one or more of those engaging fellows. Although the sisters, after Kakaako, could never have been naive about these matters, and suspected that betrayals of this sort were happening, they could not do much to prevent them. Problems of this nature affecting several girls at a time arose almost in cycles, apparently as the girls' wild responses to periods of intense frustration. Sister Antonia called those times, when "the girls wished for more freedom," attacks of "The Spring Fever." Superintendent John D. McVeigh, who arrived in 1902, found a more earthy description for those episodes: "the girls have got another wild streak on," he would report to the Board of Health. Whenever these spells destroyed the girls' usual "good spirits," Sister Antonia wrote, "the Sisters spent many a *weary* night as well as day." If a girl who slipped away in the dark did not return in the morning the sisters counted her lost. Then they grieved for her; and always they hoped that someday she would have a change of heart and come back to the Home, if only to die there "an edifying death."

Whenever such a burst of mass "ingratitude" rose to its peak, Mother Marianne and her companions felt both sad and regretful. They did not hesitate to scold the "miscreants." As a last resort, they punished or expelled the most hardened offenders. Mother tried to avoid as long as possible the actual expulsion of a girl, and did so only because she realized that the uncooperative one was endangering discipline among other inmates.

Mother did not brood in secret over those signs of wickedness. She confided her feelings in letters to Superintendent Meyer, living peacefully above the melee in his ranch atop the cliffs. "I fear it will never be the happy Home it was before," she said after the first of those out-bursts. Meyer, a decent man, and a long-suffering one when he contemplated the Settlement's populace from a distance, tried to console her with the usual platitudes. He told her, in effect, that these disturbances come and go, like squalls from the sea, and that her charges would settle down again, in good time. "The girls are foolish," he agreed, "they do not seem to realize the kindness there is bestowed upon them."

The men of Kalaupapa played the game with extraordinary restraint. Any day or night in the week they could have stormed in and, like Romans stealing wives from the Sabines, carried off the women they wanted. But Kalawao's lechers never did anything so bold—or so rash. Not fear of God or of the law deterred them, but plain good sense. A man who took a "wife," so called, had to provide her with both a house to live in and, supreme sacrifice!, with a semblance of fidelity—by Kalawao's standards. That was too great a price to ask a man to pay, thought those roaming males, well aware of the joys of staying free. Almost to a man they preferred the fun of the chase, as opportunity allowed. And so, also did many of the more attractive women and girls.

Sometimes, however, as Sister Antonia related, an especially insistent youth "would come in at night in the darkness and hide. One big fellow, Mother caught behind one of the doors. She had a big stick and rapped him soundly. He took it all without complaint and in after years . . . would say 'Mother was right; I was wrong. I had no business to be there.'"

The Franciscans did not attempt to stand guard like dragons at the gates to Bishop Home. Nor, except in times of "Spring Fever," did they check the wards during the night or scout through the yard in search of culprits. They trusted to good example, moral suasion, the inherent decency of the human being and her capacity to show gratitude for kindnesses received. A girl so happily affected, said Father Maxime André, is "formed in piety." Such girls seldom betrayed the sisters' trust.

Sister Leopoldina and several companion sisters observed how the patients in Bishop Home felt about Mother Marianne while she lived among them. No doubt the sisters were right when they interpreted the good behavior of their charges as proofs of respect and affection, presented in smiles and songs and willing assistance, and in the "happy deaths" they attained at the end.

Although death brought the only easing to the lepers' pain and disintegration, the Franciscans never were in a hurry to see their girls gain that ultimate release. Always the sisters fought to hold off death, with every means at their command, if only for a short while. At least once, when the Settlement's doctor was absent from Kalaupapa, Sister Leopoldina herself, with faint heart but the most resolute will, amputated the useless foot of a young girl, dangling from her leg by shreds of rotten flesh. (The girl survived the operation, and stumped happily around the Home for many months thereafter.)

Mother Marianne expressed her philosophy very clearly to Jean Sabate, a traveling writer, who visited the Leper Settlement in 1905. Appalled by what he saw, Sabate said to Mother (in "a foolish remark," as he later acknowledged), "it would be a mercy to put an end to such a hopeless and miserable life." An honorable man, he preserved Mother Marianne's answer to him: "God giveth life; He will take it away in His own good time. In the meantime it is our duty to make life as pleasant and as comfortable as possible for those of our fellow-creatures whom God has chosen to afflict with this terrible disease."

To all female newcomers, regardless of creed, the Bishop Home offered shelter and protection not available elsewhere in the Settlement, during those years when boatloads of frightened miserable women and girls were simply deposited at Kalaupapa's landing place.

For many of its inmates, Bishop Home was a refuge they did not leave until their bodies were carried away for burial. Others accepted its comforts for a time and then moved out, either to marry (and thereby to acquire homes of their own) or to live with friends they'd found in the Settlement.

Once a group of newly arrived women had been installed in Bishop Home, the Franciscans tried, with unlimited patience and warmest concern, to make them content, if not happy. Good example, demonstrated both by the sisters and by older patients, was the most persuasive influence they could exert upon newcomers. The Franciscans' expectations, sustained by their indomitable good will, made most of their charges respect the rules of the Home. Although "The Spring Fever" seized some of the girls on occasion, most of them conformed reasonably well to regulations. The few who would not submit, like "poor Camilla," ran away to the illusion of liberty—and usually to an early and cheerless death.

In 1957, Sister M. Rosanne La Manche, a Franciscan nurse stationed at Kalaupapa, asked several older patients to tell their impressions of Mother Marianne. All spoke of her in almost the same words: she was, they said, "very kind," but also "very strict." Their rambling reminiscences, touching upon many subjects, did indicate that Mother Marianne, determined to guard her "girls" against immorality, exercised her authority most firmly. Naturally, not everyone in the Settlement liked the procedure for proper courtship and marriage that she prescribed. And, in that place where too many men preferred to live without law, not everyone appreciated Mother Marianne's vigilance, or her influence upon her girls.

A few old patients living at Kalaupapa in 1977, who remembered courtship rules at Bishop Home during Mother Marianne's time or soon afterward, recalled that the Franciscans did allow "the girls" to visit with "the boys" whom they wished to see. Each such formal call by an approved swain lasted for an hour. With this sensible system, the Franciscan assured privacy of a sort for the Home's inmates as a group, while at the same time offering individuals, both male and female, a semblance of normal behavior according to the customs of Christian nations. Needless to say, these supervised visits at the Home were not the only opportunities for meeting that the patients enjoyed. A variety of social events, such as picnics, hikes, parties, dances, gatherings of music clubs and funeral societies, as well as promenades to and from church, helped the better adjusted residents to pretend that they were not entirely cut off from the pleasures of this world.

The sad tales of "girls who went wrong" also helped to impress upon those not yet fallen the need to reserve their places in the Home, if not the importance of preserving their virtue. Even with those weak defenses the sisters succeeded to a remarkable extent. Most of their charges did remain loyal, helpful, "good," as the Franciscans would have said. Usually the sisters did not frown upon marriage, but rather rejoiced when one of their girls found a worthy husband and wed him in the proper way, "for love." The sisters did most vehemently oppose illicit and promiscuous sexual misconduct, and they did not hesitate to turn out of the Home the few young women who persisted in disobeying the rules. Such a rebel was Camilla, the girl who almost drowned in the sea.

The sisters, then, tried to be realists in their approach to the sexual problem. Their great dread, always, was the possibility that, some dark night, the men would no longer be satisfied with standing beyond the fence, whistling, calling, serenading the ladies within the cottages. The girls, too, or those who still valued decency, feared the threat of violence. On several occasions they called in alarm for the sisters. And they, armed with cudgels, lighting the way with bull's-eye lanterns—and fortified with a moment's prayer before the altar in their chapel—dashed out into the night to rout the foe. They never found anyone there, of course and little evidence that men had been near—except, perhaps, the sounds of mocking laughter, drifting back through the night. The rescue parties had better luck at finding culprits hiding inside the cottages, as the story of honest Ilihia demonstrates.

Sister Leopoldina seems to have enjoyed the memory of those encounters. "I wish you could see the fun when I turned the bright light into their faces, the first one jumped from his hiding place, down came Mother's club on his head, out came the other long fellow and as he was turning like a flash Mother raised her club high in the air, and as it came down on his back the dust flew from his old coat, and it sounded like a gun shot in the deep stillness of the night, they doubled up like hoops and sprung from the top step to the ground and disappeared in the darkness. All this was done quietly and not a word was spoken. . . ."

For Sister Leopoldina the best part of all was the remembrance that these intruders were routed by "the fragile little hand of our Superior." In this Sister Leopoldina "could see so plainly the great power and the loving care of Almighty God."

Fortunately for the sisters, the gallants from Kalawao did not gather outside the fence every night in the week. A walk of ten kilometers on a cold and rainy night is something even the most urgent of males will sensibly forego, and such inclement evenings are frequent at Kalaupapa.

The Franciscans were rarely endangered by those invisible suitors. But once in while a man much hurt by fate, and angry with the whole world, turned his hate upon "those virgins" because they interfered with his liberties. He would conspire with cronies, and plot an attack upon the convent-fortress. Probably those bullies wanted only to frighten the sisters into going away. A few such midnight harassments did occur, marked by shouts and swearings and throwings of stones, although no one on either side of the fence was ever injured. At least once, however, if Sister Leopoldina can be believed, a leper more vindictive than all the rest actually did plot to kill Mother Marianne.

Nakipi was his name. He was the one who had lured the gentle and beautiful Camilla away, much to the sisters' distress. And then, having got her, Nakipi refused to marry Camilla as promised, or even to treat her lovingly. He abused the girl and neglected her, and apparently sold her body to favored friends. Under the effects of his cruelty Camilla soon wasted away. Nakipi and other men of his temperament, fretting over the presence of "the virgins," decided to rout them, once and for all. Fortunately, Ah Kyan, the Chinese wife of one of their friends, heard them talking in her own house, where they came to gamble, drink rum, and fan frustrations into hatred. Ah Kyan went in secret to Sister Leopoldina, saying "they plan bad things for Mother and, they say bad words how they must get red of Mother . . . they say if they get red of Mother they can go in Home and do what they like because the Sisters will be afraid. . . ." Ah Kyan explained how they intended to go to the convent at midnight of that very day, "then rap at the frunt door and when she opens the door we will stuff her mouth so she cannot scream and we can carry her off before any one can tell who we are."

Nakipi and his gang completely underestimated the power of women. Ah Kyan had already told the girls in Bishop Home about Nakipi's base scheme. "They were very excited, we have made our plans Sister, they said it will be a battle we will kill them if they come, for we will save our Mother or die." They arranged a signal—when that knock upon the door sounded, Sister Leopoldina would ring the big dining room bell "with all my strength"—and began to prepare for action. "It was interesting to see them prepairing their weapons for their battle," observed Sister Leopoldina, in cold blood. Kaheana, "a very good girl large and muskler, and she loved Mother so that she would be glad to do anything . . . sharpened a hatchet on a brick until it was shining like silver. . . . I am going to kill them dirty men if they come [she said] It made me shiver for I knew she ment it and had strong nerves, and that she would rather kill or beat some of them badly even if it would cost her life."

Sister Leopoldina "returned to the Convent and told Mother everything than she said with her sweet little smile what are you going to do? First of all Mother promise you will not leave your room tonight no matter who calls but let me answer. very well she said and what are the girls going to do?" Sister told her about the battle plans, the girls' determination, concluding bravely "and if Nakipi and his men don't run for their life pity them. that is a good plan Mother said, do the best you can, but I think more likely Nakipi will learn that the girls and woman are not on his side and they will not come, and if they do God grant they will not be hurt."

Mother Marianne was right: she guessed the sympathies of certain of the girls—and she knew the valor of the men beyond the fence. The

Amazon squad never saw action. Someone sent word to Nakipi and his henchmen. "... they never came, and we heard no more from them. Only now and then we heard of their death." The first to die was "poor little Ah Kyan."

Early one morning, not long after that night of worry, Sister Leopoldina found Camilla "on the veranda crouched down by the door ... her knees drawn up to her chin her face covered with two bony thin arms that were around her scarcely covered knees... Oh! Camilla I said you have come Home ... and I would gladly have taken her in may arms, but Oh the look she gave me when she turned her deathly face, my voice chocked I could not help it. . . ."

Camilla had not come home to stay. ". . . I have never had a happy day since I left the home [she said] now I have come just to look at you once more and say goodbye. A few days later Father told us she had received the last Sacrament and was happy to die. 'May she rest in peace.'"

As it must in all moral tales, Death soon claimed the villains too, and delayed her call for the good: "Nakipi and the Chinaman [Ah Kyan's husband] did not make any more trouble for shortly they died. Kaheana remained with us many years and she died a Saintly death. She loved Mother very dearly to the end." One faithful Kaheana more then made up for a dozen fallen Camillas.

Although Sister Leopoldina may have exaggerated the danger to Mother Marianne in the Nakipi affair, Father Leonor, far away in Honolulu, reported unadorned facts about an entirely different incident. While writing to Father Bousquet on August 12, 1890, he mentioned "serious troubles at Molokai, at the instigation of some wicked fellows." About three weeks before that date, several disgruntled patients had tied up the Board of Health's resident administrator, a thoroughly unpopular American named Evans. When Father Conrardy intervened in his behalf, the men threatened to tie him up too. In reprisal, the government sent in "a squad of policemen armed from head to toe." Arrests and trials followed. Five men were sentenced "to forced labor here for five years ... the revolt was stopped, but Father Wendelin claims that the fire still smolders under the ashes. The Rev. Mother Superior of the Franciscan Sisters showed great courage, they say, and great presence of mind; but the Minister of the Interior must take measures that that doesn't happen again, or they will have to withdraw to avoid scandals and insults. Some stones ... were thrown into their enclosure, or against them or at the girls whom they care for."

Troubles of this kind broke out sporadically for many years until, after the islands of Hawaii became possessions of the United States in 1898, the men of the Leper Settlement finally realized that law and order had gone there to stay. Enticements and seductions continued, of course, regardless of the flag that flew over the Settlement; but at least the threat of violence was abated.

NOTES on Chapter XVI

1. Record of St. Elizabeth Convent, Kalaupapa, and the *Origin and History of St. Elizabeth's Convent,* Kalaupapa, were initiated by Father Corneille Limburg. Subsequent entries were made by Mother Marianne.

2. Sister Antonia Brown at Bishop Home: in 1907, Sister Antonia was granted a certificate by the Department of Public Instruction, Territory of Hawaii, recognizing the Bishop Home School as a private one. Apparently, the teaching of English as a second language in the Bishop Home School began with her assignment to Kalaupapa. Sister Antonia also was responsible for a variety of entertainment and recreational activities at Bishop Home (lauded in Board of Health reports), such as a drill team, plays, songfests, etc.

3. Recreation at Bishop Home: A project begun in 1897, with the approval of R. W. Meyer, for Mother Marianne with the aid of the healthier residents of Bishop Home to prepare a special recreational area in Kalaupapa for the patients ended in a disheartening failure. Several hundreds of fruit trees already had been planted, waterpipes were laid, and plans were in progress for building a cottage to serve as a resting place for the "poor sick" to use to enjoy seabathing and mountain breezes. C. B. Reynolds, the new superintendent who succeeded Meyer, did not favor the recreational area which, in consequence, ceased abruptly. Father Wendelin, whose society of Hui Aloha boys had helped to fence the area, said envy was the cause of failure: "the Sisters have the nicest place and the most trees would be too much."

4. Details of the 1889 windstorm at Kalaupapa: Ethel M. Damon, 1948, *Siloama, The Church of the Healing Spring,* pp. 58–59.

5. "formed in piety": In this same letter written on February 2, 1905, Father Maxime André praised the spirit of Mother Marianne during trials with the inmates of Bishop Home: "She is still here, but she is growing old without ceasing to work with ardor. But the poor woman has many vexations in her administration with the lepers, etc. etc. Many of these women and kanaka girls grow bored to stay in Bishop Home, where the men are not admitted so they run away to prostitute themselves and the Board of Health does not have regulations strict enough to get them back. They are free to flee at the age of 16. But when they have passed 4 or 5 years in the Home they are formed in piety and after their wandering many demand to return. Charity makes it a duty for the sisters to receive the repentant ones. . . ."

6. Sabate article: "America's Exiled Heroines, The Nuns of Molokai," *The World Magazine,* October 8, 1905, p. 6.

Chapter XVII

"BEAUTY SPRINGING FROM THE BREAST OF PAIN"

EARLY IN THE morning of April 15, Easter Monday of 1889, the sisters learned that Father Damien was dead. Only a few days before Mother Marianne and Sister Vincent had gone to Kalawao to receive his last blessing. They knelt beside the pallet on the floor of his little house, where he lay because he'd never bothered to build himself a bed. Others of the Settlement's residents hastened there, too, some to ask for his blessing, some simply to be present at the passing of a holy man. At least one went to watch in coldest calculation. Dr. Swift clattered in with camera, tripod, and a boxful of glass plates, to take numerous photographs of the world's most famous leper. Gaunt and anguished, scarcely conscious, his sunken eyes dulled with pain, Damien could not protest this last indignity. He escaped into death, "after much suffering," early in the morning of the first day of Holy Week, happy to meet his God. "I have received my 'Nunc dimittis,'" he told Father Wendelin when he knew that never again would he rise from that mattress on the floor. He died sustained by the knowledge that he had brought some solace to the lepers, and happy that, after he was gone, they would receive the Franciscans' loving care.

"The poor little cart and old black horse were sent for us," Sister Leopoldina recounted, "and again Mother and I moved slowly over that lonely road, the dark clouds covered the sun while the weard sad cry of the wind as it swept over the dark gray rocks that seemed to be frowning down on us from there lofty place on the side of the great mountain. When we reached the home there was a dead silence everywhere the poor boys were in little groups . . . like sheep without their shepherd."

Father Conrardy, weeping, met them at the gate, starting Sister Leopoldina's easy tears. But Mother Marianne, cheerful and smiling, "was like bright sunshine in this gloomy place." She had come to do honor to Father Damien. And she refused to mourn because she knew that he had gone to claim his reward. It was the same reward for which she hoped—as did Father Conrardy, Brother Dutton, Sister Leopoldina, and every other devoted Christian missionary anywhere, Catholic and Protestant alike.

"We wish to get to work," Mother told Father Conrardy. Having anticipated this day, she brought all the materials she needed for that work. "In a clear place in the yard" outside Damien's little house, among the mounded graves and leaning tombstones, "they had put on two benches a rough board box in the shape of a coffin." Damien himself had made hundreds of boxes like it, during the fifteen years he served his lepers. "and then we went to work, and the skillful hands of our Mother transformed that ugly rough box in to a very beautiful casket. the outside she neetly covered with fine black serge and decorated it beautifully with silver headed tacks the inside, She padded and lined with white satin neetly [pleated] and edged with beautiful white lace. She lined the lid with white and covered it with black serge and decorated it with the silver headed tacks, we were glad to have the things to fix the casket." Those funeral trappings, probably the most splendid the lepers had ever seen at Kalawao, certainly were not bought at the Settlement's store. Mother would have been given them by friendly merchants in Honolulu, who had not forgotten her poverty and her needs. And Sister Leopoldina, always too modest to draw attention to her own part in the mission's duties, did not say that she helped Mother with this labor of respect.

"Then the Fathers after dressing the remains of the Saintly Priest in his beautiful white vestments . . . placed him in his pretty casket and carried him in his new church and what was our glad surprise to see that every trace of leprosy was gone, one could never tire looking at the peaceful happy face where one could so plainly see that his pure soul was enjoying the home of the Sacred Heart that he had loved so dearly. . . ." Sister Leopoldina was not seeing a miracle. Often, as a leper nears death or after life has ended, changes do occur in the superficial tissues of his body that resemble the initial stages in healing and clearing. Fluids are resorbed, swellings subside, discolorations fade as the pallor of death sets in, almost as if the leprosy bacilli are withdrawing to some other refuge before the grave swallows them too. Nothing, however, can repair the mutilations they have caused before they have killed their host.

"And looking in Father's peaceful face I could easily understand why Mother seemed so happy she knew his Saintly soul would add to the Glory of God through eternity. On our way home there was a light sparkle in her wonderful eyes, and her cheery words dried all my tears." They returned to the convent late in the afternoon. "Mother was really a marvel. All day she had been on her feet, and then jolting over that dreadful road and had very little of the poorest kind of food until late in the night she was triming hats with crape and making black sashes, for the next day was to be the Rev. Father's funeral."

They set out again for Kalawao early the next morning. Mother Marianne and Sister Vincent shared the cart. Sister Leopoldina walked along the stony road with the women and girls, wearing those black sashes and bands of sable crepe. They reached Damien's Church of St. Philomena—which had been finished before he lay down upon his straw pallet—in time for the requiem Mass, sung by Father Wendelin.

"When the service was over, we formed a procession for the funeral moving slowly around to the side of the beloved church where they had made a good large cement vault under the good old lauhala tree which had sheltered the Saintly Priest when he was young and strong." Complying with an insensitive decision that Damien would have deplored, "eight white lepers" bore the coffin, rather than eight Hawaiians, or a selection of men representing the assortment of races condemned to Kalaupapa.

The service reminded Sister Leopoldina of "our Holy Father St. Francis and His Lady Poverty. but the good old tree was not clothed in rags. it was clothed beautifully in white a mediera vine had sprung up under the tree and the little tender vine had crepped up all around the large drupping leaves, and covered them with downey white flowers that had filled the air with sweet perfume...."

Mother Marianne, when on May 6 she addressed her next letter to Mother Bernardina, referred to Father Damien's death: "...We visited him before he died and standing at his bedside one could imagine the Voice of God calling him to come to his reward—his was a grand and noble life of self-sacrifice, how closely he followed in the footsteps of our loving Savior living and dying for the poor outcasts. What more can a poor mortal do than give his life for his fellow creatures." Here, more than in anything else she wrote, Mother Marianne came close to declaring her own feelings about the work she had chosen to do.

Father Conrardy and Brother Dutton, on the scene at Kalawao, felt rather possessive about the boys' home, even though Father Damien had started it years before either of them joined him at the Settlement. During the several weeks before he died they assumed responsibility for the home and its 101 inmates. They managed it to some extent, in the fashion of men who can overlook mud on the floors, grease on the tableware, clothes in need of laundering and mending, the unwashed faces and dirty feet of little boys who hate to bathe. The older boys took care of their persons fairly well, and just as easily put their mortal souls in peril. But the smaller ones were pitiable specimens of neglect and woe. Mother Marianne's visits, made while Father Damien still lived, convinced her that both the home and the boys needed the kinds of attention that only women can give.

In her "Record of St. Elizabeth's Convent," begun soon after she reached Kalaupapa, Mother Marianne wrote her impressions of the first visit to the Boys' Home on November 28, 1888: "Our little boys seemed glad to see us, several shed tears—I do not like the looks of the houses and the surroundings. How much room there is for improvement in every corner and what a large field for loving hands to cultivate—the poor children, how much they need the care of the Sisters—I fairly sicken when I think of the conditions of that yard— how shocking to a sensitive person to be walking and living over the graves of the dead. The grave yard is the boys' playground. . . . The sad impressions of today will never leave me—how I pity those who live in that horrible place where everything is so repulsive and so dirty. . . ."

"Sympathy for these poor little ones," she wrote to Bishop Hermann on May 16, 1889, "prompted me to say to Father Wendelin that Sisters were needed there to improve the conditions of things."

She remembered very well her promises to Father Damien, that Franciscans would take care of the boys just as they watched over the girls. But how was she going to provide this motherly care without offending the priest and the brother? And without endangering the sisters who would be working there? Almost five kilometers separated the Convent of St. Elizabeth from the Boys' Home. Her companion sisters could not live safely, or even comfortably, in the decrepit cottages at Kalawao. She had no means of transporting them to and from Kalawao each day. The worst complication of all lay in the sad fact that she, too, like so many others in and out of the Church, simply did not approve of Father Conrardy. They all found him arrogant, contentious, opinionated—"imprudent," as Bishop Hermann adjudged him—

and much too eager to gain the world's censure for the Board of Health and its acclaim for his dedicated self. But Bishop Hermann and his associates were stuck with him because Father Damien had wanted this wandering priest, who was not even a member of the Congregation of the Sacred Hearts, to be his helper at the Settlement.

Father Conrardy was not all prickles and pride, to be sure: he performed his duties as priest and solacer without fear of leprosy; he had a liberal attitude toward the patients and their behavior; he laughed and joked and visited with them; and therefore he was much too popular to be sent away by orders from either the bishop or the Board of Health.

Before she moved to Kalaupapa Mother Marianne informed Bishop Hermann that she did not want Father Conrardy to serve as chaplain to the sisters. His Lordship, understanding her reasons, assigned Father Wendelin to that position—thereby adding another strong personality to the Settlement's managers. After she had lived for a while at Kalaupapa, closer association with the abrasive Father Conrardy convinced Mother that her instinct about him had been correct. He, alas, was no silent worker.

A fine conflict of interests and personalities seemed to be developing when, providentially, an attack of dysentery—"an old complaint," as Brother Dutton called it—forced Father Conrardy to go for treatment to the Queen's Hospital in Honolulu. With him out of the way, if only temporarily, matters fell naturally into place. Brother Dutton welcomed any assistance the Franciscans might give him. Mr. Meyer sped to Honolulu to confer with the Board of Health, and to express his support for Mother Marianne as Damien's successor in caring for the "orphans" of Kalawao. Members of the Board told him that Mother Marianne, in whom they had "great confidence," was indeed their choice as Damien's successor. The Board had already looked about for a wealthy citizen to follow the philanthropic example set by Charles Reed Bishop, and hoped to find him soon.

By the morning of April 28 everything was settled. From Honolulu Mr. Meyer wrote to Mother Marianne, telling her that the Board unanimously requested her to take "supervision of the Boys' Home, with such aid and assistance as you may require." The Bishop of Olba, Meyer added, had already approved such an arrangement. Furthermore, knowing the problems of housing and distance, the Board agreed to send a horse and carriage for the sisters to use in traveling between Kalaupapa and Kalawao.

Mother Marianne accepted the Board's request on May 2. "We

are . . . willing to do what we can to make the boys' establishment a pleasant home for the poor children. I cannot well express my views about how this can be done until we go to work." In saying this she was being tactful, for Brother Dutton's sake, and prudent, for her own. She knew very well what needed to be done at once, and probably expected to discover a whole rats' nest of complications that she could not easily define before the sisters began their labors. For the work, she concluded, "we will need two more Sisters, whose whole time can be devoted to the care of the home."

On May 16 she wrote to Bishop Hermann. Ever since Father Damien first showed her through the Boys' Home, she explained, "my heart has bled for them and I was anxious and hungry to help put a little more sunshine into their dreary lives." As a matter of form, she submitted to the bishop's authority: "If I am going too fast, I pray your Lordship to tell me so. . . ."

His Lordship responded with obvious relief on May 19: ". . . the idea meets with my most ardent desire. . . . Knowing that those Hon. gentlemen feel more or less mortified by the interference of the Catholic bishop, I prefer to keep myself in the background, leaving you the liberty of treating the matter with the Board of Health. . . ."

Inasmuch as the Branch Hospital was being vacated at last, Mother Marianne could transfer two sisters from Kakaako. Sister Crescentia and Sister Irene arrived at Kalaupapa on May 22, 1889. The three sisters who remained in Honolulu continued to serve at Kapiolani Home, which was not moved from Kakaako to Kalihi until the following year.

A horse, a sturdy new wagon, and Manuel, a healthy Portuguese man (accompanied by his wife) reached Kalaupapa along with the sisters—and a most unusual visitor as well. Manuel would take care of the horse and wagon, and drive the sisters along the rocky road between Kalaupapa and Kalawao. Sam, the horse, turned out to be fractious and dangerous, Manuel very "hot-tempered." Mother Marianne put up with both, with great forebearance, until one day Manuel, in a great fury, threw stones at Sam with such violence that "poor old Sam's leg was broken and we never seen him again for they had to shoot him. The lepers were so angry that Manual perhaps was a shamed so he packed and went away on the next steamer." Mother Marianne, Sister Leopoldina continued, "sayed how thankful we should be to get him away without any trouble a man with such a temper is very dangerous. . . ." But the sisters regretted having to "part

with his wife as she was a sweet little lady and the best help we ever
had . . ."

By mid-June the Boys' Home was being run almost as smoothly as
the Girls'. With good sense and perfect courtesy Mother Marianne
delegated to Brother Joseph Dutton responsibility for settling the more
masculine problems, keeping for herself and the sisters the general
supervision over domestic operations and the personal attentions that
women can best provide. Sister Crescentia and Sister Irene did not
actually live as yet at Kalawao. Accompanied by Mother Marianne,
they rode over each morning and returned to the Convent of St.
Elizabeth each afternoon. This arrangement naturally added to the
burdens of both Sister Leopoldina and Mother Marianne at Kalaupapa.

The same voyage of the *Lehua* that delivered Sister Crescentia and
Sister Irene to Kalaupapa landing on May 22, 1889, also brought
Robert Louis Stevenson—"the eminent literary man," as Dr. Emerson
described him in a warning note to Mr. Meyer. Stevenson was the first
of several famous men and women who would visit the Settlement
during Mother Marianne's years there. Some rushed through it in a
few hours, hurrying to get away as soon as possible. Others stayed for a
day or two. Stevenson stayed for a full week, living in a guest cottage
and taking his meals with Dr. and Mrs. Swift at Kalawao.

He called at Bishop Home each day, beginning with the morning of
May 23. He enjoyed talking with the sisters, taking lunch or tea with
them, questioning Mother Marianne about life in the Settlement.
During that first visit he offered to teach the girls how to play croquet,
using a set he had sent to the Bishop Home from Honolulu a week or
two before. His jester's antics, and the long hours of instruction,
entertained the girls but endangered his own delicate health and
caused Mother Marianne considerable anxiety. She seems to have
recognized immediately that he, too, suffered from pulmonary tuberculosis. When she cautioned him, urging him to rest, he simply
laughed and went right on playing, sometimes for three hours on end.
He wanted to make the girls laugh, he said, to forget for a while the
pain and the loneliness in which they lived. And they, knowing nothing at all about him except that he was a very kind and a very funny
man, were delighted with this comical haole, who showed no fear of
their disease, no disgust at their ugliness.

Soon after he arrived, responding to his impressions of the place
and of the people he had seen, Stevenson composed a poem. He ad-

dressed it to "Reverend Sister Maryanne, Matron of the Bishop Home."

> To see the infinite pity of this place,
> The mangled limb, the devastated face,
> The innocent sufferers smiling at the rod,
> A fool were tempted to deny his God.
>
> He sees, and shrinks; but if he look again,
> Lo, beauty springing from the breast of pain!—
> He marks the sisters on the painful shores,
> And even a fool is silent and adores.

Below the verses he wrote "Kalawao, May 22, 1889," and his signature.

No one knows when or how he presented this tribute to the sisters. He may have brought it to them during one of his visits, but that seems to be an act of egotism such as a sensitive poet would have avoided. Inasmuch as he could not bear to say goodbye to either the girls or the sisters, he probably asked Dr. Swift or some other courier to deliver it for him after he sailed away on May 29.

When, a week later, the *Lehua* returned from Honolulu she brought, Sister Leopoldina wrote, "a very grand five hundred dollar $500 piano for the Bishop Home for Girls. We never had the pleasure of meeting our good friend Mr. Stevenson again but we heard from him and now and then he sent good wishes to our Mother."

After the piano arrived (Sister Antonia identified it as "a Wetermeyer made in Tyrole") "there was always music.... The girls had beautiful voices, so that the Bishop Home was a pleasant place, all were in good spirits until 'The Spring Fever' moved them."

Sister Leopoldina, not quite the citizen of the world that Stevenson was, knew exactly how his sojourn in the Settlement had benefited him: "no doubt he carried away with him a wealth of noble enlightened thoughts as was shown in the deep meaning of the words he has written to Mother." Like everyone else who reads his poem too quickly, or who sees only its superscription, self-effacing Sister Leopoldina did not realize that he had written his tribute for her, too, and for all her companion sisters who brought solace to the sufferers in that pitiful place.

But, then, for Sister Leopoldina Mother Marianne had no equal in this world. Immediately after writing that observation about Stevenson, Sister composed her own panegyric for Mother Marianne. It is as moving a testimony as is Stevenson's, and far more significant, inasmuch as it grew out of thirty-three years of unbroken association with her heroine:

"Yes, Mother was very wonderful! one could not leave her presence with out feeling the sweet peaceful influence of her grand noble spirit. it was not what she would say for her words were few, but just her presence seemed to fill ones weary heart with new life and strenthen the fainting spirit so that one could go cheerfully on through the dark shadows of the painful part of life. I often wondered if Mother ever suffered with those dreary dark shadows, for at all times she was the same with a smile and a pleasant encouraging word. Often I remember walking slowly home with that fainting spirit after tiresome days spent in that dreadful stench of the leper cottages . . . but a glance in Mother's sweet face and a few minuets in her powerful presence [were] so soothing. A new life of joy and sweet peace would be mine. Oh sweet and blessed years that I spent with our Mother."

NOTES on Chapter XVII

1. Lauhala tree and Madeira vine: the lauhala tree and the Madeira vine (probably a kind of mignonette introduced to Hawaii from Ecuador), whose white flowers eventually turn a funereal black, died and rotted away long ago. The vault remains, empty now: the headstone above it marks a cenotaph, not a grave. In 1936, at the request of the Belgian govenment, Father Damien's bones, lying in the casket decorated by Mother Marianne and Sister Leopoldina, were removed to Louvain, and rest now in the chapel of the seminary in which he studied. "He would not have willed it so," said Sister Antonia Brown.

2. Dutton and Baldwin Home: Dutton liked his penitential life so much, in fact, that he stayed with his "boys" for the next forty-four years. He left Kalawao for Kalaupapa only three times after the death of Father Damien in 1889 until hospitalization in the 1930s, once on business about the Boys' Home (in 1891), once to send the effects of the leper priest to Belgium (on April 15, 1893), and, once, for eye surgery. In July 1930 he was moved to St. Francis Hospital in Honolulu and remained there until his death on March 26, 1931. His final resting place is in the churchyard of St. Philomena's at Kalawao, Molokai, the place he loved.

3. The manuscript of the poem written by R. L. Stevenson is preserved in the Motherhouse in Syracuse. Details of Stevenson's visit to Molokai Leper Settlement: (a) Stevenson, *The South Seas*. pp. 181–204; (b) Sir Sidney Colvin (ed.), *The Letters of Robert Louis Stevenson*, pp. 125–135.

Chapter XVIII

"THE SWEET AND BLESSED YEARS"

THE YEARS at Kalaupapa passed, bringing their succession of labors for the lepers, their muted joys and insistent worries, the trials that Sister Leopoldina called "the dark shadows of the painful parts of life." And, during a climactic period of great stress, they brought a season of physical and spiritual travail for both Mother Marianne and her companion sisters. The dark shadows were lighted only by the Franciscans' knowledge that they did bring some sunshine into the lepers' crowded wards, some relief from despair into fainting spirits and sickening bodies. But the price those years exacted of the sisters was heavy and cruel. In spite of every intention and resolve they suffered in body and spirit, often without quite realizing what had gone wrong with them and their vocation. And always, above all else, the years brought the Franciscans perpetual reminders of mortality in the frequency with which death carried away so many of their patients, associates, and friends.

In the Leper Settlement Sister Death was always near. A compiler of statistics could almost believe that because she was so much occupied at Kalaupapa she spent less time at other places in Hawaii. After 1900 she filled the Settlement's graveyards faster than Sister Leprosy filled its cottages and wards. The number of patients confined to the Leprosarium reached its peak in the decade between 1889 and 1899, when the annual census ranged between 1,000 and 1,100. In 1900, that great turning point in so many of Earth's affairs, the census fell below 1,000 for the first time since 1888. After that the number of new cases of leprosy discovered each year declined, slowly but definitely. Epidemiologists today believe that a number of factors contributed to this merciful conclusion. But they agree that the policy of segregation was very important among those factors. Enforced more or less rigorously since 1866, it yielded its one reward. The Board of

Health could hope that some day, in a distant future, Hawaii's epidemic of leprosy would reach an end. Most of the vulnerable residents in the islands were already infected or already dead. Because the Given Grave at Kalaupapa, whether in the ground or above it, had swallowed them and their leprosy bacilli, the infection was not being transmitted as frequently to susceptible individuals on other islands. They might be vulnerable still, but their chances of being spared were increased because segregation broke the contacts between them and the carriers of those devouring germs. Sister Death, "the Sure Deliverer," was being kind to both the clean and the unclean.

Nonetheless, in 1890 the Board of Health's physicians still shipped patients enough to the Settlement to require the Franciscans' ministrations for years to come. Mother Marianne did not have to think about their being sent home to Syracuse for lack of work to do at Kalaupapa. Although Father Leonor in Honolulu still made gloomy prognostications—"Our government," he wrote to Father Bousquet on March 13, 1890, "annoyed by the reputation and often by the exaggeration on the subject of Father Damien, seems to want to try to oppose us with regard to the Franciscan sisters at the leprosarium, and to avenge themselves because the Catholics have all the honor"—Mother Marianne knew that neither Calvinist vendetta nor legislative parsimony threatened her mission.

Nor, surrounded as they were by the doomed, the dying, and the dead, did the Franciscans fear Sister Death. For them she could hold no terrors.

As sickness, exhaustion, anxiety, or death robbed them of companions in Hawaii, other sisters came—eventually, but never in sufficient numbers—to fill those empty places. All save one came from the Motherhouse in Syracuse. The one exception stepped forth from the kitchen of the Convent of St. Francis in Kakaako. Olinda de Jesus Gomes, the girl from Madeira who had been working for the sisters almost since the day she reached Honolulu in October 1884, asked to be allowed to join the community. Mother Marianne happily encouraged her interest. In December 1888, having obtained permission from Syracuse to accept her, Mother sent Olinda-Louisa to the Convent of St. Anthony in Wailuku.

There, with Sister Bonaventure as directress, the young woman spent her required year as a postulant (the term having been extended by then). In December 1889 she was accepted as a novice, and on

February 3, 1890, was invested in the habit of St. Francis, receiving
the name Sister Mary Elizabeth. Mother Marianne journeyed to Wailuku to be present for that happy event.

A little more than a year later, on April 9, 1891, Sister Elizabeth
pronounced her vows in the presence of Father Gulstan Ropert. The
community's officials in Syracuse recommended that her profession
should be binding for two years. In that same month of April 1891
Mother Marianne called Sister Elizabeth to Molokai. Sister Renata
(who had been serving at Kalawao since March 1890) returned to
Wailuku. Mother kept Sister Elizabeth at her side in Kalaupapa when
in May she assigned Sister Irene to kitchen work for the new service
the Franciscans had assumed in the Boys' Home at Kalawao. Once
again Sister Elizabeth worked in a convent's kitchen.

After many delays caused by "rain and more rains," the Home for
Boys at Kalawao was completed late in the spring of 1890. On May 15,
the Feast of the Ascension, Sister Crescentia, Sister Renata, and Sister Vincent took possession of the new Convent of Our Lady of Mercy
at Kalawao, and assumed charge of the Boys' Home. Mother Marianne
appointed Sister Crescentia its "Directress." The foundations of this
convent had been blessed by Father Conrardy in January. Bishop
Hermann, making a pastoral visit to the Settlement from May 5 to 9,
inspected the institution just before it opened. As he wrote to Mother
Marianne earlier, on January 6, His Lordship expressed his happiness
that "the boys of Kalawao would enjoy your motherly care more than in
the past."

The sisters' convent stood across the street from Father Damien's
Church of St. Philomena and from the cluster of houses in which the
boys lived, next to the Church—and still surrounded by graves and
tombstones.

Six weeks before the construction crew finished its work Mother
Marianne asked Rudolph Meyer to approve building a cottage within
the sisters' enclosure, "for the very small boys," he explained to the
Board of Health, "which she wishes to separate from the larger
ones . . . and have them more under the direct care of the Sisters."
Meyer thought the request a good one and advised the Board to "have it
granted." He and the Board soon changed their minds about this,
however, and decided to "await developments" because the planners in
Honolulu were discussing the possibility of moving the whole Settlement from the Kalawao side of the peninsula to the Kalaupapa side. As

a result, the Franciscans did not receive those special accommodations for the smaller boys until 1892.

Brother Dutton, reporting to Father Daniel Hudson in June 1890, said "all goes nicely," but added: "The good Mother feels it to be a hard trial to have the boys home—as well as the girls—but I hope all will go so smoothly and easily that she will be fully reconciled to it. It seems for the best. . . ."

The arrangement whereby the Franciscans took charge of the Boys' Home, although practicable in theory, was unworkable in fact. Some of the difficulty arose from Mother Marianne's belief that the sisters could work safely at Kalawao only during the daytimes, and that they must return to spend each night at Kalaupapa. The Convent of Our Lady of Mercy was to be used, the Board of Health agreed, as "a suitable cottage of moderate size for the occupancy of the Sisters while there during the day, that they may have a suitable place to secure privacy when they desired." But the road between Kalaupapa and Kalawao was so bad, even on the best of days, that the sisters spent at least an hour in traveling each way. They did not arrive at Kalawao until ten o'clock in the morning, and had to begin the return trip at 4 o'clock in the afternoon. Some days, when the weather was stormy or the carriage was "out of order," they did not go to Kalawao at all.

Brother Dutton, too, complicated matters by misunderstanding the part Mother Marianne expected him to play, and did not bear his share of the load. She assumed that he would continue to serve, both day and night, as the boys' leader and disciplinarian, while the Franciscans would "keep order" and do the necessary sewing and housekeeping during the hours when they were present in the Home. Dutton, however, limited himself to "business matters" and to dressing the sores of the boys and of other sick patients lying in Kalawao's grim hospital.

Rudolph Meyer learned about this situation almost immediately. He wrote to Mother Marianne on May 16, 1890, using a pen dipped in acid: "The management of this Home, since, as I learn, from Father Wendelin our kind Mr. Dutton has, to a great extent, withdrawn his helping hand must be, I fear, quite a task to you and the Sisters and I am studying how to make this matter easier—and hope to succeed—although it may not be a very short time."

The three principals, in time, with sensible discussions and without ill feeling, did rearrange responsibilities, whereby Dutton assumed a stronger part in managing the boys, if not the Home as such. But, as time—and watchful critics—would tell, this division of labor was never satisfactory to anyone. By 1894 the system's faults caused everyone involved to seek another solution to the problem. In the interval, the Franciscans struggled with the Boys' Home's many problems as best they could.

On September 3, 1891, Mother Marianne wrote to Mother Bernardina: "The past two years have been hard ones for me. . . ." The Bishop Home housed seventy-seven patients, she explained, the Boys' Home eighty-four. "I usually go there once a week and spend a few hours with them. . . ." After referring to her work, and to the fact that she must write letters late at night, "after the Sisters have retired," she inserted a personal note: "I am getting old, you know, and cannot well stand sitting up nights. . . ." But she has some compensations: Sister Leopoldina and Sister Elizabeth are loyal helpers at the Bishop Home. Sister Elizabeth "made her profession for two years, to renew it after that time has expired, and we are satisfied to have her do so. So far I am well satisfied with her."

In Honolulu, meanwhile, the mission's affairs did not progress as well. On September 10, 1890, at Kapiolani Home, Sister Martha Kaiser died "without a struggle," after being "confined to bed only a few days." (Years later, Sister Bonaventure expressed the opinion that tuberculosis had killed Sister Martha.) Now Sister Benedicta managed the Home almost unaided, "Poor Sister Rosalia being a worry and cair instead of help."

During that same week the Board of Health was reacting to a personality problems at the new Receiving Station, hidden in a thicket of algaroba trees on the beach at Kalihi. Miss Amy Fowler, a much-lauded English nurse—who, as a secular Third Order Dominican, preferred to be addressed as "Sister Rose Gertrude"—had arrived early in 1890, amid fanfares sounded from London to Honolulu, announcing that she had come to take care of the lepers. Not knowing what else to do with her, the Board of Health put Sister Rose Gertrude in charge of the Receiving Station. She lasted about five months and by September 1890 decided that she'd had enough of that dismal service, and resigned.

In mid-September 1890 these several crises beset Sister Benedicta as well as the Board of Health. The Board, thinking principally of economies, informed her that it wished to close Kapiolani Home. The girls could be lodged in boarding schools at far less cost to the treasury;

or, even better, they could be sent home to relatives with no expense at all to the government. Furthermore, closing the Home would allow the government to demolish the big building at Honolulu's very front door, that much too visible reminder to tourists of the kingdom's mortifying shame. Earlier in the year, to the general satisfaction of the community, workmen had improved the waterfront's appearance by moving away the eyesores of the old Receiving Station. They sent some knocked-down cottages to Kalaupapa and towed others away "on a large scow," Sister Leopoldina wrote, "down the beach many miles" to Kalihi, where grew "a thick forest of algaroba trees. . . . In this forest the Leper Receiving Station is heden away from all view not only of the lovely ocean but from everything. . . ."

Kapiolani Home stood next on the businessmen's list of disposable items. They did not reckon with redoubtable Sister Benedicta. "No Sister told them. I was not the one who started this Home, and I shall not do anything to brake it up." Sister Benedicta's talents as a politician were as formidable as her reply. She employed the convent's telephone to organize powerful help from all sides, most especially from Bishop Hermann and Father Leonor, who still had access to King Kalakaua and Queen Kapiolani. "When [the legislators] learned that it was Mother's wish to keep the poor unfortunate girls of leper parents who were more to be pited than orphans there was never a word about braking up of the Home again."

Amy Fowler's resignation led the Board to propose another arrangement to Sister Benedicta: why not move Kapiolani Home to the Receiving Station in Kalihi, and put her in charge of both institutions? Once again Sister Benedicta refused to accept a plan so inconsiderate of her healthy girls. The Board solicited Mother Marianne's help in resolving the deadlock. On September 18 she wrote to Bishop Hermann, telling him about the problem, saying that "we look to you for advice and approval," and authorizing Sister Bonaventure, assisting Sister Benedicta at the time, to confer with His Lordship "and to act for me."

The negotiators worked out a compromise that was considerate of everyone except Sister Benedicta. But she, like Mother Marianne never thought of herself first, would never say no to a plan that took care of the needy lepers as well as her clean charges. She agreed to direct both Home and Receiving Station, provided that "a place could be prepaired so [the healthy girls] could be protected from the desease." Happy to oblige, the Board of Health constructed a new

Kapiolani Home in Kalihi at a safe distance from the Receiving Station: "a large one story building... with a wide pleasant verandah a large yard and playground, and neet little two story convent... and it was all enclosed with a very high close board fence to protect them from the leprosy."

While the new Home was being built Sister Benedicta, "always so brave and courageous," rode each morning in a hired hack through the slums of Honolulu and across the dusty plain of Kalihi to reach the Station, about five kilometers away. Sister Bonaventure having returned to Wailuku, Sister Rosalia, well or ill, was entrusted with managing the old Home during the day. After "attending the sick and dressing the sores" at Kalihi, Sister Benedicta rode back to Kakaako in the late afternoon, to face the problems that Sister Rosalia could not handle. Sister Benedicta had good reason to rejoice when finally she could move her girls and Sister Rosalia to the new compound at Kalihi.

This compromise by no means ended the saga of Kapiolani Home and Sister Benedicta's battles with the Board of Health. The success with which she fought those engagements won Mother Marianne's approval. She saw how, of all the companions who served in Hawaii, Sister Benedicta most resembled her in strength of purpose and in the courage to sustain the work of the mission. Mother watched this treasure from afar until 1916. Then, as her own health failed to the point where she knew that Sister Death was drawing near, she sent for Sister Benedicta to be her successor at Kalaupapa.

The great world beyond the horizon intruded but little upon the sisters at Kalaupapa. They learned eventually, and only incompletely, about events that shook the kingdom: the death of King Kalakaua in San Francisco on January 20, 1891; the accession of his sister, Princess Liliuokalani, when the sad news reached Honolulu on January 29; the Revolution of 1893 that deposed her and ended the monarchy in favor of the efficient businessmen who preferred their kind of autarchy to hers.

When King Kalakaua died the sisters would have recalled the many occasions at which they met him, especially the last. One day in August 1890 he arrived at Kalaupapa, unannounced, aboard "a very large steamer," probably a British warship. His Majesty, accompanied by "3 or 4 of the english officers," walked through the Settlement, looking for a place in which to raise a memorial to Father Damien that the people of Great Britain wished to present. The royal party called upon Mother Marianne for advice. She suggested "a spot just outside the Bishop Home grounds, and close to the Damien Road, as the monument could be seen there from any boat passing close to the shore." According to Sister Columba O'Keeffe (who heard this story many years later), Mother conducted the gentlemen to the place and they accepted her suggestion. The monument, generally known in the Settlement as "the Celtic Cross," was erected in September 1893, upon the site Mother recommended. Today, because of Kalaupapa's vegetation, it is invisible to ships at sea—and to visitors by land as well, until they discover it in its bower.

And when, with another bloodless revolution much more ruthless than the one of 1887 by which they restrained King Kalakaua and routed Walter Murray Gibson, Honolulu's impatient businessmen forced Queen Liliuokalani from the throne on January 17, 1893, the sisters remembered the few times they had met her, in Honolulu, in Wailuku, and most recently in Kalaupapa. Her Majesty came to the Settlement in 1892, to visit her suffering imprisoned people. Sister Leopoldina thought her "hard faced" and "cold," singularly unmoved by the attempts of the Bishop Home girls to entertain her with songs and recitations. She was not at all like warm and compassionate Queen Kapiolani. Where Kapiolani would have wept, Liliuokalani sat as stiff as a statue. The girls wept instead of the queen, feeling that she rebuffed them. No one was kind enough to think that the poor troubled queen might have been so affected by the experience that she dared not weep. But certainly she was grateful for the respite from misery and sorrow the Franciscans offered her, as she sat for a while in the blessed peace of the convent, in the company of the immaculate sisters.

The swift succession of regimes in Honolulu—first the Provisional Government of 1893–1894; then the Republic of Hawaii from July 4, 1894, until August 12, 1898; and finally, after that fateful day, when the United States formally annexed the islands, the Territory of Hawaii—did not disturb the Franciscans much. Except for Sister Leopoldina perhaps, they were not such romantics, or such fervent patriots, whether American or Hawaiian, that they rejoiced or sorrowed so openly over changes in temporal rulers. They worked for a different lord, in hope of entering another kingdom.

Mother Marianne expressed her sympathies about annexation in a letter to her nephew in Chicago. "We are Americans now, these islands have been annexed. I hope for the best," she wrote to Paul Cope on 25 August 1898, thirteen days after the great change was marked in

Honolulu. "The poor natives feel very bad about losing their country. We have lived here since Nov. 1883. . . . "

As did many others of Hawaii's residents during that time of transition, Mother Marianne seems to have believed that, as a consequence of annexation, everyone living in the islands automatically became a citizen of the United States. In making this assumption she—and many other hopeful residents—were mistaken. The Organic Act which established the Territory of Hawaii in 1900 carefully specified that American citizenship would be granted outright only to people who had acquired Hawaiian citizenship either by being born in the islands or by being naturalized. Aliens to Hawaii remained aliens to America. Looking ahead, the generous politicians who drew up the Organic Act, allowed certain estimable folk among those aliens to apply for American citizenship. (Naturally, members of the "colored races" and lowly plantation laborers of any complexion were not regarded as acceptable. The problem of dealing with 29,000 sun-tanned native Hawaiians was resolved with the aid of Science: Congress declared that they were Polynesian representatives of the superlative Caucasian race.)

The list of applicants for American citizenship who qualified for the honor is very short. It presents the names of only a few women. None of the Franciscan sisters is among them. (Sister Leopoldina and those of her associates who had been born in the United States did not lose their citizenship, of course, when they moved to Hawaii). Obviously, in that era of unequal rights, most of the eligible women living in the new territory simply did not bother to apply for a prize that would bring so little reward.

Mother Marianne's own American citizenship had been gained when her father became a citizen sometime before the Census of 1855. Whether or not her official status was known to her we do not know. Being a woman she would not have been able to vote, so there is no reason why she would ever have considered or referred to the fact that she was a citizen or have known of her automatic citizenship.

More than likely, Mother Marianne herself gave little heed to the business of citizenship. She had too many other claims upon her time and energies. Even so, after spending almost all the years of her life in New York state and in the scarcely less Yankee province of Hawaii, in her thoughts and loyalties she must have regarded herself as an American. But thoughts, memories, loyalties, habits are of little importance compared with her deeds. With those she transcended all such narrow bounds as nations try to impose upon their citizens.

The Franciscans rejoiced or grieved over people. They sorrowed for Queen Kapiolani, their best friend among the members of the royal family, when she lost her husband. A girl from Bishop Home who fell into sin hurt them more than did the fall of the monarchy. A repentant sinner who returned to the Home—and to the Church—in time to die "a Saintly death" encouraged them more than did the ceremonial raising of the Stars and Stripes over Iolani Palace, proclaiming to all the world that now these islands belonged to the United States of America. The sisters thanked God when a patient accepted the One True Faith in which they believed. For the many lepers who told them "I thank God for giving me this sickness, because it has helped me to save my soul," the sisters, too, sent up prayers of praise and thanksgiving.

But they were not so unworldly as to be indifferent to the consequences of political changes occurring in Honolulu. They realized the benefits that American ownership would bring to the islands. Thus, on September 11, 1898—when, in a fussy little ceremony of showing the flag, a set of American commissioners landed at Kalaupapa and, in the shortest possible time, saluted the Stars and Stripes flying from a pole beside the superintendent's house, toured the Bishop Home with Mother Marianne as guide, and then dashed off to invade the next hamlet farther along the coast—Sister Leopoldina reacted as if the millenium had begun. "The whole Settlement was in silence," she observed, understanding how deeply Hawaiians mourned the death of their nation. But she herself, a child of America, glowed—no doubt for all the right reasons: "Oh how happy I am! to know that our dear old flag our glorious Stars and Strips will protect the poor Hawaiins I was sure great blessing would come with it . . . our blessed country never fails, victry is always ours. . . ."

For that festive day the Franciscans made little American flags for the patients to wear in hats or on dresses. Most Hawaiians rejected those symbols of the new authority, despite Sister Leopoldina's enthusiasm for "the great magistical stars and strips," despite Mother Marianne's talks as she "tried to have them understand how much better they would be cared for." Sister Leopoldina could not ignore the girls' reactions: "it was dreadful to see the expressions change on their disfigured faces, anger and sadness narrowed their eyes, and made them look deathly, yet no words, through it all they were silent, and I quickly learned I too should be silent. . . ." When she and Dr. Richard Oliver found one of those tiny flags trampled in the mud they became terribly upset. The doctor, raging at such an insult, cried out to

Mother Marianne that the patient who did that should be shot.
". . . but Mother's peaceful expression did not change, she said very
gently, Dr. I could never hurt the poor afflicted creatures when they
are down, now they love their country and their flag it is not easy for
them to give up but let us wait a while. Uncle Sam will teach his poor
afflicted children to love the dear old flag, so that they will be ready to
give their life for it. . . . " Dr. Oliver and Sister Leopoldina accepted
that instruction in generosity.

Mother Marianne's own generosity had been strengthened years
before, long before she left Syracuse. In the scrapbook she kept during
her years there she pasted a quotation from St. Philip Neri that she
honored: "When the service of our neighbor is in question we must
reserve to ourselves neither time nor place."

The Franciscans sorrowed over the sudden death of their august
friend and protector, His Lordship the Bishop of Olba. In Honolulu
Bishop Hermann suffered a stroke on February 18, 1892, and died four
days later, at the age of sixty-four. And the sisters were delighted
when, early in June, word reached them saying that the Holy See had
chosen their good friend from Wailuku, Father Gulstan Ropert, to be
the next Vicar Apostolic in the Hawaiian Islands. Bishop Gulstan,
consecrated in San Francisco on September 25, received the title of
Bishop of Panopolis.

On the day after Bishop Hermann died the Very Reverend Father
Francis Neubauer arrived in Honolulu. In October 1889 he was elected to succeed Father Joseph Lesen as Provincial Minister of the Third
Order of St. Francis in North America, and in that capacity came from
Syracuse to inspect Mother Marianne's mission in Hawaii. In person,
character, and manners Father Neubauer was very different from any
of the provincial ministers with whom Mother Marianne had worked
in Syracuse. He certainly was the very antithesis of Father Lesen.

He seems to have been one of the Franciscan officials in Syracuse
who, from the beginning, opposed Mother Marianne and Father Lesen
in their willingness to send a mission to Hawaii. In his letters to her
after she settled in Honolulu, Father Lesen's several allusions to adversaries within the Order who might someday replace him as provincial minister probably were written with Father Neubauer very much
in mind. In 1892, three years after he did succeed to Lesen's high
office, Neubauer had not changed his attitude toward Mother
Marianne's mission when, very reluctantly, he journeyed out to

Hawaii to inspect it. She did not help to soothe him when, in the spring of 1891, she sent him a bank draft to pay for the expenses of his visitation. "You have done a very foolish thing," he scolded on May 28, 1891, "in ordering that money, to be sent to me. . . . You knew, that I wanted you home for the Chapter [to be scheduled for later that year], which idea you disliked and to check its possibility, you thought to put up a draft for me. You ought to know me better. . . ."

Nonetheless, he did not return the bank draft. And almost a year later he ventured forth from Syracuse. Still grumbling, he descended upon Kalaupapa. The few references the Franciscans in Hawaii made to him in letters and reminiscences indicate that he began his visitation by being cold, hypercritical, demanding, and unbelievably blind to the difficulties that plagued the sisters from every side. He must have caused Mother Marianne a great deal of distress. An entry in the journal she kept at the time implies as much: "Father talked with me today—his language and his manner was hard and heartless. *Fiat.*"

Inasmuch as neither she nor anyone else ever explained why he should be so hard with her, we can only wonder about his motives. Mother Marianne, who never indulged in self pity, had no cause to invent that summation of her interview with the powerful provincial. His own letters, written after he returned to America, indicate that he still found things to disturb him. He seems to have wanted her to come home to Syracuse, where she might put to better use for the community her abilities as administrator and leader. In Hawaii, on the other hand, he criticized "the melancholic spirit" he detected among the sisters at the several convents. If, indeed, he did chastise Mother Marianne for allowing this "certain sadness," instead of helping her and the sisters to ease it by praising them for their labors and by sending them more help from Syracuse, he heaped further tribulations upon spirits already heavily laden.

The experience of having to live for a whole week in the Leper Settlement was a great trial for him, yet he appears not to have understood that his own impressions of the place were shared by the sisters who spent their lives there. He arrived at Kalaupapa aboard the sickening *Lehua* on March 18, after having made a short visit to the convent in Wailuku. Father Wendelin put him up in the guest room of his little house, and Sister Elizabeth at the convent prepared most of his meals—which he ate in solitude. ". . . he did not relish the food and complained," wrote Sister Antonia Brown. "but one day he happened to come out when the Sisters were dining. He saw their scanty table.

(They had given him their best) and he just stood in silence and from that moment he never again complained of food." He was beginning to notice some of the facts of living at Kalaupapa, where food was never plentiful or varied enough to please the palates of spoiled Americans.

Apparently during his long sojourn in Honolulu Father Neubauer discussed a number of matters with his hosts at the Sacred Hearts mission. Some of the fathers fretted over the presence of Father Conrardy and "Brother" Joseph Dutton at Kalawao because they did not belong to a proper lay or religious organization. Father Neubauer resolved that difficulty. At the request of Mother Marianne (as Dutton himself testified in 1925), "Mr. Dutton was invested in the Habit of the Third Order," she wrote in her journal on March 19, St. Joseph's Day, and the day after the Provincial Minister reached the Settlement. (Dutton's official name in the secular Order was Brother Francis Joseph, but he preferred to be known as Brother Joseph because Father Damien had called him that. Mother Marianne, however, following custom, always referred to him as "Mr. Dutton"). Three days later, after due appraisal of the controversial priest, Neubauer also accepted Father Conrardy into the Third Order, thereby relieving the Sacred Hearts missioners of an anomaly, if not an irritation.

On that same March 22, Mother Marianne noted in her journal, Father Neubauer declared Sister Crescentia "Superior" of the convent at the Boys' Home. And he told Sister Elizabeth the "canonical terms" which ended her probation. The next morning, after Mass and Holy Communion, "Father Provincial received the Profession of Sister Elizabeth. Thanks be to God that she is settled." The day should have been a joyful one for Mother Marianne, but he spoiled it with that "hard and heartless" talk. *Fiat,* she wrote, underlining the word: "Let it be done."

During the return voyage to Syracuse, Father Neubauer thought a great deal about what he had seen in Hawaii. ". . . I am home sick for the Islands," he confessed in his letter to Sister Bonaventure. "I am not at home in my mind and when I come to reflect on the Islands, tears fill my eyes. . . ." His week's stay in the Settlement, he believed, "was undoubtedly, in the midst of all human misery, notwithstanding of the pleasantest kind and most interesting for a curious mind like mine. Kindness on all sides from the good priests Wendelin & Conrardy certainly in an extreme measure from our good Sisters and every body."

He made amends to Mother Marianne. On June 6, 1892, in a long circular letter preparing all Franciscan houses for the General Chapter to be convened on July 25, he introduced a paragraph that praised the sisters in Hawaii: "Since nearly 9 years have our good Sisters under the quiet and energetic guidance of Moth. Marianne worked heroically among the Hawaiians in schools, hospitals and in latter years in the Fath. Damien and Bishop's Home on Molokai for the poorest of humankind, the lepers. Not the spirit of vagrancy or vain curiosity has prompted me, to risk the dangers of steam and ocean to investigate their work and see with my own eyes and judge unbiasedly whether it be advisable, to recall them from their post or encourage the continuance of their labors and sacrifices. To my happy surprise it has pleased God, to bless their work and give them that noble spirit, to consume to the very end their noble holocaust. Not one is willing to return and all on the Islands venerate them as Saints, whose departure would be deplored as a dire calamaty. To the cause itself and its heroical supporters I owe a duty, which makes me send out among you an appeal for help, that such who feel it their vocation will come forward and join them in their saintly life. . . ."

Many sisters in Syracuse—having assumed that, according to their constitutions, Mother Delphina could not be elected for a third consecutive term—kept asking Father Neubauer why he did not recall Mother Marianne. "All feel sorry, but not I," about her staying in Hawaii, he reported to Sister Benedicta on July 10, 1892. "I envy [Mother Marianne] for her quiet position and separation from a stormy world. Likewise I envy you and everyone of our Sisters in the Islands for the enjoyment of the extraordinary blessings, which they enjoy from the hand of God."

Nevertheless, he would not permit doubly blessed Sister Benedicta to hire a servant for Kapiolani Home until she had at least thirty girls in her care. As he told her earlier, "She who serves the lepers, earns no more than she who sweeps the floor. . . . A true religious is simple like a child."

This complex man did not allow sentiment in any heart to deter him from making certain administrative decisions. Upon returning to Syracuse he insisted that the Franciscans in Hawaii "voluntarily and spontaneously renounce all possible privileges and rights of election or being elected in the Provincial Chapter of our Lord 1892." As evidence of her compliance with this order, each sister in the islands had to sign the declaration. Although Father Neubauer probably intended only to be practical, considering the distance between Syracuse and Hawaii, the language in which he imposed this measure upon them could not fail to make the sisters feel that he had devised one more way of cutting them off from home.

On February 17, 1893, almost a year after Father Neubauer left the Leper Settlement, he addressed a letter to Mother Marianne. In reviewing "the impressions which I have received there, I must say that there is a certain sadness spread over the houses of our Sisters. That I noticed in Kalihi, Wailuku, Kalawao and even Kalaupapa not excepted. The surroundings are certainly not encouraging, the life too monotonous, the climate too depressing. . . . This melancholic spirit I noticed not only in some Sisters more particularly than in others, but also in the priests and Mr. Dutton. In you alone I observed that happy cheerful disposition to make it serene and happy for every one and every where, by every word and every step. Not one is like the others and those, who have it, let them thank God, and also let others enjoy its blessing! . . ."

Mother Marianne, the receiver of this letter, destroyed the original after having copied it in the notebook in which she preserved correspondence important to the history of her mission. In this copy she used initials rather than full names, hoping thereby to disguise identities of people mentioned—especially herself, the receiver of such praise.

Happily for the sisters, they found a more sympathetic friend closer to home in Bishop Gulstan Ropert. He made his first pastoral visit to the Leper Settlement on October 25, 1892. Father Wendelin, Father Conrardy, and a delegation of patients, all on horseback and bringing spare mounts for the visitors, met the bishop and his party of priests and laymen at the foot of the pali and conducted them through the Settlement. During the afternoon His Grace called at the Bishop Home. "After a short visit to the Sisters," Father Wendelin reported to Paris, "the boarders (about 80) all lepers paid their respects to His Grace by songs, compliments, etc. All the houses . . . adorned with greenery etc were visited by His Grace and were appreciated by the boarders, more or less disfigured by the disease." The girls of Bishop Home did not feel rejected that day. The next morning "Confirmation for Kalaupapa took place after High Mass. It was the first time Msgr. administered the sacrament and His Grace will probably not forget that the first person he confirmed was a leper."

Bishop Gulstan expressed surprise "at seeing Kalaupapa so populated. 'When I visited the leprosarium in 1886 there were almost no houses here, the lepers were living at Kalawao.'" Now, in 1892, Father Wendelin replied, about 1,100 patients and 200 nonlepers lived in the Settlement, but only about one-third dwelled at Kalawao. "'At the time of my visit in 1886, there weren't 700,'" said the bishop. "'The majority of those people are probably dead.'" For answer Father Wendelin pointed to the several crowded cemeteries, spreading like lesions upon the body of a leper, in the wide green meadow between Damien's church and the brink of Kalawao Bay, upon the slopes of Kauhako crater, and now, the newest, extending along the shore at Kalaupapa.

On the third day "Father Conrardy, myself, and some Canaques . . . accompanied Msgr. At the foot of the mountain, we had to separate. Msgr. went up (with several nonleprous canaques) to return to the world and we turned the rein toward our dear solitude . . . to devote ourselves with renewed courage to the work of the lepers. . . ."

Even though governments might change in Honolulu, they caused Mother Marianne no anxiety about the Franciscan's tenure at the Leper Settlement. She knew that no one else could be found to take their place. Rumors that Anglican nuns were being recruited to supplant Catholic sisters were heard no more. And Miss Amy Fowler's eccentricities, which made her an object either of ridicule or of scandal in Honolulu, convinced the Board of Health that laywomen could not be trusted to do the work.

Letters of visits from members of the Board and from successive Ministers of the Interior, whose names might change but whose policies differed not a whit, assured Mother that she and her hard working group were too well esteemed to be in danger of dismissal. Thus, S. M. Damon a member of the Board of Health (and a staunch Congregationalist), wrote to her on August 3, 1891, expressing "admiration and reverence for those engaged in Christian services that you . . . render cheerfully as your daily task." W. O. Smith, a lawyer who had opposed King Kalakaua and Queen Liliuokalani, and who served in a number of posts for the several oligarchies that replaced the monarchy, regularly sent Christmas greetings to Mother Marianne and her sisters. In November 1894, as President of the Board of Health, he wrote to say that during a recent visit to the Settlement the members of the Board were "so impressed with the magnitude of the work being performed by yourself and the Sisters [that] we feel you should have more assistance." He assured her that the government would gladly support four more sisters. On March 20, 1899, as he left the presidency of the Board, Smith sent her a letter of thanks: ". . . I wish again to express my love for you, and appreciation of your work and devotion. . . ."

The patrons of the two Homes at the Settlement were equally loyal. Charles R. Bishop never visited the Leprosarium, but Henry P. Baldwin (who endowed the Boys' Home) went there several times as a legislator and a member of governmental committees. Both philanthropists appreciated the good use to which their gifts of money were being put and always supported such improvements as Mother Marianne or Brother Dutton requested. For their part, Mother Marianne and Brother Dutton never failed to express their thanks to Mr. Bishop and Mr. Baldwin with letters, drawings or photographs of the institutions and their inmates, and with prayers offered in private.

Where Honolulu gave, Syracuse withheld. The Motherhouse, too, had its share of problems: the number of novices and professed sisters was never great enough to meet the needs of the community's network of convents, hospitals, and schools in the United States. And, in the perennial story of all religious institutions at the beginnings of their histories, money and facilities that money might buy were always lacking.

At last, on November 30, 1892, Mother Marianne received a third company of reinforcements when Sister M. De Sales Waldburger, Sister M. Hieronyma Braun, and Sister M. Albina Sluder arrived in Honolulu. All had volunteered to join the mission, probably in response to Father Neubauer's exhortation. Although he had urged Sister Hieronyma *not* to go, thinking her not quite ready for the life of heroic devotion that Hawaii required, she opposed his advice, if not his will, and set forth anyhow. Sister Albina was so eager to come that she was still a novice. The three newcomers stayed for a few days with Sister Benedicta in the Receiving Station at Kalihi before Mother Marianne brought them to Molokai, on December 7.

There Sister Hieronyma—or Sister Jerome, as companions called her—soon realized that she could not bear to work with lepers. Sister Rosalia had not made the process of adjustment any easier. "No sooner had they . . . arrived at Kalihi," Father Neubauer fumed in a letter to Mother Marianne on February 17, 1893 (the same in which he complained about "the sadness spread over the homes of our Sisters"), "than wickedness commenced to belabor them, and one of the older Sisters there thought... to pour out all the imaginary evils and halucinations on the newcomers as a welcome means to treat them in her own fashion like so many others...."

Father Neubauer condemned Sister Jerome as a troublemaker, and wished that "she were the only one of its kind." Genial Bishop Gulstan found reason to agree with this diagnosis: when he suggested that she serve as teacher or nurse in Wailuku, Sister Jerome refused to accept either alternative. She wanted only to escape from these dreadful islands, to go back to America. Mother Marianne could do little else but send her home.

Realizing that poor Sister Rosalia was on the verge of becoming more than "a mental case," Mother sent her too home, with Sister Jerome for guardian and companion. They departed from Honolulu on April 26, 1893.

Sister De Sales lasted a little bit longer. She was assigned to Wailuku on May 24, 1893, did not like the place, and was reassigned to the Kapiolani Home in Honolulu on June 3, 1893. She returned to Syracuse on April 23, 1896. Sister Ludovica Gibbons, who had accompanied Mother Marianne to Hawaii in 1883, went with Sister De Sales. Mother was present in Honolulu when these two sisters departed.

Of the three "newcomers" of 1892, only Sister Albina showed no fear of lepers and spent the rest of her life serving in Hawaii. At Kalaupapa, in the tiny chapel of the Convent of St. Elizabeth, "Our dear Sister Albina made her profession on the 12th day of August, feast of St. Clara," Mother Marianne informed Mother Delphina on August 17, 1893. Reverend Father Wendelin received her vows, Sister Leopoldina, Sister Elizabeth, and Mother Marianne were witnesses. "It was not a grand profession, but it was none the less impressive.... I had almost forgotten what to do on such occasions. I made Sister a wreath of Smilax (which we have growing here) with white flowers entwined...."

Mother Marianne directed the mission from her little office in St. Elizabeth's Convent. Once or twice a year, until 1899, she forced herself to brave the discomforts of the sea as she went to Wailuku or to Honolulu to see how the sisters fared, to settle problems of policies or personalities that arose even in such small outposts. In Kalaupapa she sat at her little desk whenever she could find the time from other duties—during rainy afternoons, late at night, far into the early hours of a morning—writing instructions to her deputies, giving advice, making inquiries, sending acknowledgments, composing reports to the Board of Health, to the Motherhouse, to bishops and to father provincials. Once in a rare while she snatched a few moments for writing a personal letter, to Mother Bernardina, or to a relative never seen but fondly claimed, such as young Paul Cope, the nephew troubled about his vocation. And always, for the sake of keeping records in good order, she devoted countless hours to making copies of official letters received or sent, and lists—lists of patients in the Home, lists of items to be purchased from Honolulu's stores, lists of things not received even after weeks of waiting. And filling out forms, endless numbers and kinds of forms, to appease clerks in Honolulu. And, stupidest exaction of all, each month in every year she must write a formal letter acknowledging the receipt of pay warrants sent to the sisters by those same clerks in Honolulu.

Quite aside from the fact that she suffered from seasickness on those trips to Oahu or Maui, Mother Marianne preferred to stay in Kalaupapa for other reasons. Her "children" were there: with them she found everyone she loved and everything she needed to fulfill her convenant with God. In contrast, Honolulu and Wailuku stole precious time and energy which might better be given to the people who most needed her care. " . . . her heart and thought were all for Molokai," wrote Sister Antonia Brown, who served with Mother on Molokai for twelve happy years. "The girls were her treasures. No Mother could love her child more than she loved those, she never called them 'girls' but 'children,' no matter how old they were, to her they were just 'children.'"

In this willingness to stay in Kalaupapa she was not indulging herself. The duties she performed each day in the wards of Bishop Home can never have been exercises in self indulgence. Even after five years of daily association with the lepers at Kakaako, the sight and the smell of them still affected her: "I suffer when I go to church," she confided to her "Record of St. Elizabeth's Convent" on December 2, 1888, soon after the move to Kalaupapa. "the smell and the sight of lepers everywhere is disagreeable. . . . How glad I was to get outside to breathe again the fresh clean air. We met many of our old patients outside. All were anxious to shake hands—something that makes me shudder—yet we did it . . ."

Sister Leopoldina confirmed this reaction: "Poor dear Mother how she suffered being subject to sick headaches often she would be days that her stomach could not retain anything, so the dreadful mixture of iodoform, leprosy, and strong perfume on hot summer days was almost more than she could endure." Father Wendelin, too, was so bothered by the effluvium that as soon as possible he enlarged the painted church, in order to ventilate it more effectively.

That entry in a journal intended for herself alone to read is the most personal and the most revealing comment about her work that Mother Marianne has left. Its last clause presents her spirit exactly: "Yet we did it." Courage, resolution, sheerest indomitable will: whatever the attribute is called, in it lies the explanation for her strength.

The whole course of her life, after she saw the plight of the lepers at Kakaako, is implicit in the opinion she expressed so often to her companion-sisters: "charity is the greatest of all virtues." In charity she would dedicate herself to the service of lepers, those most feared and rejected of men. After making the decision, amid the uglinesses of Kakaako, she knew what road she must walk into the future. She never lost her way along that road, just as she never lost her faith. But, as she must have learned with almost every step along the way, charity alone was not enough to sustain her. She needed the strongest of wills to help her, and the most unshakable faith in the examples of Christ and St. Francis. In keeping her faith, she trained that will and found the strength to go on.

Few of her companion sisters would be as strong. At least four would falter and fail. Sister Jerome refused even to set foot upon the path. Sister Rosalia, who at least tried to take that path, found escape from it in madness. Sister Vincent probably was the greatest disappointment of all to Mother Marianne. She who had given her obedience so readily, just before the departure from Kakaako, showed signs that she regretted her fate as soon as the three Franciscans reached the landing place at Kalaupapa. On November 24, their tenth day in the Settlement, Mother Marianne wrote in her private journal: "Sr. V. looks bad is either sick or sulky. I do not know how to treat her, I do not understand her changeable disposition. . . . There is much we might do if we all worked together with a cheerful spirit—" On December 10 she added another line of worry: "Sr. V. one of her spells— do not understand her. I pray God to inspire me what to do." December 12 brought a similar entry.

These expressions of concern, and many others like them, indicate that Mother Marianne did suffer "dark days," as Sister Leopoldina called them, did feel the "dreary dark shadows" that events and people at the Settlement cast over her. Sister Leopoldina may not have known about them, but those times of disappointment and doubt happened oftener than Mother's companions realized. The entry in Mother's journal for Christmas Eve 1888 is saddening: "Filled the Sisters stockings—Neither of them said anything about it. I have never spent such a cold Christmas." Sister Leopoldina would have been distressed had she known how she herself caused Mother to feel such sadness. But Sister Leopoldina, too, was unhappy during that cheerless season. She, too, was suffering the miseries of adjusting to Kalaupapa and trying to suppress her dread of catching the loathsome disease. But she recovered fairly soon, precisely because she talked about her troubles with Mother, and rose to become one of her most faithful assistants. Sister Vincent never did overcome her miseries, whatever may have caused them. She endured them for twelve long years before she broke free from Kalaupapa—and from the powerful hold of her concept of the duty she owed to the Franciscans and to her God. Sister Leopoldina climbed the pali of tribulations to gain the top. But poor Sister Vincent, faint with fear at the prospect wherever she looked, lay down by the wayside and despaired.

Mother Marianne, a woman of strongest will, never permitted herself the misery of fearing the lepers or doubting her mission. On December 9, 1888, while Sister Vincent retreated into one of her "spells," while heavy rains fell all the day long from gray skies, Mother looked beyond the confines of the Leprosarium: "Several beautiful waterfalls from the Mountain. How grand are the works of God. I prayed much and earnestly today for the conversion of Hon. C. R. Bishop and Mr. S. Damon."

Wherever possible she put aside detail in order to follow the greater rule elected by servants of God. The field was large, as she had seen, almost in a vision, while sitting at her desk in Syracuse. In Hawaii she found how large the field was in fact—and how heavy would be the yoke she wished to assume. In going to Kalaupapa she did not forsake the larger field for the smaller one. On the contrary, in the Leper Settlement, because of the policy of segregation, the whole large field was concentrated in the one small place. And in this one place, this concentration camp for the doomed, she could help the largest number of leprosy's victims with the least waste of time and energy.

The five years she spent at Kakaako taught her to conserve energy.

She was growing old—as she said in letters to Mother Bernardina. And, as Sister Leopoldina emphasized, she was "suffering most of the time"—a fact that Mother Marianne would not admit to anyone until she was more than sixty years old. Nonetheless, at Kakaako (if not in Syracuse) she resolved that mere sickness of the body would not make her as unreliable as Sister Rosalia, as weak as Sister Martha or Sister Charles. She had too many important things to do in this life, and she would not submit to the tyranny of an ailing body. By acts of will she forced herself to work even when that weak body protested so much that it would scarcely walk at her command. Sister Leopoldina's description of Mother, faint and ill during the morning of their departure for Kalaupapa, and yet utterly resolute, is the paradigm of her life during the years she spent in Hawaii.

That strong will, sheathed perhaps in soft words and cheerful smiles, she turned upon her companions when they were well. She had the grace to use it kindly, almost always with thoughtfulness and humor. When they were ill or unhappy, she worried about them, coddled them, endured with admirable patience their "spells," even their disobediences, because she accepted the sisters, too, as part of her burden. In Hawaii, as in Syracuse, she gave cheerfully, to sisters, to lepers, to officials of church and state. And, somehow, she found the energy to complete a thousand tasks each day, even when she was harried and sick. When she felt well—or, rather, relatively well—she was "a marvel," as Sister Leopoldina said. Sister Antonia, visiting Kalaupapa on "a working vacation" in the summer of 1889, found her "hard at work full of energy. She was all over."

She must have found means of restoring that ailing body's reserves of energy in meditation, in prayer, in "dressing the altar," even in work itself. Most certainly she taught herself, with the wisdom of the sickly, how to conserve energy as she worked at ordinary tasks. Robert Louis Stevenson was such an artful saver of energy. When he taught the Bishop Home girls how to play croquet, and at times appeared to be a veritable whirlwind of activity, he was careful, as Sister Leopoldina noticed, to "fling himself down upon the grass" while his pupils took their turns at the wickets. He might be calling instructions, or making funny remarks, but he was also resting his sick lungs for a few moments, and easing the scrawny muscles that depended so much upon the air those treacherous lungs drew in. Mother Marianne would have known that secret too, whereby a strong will and good sense reinforce each other in sustaining a body despite its weaknesses.

Above all, she learned the uses of silence. She did not talk much, as several sisters have remarked. She was a silent worker in more ways than one. She had learned, not only from keeping the Rule of Penance, how the chattering tongue, like the chittering mind, is a terrible waster of energy. An inner quiet, a salving peace, dwelled within her. And this gave her the look of serenity that impressed everyone who met her.

As a boon of the kind Mother Marianne could never have expected to receive, she acquired two gift-children to keep for her very own. She had scores of leprous "children" in the wards of Bishop Home, but she did not hesitate to take two healthy babies when they were offered to her. They were sisters, those two. Their parents were Japanese immigrants who came to Hawaii in 1890. The Board of Health employed them to work for Mother Marianne at Kalaupapa. The Franciscans "adopted" the first girl soon after she was born on June 21, 1891. Sometimes Mother Marianne put the baby in a rocking chair, tied a cord to the chair and her foot, and rocked the improvised cradle whenever the child cried, the while Mother worked at whatever task she happened to be doing. In that household the child must have a Christian name, of course. And so, not surprisingly, Mother named her Mary. For a surname the girls were given the personal name of their father, Kiyoji.

A second daughter born on August 30, 1893, the Franciscans called Rose. The two girls were raised by the sisters until, on July 29, 1899, when Mary was almost eight years old and Rose six, Mother Marianne sent both children with Sister Benedicta to stay at Kapiolani Home in Honolulu, in order to remove them from the contagion so prevalent at Kalaupapa.

In 1906, at the age of fifteen, Mary returned to Kalaupapa, to assist in the convent household. In March 1911 Mother Marianne recommended to Syracuse, as a postulant for admission to the Franciscan community, "our Mary the Japanese girl . . . well known and well loved by all the Sisters in the Islands." Mary and another island girl began their novitiate in Honolulu because the Provincial Superior at the time, Mother Johnanna Kaiser, believed that "they could never endure the climate" in Syracuse. But by November 1913, as Mother Marianne wrote, "on account of poor health and other reasons," Sister Mary Aloysia, "our little Novice . . . was obliged to lay off the Habit. . . . She will come back to us—she has no desire to live in the world." Mary returned to Kalaupapa soon after April 7, 1914. About the same time her sister Rose, a helper in the Kapiolani Home kitchen since the time of her schooling, returned to Bishop Home. Rose went back because Mother thought Mary was "lonesome for her."

The Franciscan sisters who worked with Mother Marianne on Molokai also received her love and care—provided they would accept that attention. "It was delightful to live with Mother," Sister Antonia remembered. ". . . her long life had taught her many things and she loved to impart her knowledge to the Sisters. This made life on Molokai one of paradise. The hardest trial of my life was to leave Mother & Molokai. I thought to be burried there."

The testimonies of Sister Leopoldina, Sister Antonia, and others help to explain how Mother won their love and loyalty. "To make the Sisters happy was her aim," said Sister Antonia. Mother guarded her companions against unfair attack, sometimes with refreshing tartness. "No one dare say a word against the Sisters. One visiting priest tried to find fault with some of the Sisters on one of the other Islands. She answered, 'It is too bad that God did not make a model and have all the Sisters made after it.' He said no more. Needless to say she was not bothered again with fault finding. . . . She never wanted anyone to speak lightly of her Sisters. She said Who touches them touches me." As Sister Benedicta explained, Mother also extended this charity toward priests and laymen if ever the sisters tried to criticize them.

She also expected her companions to be above criticism, whether from priests and laymen or from herself. When a sister did need chastening Mother applied a superior's pressure, delicately, even humorously—and therefore all the more effectively for most, if not all, her charges. Sister Antonia thought that in her relationships with the sisters Mother was "very elegant in manner. I think that this elegance can be summed up in the statement Mother [studied] the feelings of others and never pained a sensitive nature. When obliged by duty to give a correction it caused her eyes to fill with tears. For myself I would rather do anything than cause her pain. The most pleasant memory of my life is the knowledge that she loved to have me with her when she was old and feeble."

Mother Marianne made effective use of quiet humor. "She had such a quaint way of giving a Sister her 'obedience.'" When in 1888 Sister Bonaventure brought her from Syracuse to Honolulu, Sister Antonia expected to be assigned to duty on Molokai. "But she had other plans for me and one day . . . said Sr. Bonaventure has taken such a fancy to you that I must ask you to go to Wailuku for a while. The 'while' lasted 15 years. In school and I wished to be a nurse."

Delicacy, and grace, courtesy, thoughtfulness, lightened with gentle wit, characterized Mother's easy rule. And yet, because she saw clearly what must be done, for the lepers' comfort and for God's glory, she also must have been very clear in giving instructions to the sisters, and not at all hesitant in admonishing them when they did not perform their duties according to her standards. She seems to have been the best kind of commander: attentive without being possessive, leading but not driving. All the sisters who ever wrote about her reveal, either directly or by implication, her great gifts as a leader. One of the strongest of those virtues seems to have been a willingness to allow her companions considerable freedom of speech and action. According to Sister Elizabeth Gomes, "she never did anything without consulting the Sisters first." She trusted them as grown women and as responsible religious. She asked them to remember, always, that they were Brides of Christ. The Convent of St. Elizabeth was not a grim and silent house. She could not have ordered it so if she wanted to keep the loyalty and preserve the sanity of her companions in that desolate prison of Kalaupapa.

For most of her companions Mother Marianne's methods were just and right. Those sisters thrived under her regimen—and gave her devotion as well as obedience. But such a generous leader also allows weaklings, dissenters, and misfits too many opportunities to take advantage of her and to cause trouble. For at least four of Mother's sisters her system did not work.

Nor did it work for all the men and the boys, accustomed to doing exactly as they pleased—especially when women tried to steer them in directions where males did not wish to go. Her quiet virtues, firm enough to keep a convent in peace and a compoundful of ailing women in reasonably good order, did not please strong-minded men or certain priests who had definite ideas of their own about how the Home for Boys should be managed.

Throughout the whole Settlement lawlessness still prevailed, made worse as even the memory of Father Damien's strong scolding voice faded away in a populace who had never seen or heard him. The two opinionated priests, who succeeded Damien could not take his place as the conscience of the Settlement. In their frustration over larger issues they found fault with smaller problems. And, naturally the most convenient object of their complaints was the Baldwin Home for Boys.

In June 1893 Rudolph Meyer suggested that, after its completion, the new Boys Home be named for its donor, Henry Perrine Baldwin, an American missionary's son and a prosperous sugarcane planter on the island of Maui. Using the funds he provided, the Board of Health, in 1892, began to develop an extensive complex in a wide sloping field opposite Father Damien's church in Kalawao. At its opening, in 1894, the new Baldwin Home consisted of twenty-nine separate structures, (compared with twenty-six assorted buildings at the Bishop Home). Most were constructed of new materials, a few were cottages moved across the street from their original location adjoining the cemetery. As the years passed, even more cottages were added, until ultimately the Baldwin Home numbered about fifty buildings. All were arranged along the sides of a large grassy quadrangle. No more would the boys have to play amid tombstones and sunken graves. Most of the buildings were simple cottages for patients to live in, and resembled the wards at Bishop Home. Inmates shared a cookhouse, dining hall, and the usual outhouses and sanitary facilities. The Franciscans' Convent of Our Lady of Mercy—"a handsome residence," as Mr. Meyer called it— stood at the lower left corner of the quadrangle. It was enclosed by a board fence and provided with a gatehouse, presumably guarded by a "porteress."

Discipline in the Boys' Home, despite the Franciscans' attentions and Brother Dutton's soldierly efforts, was maintained only with difficulty. Reasons for this were not hard to find: the more active boys were bored. And, as they grew into manhood, some objected to the rules and regulations the Board of Health tried to impose upon them. The priests argued between themselves about remedies for correcting this situation, but could agree upon only one premise: a corps of strong Christian men must be put in charge of the Home. Most especially, they must be present in the Home at night.

They disagreed, however, about who those men should be. Father Wendelin was bothered by the possibility that Father Conrardy's attempts to persuade the Board of Health would bring in almost any one who cared to take the job, thereby displacing the Sacred Hearts community in the Settlement. And Father Conrardy did not assuage his colleague's fears by actively recommending himself as the man who would supervise the Baldwin Home.

Father Wendelin, who had a trusted relationship with Mother

Marianne, must have talked with her about the problem. More than likely he and others kept her fully informed about the difficulties at Kalawao and about the solution the two fathers advocated. Toward the end of 1893 Father Wendelin carried his estimate of the situation to Bishop Gulstan. His Grace reported all this to Paris on January 5, 1894. Father Wendelin is "a little discouraged at Molokai," he wrote. "He wants Father Conrardy replaced. He wants himself replaced. He flares up against the good Mother Marianne... whom he says lacks the energy [strength] to maintain order among the boys. He is advertising loudly for brothers of the Damien institute; then he seems to be afraid—what to do!..."

Mother Marianne, as practical as ever, agreed with the priests that men should supervise the Baldwin Home. She had fulfilled her goal of bringing adequate housing and proper care to the boys. Just as she knew when to fight for a cause, so also did she know when to let it go. Conditions had changed since 1889. In August 1893 Bishop Home sheltered 103 girls and women, many more than she and Sister Leopoldina could take care of. She was happy to be relieved of part of the labor at Kalawao. But not all of it.

On November 30, 1894, in reply to his request for her suggestions about managing the Home, she wrote to W. O. Smith, President of the Board of Health, with both frankness and generosity: "more male help is needed, three more Mr. Duttons—to assist in the care of the sick and to superintend and instruct the boys in farming and carpentry work. Our good Bishop Gulstan could obtain Brothers to fill this department." With this mention, of course, she supported Father Wendelin's hope that the Sacred Hearts congregation would be kept in control of the Catholic presence in the Settlement. She herself, Mother added, planned to ask her community in Syracuse for more sisters.

She had told Mr. Smith on March 30 how she intended to employ those new sisters, if ever they arrived. As soon as a building being constructed for the Baldwin Home was finished, she wrote, "we propose to open a school in the new Hall." In additon to all their other duties, she and Sister Leopoldina were supervising a school for girls at Bishop Home, started sometime in 1890. "Beautiful Annie Joe" taught the pupils—in Hawaiian—in that little school. Now in 1894, Mother wanted to bring in new sisters to teach the boys as well as the girls.

Bishop Gulstan sent word of the accord to Father Bousquet on February 15, 1895: "... mission, government, and Sisters think that the establishment for young men must be confided to men and that is the reason why the Minister [of the Interior] came to me to implore me to procure for him at least four brothers to begin. . . ."

With everyone being so cooperative, arrangements proceeded smoothly. The government, following the model of contracts engaging the Franciscans twelve years before, would pay costs of transportation for the brothers, monthly salaries of $20 to each, and the usual perquisites of housing and food. W. O. Smith himself, afraid that if he selected Father Wendelin to be superior at the Baldwin Home "it might create dissatisfaction among the Protestants at the Settlement," decided that Brother Joseph Dutton should be appointed "the Director of the establishment while the other newly arrived brothers will be his aides. Mr. Dutton's experience and faithful, effective service show that he is worthy of this position of confidence."

Bishop Gulstan, about to embark upon his required *ad limina* visit to Rome, decided to go in person to ask for the brothers at the Damien Institute of the Congregation of the Sacred Hearts in Louvain, Belgium. He sailed from Honolulu on May 2, 1895, and returned on November 16, accompanied by four brothers and by a very special priest—Father Pamphile de Veuster, elder brother to Father Damien. On November 30 Bishop Gulstan brought the group to Molokai.

Thanks to Father Wendelin's efforts, signs greeted them in several places: "Welcome to Molokai," at Kalaupapa's landing; "Benedictus qui venit in nomine Domine," Blessed is he who comes in the name of the Lord, atop Kauhako crater; and, before the Baldwin Home, "I was sick and you visited me."

Anticipating the brothers' arrival, the three Franciscan sisters had withdrawn to Kalaupapa, leaving a clean and fully furnished house for the newcomers to occupy. Mother Marianne, concerned for their continued comfort, offered the help of her group in sewing more linens and other such articles as they might need, both immediately and in the future.

Father Pamphile's presence in Kalawao enabled the Board of Health to remove Father Conrardy (with Bishop Gulstan's tacit approval). Unwilling to tolerate any longer his mania for publicity, always at the government's expense, or his propensity for extending his own lines of influence within the Leprosarium, the Board ordered Father Conrardy to leave. He departed from Kalaupapa on December 27, 1895, and sailed from Honolulu for Japan on March 25, 1896.

When the Franciscans withdrew from Baldwin Home, Sister Crescentia and Sister Vincentia came to Bishop Home. In all, Mother gained only one assistant. On December 12, 1895, Sister Albina left her side, returning to Honolulu with Sister Irene to help Sister Benedicta at Kapiolani Home and the Receiving Station. The four new sisters Mother hoped to draw from Syracuse—and whom the Motherhouse had promised to send—did not come. The Board of Health decided to "defer" sending for the sisters, claiming that supporting four Sacred Hearts brothers took care of its obligations to the younger patients in the Settlement.

NOTES on Chapter XVIII

1. Since the introduction of effective chemotherapy in 1947, Hawaii's epidemic of leprosy has ended much more quickly and more dramatically than anyone could have imagined in 1900. In 1980 the number of new cases occurring each year among all residents, of any race, is four—or less. Moreover, most of these new cases develop not in people born and raised in Hawaii but in recent immigrants from Pacific islands or Southeast Asia. Usually these new cases are not hospitalized but are treated at home, as outpatients. The Settlement at Kalaupapa is still maintained, out of consideration rather than need: it is home for about 125 older patients, most of whom have spent more than thirty years there as inmates. They are cured of the disease but, because they have been affected physically or psychologically, prefer to spend the rest of their lives at Kalaupapa.

2. Investing and Temporary Profession of Olinda Gomes (Sister Elizabeth): (a) Chapter for acceptance into novitiate, *Investing and Profession Chapters,* 1870–1921, insert between pp. 72–73; (b) Chapter for Profession of Vows: the question arose at the Chapter held in Wailuku, Maui, as to whether the novice be allowed to make profession for life, or for a period of two years. The latter was decided upon, according to an insert between pp. 76–77.

3. Details of opening of new Convent at Kalawao and of the sisters assuming charge of Boys' Home: Mother Marianne, *Origin and History of St. Elizabeth's Convent,* Kalaupapa.

4. Accommodations for the smaller boys: another reason for the delay in expediting this request made by Mother Marianne in April 1890 was the appointment in 1891 of a new resident superintendent, William Tell, whom Meyer said had "animosity" toward the sisters. The resident superintendent aroused the owners of produce growing on the needed land to oppose selling it, so that the sisters would not have use of the property. Tell was removed by the Board of Health from the Leper Settlement in late 1892, at the request of Meyer, who expressed dissatisfaction with him in several respects. Meyer in correspondence with the Board inferred that the wards for the smaller boys were in use in 1893. He suggested also that further expansion be made on the other side of the road, near the sisters' residence, for their convenience. In regard to Tell and the sisters, Meyer could

not give any precise reason to the Board for the "unfriendly feeling" that he held toward them, but was "convinced that he had it." (Not the least of the sisters' problems during Tell's administration was the decreasing number of girls entering Bishop Home. Complaints were made to the Board of Health that people were allowed to prevent newly arriving leper girls from entering the Home. As a means of furthering cooperation, Meyer arranged with the Board that the resident superintendent be personally responsible for placing all minors, both male and female under 16 years of age, in the respective Homes maintained by the sisters, as soon as possible after their arrival, unless they were housed by their own parents at the Settlement).

5. Amy Fowler or Sister Rose Gertrude: (a) "To Molokai," *Feuilleton de L'Universe,* February 1, 1889; (b) *Notes of Sr. Flaviana Engel.* The impression given in these references is that Miss Fowler was a member of the secular Third Order of St. Dominic. Miss Fowler often wore a religious habit in public, which caused some confusion about whether her status was secular or religious.

6. From the time of their arrival in Hawaii, the Franciscan sisters were known as Americans; e.g. in November 1885 after the opening of Kapiolani Home at Kakaako, J.W. Putnam, Consul General, H.I., sent a dispatch to the Department of State in Washington: "Knowing the pride Americans feel in the achievement of the citizens of the Republic in every field where fame or good can yield results," they would be glad to know of the good work "being undertaken by a little company of American ladies of the Sisterhood of the Franciscan Convent of Saint Anthony, Syracuse, N.Y." *Dispatches From U.S. Consuls in Honolulu 1820-1885.* National Archives. Library of Congress, Washington, D.C.

7. Dutton in secular Third Order of St. Francis: (a) *Record of Third Order Members,* Church of the Assumption, Syracuse, N.Y., p. 64; (b) *Record,* April 27, 1925 (AH).

8. Final Profession of Sister Elizabeth Gomes: *Record of Professed Sisters,* insert between pp. 256–57.

9. Letters of Father Francis Neubauer: his letters to the sisters and to Brother Joseph Dutton were shared with Mother Marianne, who wrote in a copybook the important ones relating to the Franciscans' Hawaiian Mission.

10. Sister Rosalia: According to the Order's records, she "was sent to St. Anthony Convent, Louisville, Kentucky. She was then transferred to the Motherhouse where she remained, until mentally sick, it became necessary to place her in a Sanatorium, where she remained several years. Finally she was pronounced cured and dismissed by the authorities of the Sanatorium. She refused to return to the Convent, but asked for Dispensation of her vows, this was granted to her, and she remained in the world." The circumstances of her life after that time and of her death are not known.

11. Profession of Sister Albina Sluder: (a) Chapter for Profession of Vows, *Investing and Profession Chapters* 1870–1921, insert p. 82; (b) Profession of Vows, *Record of Perpetual Vows* 1884–1915.

12. The desk that Mother Marianne used at Molokai is preserved in the Motherhouse in Syracuse.

13. Peter Kiyoji Morita (converted to Catholicism on September 29, 1897), his wife

Kishi (converted on March 1, 1897), and two younger children left Kalaupapa in October 1901. Later the older Kiyojis returned to Japan.

In 1944, at the height of World War II, Rose became seriously ill and needed major surgery. She was flown to Honolulu for an operation performed at St. Francis Hospital. Mother M. Jolenta Wilson sent for Mary to come and stay with Rose. Neither returned to Kalaupapa. Mary died January 3, 1974, followed by her sister Rose on May 16, 1983. During their last years, both women lived in a cottage near St. Francis Hospital, enjoying the special concern of the Franciscan sisters.

14. As Father Wendelin rather guessed, Father Pamphile did not stay long at Kalaupapa: on August 19, 1897 he left the Settlement, going home to his proper place in Louvain.

15. Father Conrardy ultimately achieved in China the distinction he came too late to Molokai to gain. He founded the Lepers' Asylum of Shek-Lung near Canton, and served as its priest and director for many years. In 1913 he wrote to Brother Dutton, giving belated credit to the Hawaiian government for having done so much to help its lepers. "Was I a leper," he admitted, "I would like to be at Molokai." In China, he had learned the hard way, the government did nothing at all to take care of the nation's many lepers. He died in Hong Kong on August 24, 1914, honored by fellow religious as "the example of those noble virtues that formed his characteristics: mortification, charity, energy."

Chapter XIX

"DARK DAYS"

AS SHE MARKED her sixty-first birthday, on January 23, 1899, Mother Marianne might reasonably have expected that the years of hard trials were ended, that the future would bring only quiet fulfillment. Her dominion over Bishop Home was firmly established, routines she had developed were being followed, the girls were usually under control, except for those sporadic attacks of "The Spring Fever." And, except for the mean little persecutions arranged for her by two small-hearted resident superintendents who succeeded Rudolph Meyer after he died in 1897, the Franciscans' life in the Settlement was quiet and peaceful.

But the years of trial were not yet ended. The period from April 1899 through October 1900 subjected her to new and different testing. "Dark days" were given to her in full measure—so much so that, for a while, Sister Leopoldina feared that they would be "fatal days." Sister Leopoldina and her companions marvelled that Mother survived them.

The ordeal of the body began during the night of April 14, 1899. Mother had been ailing for several days. Everyone thought that her weakness and uncharacteristic listlessness were signs of "the grippe," then epidemic in the Settlement. "I could see how she was failing," Sister Leopoldina remembered, "her voice was growing weaker and her step slow. One evening she said in a cheerful way I am so tired I think I shall sleep well tonight   Oh Mother I pleaded if you would only go to bed now and have one good night's rest it would do you so much good, but we could never persuade her to do that   she would only smile and tell us the night would be too long but that night she seemed so very week that it required an efferet for her to speak,   after nine oclock night prayers she went slowly to her room   as there was only a board partition between her room and mine I could hear her moving about a little more than is usual   but after a little while everything was quiet only that continual cough, and being so accustom to hearing it I was soon in the land of dreams.

"The next morning Mother was very pale and there were great blue rings around her eyes. as we observe silence during the morning and I was obliged to rush away to the lepers I had no chance to see her again until near eleven oclock, on returning from the lepers I found her in the little room near the chapel, she looked at me with a little smile and pointed to a large white wash boll nearly full of blood she cheerfully said do not be afraid it is not siirous you know. I was so shocked it seemed everything was whirling.

"Oh Mother I pladed why did you go to work in that hot storeroom? You know you was sick. that is why I did it, she said. I thought perhaps I could work it off but it came again. Came again Mother! did you have it before? Yes last night when I went to my room I was so tired I went quickly to bed thinking to have a good restful sleep but as soon as I put my head on the pillow it came, the room was verydark but the blood was rushing so fast I could not get the light, Oh Mother why did you not call me? Just a little rap on the wall, and I would be with you. Oh Sister how could I do that knowing so well all the work that is depending on you, and if I had called you, not one of the Sisters would sleep the whole night. I took my big black cloak wraped myself in it and sat at the foot of my bed until morning, the night seemed very long   I was so cold, how anxious I was to get out of that room as every thing was covered with blood.

"I listened to that sad little story that she told me so cheerfully, of her dreadfull nights suffering but it was so sad I could not trust myself to speak   I went quickly to find Sister Crescinta to see what we could do and found her at the wash tub, She was pale and anxious. What will we do she said we must get the Doctor. I never thought any one could have so much blood in their body   a large tub was packed with bedding that she was about to hang on the line, all this she said was soaked with blood. She cannot live through an other hemorrhage we must get the Doctor. But what are we to do? Our good Doctor Oliver was in Honolulu. . . ."

Despite Mother's claims that "it was not serious," the sisters put her to bed and "begged her to remain very quiet." Sensible at last, she obeyed them. "although she was so cheerful and trying to be indifferant yet she was greatly in dread of an other hemorrhage." Fortunately, another one did not come.

A few days later the peripatetic Dr. Oliver returned to the Settlement in response to an urgent message from Father Maxime. He continued for more than two months the regimen of "rest and perfect quiet" the sisters had begun. He visited the convent "every day to see that his orders were obeayed." When finally the doctor allowed her to move about "she could be dressed and seated in an easy chair in a cool room where we could visit her often to receive her instructions." Mary and Rose Kiyoji, too, would slip in to see her as often as they were allowed, bringing her the pleasure of their little attentions.

Rest, the "solace of sisterly support," and a strong will helped Mother Marianne to recover from this severe bout of hemorrhaging. When the attack occurred, she must have been very close to complete exhaustion, both from overwork and the pulmonary tuberculosis, if not from a superimposed infection with "the grippe" as well. This period of enforced inactivity helped the ailing body to mend. Apparently her lungs healed sufficiently well to prevent further hemorrhagings, since no similar episodes are mentioned during the nineteen years of life that remained to her. Yet a dread of further attacks worried her and the sisters for years to come. Mother did not oppose him when Dr. Oliver warned her that she must not travel anymore upon ships, because of the possibility that seasickness might provoke another round of hemorrhages. She never left the Settlement again. "We were very thankful," wrote Sister Leopoldina, "that she was willing to give up those painful trips." After April 1899 she managed her mission by correspondence and by asking sisters to be her emissaries. When necessary, they came from Honolulu or Wailuku to consult with her.

She had learned to dislike publicity, newpaper accounts, prying reporters, insistent photographers, any one or any thing that would intrude upon her privacy or draw attention to herself. Once upon a time, in Syracuse, she had turned to newspapers for their help with publicity about events being held for the benefit of St. Joseph's Hospital or to print her letters of thanks for favors the hospital received. In Hawaii she shrank from any connection with newspapers, possibly because she did not need them, probably because the unhappy experiences of Walter Murray Gibson, King Kalakaua, Queen Liliuokalani, Father Damien, and Father Conrardy taught her how shallow is the world's acclaim and how foolish are people who strive to win it. She said as much, many times, to her companion sisters, and meant exactly this with the declaration, often repeated, that she wished only to be a silent worker. She also told government officials about her attitude toward publicity. Thus, in January 1895 she wrote in private to W. O. Smith, as President of the Board of Health, rather than to one of his assistants, simply because she wanted to keep her name and business "out of the newspapers."

And once, as Sister Antonia reported, Mother declined to pose with Bishop Libert Boeynaems, who was making a pastoral visit to Kalaupapa. The picture "would be in every magazine in the country," she declared. In her stead she put shy Sister Elizabeth beside the bearded bishop.

In 1899, however, after she recovered from the pulmonary hemorrhages, at least two visitors bearing cameras did succeed in photographing her. The first must have come to Kalaupapa toward the middle of May. He persuaded Mother and the four Franciscans who served with her at the time to pose for a rather formal group picture. She stood at the center of the row, with Sister Leopoldina and Sister Crescentia at her right, Sister Elizabeth and Sister Vincent at her left.

The second visitor can be identified precisely: "Dr. Dom Sauton, a Benedictine abbot and specialist from France," as Father Wendelin called him, arrived at Kalaupapa on November 10, 1899. "The little Benedictine priest," wrote Sister Albina, "wanted to take Father Wendelin's and Mother Marianne's picture, but he knew it would be useless to ask them to pose for it. He watched his chance, and while Mother was speaking to Father Wendelin who sat on the stump of a tree in the Sisters' back yard, he moved quietly back and then snapped Mother and then snapped Father Wendelin. He was so pleased that he got both of them that he rubbed his hands and almost danced as lame as he was. . . ."

Mother Marianne, photographed unaware, seems also to have been visited by surprise. She is wearing an apron over her habit, probably because she was "doing the wash" when the two fathers arrived. Her hands are clasped at the waist, and she is listening, with a faint smile, to Father Wendelin. She is thin, small, weary. Her body, down to its very bones, is tired. Spectacles with metal frames obscure the eyes. The nose is prominent, almost a beak. She leans slightly to the left. This bending and the spectacles are discernible in photographs Gibson commissioned at Kakaako in 1886, but now in

Kalaupapa they are much more evident. Her beauty is gone. The wan old woman depicted in this candid snapshot bears no resemblance at all to the beautiful young Mother Provincial seated in a photographer's studio in Syracuse in 1878, carefully posed for the official portrait that would mark her first term as the community's leader.

The contrast between the two pictures shows the price her body had paid during the years she had been working for God and the lepers in Hawaii.

The end of 1899 brought a pleasant change when the Mother Provincial of the community journeyed all the way from Syracuse to inspect the mission in Hawaii. Mother Delphina Mueller accompanied by Sister Robertina Lange and Sister Susanna Perin, reached Honolulu on December 20—at a time of great peril for everyone in the capital. The first case of bubonic plague ever to occur in Hawaii had been recognized in Honolulu on December 12; and on Christmas Eve the Board of Health had "the melancholy duty" of announcing that an epidemic of the Black Death was being visited upon the city.

Infected rats aboard ships arriving from the Orient, where the disease raged at the time, stole ashore in Honolulu harbor and passed their fleas and plague bacilli to local rats which transmitted them to human beings. Sister Leopoldina recalled the fear with which islanders heard the terrible news: " . . . the black plague broke out sending that dreadful boom of fright and horror throughout all the Islands, people were in deathly dread, ships were not allowed to land their passengers or freight. . . ."

The Board of Health published regulations controlling interisland shipping, in order to prevent the spread of the pestilence from Honolulu to other islands, but did not impose the quarantine soon enough. Ships, people, rats, and fleas escaped from Honolulu—and introduced the plague to the port of Kahului on Maui and to the town of Hilo on Hawaii. Unaccountably, the islands of Molokai, Lanai, and Kauai were spared.

Mother Delphina and her companions fled from Honolulu just before that port was closed, and arrived at Kalaupapa on December 27, the very day upon which a complete quarantine was imposed. The government's interdiction of all interisland shipping marooned the visiting Franciscans in the Leper Settlement for nine long weeks.

The unplanned vacation at Kalaupapa passed pleasantly for all the sisters. Mother Delphina, in the midst of an unprecedented fifth term as Provincial, brought none of the conflicts and tensions that Father Francis Neubauer had introduced in 1892. The permanent complement of sisters always had plenty of work to do for their female patients, not to mention sewing for the boys and brothers at Baldwin Home. The visiting sisters would have helped as much as they could, in ways that relieved for a while the burdens upon Sister Leopoldina, Sister Crescentia, Sister Vincent, and especially Sister Elizabeth, drudging away in the kitchen. Mother Marianne, having recovered amazingly well from her sickness in April, found time and energy to perform all her usual duties, even to keeping a journal again, after a lapse of almost seven years.

The journal of 1900, begun on January 1, is very different in style and content from the Record of St. Elizabeth's Convent begun in 1888. In the Record she was responding to the stimulus of novel impressions gained from living in a new place. The entries of 1888 were long, flowing, not sparing of words, and often presented her own personal thoughts. The new journal, on the other hand, is dutiful, impersonal, dull, as she makes the flattest and briefest of statements about the weather, callers, things done during the day. She says nothing about important matters she must have discussed with Mother Delphina, such as decisions about the prospects for the mission or problems relating to starting the new school they planned for Hilo. Whereas in the Record Mother Marianne appeared almost relaxed about herself as a person, almost willing to reveal something about her self if only to herself in this most private of ways, in the journal of 1900 she is as objective, as noncommittal, as ego-less as an automaton. It is intended to be nothing more than a reference, a means for keeping records.

Sister Leopoldina had no inhibitions about wearing her big heart on her sleeve. In 1899 she was forty-four years old, grown heavy and vastly imposing, no doubt still flashing of eye, quick of tongue, and hearty in laughter, but no longer as beautiful or as naive as she was when she arrived in Hawaii in 1885. Her mention of the visitors' sojourn in 1899–1900 is informative: "It gave us great pleasure to be with our dear Mother [Delphina] again even for a short time, and it was good to see her enjoy every minuet of her stay with the lepers. She was much surprised to see them enjoying life, being so sadly afflicted."

By late February 1900 the epidemic of bubonic plague appeared to have run its course in Honolulu. The government, realizing that people on the outer islands were desperate for mail and supplies of food, kerosene, and building materials, relaxed its ban upon shipping and allowed a few vessels to leave Honolulu. The most exciting entry in Mother Marianne's journal was written on March 4: "Father [Wendelin] informed us that a steamer is coming—Mother Provincial Srs Susanna, Robertina left at 8 for Maui—This is indeed a sad and lonely day. How painful it is to be thus separated. It is hard to be resigned."

Mother Delphina and her companions intended to visit the Franciscans in Wailuku, Maui. But when the *Lehua* approached the pier at Lahaina in the afternoon of March 4, Sister Leopoldina related, "there were crowds of horror stricken people at the wharf with clinched fists high in the air they shouted no passengers will be landed here." The captain tried to ease their fears by saying that the sisters were safe, inasmuch as the plague had not affected Molokai. But still the aroused citizens "screamed we will not allow them to land!" Whereupon the exasperated captain told them that either they allowed the sisters to land or he would not unload the freight they wanted. "that quieted them as they were anxious for their mail."

As Mother Delphina left the ship, "in all that excitement," one of her legs slipped between the heaving boat and the pier. It was badly injured, and Mother was obliged to stay abed for several weeks at Malulani Hospital while a physician and the sisters treated the wounds. She recovered without complications and on May 1 sailed for Hilo with Sister Susanna. Sister Robertina remained in Wailuku, to teach at St. Anthony's School.

In Hilo Mother Delphina, in correspondence with Mother Marianne, organized matters relating to the establishing of yet another Franciscan enterprise in the Hawaiian Islands, St. Joseph's School for Girls. Then at last Mother Delphina was able to start the journey home: she sailed from Honolulu on June 13 and reached Syracuse early in July. St. Joseph's School opened on September 10, 1900, with "about 180 girls to form and instruct." Sister Susanna was in charge, with Sister Flaviana Engel and Sister Albina as her assistants. Sister Irene served as housekeeper. On December 13 Mother Marianne wrote a letter of welcome to Sister Ephrem Schillinger, just arrived in Honolulu, in which she assigned the newcomer to duties in Hilo. After Sister Ephrem was settled in Hilo, Sister Albina returned to Honolulu.

Mother Marianne was tested now by an ordeal of the spirit. This time of emotional travail was not an experience of her own making, but was imposed upon her by other people. She had found her role in life many years before. She was predictable: the lamp of her devotion burned with a steady flame. And she thought she had gained the peace that comes with achieving perfect control over the assertions of self. The sisters who served with her, the priests at Kalaupapa, even cold and critical Father Neubauer, remarked this quality in her. All chose the word "serene" to describe her manner, thinking that in observing her composure they perceived the spirit within.

She was serene, most of the time, at peace with herself and the world. Had she lived as a recluse, or been surrounded by companions as dedicated as she, perhaps no distress of the spirit would have assailed her. But, unfortunately, too many of the sisters, priests, and brothers around her were not as content to work for God as she was. And often they "painfully surprised" her, as she said, with their weaknesses. In 1900 two sisters at Kalaupapa proved to be so weak—or so willful—that they tried her to the point where she suffered both for them and for herself.

For years she had borne with kindness and patience the weaknesses of her companions. Sister Rosalia, whose alternating spells of usefulness and uselessness must have been a continual cause of apprehension for everybody, she treated with the greatest consideration for more than ten years, until finally the signs of progressing madness could no longer be ignored. Sister Charles and Sister Martha, genuinely sick in body if not in spirit, worried but did not dismay her. Even a doughty rebel like Sister Dominica Cumming, contentious and confused in Syracuse, she could manage with understanding and charity.

The distinction of being the ones who most seriously disturbed Mother Marianne belongs to two sisters who served in Kalaupapa in 1900. One, relatively new to the islands, coming from Germany by way of Syracuse, was Sister Bonaventure Oechtering. She and Sister Flaviana Engel reached Honolulu on February 17, 1899 and, after a brief visit to Kalaupapa to receive Mother Marianne's blessing and instruction, went to Wailuku on March 1, to work with Sister Bonaventure Caraher.

Because Sister Bonaventure Oechtering turned out to be too "difficult" a person for the Wailuku sisters to tolerate, Mother Marianne brought her to Kalaupapa, where she arrived on May 23, 1900. Within two weeks she'd upset everyone in the convent. Father Wendelin— who referred to her as "Sister Bonaventure II"—wrote in his diary that

Mother Marianne considered her "mad," without a qualifying adjective or adverb.

Sister Bonaventure II was like the proverbial rotten apple in a barrel of good fruit. She brought out the worst in ailing Sister Vincent McCormick. Although Sister Leopoldina wrote not a word about this period, life in St. Elizabeth's Convent could not have been pleasant for anyone during the months Sister Bonaventure II stayed there.

Sister Vincent had been a cause of worry to Mother Marianne (and to Sister Leopoldina) from the day they reached Kalaupapa in November 1888. Overnight the young sister, so obedient in Honolulu, became moody and "sulky" in Kalaupapa. One glimpse of all those lepers gathered in the Settlement was cause enough to make her regret having come to Molokai. She probably had personality problems as well. A clue to them is hidden in a letter Father Neubauer wrote to her at Kalawao on May 20, 1892, soon after he returned to Syracuse. At the time, Sister Vincent was working at the Boys' Home, and Sister Crescentia was her superior.

"What you write to me and ask of me," Father Neubauer said, "gives me great Joy and Happiness and my happiness will be still greater, when ever I hear that my dear Sisters on the Islands live like good humble children for the great and best object of life. . . . Now my dear Sister V—do your share and show your good will: it matters not, who our Superiors are if we only reverence and acknowledge them as representatives of God, and mind whatever they either tell us to do or express their wish, what should be done. I know the climate of the Islands is very enervating and taxing on the human system and an illy or weakly disposed body may not always be so prompt and ready as might be expected; but nevertheless a good will, will always predominate and prevail and make our work and our assistance ever so small, acceptable. It makes me happy that your occupation is dear to you and precious. . . ."

Whatever may have caused Sister Vincent's attitudes, her reactions were not so serious that she found life in the Settlement unbearable—until Sister Bonaventure Oechtering arrived. By that time Sister Vincent had served in the Settlement for twelve years.

Then Sister Bonaventure II descended upon Kalaupapa like a devil-wind from Pelekunu. She did not like Hawaii, she said. She did not like Molokai, she declared. She wanted to go home to Germany, she cried. Given that fine example of perfect obedience, entertaining second and third thoughts about her own vocation, Sister Vincent fell apart. Within a week of that Black Wednesday her physical and psychological breakdown was apparent. Successive entries in Mother Marianne's journal present the picture of "melancholia" claiming the body and the spirit of an unhappy woman. "Sr. V.—silent." "Sr. V. ugly." "Sr. V. spent most of the day in her room." "Sr. V. did not work for the B'd of Health nor for the order." When Mother reproved her she either sulked even more or, in the typical response of a manic-depressive, compensated for days of sullen silence in a spate of un-stoppable chatter.

Mother consulted Dr. Oliver, who recommended that Sister Vincent be sent to Honolulu for observation and treatment. Despite the hazards to her own health that a sea voyage invited, Mother decided to take Sister Vincent to the capital city. Mother Delphina, she knew, was still in Honolulu, waiting for a ship bound for San Francisco. Between the two of them, Mother Marianne hoped, they might work out a plan that would take care of both Sister Vincent and the even more troubled Sister Bonaventure. On Friday June 8 she told Sister Vincent to prepare for the trip. "She refused outright. Her conduct and her words pained me deeply."

Sister Bonaventure's conduct was even meaner. She refused to work, hid in her room for days on end, "crying, no one knows why," did not appear even for meals. "She is not nice—full of suspicion about letters." She claimed that she was "sick" or "upset," or simply "indisposed." For several weeks she did not go to confession or receive Communion. Later, when Sister Vincent refused to obey Bishop Gulstan's orders to come to see him in Honolulu, Father Wendelin had to impose upon her a form of discipline in which he withheld the Sacraments of Penance and of the Holy Eucharist.

Fortunately for everyone, good days might follow upon the bad. Sister Bonaventure and Sister Vincent actually emerged from their cells, did the work expected of them, seemed to be recovering from their maladies. Mother and her more sensible companions could hope that the worst was over, that everything was going to be all right. But then, after a short season of relative harmony, the evil mood would seize Sister Bonaventure or Sister Vincent once more, and the whole hysteric round would begin again. "Sr. B. is talking and acting strange," Mother observed on September 17. "Sr. B. talked strangely.— I am anxious about her," she wrote soon afterwards.

During those months of turmoil Mother Marianne treated the two difficult sisters with great forebearance, hoping that with time, prayer, mild penances, and God's favor they would improve in health and attitude. But the changes she yearned for were very slow in arriving. "I feel sad and troubled about our future," she admitted on August 12. "Two Sisters refused to come when I sent for them. I feel hurt at their conduct," she wrote on September 21. And, on October 6, "I am full of worry, not one well Sister here."

She, too, felt the strain of this prolonged disaffection. In the best of times, she seldom slept more than four or five hours a night. Now even this short rest was broken. "I am very tired," she confessed on September 28.

Sister Bonaventure II, that Teutonic fury, would not give up. Since the day she arrived at Kalaupapa she had been begging for permission to go home. As the weeks passed, and Mother—waiting to learn the decision of the Order's superiors in Syracuse—still could not give her permission to go, Sister Bonaventure, far from subsiding, grew all the more insistent. After talking with her once again on October 11, Father Wendelin wrote in his diary: "Sister Bonaventure violently wants to return to Germany." Nothing Mother Marianne or he said could silence that wail.

The forces for good did not win. On Thursday, October 11, Mother wrote: "Spent half the night sitting up and worrying about Sister B. . . . Sister B—was bound to go today. Father called—had a long talk with Sister—he could not influence her to change her mind. I talked to her and succeeded in having her wait another week. . . . This has been a very sad day." The next day she "sent a long letter regarding Sr. B. to Mother Provincial."

Sister Bonaventure served the exacted week less than honorably, showing "a very bad determined spirit," and severely straining Mother Marianne's patience.

On October 17 Mother received a letter from Bishop Gulstan, His Grace wrote that he had been hoping that, under Mother Marianne's "motherly care," Sister Bonaventure would regain her "mental strength." He knew that Mother Delphina, clearly aware of the problems presented in the two troubled sisters, had decided against taking them with her when she sailed from Honolulu in June, "fearing that their presence in Syracuse . . . would have a bad effect on those wishing to come here." In view of their intractability—" . . . to reason with such a person is useless . . ."—Bishop Gulstan suggested that Mother Marianne send the two sisters to Honolulu. From there he would arrange to transport them back to Syracuse.

"The Bishop's letter gave me a shock," Mother wrote in her journal on October 17, apparently because she had not known how Father Wendelin was communicating so fully with His Grace. "I spoke to Sr. V but oh—Sr. V had a talk with Father—" The dejected "oh" meant that Sister Vincent refused to accept the bishop's summons to Honolulu.

But Sister Bonaventure, having heard of His Grace's suggestion, seized her chance. On Friday, October 19, the next steamer arrived at Kalaupapa. "Sr. B. is beside herself with joy. . . . Sr. B. aggravated me many times today and made me say hard words to her.—"

Sister Bonaventure sailed from Kalaupapa that evening, "sans obedience," as Father Wendelin wrote in his diary. His meaning is clear: she went without permission from Mother Provincial Delphina in Syracuse.

For a few hours Mother Marianne could hope that, after Sister Bonaventure left the house, grace for Sister Vincent had flowed back into it. On the morning after Sister Bonaventure's departure "Sr. V. asked pardon on her knees for the first time in twelve years—She expressed herself in a very humble way—I was pleased thinking she would change—She had a talk with Father Wendelin. [B]y all appearance she made a good impression on him at 5:15 P.M. he heard her confession—But oh, this evening she held fort again and expressed herself in very unreligious manner—what next—I found it hard to keep still—" She kept still because she recognized the symptoms—and understood that they were beyond her ability to cure.

Father Wendelin also believed that the contrite sister would be a good member of the community once more: "Sister Vincent is sorry and will be obedient to the Bishop. Because of this I allowed her to go to Confession."

Sister Vincent's story did not have a happy ending. Sister Bonaventure's influence, her *contagion,* had infected Sister Vincent beyond recovery. Four days later on October 24, Sister Vincent's twelve years of durance on Molokai ended. "Sr. V. left at 6 o'clock.—She left without a tear.—I am sorry for her," wrote Mother Marianne. As he had done for Sister Bonaventure only five days before, Father Wendelin obtained the necessary Board of Health permit for Sister Vincent to leave the Settlement.

In Honolulu Bishop Gulstan loaned the two sisters money to return to Syracuse. They reached the Motherhouse on November 13.

Three days later, Sister Bonaventure, unwilling to wait for dispensation from her religious vows, left the Motherhouse. She sailed the next day from New York City, going home to Germany.

Sister Leopoldina, who could never bring herself to say anything that was not nice about her colleagues, scrupulously avoided all mention of this difficult period in the history of the mission. But surely the sisters, after recovering from the initial shock, must have welcomed the peace that entered into the Convent of St. Elizabeth.

Mother Marianne's diary says nothing direct about her own feelings after that fateful October 24. In her entry for October 26 she wrote: "I worried much about Sr. Vincentia.—I do not feel well." She did not expunge from her thoughts all memory of the absent sister. Nor did Sister Vincent forget her companions at Kalaupapa: she sent them several letters, as Mother noted in the diary—although she said nothing about their contents.

Mother Marianne did receive at least one "Letter from Ex. Sr. Bonaventure," on January 16, 1901. Whether it brought an expression of contrition or a blast of recrimination is not known.

After those stormy months, which brought the hardest of the trials Mother Marianne would have to bear in Hawaii, peace came to her at Kalaupapa. Only then could "The Sweet and Blessed Years" begin.

NOTES on Chapter XIX

1. Sister M. Flaviana Engel and Sister M. Bonaventure Oechtering spent much of the summer of 1899 at the Leper Settlement. Sister Bonaventure arrived July 29 and another sister "teacher in Wailuku" arrived at Kalaupapa August 4. On September 5, 1899, Father Wendelin records that he went over the pali [to depart] with "Sisters Flavien and Bonaventure II."
2. Details of the Sister Bonaventure II–Sister Vincent problem: (a) Journals of Mother Marianne 1900, 1901, in AS; (b) Diary of Father Wendelin Moellers, 1895–1907, in Roman Catholic Chancery Archive, Honolulu.
3. Sister Bonaventure Oechtering leaving Franciscan community: *Council Meetings* 1891–1905: November 16, 1900, pp. 34–36.

Chapter XX

"DEEP HUMILITY AND SWEET GENTLE PATIENCE"

SHE HAD earned those years of peace. She who asked for nothing for herself, except a little corner in heaven, received much love here on earth. After the troubled months of 1899 and 1900 no rebellious daughters and very few unfriendly patients wanting to drive the Franciscans from the Settlement disturbed her: And not until near the very end of her life did she suffer from illness severe enough to interfere seriously with her work.

Lesser problems continued to arise, of course. They would always be there, in that village full of nosy gossips, complaining patients, contending sectarians, and busybody officials in Honolulu. But they did not especially bother her, who had faced and solved greater difficulties. She never had enough help, to do all the work that people in and out of the Board of Health wanted her to do. Thus, she had to decline, with great regret, a request that the Franciscans take care of the non-leprous little boys who still lived in the Settlement. And, every now and then, she had to assure the changing overlords of the Board of Health that, yes, the girls of Bishop Home had always enjoyed, since the beginning, the privilege of going for walks "for recreational purposes" through the pastures and valleys near the cliffs of Kalaupapa. And that no, the Franciscans did not bar Protestant pastors and Mormon elders from visiting patients belonging to their faiths who lived as wards of the Bishop Home.

During most of those years she enjoyed fairly good health, although references in her letters and in reports from other people indicate that in 1908 and 1909 she was sick enough to cause worry even to herself. On January 7, 1910, in her seventy-second year, she wrote (probably to Sister Helena Haas in Wailuku), "I am doing nicely but am in constant fear that I may be visited again by the unwelcome visitor that has given me much trouble during the past two years." No one ever described the symptoms of this "unwelcome visitor." Sister Leopoldina's mention of her "repeated hemorrhages and continued racking cough" suggest that it probably was a milder recurrence of the pulmonary trouble she had experienced in 1899. But it may just as well have been an exacerbation of the spinal arthritis that was twisting her back, or a plaguing rheumatism, or any one of a dozen other complications of aging. In any event, whatever the sickness was, it did not confine her for long, and seems not to have interrupted her ability to work. "She was never known to complain, but [was] always at her post," said Sister Leopoldina.

Mother's achievements, founded upon completest dedication, won the esteem of everyone who knew her personally. Sisters, priests, brothers, government officials, patients, and visitors gave her reverence or respect. And yet because she was modest and shunned publicity of any kind, very few people beyond the limits of the Leprosarium knew about the Franciscans' efforts in Hawaii. The world, having discovered, admired, and lost Father Damien, went on believing that he was the only one who gave up his life for the lepers. It paid no attention to Mother Marianne and her Franciscans. Nor did it heed the quiet Sacred Hearts brothers, the Catholic priests and Protestant pastors, who followed in Father Damien's footsteps. It soon forgot the lepers of Molokai and ignored the followers of Christ as they ministered to the patients' bodies and their souls.

Mother Marianne did not mind the world's inattention. She lived true to herself, in the fortress of her spirit, continuing to work for the benefit of her "children." She could hide herself in Kalaupapa, but she did not hide her love of God. Because she loved God with all her heart and all her soul and all her strength, because she strove to fulfill His Will, peace flowed from her, filling with serenity the Convent of St. Elizabeth and the cottages of the Bishop Home for Women and Girls. She herself became like the saint she held up as example to her sisters: "that Saint who begged our Lord never to let him know the good he would do."

As her days neared their appointed goal, and companions and patients saw that soon Sister Death would be coming for her, too, they understood how desolate a place Kalaupapa would be when she was gone. Some of the love she had given so generously flowed back to her, as streams will find their way to the sea.

Her life had the happiest of endings.

The mission's work went on under her direction. At infrequent intervals younger sisters came from Syracuse, to begin their service in

Honolulu, Wailuku, or Hilo, but not at Kalaupapa. Only later did she bring some of those newcomers to the Leper Settlement, after they had been well tested in less trying settings. All newcomers joined the Hawaiian mission as volunteers; and apparently all were so carefully selected in Syracuse that they presented her with no more "trouble-makers" like Sister Jerome and Sister Bonaventure II. As the years passed, a few sisters, worn with labor or ill or needing a change of climate, returned to the Motherhouse. Until 1916 Mother Marianne herself supervised the mission from Kalaupapa, although after 1910 she did this with the help of a deputy. Her faithful lieutenants on Oahu, Maui, and Hawaii presented her with few unexpected problems.

Nonetheless, a few did arise, inevitable in the managing of institutions amid the usual differences of opinion that people will contrive. Mother Marianne reported some of these difficulties to Mother Johanna Kaiser, Fourth Provincial Superior, in Syracuse on June 2, 1908: ". . . You are aware that we out here are growing old and consequently are not able to go on with the heavy work we have been doing in the past. In Honolulu at the Kapiolani Home are three sisters, all three worn out and more than half sick. They have 56 children to care for many of them mere infants who require care night and day. . . . Here at Molokai we are five Sisters and have our hands full. I am over 70 years old. You can judge from that I cannot do heavy work, in Wailuku there is trouble—The two teachers are not satisfied. They do not let me know what they really want. . . ." Once again, as she did in 1875, when Mother Provincial Bernardina and she had had to explain to an alarmed bishop in Albany the defection of five unhappy sisters in New York, Mother Marianne recognized the reason behind the dissatisfaction of the two teachers in Wailuku: "the spirit is not that of humble Franciscans, but independent Sisters." Apparently they wanted to be independent of the sister superior in charge of Malulani Hospital, maintaining that the rules established for nurses were different from those required for teachers.

Mother Marianne did not approve the separation. Always her message, to all her daughters, would be the same. We have so much work to do. Therefore, let us do it together, and not waste time and energy with needless concerns over trivial matters. "I am certain the Sisters will do their part faithfully. Let us try in the name of God and do what we can for His greater honor and glory," she wrote on January 7, 1910, to Sister Helena Haas, superior of both convent and hospital in Wailuku, who had been referring to her many questions about hospital regulations. In that same letter she approved Sister Helena's plan to accompany ailing Sister Eulalia home to Syracuse. "I do not regard your expenses traveling with a sick Sister heavy—I wished you [to] have the best accommodations. . . . You know where to call for money. Sister Benedicta is our Treasurer. . . ." Unmurmuring Sister Benedicta, in addition to all her other duties, disbursed funds for purposes approved by Mother Marianne and paid the bills for goods and services provided by Hawaii's merchants.

Of Mother Marianne's numerous relatives, she saw only one during the thirty-five years she spent in Hawaii. He was Father Alphonse Lehrscholl, the seventh among the eight children born to her older sister Eva. Father Alphonse was a man Mother Marianne could be proud of. He, too, had joined the Franciscan Order. When he came to visit his aunt at Kalaupapa in August 1905 he had already served from 1895 to 1899 as Assistant Minister Provincial of the Order of Friars Minor Conventual and been pastor in two of the biggest parishes in New York State. In 1905, probably more out of the hierarchy's consideration for Mother Marianne than out of any administrative need for him to make the journey, he accompanied Father Louis M. Miller, the incumbent Minister Provincial, upon a visitation to inspect the Hawaiian mission.

Father Louis was a happy contrast to Father Francis Neubauer, the Provincial Minister who inspected the Hawaiian mission in 1892. The communication of June 11, 1905, in which Father Louis announced to Mother Marianne his forthcoming visitation, is brief, cordial, unsanctimonious. And a letter to Mother, written on February 15, 1906, months after he returned to Syracuse, is a mixture of generous reminiscence about Kalaupapa's patients, genial reference to someone named "Kicke" (who doesn't write to her and who probably is Father Alphonse), and genuine interest in the work of her mission. The most significant part of his letter is serious and heartening: ". . . Most assuredly your work deserves appreciation. God's reward will certainly be yours, but every man or woman with a human heart must also acknowledge the martyr-like sacrifice not only of a day, but of a whole lifetime. My prayers are with you daily. . . ."

In November 1908 the Franciscans celebrated the twenty-fifth anniversary of their arrival in Hawaii. Without Walter Murray Gibson to promote interest in the occasion, few people noticed it. The latest in the line of Vicars Apostolic for the Hawaiian Islands, Right Reverend

Bishop Libert Boeynaems, titular Lord of Zeugma, sent Mother Marianne a gratulatory letter. So also did Father Wendelin Moellers—from his newest parish in Hilo. The latest—and by far the most popular—in the long series of superintendents the Board of Health appointed to manage the Leper Settlement, John D. McVeigh, wrote Mother a most pleasing message. He, better than anyone else in Hawaii, knew the value of the labors the Franciscans performed at Kalaupapa.

At St. Elizabeth's Convent the Franciscans attended the commemorative Mass in their new chapel, not the tiny room that served them as an oratory during the first seven years of their stay in the Settlement. Father Wendelin and a crew of patients, following the example set by Father Damien and his "boys," built this more spacious chapel in the yard to the left of the convent. They began construction on the day after Christmas 1895 and finished painting it on March 4, 1896. Father Wendelin undertook the project with pleasure, enjoying not only the actual labor but the challenge of planning and furnishing the chapel. The enterprise gave him and his men the experience they needed for erecting a big new parish church at Kalaupapa, to replace the painted monstrosity he'd found there in 1888. When this commodious—and well ventilated—new church, modestly ornamented and painted, was completed, Bishop Gulstan Ropert consecrated it on June 29, 1900. His Grace surprised and delighted the sisters by dedicating it to St. Francis of Assisi.

In 1910 members of the Provincial Chapter, meeting in Syracuse, expressed concern about Mother Marianne's health and inability to travel. They passed a resolution calling upon the sisters in the islands to elect a deputy to assist Mother Marianne. The deputy-elect, after being approved by officials in Syracuse, would help to lighten Mother's administrative duties related to establishments on islands other than Molokai.

Surviving letters-patent name two such deputies for the years before 1918. The first served until 1916, the second from that year onward. On February 10, 1911, Sister Helena Haas was named Deputy Commissary of the mission in Hawaii. Since February 23, 1906, she had been serving as superior in Wailuku. Mother Marianne herself gave Sister Helena that office in order to afford some relief to Sister Bonaventure Caraher, who had been suffering from "heart trouble" since 1895.

The letter appointing Sister Helena as Deputy Commissary identified the chief worry of the hierarchy in Syracuse: "In the event of the illness or death of Mother Marianne," wrote Mother M. Johanna Kaiser, Fourth Provincial Superior of the Order, Sister Helena "is empowered to transact business and to act in her place until the next chapter."

The reasons behind this move can be inferred, although they are not stated in surviving documents. Syracuse was assuming control over the Order's outposts in Hawaii, recognizing that the mission's primary goals had been achieved. Henceforth, the Franciscan establishments in Hawaii would be considered not as parts of a mission struggling to survive among pagans in a foreign land, but simply as the community's westernmost installations. Time, technology, and nationalism made this conclusion both sensible and feasible. Hawaii, belonging now to the United States, had become as American—and as safe—as New York State. Father Provincial Francis Neubauer's edict prohibiting the sisters in Hawaii from participating in their community's general chapters expired soon after the United States annexed the islands in 1898. By 1901 the names of sisters serving in the islands were restored to the rolls of eligible voters in Syracuse. Father Neubauer's immediate successors could not use distance as an argument for excluding the sisters in Hawaii from participation in the Order's general affairs. Improvements in means of communication assured their return to the fold. Telegraph lines crossing the continent and transPacific cables laid upon the ocean floor could transmit messages from Syracuse to Honolulu in a matter of seconds. Father Louis Miller understood the value of improved communications at the Chapter of 1907, when he wanted the sisters in Hawaii to vote by cable, instructing their proxies in Syracuse by this wonderful means. Soon luxurious ocean liners could speed sister-delegates to Los Angeles or San Francisco in six swift days. The ties that bound the Franciscans in Hawaii to Syracuse were strengthened in every respect.

Steamers, trains, and miracles wrought by electricity notwithstanding, the sisters did not forget the old ways. In Syracuse, on October 19, 1913, Mother Margaret Haskin, Fifth Provincial Superior to be elected to that position, had letters sent to all houses of the community, asking them to present special Masses on November 19, St. Elizabeth's Day, to commemorate the fiftieth anniversary of Mother Marianne's and Sister Norberta's profession.

In August 1915 Mother Marianne and her deputy, with the approval of Syracuse and the help of more sisters, added still another function to their services in Hawaii when they accepted an invitation from the trustees of Hilo Hospital to provide nursing care for its patients. As early as 1897 the Board of Health had tried to gain the Franciscans' help for the second largest town in the islands. Mother Marianne, in replying to W. O. Smith, said "I am in favor of assuming the work . . . if the Board of Health will authorize me to invite three Sisters from our Motherhouse . . . to assist in the work." The Franciscans did not assume the work at that time, because the Board of Health withdrew its request.

The association with Hilo Hospital begun in 1915 did not last, because of differences over policies the Franciscans could not accept: "after four years of successful work," Sister Columba O'Keeffe wrote, "the sisters were withdrawn to the great regret of the trustees and the public generally."

Early in 1916, Mother Marianne's seventy-eighth year, she wanted to inform Syracuse once again that she could no longer manage the community's affairs in Hawaii. According to Sister Albina, Mother had asked to be relieved from office during Mother Johanna Kaiser's second term (which ended in August 1913). "A letter came refusing to take her out of office. When it was near time for another chapter [in 1916] she intended writing again, but the sisters with her begged her not to think only of herself but them and she did not write again."

In this, as in other matters, Sister Albina was remembering things from a purely conventual point of view. Far more likely is the sensibility with which Mother Marianne discussed her wishes and needs with Mother Margaret, Superior General (as newer Constitutions entitled her to be called) who visited the Hawaiian houses in November and December 1915. By that time (as Sister Leopoldina would write), Mother "could easily realize how unable she was to continue her work." Early in 1916 several sisters were transferred to new positions. On February 3, 1916, Sister Benedicta moved to Bishop Home at Kalaupapa, and Sister Helena of Wailuku took her place as "Matron" at Kapiolani Home in Honolulu.

"Often [Mother] said to me," Sister Leopoldina recorded, "I wish Sister M. Benedicta to take my place I have always had her in view for the work. She is so selfsacrificing and corragous, there is nothing too hard for her She shrinks from nothing. I know she will be able to continue the work."

At about that time, too, Sister Elizabeth—who had been at

Mother's side in Kalaupapa since she professed her vows in 1890—was moved to Kapiolani Home. She stayed there until August 1917, when Mother Marianne wanted her to come back to Kalaupapa. Sister Elizabeth's return to Bishop Home cost Sister Antonia Brown her place beside Mother in "the Paradise of Molokai."

On August 8, 1916, Mother Margaret in Syracuse appointed Sister Flaviana Engel as "Vicaria of the Hawaiian Islands until further disposition." In a letter accompanying the formal appointment Mother Margaret stated: ". . . as Mother Marianne is not able to transact business and travel from one island to the other, Sister Flavianna is authorized to [be the] representative of the Mother General, hence all transactions should be made through Sister Flavianna."

The logic supporting this arrangement can be imagined. The hierarchy in Syracuse wished to honor Mother Marianne to the end of her life. Instead of following the usual practice and allowing her to retire, it kept her in the office of Mother Commissary to the mission she had created, while at the same time relieving her of most of the administrative drudgery that went with the position. Sister Flaviana, an excellent administrator, had been teaching at St. Anthony's School in Wailuku since 1909 (after having taught at Hilo since 1900). Upon becoming Vicaria in 1916 she directed the five Franciscan institutions in Hawaii—although probably, with fine tact, she left the convent at Kalaupapa to Mother Marianne's supervision. In 1918 Sister Flaviana moved from Wailuku to Honolulu, a more convenient location.

Few events of any consequence ever happened to the patients in the Settlement—except for the most important one of all, compared with which nothing else mattered. For the most part, day in and day out, they lived in the peace of the graveyard. As the administration of the new government called the Territory of Hawaii improved physical conditions of housing and medical care, most patients found little reason to complain about being neglected by officials in Honolulu. With contentment came an increasing respect for law and order, at least ostensibly. The Settlement's populace, whether clean or leprous, learned to show more discretion, if not a genuine elevation of morality, in their floutings of the edicts promulgated for God and men.

Both Catholic and Protestant inmates regretted Father Wendelin's departure in 1902. He left after an extended controversy with the Board of Health about a number of matters. The immediate cause of the confrontation lay in his outspoken criticism of the manner in which the Board's leprous constables mistreated leprous prisoners thrown into Kalaupapa's jail. Protests from Father Wendelin and a number of patients forced the government to investigate "this heartless and illegal treatment." As a result, C. W. Reynolds, superintendent of the Settlement, and Dr. Oliver were discharged for "official neglect." Father Wendelin could see some hope of correcting that kind of brutality. But other causes of discontent reduced him to despair. At first the Board, as irked by his denunciations as it had been by Father Conrardy's, wanted to expel the crusading little Westphalian from its precincts at Kalaupapa. It did not hesitate to correct wayward physicians or patients, but it did resent being censured for its own shortcomings. Bishop Gulstan, that "lover of peace" at almost any price, persuaded the Board to reconsider its verdict about his priest. It did—provided that Father Wendelin keep quiet and "attend strictly to his clerical duties in the future. . . ." To this stipulation Father Wendelin retorted that he could hardly "strictly adhere to his clerical duties without preaching against immorality and the breaking of the Sabbath."

A close reading of Father Wendelin's diary—which he kept in German, French, and English, with an occasional Hawaiian entry for variety—leaves no doubt that he seized the excuse to escape from stifling Kalaupapa. Serving the lepers did not bother him, combating immorality in all its forms he accepted as part of his duty. But confinement in that infinitesimal peninsula did weigh heavily upon his spirit. After having spent nearly fourteen years in that microcosm of predictable deeds, unimaginative conversations, and unvarying sins he had become so bored, so frustrated intellectually, that he could scarcely bear to look at the place or be polite to its inhabitants. He is one more example of the overeducated, overcultivated, highly intelligent European whose mind seems to be wasted upon a missionary effort among an afflicted people who have lost all interest in concerns of the intellect. The lepers' relaxed notions about morality did not defeat him. Boredom was his enemy, not the Board of Health. He must have recognized himself in Father Pamphile de Veuster, when he analyzed that misplaced scholar.

Father Wendelin ascended from his private hell on September 23, 1902—by way of the trail up the pali. In a farewell tribute his fond parishioners "presented him with a beautiful gold chalice procured from Paris, France, as a token of esteem, good will, and gratitude for his many kindly acts and spiritual comfort in their affliction." Sister Antonia Brown (who met him in 1889) conferred upon him her fervent accolade: "a Saint that is not in the liturgy!"

Father Maxime André came from Hilo to take Father Wendelin's place at Kalaupapa. Endowed with a different intellect and personality—Dr. Mouritz called him "a saintly Priest of the old school, beloved by all his flock and others"—Father Maxime spent the rest of his long life in the Settlement.

Dr. Oliver's successor, Dr. W. J. Goodhue, equally content with the place, would be the Settlement's physician for twenty-three years.

Kalaupapa was being transformed, thanks to forty years of effort on the part of Hawaii's governments and to the work of dedicated people like the resident priests, physicians, the Franciscan sisters, and the Sacred Hearts brothers. No longer a bleak and comfortless prison, it was becoming a beautiful refuge from strife and turmoil in the world beyond—for lepers and clean people alike. "Our abode has been called 'Molokai the Blest,'" Brother Dutton acknowledged to the governor of Hawaii in 1908.

Father Wendelin's liberation spared him the grief of seeing his big wooden church burn to the ground during the afternoon of August 12, 1906. In October 1907, Father Maxime and Father Joseph, the Catholic Mission's Provincial from Honolulu, began the task of replacing the destroyed church. With the aid of a dozen Japanese workmen imported from Honolulu and a few resident lepers they built a massive structure made of reinforced concrete, proof against both fire and storm. Its arched portal opened upon the wide unpaved plaza at Kalaupapa landing, welcoming patients as they came ashore. Its congregation, gathered within, facing the curved apse, looked to the east, toward Kalawao, and beyond that toward the rising sun and the promised resurrection. Bishop Libert Boeynaems consecrated this new edifice on May 26, 1908, and dedicated it, too, to St. Francis.

Never had the people of Kalaupapa and Kalawao known such excitements as 1908 gave them, at almost a frenetic pace. That was the year when Uncle Sam manifested in splendid style his awareness of his leprous citizens. Until that year "the better care" that Mother Marianne had promised with such confidence at the time of annexation, in 1898, had come to the Settlement rather slowly. After all, his assistants explained, the Great White Father in Washington had to attend to a great number of more pressing details as he assumed stewardship over these islands in the middle of the sea.

But by 1908 he was ready to shower his munificence upon the people of the Settlement. He practically overwhelmed them with proofs of his concern for leprosy. They watched in utmost awe as construction crews from Honolulu swarmed in and, with heroic effort, brought ashore and stacked on Kalawao's green field boatload after shipload of lumber, cement, sand, glass, pipes, and wire, and all the tools the men would need for assembling those materials into buildings. For almost two years the Settlement's people looked on, in amazement and envy, while the workmen built a sprawling complex of hospital wards, research laboratories, palatial verandahed dwellings for physicians, technicians, their families, and thirty-two Chinese servants, even stables for horses to be ridden and cows to be milked. This huge institution, which cost $300,000 by the time it opened, was the largest and most expensive facility of any kind ever built in Hawaii for civilian use before the 1920s. The Congress of the United States had authorized it at the request of the United States Public Health and Marine-Hospital Service—after some prodding by far-sighted businessmen in Hawaii, no longer willing to pay all the costs of caring for the territory's lepers. Its planners conferred upon it a proud name: The United States Leprosy Investigation Station.

Beyond question their purpose was laudable: they wanted to study every aspect of leprosy, especially to isolate and identify the microbe that caused the infection, to improve methods of treating diseased people, above all to find a cure for this most fearsome of man's afflictions. The federal government, agreeing with the USPHS, spared no expense: it gave the USLIS every piece of equipment a medical research institution needed in those days, and the finest minds in the nation to use all that shining apparatus. The USLIS lacked only one thing: a director who understood the psychology of Hawaii's lepers.

The foundations for all the USLIS's many buildings had scarcely been laid when Uncle Sam sent the people of the settlement an even more spectacular—if also more fleeting—display of his solicitude. On July 16, 1908 America's "Great White Fleet" steamed past the peninsula, while on its way to Honolulu (Pearl Harbor not yet being ready to accommodate so many huge vessels). President Theodore Roosevelt, speaking softly the while he brandished that big stick, was sending the Atlantic Fleet on a journey around the world, to instruct other nations in the quality of America's naval might. In response to an inquiry from Brother Joseph Dutton, more pronounced a patriot than ever after twenty-two years at Kalawao, the governor of Hawaii asked President Roosevelt to give the patients at Kalaupapa a closer view of the great ships of war. The generous president instructed the fleet admiral to divert his spotless ships from their course by a few kilometers. And so, on that brilliant sunny July 16, the Settlement's people turned out in their hundreds to see the sixteen gleaming battleships sail grandly by—"passing in parade in our front yard," as Brother Dutton wrote in his letter of thanks to the governor.

The Franciscan sisters, too, standing on the porch of their convent or on the verandahs of the patient's cottages, would have been thrilled by this spectacle—not because of the powerful ships themsleves, but because it gave visible proof to their statement that Uncle Sam cared for even these least of his people.

One evening in October or November of 1909, as construction upon the USLIS neared its end, engineers gave the Settlement's population another glittering treat when they tested the machines that generated electricity for lighting the many new buildings. Hundreds of patients went to stand on Kauhako's eastern flank or outside the double fence at Kalawao, to marvel at the beauty of the scene when the lights were turned on for the first time.

Although no one guessed as much, that evening of illumination marked the USLIS's most successful performance. Despite the usual good intentions that accompany America's emissaries of culture and technology, the Station's scientists managed to bungle every human relationship from start to finish. At the official opening of the Station on Christmas Eve 1909, all members of the staff and their families attended the flag-raising ceremony, listened to the speeches, enjoyed the festive repast served in the spacious dining hall. But no one of the Settlement's inhabitants was invited to the occasion. Not even patriotic Brother Dutton and flag-waving Sister Leopoldina of the ever-loyal heart were allowed to enter the compound, just to see the fine hospital beds and the sparkling laboratories. Nor did Mother Marianne or Father Maxime, those champions of probity and morality, tour the USLIS either before or after its grand opening.

No one from the Settlement, whether clean or leprous, was permitted to pass through the locked gates in the two high barbed-wire barricades that protected USLIS personnel from unguarded contact with lepers or prospective lepers. The American scientists, men of intellect perhaps, but not of sensibility, had not the slightest idea how elaborate precautions to safeguard themselves affected the lepers they had come to study. Those double fences, the locked gates, the big signs warning KEEP OUT, the face masks and rubber gloves the doctors wore, the many basins filled with reeking solutions of carbolic acid for washing those gloved hands: all these and more, and above all else the Americans' determination never to emerge from behind the physical and psychological barriers they raised around their encampment, insulted the lepers beyond remedy. "We are not interested in you as people," the Americans demonstrated in every regulation and in almost every act. "We look upon you as animals to be used in our experiments," proclaimed the antiseptic hospital rooms, the impersonal laboratories, the masks covering the invisible faces of doctors carrying sharp scalpels in their gloved hands.

Ever sensitive and always proud, the lepers refused to enter the USLIS when the doctors sent word into the Settlement that now they were ready to admit volunteers under guard. In two years exactly nine patients in a population of about 700 lepers consented to participate in the research program. Not one of the nine stayed in the cold hospital for more than a few days. The scientists did not mistreat them, of course. But neither were they "friendly." And, the lepers thought, they carried their dread of the infection to ridiculous extremes.— Those masks and gloves! Those basins full of germ-killing chemicals!—With "nothing to do" in those bleak hospital rooms, no companions to entertain them, "no moa fun" as Hawaiians say, to while away the dull hours, the volunteers almost perished of supervening boredom. Even worse, the volunteers resented being treated like guinea pigs, animals they'd never seen but had heard enough about. A smoldering hatred for the powerful nation that had appropriated their own little country flared up once more among Hawaiians, after forgetfulness had all but smothered it. Almost as soon as they'd entered the hospital the volunteers picked themselves up and left the grim confines of that Temple to Science.

As Father Damien and Mother Marianne had learned very soon, lepers judge the quality of a clean person's character by testing his willingness to shake their hands. The USLIS scientists failed this test—and almost every other criterion by which humane men are measured.

For almost two full years the scientists sat there, baffled, with all their advanced ideas and all their fancy equipment, waiting for the patients who never came. Seven hundred hard-headed, stony-hearted lepers defeated a corps of the world's best pathologists, bacteriologists, and chemists. In rejecting the condescending scientists the lepers declared their preference for the loving kindness of the Franciscan sisters, of Joseph Dutton and Father Maxime and the Sacred Hearts brothers. The Catholics who ministered to them had little more to work with than soothing ointments, strips of rags, and smiles, but their fearlessness and compassion always won the patients' respect, and often their love. The scientists drew only their scorn.

At last, late in 1911, scientific intelligence put an end to this tragedy of errors, this lost opportunity. Recognizing defeat (but not admitting the causes of it), the scientists sailed away, going back to "civilization" and safety. They left behind a lone agent to close the useless USLIS, to send the more expensive apparatus to Honolulu, to shut windows and doors upon all the rest. The research group set up a smaller laboratory in the Receiving Station at Kalihi. There, fortunately, the team was somewhat more successful than it had been in the glamorous establishment at Kalawao. On August 7, 1913, his duties done, the caretaker-agent closed for the last time the doors to his fine home, locked the gates in the double fence, and left Kalawao, to join his colleagues in Honolulu.

For sixteen years the haughty imperial buildings stood there, dark and dead, rotting away, upon the field beside the cliffs above Kalawao's bay. For sixteen years the lepers hated the place so much that they did not bother to steal the valuable lumber and priceless plumbing and useable furniture, all accumulating coats of dust from the land and salt spray from the sea. Finally, in 1929, the Board of Health and Hawaii's governor persuaded Washington to approve dismantling the station. A gang of laborers came from Honolulu to tear it down. "Now at last the USLIS was of some use to the lepers," a sardonic antiquarian has written. "Each day lumber salvaged from the old weather-seasoned buildings was carefully stacked by the workmen recruited for the task. And each night the lepers came from Kalaupapa, to take whatever they wanted from the unguarded hoard."

Mother Marianne left no private record of her thoughts and attitudes during her last years at Kalaupapa. After 1901 she did not keep consistently either a journal or a dutiful diary, although once in a while she began one for a few days and then, for no clear reason, stopped. Probably she saw the futility of keeping such things. By 1902, with no difficult sisters to agitate her, the usual round of days and obligations at Kalaupapa must have been as unvarying as is the unruffled sea on a windless day. And she, grateful for this calm, unwilling to commit anything about her private self to paper, simply dropped the business of keeping unnecessary records. It claimed time and energy better spent upon worthier tasks. She contented herself with preserving important letters—or copies of them—that might be significant in understanding the development of the mission.

A few letters from her hand do survive, however. They indicate that aging brought no change in her philosophy or in the strong faith that sustained it. These letters affirm that she had found her place in life, in relation to God and the work she was doing for Him. She had no reason to change her thoughts because she had not the slightest doubt about either faith or vocation. Awareness joined with experience to make her wise. And, like a good missionary and a loving Mother, she tried to share that wisdom with people still searching for a way to peace.

On January 16, 1902, for example, in her role as his "devoted Aunty," she wrote a long letter to Paul Cope. After apologizing for not writing oftener—and mentioning just a few of the daily chores that prevented her from doing so—she told him a very little bit about herself: "—before this reaches you I shall have reached the good old age of 64 . . . Of these 64 years I have spent 40 years in religion. I am wondering how many more our dear Sweet Lord will allow me to spend for Him. I do not think of reward, I am working for God, and do so cheerfully." The thoughts, the phrases, the very words: they are the same in 1902 as they were in 1883, when she addressed her fateful reply to Father Leonor. "How many graces did He not shower down upon me," she assured Paul Cope, "from my birth till now—Should I live a thousand years I could not in ever so small a degree thank Him for His gifts and blessings.—I do not expect a high place in heaven—I shall be thankful for a little corner where I may love God for all eternity." In a lazar house filled with woe she could thank God for having been good to her. The words, the phrases, the thoughts: they are utterances of a holy woman who has received blessings beyond the imagining of most people in this world.

Remembering Paul's uncertainty about his vocation and thinking of his father, her brother Mathias, whom she had not seen since he left Utica more than forty years before, she added: "Oh, how my heart yearns and cries for the Salvation of all my dear relatives—Brothers, sisters, nephews and nieces—I daily pray with a bleeding heart for the conversion of those who have lost the way—May the good Shepherd bring them safely back to the fold—"

The Sisters of St. Francis found an outlet for expressing simple affection in sending name-day cards, letters, even small gifts, to favored recipients on such anniversaries. Mother Marianne herself sent many such messages whenever she found a few minutes to do so—and all too often posted them too late for the days they were supposed to celebrate. Naturally, she also received many name-day greetings, not only from sisters in Hawaii. In 1903 "a prettily worded letter and the appreciated present, the work of your hands," came from a sister, probably one of those teaching at St. Joseph's School in Hilo. In thanking this unnamed daughter on August 21, 1903, Mother Marianne concluded "I wish you all the blessing you may stand in need of to become a perfect child of St. Francis—that you may say with him in all sincerity—'My God and my all. . . .'" In this one sentence she summed up her definition of the true religious—according to a Franciscan's beliefs.

Mother Bernardina Dorn never forgot this most distant of her spiritual daughters. In the fall of 1903, apparently to commemorate November 19, 1863, the day upon which Sister Mary Ann professed her vows in Syracuse, Mother Bernardina sent a gift made with her own hands. On November 5, Mother Marianne, expressing her gratitude for "a beautiful and much appreciated Burse," said: "On the 14th, it will be 15 years since we came to the Leper Island. How the time slips away from us. How many more years will it please God to permit us to work for Him is a question ever before me. I am not well, neither am I sick—but I am growing old and am not able to do as much work as I wish to do. We four have to pull hard to keep the cart going. Please pray for us that God may help us in the future as he has so mercifully done in the past years we have spent here among the unclean. . . ."

Yet Mother Marianne could be firm—and fortifying also—when the need arose. No letter so well illustrates both her own philosophy and the directness with which she counseled her companions as the one she wrote to an unidentified sister on February 23, 1905. The receiver probably is Sister Albina, inasmuch as she kept this letter among her treasures: ". . . I have made up for my silence in writing by offering my poor prayers for you, asking our dear Lord to give you the necessary grace to work out your salvation in deep humility and sweet gentle patience. Pride, you know, is the cause of all sin and is the dark cloud that hides from our view Jesus' bleeding and suffering for us, and closes our ears to our sweet Saviour's call, 'Take up thy cross and follow me'—not on a path of roses. No, no, not on an easy road, but one that is full of thorns and rocks. We followed the call of Jesus to come to Him as His Spouse, and since we are numbered among His chosen ones, it behooves us, to take up our cross and follow Him. Our own dear Saint Francis, the Saint who followed so closely our dear heavenly Spouse in deepest humility, he was ever ready to obey the simplest novice. How will our life compare with his. Try to accept what God is pleased to give you—no matter how bitter. God wills it is the thought that will strengthen you and help you over the hard places that we all have to experience if we wish to be true children of God. . . . I shall offer up Holy Communion for you. I trust God will grant you the graces that you need to sanctify yourself. Time is flying. Let us make use of the fleeting moments. They will never return."

The manner in which she arrived at decisions upon worrisome problems is described in a letter to an unnamed sister written on May 25, 1909. Internal evidence suggests that the recipient was Sister Helena Haas, superior at St. Anthony's Convent and also of Malulani Hospital in Wailuku since February 23, 1906. In the spring of 1909 she was so upset by problems arising from certain administrative policies at the hospital that she had written four letters to Mother in five days. ". . . Since I have read your letters," Mother replied, "I have been thinking, thinking, thinking and I am still thinking what to do. I offered up my Holy Communion asking our dear Lord to inspire me with the right thought, but no other thought presents itself but to patiently await the outcome of all the new ideas." God's will is not always clearly apparent, even to her, she is saying, as she declares that she trusts to Him to make known His purpose in good time. "Deep humility and sweet gentle patience," she is recommending again, in 1909 as in 1905, as always. These are the virtues that prepare us to hear the voice of God when He speaks. How can we hear Him, she is asking, when pride or alarm provoke us into making such a clamor that head and heart are abuzz with noises—rather than listening in expectant silence?

She could be grateful—and gentle—toward a faithful daughter who added no worries to her burden. "Accept my most hearty congratulations for your Silver Jubilee," she wrote to Sister Cyrilla on August 1, 1911. "I have no silver or other fine gifts to offer you but instead will offer my poor prayers, Holy Communion and Holy Mass for you, asking God to bless and reward you for the good work you have so faithfully performed during the past twenty-five years. May it please God to grant grace and strength to continue to serve Him in His poor suffering members. . . . Some day you will serve Him in Molokai."

The number of surviving letters from Mother Marianne diminishes markedly after 1914, no doubt because she did not write many after that year. The miseries of age, including failing health, were reasons enough to explain a disinclination to take up her pen. ". . . I am poorly—cannot [do] much but am up and about directing the poor Sisters," she said in a brief letter to Mother Superior Margaret Haskin on April 28, 1914. "All are hard workers have been for years." Sister Crescentia, she reminded their Superior General, has been serving in Hawaii since 1883, Sister Leopoldina since 1885, and Sister Antonia since 1888. "Sister Elizabeth came to us a Helper in 1884 . . . all these years she has been our Cook—She is worn out and cannot work much longer—"

On October 3, 1916, writing to a sister in the islands, Mother Marianne had little to report but miseries: "Poor Sister Leopoldina suffers much with her feet. I manage to get about 4 hours sleep every night consequently I am poorly—" This is not meant to be a complaint, nor a device to pry more help out of Syracuse. As with everything else she wrote or said, it is a statement of fact.

She gave highest praise to a few sisters. On a date unknown, to a sister unnamed, she expressed her heart's esteem for Sister Crescentia, that most faithful and inconspicuous of companions: ". . . I believe she is closely walking in [St. Crescentia's] footsteps, and is on the way of becoming a Saint. . . ."

Not surprisingly, Sister Leopoldina provided an insight into Mother Marianne's thoughts such as Mother herself would never have committed to paper. At the start of Chapter XXXII of her chronicle, entitled "Mother's painful trials and consolations," Sister Leopoldina wrote:

"Was it the dread of the filthy disease that caused our gentel Mother to suffer? No her unwaverin confidence in Almighty God never could allow her to doubt but that He would protect her and her Sisters from that great trial. Was it the frightful immorality that was than too shamful for one to ever write about? No because she was in hopes that we could teach God's afficte ones to love Him so dearly that He would mercifully cast from them the impure spirit. Was it the starvation, want of water and many other supplies? No for she knew in a short time Uncle Sam would supply all their wants. The cause of our angelic Mother's painful trials were deception and ingratitude of many of the unfortunate creatures. . . ."

Mother Marianne, too, received a small share of praise—which she neither wanted nor recorded. In Honolulu in 1917 Governor C. J. McCarthy hailed her publicly as "a Silent Worker" and, as a token of the Territory's gratitude, forced upon each of the Franciscan sisters and Sacred Hearts brothers a doubling of their monthly salaries. Also in Honolulu on July 26, 1917, Captain Henry Berger, the Prussian musician who had directed the Royal Hawaiian Band ever since King Kamehameha V invited him to the islands in 1872, presented the premier performance of "An Ode to St. Anne," created in honor of Mother Marianne and her patroness. Berger composed the music for the ode, and his sister-in-law, Mrs. Therese Bowler Hughes, wrote the words. Inasmuch as Captain Berger helped Brother Dutton to organize "the Leper Band" for musical boys at Baldwin Home, and released to Kalawao whatever ancient instruments the Royal Hawaiian Band could afford to discard, Mother Marianne probably heard "An Ode to St. Anne" more than once. She must also have heard "The Mother Marianne Hymn," which Captain Berger composed several years earlier. This hymn, according to Berger's son-in-law and biographer, was "very popular" among the Leprosarium's patients until about 1940. The original copy of "An Ode to St. Anne" is preserved in Syracuse, but the music for "The Mother Marianne Hymn" seems to have disappeared, along with the memory of its melody.

She was very old, very weary, but she still kept an active mind and busy hands. In 1915, when Mrs. Katherine Fullerton Gerould, an American journalist and novelist, visited Mother Marianne, she described a woman advanced in years, perhaps, but still impressively in command of her faculties:

" . . . [H]ere, even in the sisters' tiny cottage facing out on their green compound, was the authentic convent atmosphere. Mother Maryanne, in her little parlor, was the blood-kin of all superiors I have ever known: the same soft yellowed skin, with something both tender and sexless in the features; the same hint of latent authority in the quiet manner; the same gentle aristocratic gayety; the same tacit endeavor to make human pity co-terminous with God's. Like other superiors I have known, from childhood up, she seemed an old, old woman who had seen many things. It was only when one stopped to think of the precise nature of those things which, in thirty years on Molokai, Mother Maryanne has seen, that the breath failed for an instant. The parlor was half filled with garments ready to be given out to lepers, and if one but glanced through the window, one saw the pitiful figures on the cottage porches across the compound. Yet those eyes of hers might have been looking out on a Gothic cloister this half-century.... 'You wouldn't think we'd be busy here,' Mother Maryanne ventured, smiling, 'but there is a good deal to do.' So natural has it come to seem, to five sisters, to manage life for some eighty odd lepers.... It was not hard to imagine the sisters busy. As we walked out across the compound, set round with cottages, a sister pink-and-white and blooming—waved her free hand at us from a porch. The other held the bandaged stump of a leper...."

Mrs. Gerould saw Kalaupapa through the eyes of an outsider, and she described Mother Marianne with the rather patronizing attitude of a worldly woman who would never have immured herself in a convent or devoted her life to caring for sick people in even the cleanest of hospitals. But another witness from about that time keeps a different memory of Mother Marianne and the Franciscan sisters of Kalaupapa. She is Mrs. Victoria G. Forrest, the daughter of Dr. W. J. Goodhue who in 1902 accepted the position as the Board of Health's resident physician in the Leper Settlement.

Victoria lived with her parents in the Doctor's House from 1906, when she was born in Kalaupapa, until about 1914, when she began formal schooling on "topside" Molokai. Because her mother was the daughter of Henry Meyer (a son of Rudolph W. Meyer), Victoria lived up there with her Meyer grandparents and returned to the Settlement, by way of the trail down the cliffs, during the usual school vacations. She left Molokai before Mother Marianne's death in 1918, in order to enter a boarding school in Honolulu. During most of her first eight years, and certainly after the last family of the USPHS staff departed in 1913, Victoria was the only healthy Caucasian child in the village of Kalaupapa, and one of the very few nonleprous children of any race to live in the Settlement. Her cautious parents guarded her at all times against contact with patients of any age. For want of playmates, Victoria knew only the company of her parents and of the few clean elders who were their neighbors.

Because the Franciscan sisters shared this isolation, they understood the loneliness of both the little girl and her mother. Mrs. Goodhue—the doctor's "beautiful young wife," as Sister Leopoldina wrote of her—found some relief from Kalaupapa's solitude in the Franciscans, "My mother would take me to the sisters' home," Mrs.

Forrest remembers, "and sometimes the sisters would visit us."
Mother Marianne "stayed at the Home," wanting to be available if any
of her girls needed care.

Victoria went to the convent often enough to recall Mother
Marianne with affection: "I grew up with her . . . a lovely, wonderful
person. She was a saint—so wonderful. Everyone loved her. . . . She·
was a very learned lady. . . . Mother was very kind—especially to me.
Whenever we had a birthday in our home, there was a sister who could
bake well at the [Bishop] Home, and she'd send a cake. Sometimes
there would be a surprise in it, such as a ring. . . . My father thought
very highly of her—and of all the sisters. They were at the top of his
list."

So, through the eyes of a sensitive child, who saw Kalaupapa from
the inside, is preserved yet another impression of Mother Marianne and
her sister-companions. Sister Elizabeth's delectable birthday cakes may
have won the little girl's interest while still she lived at Kalaupapa. But,
in 1980, Mrs. Forrest remembered best the kindness and thoughtfulness
of the sisters, their "dedication to the care of the lepers," and, above all,
the grace in the woman who led them.

NOTES on Chapter XX

1. Health of Mother Marianne: Near the end of 1909, on November 28, Father
   Maxime André alluded to her condition in a letter that he wrote to his Superior in
   Rome: "The good Mother Marianne who has been very ill for a year and on the
   point of death is pretty well for the moment; although weak she does not wish to
   leave her post at the leprosarium. She is a saint."
2. Mother Marianne had, in 1991, numerous living relatives. Her older sister, Eva
   Lehrscholl, and her brothers, Mathias and John Peter, all have a large number of
   descendants who reside in various parts of the United States. It is unknown
   whether her two younger sisters, Elizabeth Miller and Catherine Murphy
   McPhael have descendants. Interestingly enough, one of Eva's descendants, Dr.
   Paul De Mare, did his medical internship at St. Francis Hospital, Honolulu, and
   now is a practicing radiologist in Hawaii.
3. R. W. Meyer died quite suddenly in Honolulu on June 12, 1897. Several corrupt or
   inept superintendents followed him before McVeigh took the position toward the
   end of 1902.
4. Bishop Gulstan Ropert died January 4, 1903, at the age of 64.
5. In spite of an ailing heart, Sister Bonaventure I "labored faithfully for forty years
   in this missionary field," as the Order's records state, and died in Honolulu on
   April 21, 1923, at the age of 79.
6. Mother Delphine Mueller, Third Provincial Mother, died on May 8, 1908, after a
   cerebral hemorrhage at the age of 58.

7. After Mother Marianne's death Mother Flaviana became the Franciscans' leader in name as well as in fact. In that capacity she helped to found St. Francis Hospital and St. Francis Convent in Honolulu. She served as the hospital's first administrator from 1927, through the time it opened on May 8, 1927, until 1929, when she went to relieve aged Sister Benedicta at Kalaupapa. Sister Flaviana served for six years at Molokai, returning in 1935 to St. Francis Hospital in Honolulu. She resided there until the time of her death on April 15, 1939, at the age of 72.

8. Father Wendelin's retort to the stipulation of the Board of Health is taken from Father R. Yzendoorn, *History of the Catholic Mission in the Hawaiian Islands,* 1927: p. 232, and the quotation about his farewell tribute from Mouritz, 1943: p. 67. After serving happily in successive parishes on Molokai, Maui, and Hawaii, Father Wendelin died in Honolulu on September 1, 1914, at the age of 65.

9. Father Maxime André remained at "his post of honor till his death on Jan. 1, 1927, in the ripe age of 83 years," wrote Father Yzendoorn, 1927: p. 232.

10. O. A. Bushnell, "The United States Leprosy Investigation Station at Kalawao," *Hawaiian Journal of History* 2: 76–94, 1968.

11. Paul Francis Cope found his vocation in the field of medicine. He graduated in 1906 from the Fort Worth School of Medicine in Texas, and in that same year was licensed to practice in Nevada. He moved home and practice to Missouri in 1912. According to his obituary in the *Journal of the American Medical Association* 209 (6): p. 951, August 11, 1969, he was born in Chicago on 25 September 1878 and died in Kansas City, Missouri, on 1 May 1969, at the age of 90.

     Paul Cope preserved his letters from Mother Marianne in a packet labelled "Mar. 12, 1896 to Jan. 16, 1902." With these letters he included the photograph she had sent him in 1899, a holy card of St. Anthony endorsed "For Paul Francis—From Sr. M 1898—," and an obituary notice that appeared in a Kansas City newspaper at the time of her death in 1918. Sometime before 1902, apparently, he stopped writing to his distant aunt. In 1974 Dr. Cope's widow, Virginia, contributed his packet of letters from Mother Marianne to the Franciscan Archives.

     Mathias Cope, Mother Marianne's older brother, worked as a butcher in Chicago for many years. He died there on 13 February 1912, at the age of 76, of complications following an attack of apoplexy.

     Mathias's first born son Louis (Paul's brother), born October 16, 1867, traveled widely as a representative of Swift's Soap Manufacturing Company. Apparently affluent, he was living in South Harwich, Massachusetts, in 1935. Another son, Richard, born May 31, 1869, worked as a "storekeeper" in Chicago. According to his death certificate, he died on September 10, 1931, a victim of a robbery from "gunshots of chest and abdomen—shot, wounded and killed by persons unknown. . . ." Mathias's youngest child, Rose, born November 24, 1882, joined the Congregation of the Sisters of St. Joseph of Carondelet at St. Louis, Missouri in 1905, and received the name Sister M. Lucretia. Like her aunt, she was "silent about self" and a "tireless mission worker." She died at Nazareth Convent, Lemay, Missouri, on October 1, 1939, at the age of 57.

12. Mother M. Bernardina Dorn died at St. Joseph Hospital in Syracuse on April 15, 1908 at the age of 74.

13. Through the efforts of Mother M. Margaret Haskin, the Franciscan sisters at Syracuse became a Pontifical Institute in 1923. After that time, they were no longer under the jurisdiction of the Conventual Franciscan Fathers.

14. Henri Berger: article in *Encyclopedia of Hawaiian Music*.

15. Mrs. Gerould's observations were published in 1916 in a book entitled *Hawaii, Scenes and Impressions*. A chapter from the book, "Kalaupapa: The Leper Settlement on Molokai," appeared in *Scribner's Magazine* vol. LX, no. 1: pp. 1–18, July, 1916. This quotation appeared on page 15 of that issue. One guess will identify the "pink-and-white and blooming" sister.

Chapter XXI

SISTER DEATH

MOTHER MARIANNE'S life drew to its end in the summer of 1918, slowly and with as much kindness as an aged ailing body can grant. On January 23 of that year the sisters at Kalaupapa celebrated her eightieth birthday. Upon that festive day she no longer resembled the "typical" Mother Superior whom Mrs. Gerould had seen in 1915. Her body, so long overworked for God's sake, so generously offered to Lady Poverty's rule, so relentlessly chastened at humility's orders, broke at last. Her heart and kidneys began to fail more than three years before she died. Like St. Francis—who neglected "Brother Ass," his body, with even fiercer disdain—she, too, suffered from dropsy.

The dropsy made her swollen and heavy, filling the body's tissues with accumulated fluids until it weighed almost 200 pounds. Because she walked with difficulty, the sisters put her in a wheel chair loaned to them by Dr. H. T. Hollmann, one of the two government physicians assigned to the Settlement's new hospital. The sisters or Mary or Rose Kiyoji rolled Mother about in this conveyance, taking her to the parlor, or the refectory, or along the verandah when she wanted to enjoy a breath of fresh air. The wheel chair served this purpose for about three years.

"She was pleased with it," Sister Leopoldina said. The sisters, too, liked the arrangement. ". . . We could wheel her from one room to another, and have her with us." But Sister Leopoldina also refused to accept for a while the significance of that mobile chair. "As my work took me away with the lepers most of the time, it never seemed to me that Mother was going to leave us. in fact I could not think of it. yet we could see her going. and many times I asked myself how can I live without her? We never had a death in our little Convent home, no words could tell how I dreaded the dark angel of death to visit us, and the shadow of sadness to meet us. . . ."

The dying Mother, who welcomed death, shielded Sister Leopoldina, not yet prepared to believe that the dark angel drew near. ". . .[A]t every turn, Mother would never speak of death or of any thing gloomy, and when I would speak of dying or where we were to be buried she would always say funny things just to change the subject."

Sister Crescentia, ". . . being Mothers lifelong companion . . . remained with Mother nearly all the time night and day . . . no one could do as well for Mother . . . when we would beg to take Sisters place, just so she could have a little rest, No Mother would say   She knows just what to do for me, and besides it would hurt her feelings to have any one take her place . . ."

". . . [E]very time I came home from the lepers Mother seemed to meet me with more, and more, love, and welcome, in her kind loving face. One evening I said, Mother I wish you would allow me to stay with you to night, You are not as well as usual. I can see you are suffering. No Sister she said, you must not ask to remain up at night, you know the work that depends on you, and if you can not rest nights, how can you do justice in your work with the lepers?"

Each evening, as the shadows of sadness closed in upon the convent, Sister Leopoldina's greatest happiness came when she could wheel Mother along the verandah. Mother, understanding this, would bestow that little pleasure with touches of her gentle wit. Once Sister Leopoldina asked "will you please tell me true, are you not doing penance by coming out here"—referring not to the ride but to the possibility that her conversation might be tiring. Mother consoled her with the most comforting answer she would permit herself to utter—and, characteristically, turned the habitual teasing into a blessing: "there was a little of the old time glee in her kind lovely face. Why Sister what penance could there be to have a little ride. May God bless you for this delightful fresh air. . . ."

Sister Leopoldina lived for moments like these. "I was a favored creature," she believed, "to be not only her subject but her confident companion more than thirty years."

Yet Sister Leopoldina could not shake off her dread. "She was going," Sister wrote, in a refrain often repeated. "We could see her growing weaker every day, soon she would leave us forever in this world. All the happy years we had been together all that she had done to spair me, was passing through my mind. Often I found myself wondering can I live without her. She seemed always to know just how to sooth one. Many years ago when we first came to Molokai it was such a deathlike barren place, like leprosy everything only reminded me of the horrors of the grave [but] Mother was always cheerful." Like St. Francis, she knew how to be grateful for the gift of life, for the joys that came with serving God, for the promise that attends even the sorrows that He sends to test us.

In the long and loving farewell for Mother Marianne that ends her chronicle, Sister Leopoldina recalled how "one day at the dinnertable She told us about a Saint she admired very much. This Saint begged our Lord never to let him know the good he would do. so our Divine Lord answered his prayer by letting a great blessing follow him and wherever his shadow would fall great miracles were wrought, but the St. did not know it was his own shadow that did it. And so it was with our dear Mother. the good she did was hidden from her."

Sister Leopoldina, in her old age, remembered with smiles and happy tears the precious little mystery wrought for herself alone many years before 1918. "One beautiful evening after having spent the hot sultry day in the leper rooms where the air is anything but sweet I was tired when I went to my room. how surprised I was to be met, by the cool fresh air filled with the sweetest perfume... the little room seemed to be changed to a paradise, how can this be I thought... it must be the angels   I will keep my secret and so I did, but every evening about the same time at twilight the room was delightfully perfumed, this is a mistry I can keep it no longer Mother surly knows somthing about it, and I went so ceriously to Mother and told her my secret. The angels are visiting my room every evening at twilight. I can always see her dear face, so full of Laugh[ter] even her wonderful eyes were smiling. come, she said, I will show you the angels that visit your room. She had planted a little Japanese flower under my window. it was a little thing not more than a foot from the ground but it was full of those sweet little cups   only in the evening they open and send out there sweet perfume. Why Mother I did not know it was there. how lovely of you to do that. She only laughed and said, it is your angel.

"How often I have thought of that little plant, and of the many acts of charity in our Mother's daily life, how very dear she must be to the loving Heart of Jesus."

Sister Albina Sluder—who also was "very dear to Mother"—came from Kapiolani Home on July 4, 1918, to spend a few weeks at Kalaupapa and especially to celebrate on August 12 the twenty-fifth anniversary of her profession, made under Mother's direction in the convent's chapel. Sister Albina, keeping pace with modern inventions, brought a camera from the big city of Honolulu.

"Mother was never willing to have her picture taken," Sister Leopoldina related, but when, on August 1, "Sister Albina told her, Mother I am anxious to take your picture, we were surprised that she so willingly and lovingly said you may take it."

Sister Leopoldina described that occasion: "One bright day we had the men carry her in her big wheel chair, how happy she looked when we placed her in the shade of the old kamane tree, that she had planted so many years ago, the Sisters were standing back of her chair, and her poor little leper girls nestled at her feet   her dear face was filled with joy. She reached her thin feeble hand to the little ones, they moved closer to her, but did not touch her hand, as they know *unclean! unclean!* Mother let her hand drop on the arm of the chair and her eyes rested lovingly on her little outcasts. She had not been able to be with her little ones for more than a year so it was a day of great joy for them. . . ."

Several photographs taken that day are preserved in the Franciscans' archives at Syracuse. They are studies in deterioration, causes for sorrow. Time has laid grievous marks upon Mother Marianne and upon all the sisters. Mother, bent and broken, sits sagging in a corner of the wheel chair. Her face is bloated, with huge pouches under the eyes and jowls hanging heavy upon the white collar of her habit. The hands are mottled, gnarled, misshapen. Age and illness have disfigured her, as if she too had caught the leprosy. In this saddening ruin can be found no trace of the beauty that once distinguished her. Even with their tumorous faces the six adolescent leper girls gathered near her are beautiful in comparison. Dr. Swift's photographs of Father Damien dying upon his pallet are not more horrifying than are these snapshots of Mother Marianne taken by the brutally exact camera of Sister Albina. In these portraits of feeble mortality, we can suspect, lies the meaning behind Mother Marianne's willingness to sit for Sister Albina's recording camera. "Look upon me and learn," she is saying. "This, too, is God's Will."

And in these portraits of her dying self lies confirmation of Sister Antonia Brown's lament: "I would look at her feeble body and bent shoulders thinking what a pity that you wore out your frail body doing work befitting the strongest man. But her heart and thoughts were all for Molokai."

At least once before this "day of great joy" in 1918 Mother Marianne had sent this message to Paul Cope. On June 8, 1899, less than two months after her siege of hemorrhagings, she wrote a brief note to her nephew. After telling him, with clinical dispassion, the nature of her illness—"I had severe hemorrhages and for weeks after raised blood whenever I coughed"—she continued: "I am better, thank God, and the Doctor tells me that I am out of danger for the present—my lungs are very weak, therefore I have to be careful. . . ."

During the period of convalescence in 1899 a visitor managed to take her photograph, standing at the center of the row of companions who served with her at the time. From this group picture she cut out the figure of herself to send to Paul. "I enclose a picture of myself," she told him, "so you can see how old and worn out I am—" The sentence sounds coy. But she who did not know the meaning of that word was being deadly serious—about herself, for Paul Cope's sake. *Look upon me now, in my age,* she was telling the young man, *and think ahead, to the hour of your death. . . . For all flesh is but as grass. . . .* Because of the evidence in the enclosed photograph, because of the nearness of death, hovering close during the time of hemorrhages, Paul's "devoted Aunty" concluded this letter: "I think of you and pray much for you every day. I hope our dear Lord—if it be His holy will, will help you to enter the religious state so you may give yourself wholly to His service—" Only in His service, she believed, could Paul—or any one else—find purpose in life and preparation for death. "The prudence of the flesh is death," she reminded Paul in his patron saint's message, "but the prudence of the spirit is life and peace."

Paul kept the photograph (and the letter) she sent him in 1899. If ever Dr. Paul Cope saw the picture of his martyred aunt taken on August 1, 1918, he would have had good reason to wince at sight of it—and to marvel at her unshakable faith in God's Will.

Sister Albina's photographs also show how the years of sacrifice have affected the other Franciscans. Sister Leopoldina, massive, bespectacled, towers above the wheel-chair's high straight back. Little Sister Crescentia, standing to the left of the group, shyer than ever, hides her face behind the fall of the veil. Sister Benedicta, even shorter than Sister Crescentia, looking like an alert terrier, challenging the camera and the world beyond it, lays a protecting hand upon the wheel-chair's arm. Sister Elizabeth, bent and weary, gazes wistfully upon nothing. Slightly taller than Sister Leopoldina, Sister Albina—once upon a time a dazzle of white teeth, smooth skin, peaches and cream complexion, and eyes glinting with merriment—stands as straight and lean as a fence post, leathery and sere. The price the sisters have paid while working for God has been drawn from their very flesh and bones.

We who stare in dismay at these photographs can draw from them only one comfort: those women were willing to pay that terrible price in flesh and bones and blood for the sake of the spirit within. Their bodies may be exhausted and wrinkled and bent, but they are not broken in spirit. Unlike Sister Bonaventure II and Sister Jerome, these slaves to a mission worked for God, and followed in the path of St. Francis, to the very end of their long lives. They found sustenance in the sacrifice—and in the promise of reward for work well done.

As we study these portraits of those humble servants of the Lord, pity gives way to admiration—and to envy, for them in their faith.

The leper girls wanted to present a program for Mother on the occasion of her patron saint's feast day, July 26. Sister Albina wrote about the event: "The sisters and patients made a novena for Mother to her dear patron St. Anne. . . . On the eve of her feast she was too ill to go to the front verandah to be with them. She did not want to disappoint them and was quite relieved when sister Ben. suggested her going to her cell and the girls would sing outside near her window, while she was resting. This they did and dear Mother enjoyed it more than I can say. They did sing sweetly, God has given them music as a gift. One piece was particularly touching: a duet sung by Teresa and Little Emma Kia. Emma is blind and has not a finger left but she accompanied the song on the autoharp and played wonderfully by tying a little stick to her poor stumps. It was pathetic to see them. Teresa did not show the sickness much but our dear little saintly Emma was too sad a sight to describe. Though she had neither eyes nor fingers her voice was clear and sweet."

Although her body's strength was failing, Mother Marianne's consideration for others continued until she drew her last breath. She still thought first of her daughters, just as they found comfort in taking care of her. All too well acquainted with the exactions of Sister Death, they did not grieve for their Mother, soon to be released from pain and suffering. They sorrowed for themselves, knowing that soon they would be left without the leader who, as the instrument of God's Will, had given meaning to their lives.

Sister Leopoldina, after working all day long with her "girls," would hurry home to claim the chance to visit with Mother as she wheeled her along the convent porch, giving her a breath of fresh air, a view of the tall trees and beautiful flowers that had grown since she planted them almost thirty years before—and perhaps a bit of gossip about the patients in the wards across the yard. Sixty-three years old at the time, stout and heavy, with feet that hurt under her bulk and a back that ached from leaning all day over lepers' sores, lepers' beds, lepers' agonies, Sister Leopoldina was still as cheerful as ever and, in some respects, just as girlish as if she had only recently entered the novitiate in Syracuse.

During the "lovely cool evenings," Sister Leopoldina, "rolling the chair slowly . . . I could walk by the side and we chated on until I feared I was tiring her." Mother would reply, "how could I get tired in this lovely fresh air? but take me in I know it is too much for you, after your busy day, and you are not yet finished. Mother dear it gives me so much pleasure we will go five times more up and down the veranda she enjoyed the little chats and it seemed to give her pleasure, and what a comfort for me. . . ."

But on the day of Sister Albina's picture taking "we all knew it would not be good to tire Mother, and after the pictures were taken the children all scattered and the Sisters went to their work. Mother seemed interested as she looked from one cottage to an other." Sister Leopoldina asked "would you like me to wheel you around the yard? it is so long since you were able to be out. No Sister not to day I am so tired please take me in. She was not sad but I fancied I could see she realized she would not be with us long. . . ."

"Her limbs were terribly swollen, so she was nearly helpless," reported Sister Albina. "She saw how hard it was for the sisters so one evening after great difficulty in helping her from the wheel chair she said 'There ought to be a nurse.'" Sister Leopoldina added that Dr. Goodhue, who served as Mother's physician, "had long before given Mother up, on account of her age. There is nothing can be done . . ., he said, only make her as comfortable as you can."

"One evening, about a week before Mother died," Sister Benedicta met Sister Leopoldina as she returned to the convent from the patients' cottages. They went to Dr. Goodhue's house nearby. "Mother is failing so fast. We have come to ask a favor," Sister Benedicta said. "Mother has expressed a wish for Sister M. Magdaline [sic] and I would like to get her help if you can help me."

Sister M. Magdalene Miller worked at Malulani Hospital in Wailuku, on the island of Maui across the channel from Molokai. Sister Benedicta decided to go and get her, and bring her back in time. With the doctor's help she did exactly that. Dr. Goodhue sent "a wireless" to Honolulu, asking the next steamer bound for Maui to stop off Kaunakakai, the port on Molokai's southern coast. He also telephoned to Kaunakakai, ordering an automobile to meet Sister Benedicta the next morning, at the head of the pali trail.

"'Sister Benedicta is brave and will never shirk,' Mother often said," testified Sister Leopoldina. Early next morning, soon after daybreak, Sister Benedicta started upon her journey. Accompanied by George, a healthy kokua and a Mormon, "one of the best men in the Settlement," she climbed the cliff for the first time in her life. At the top of the trail she parted from George. In the hired car she sped down the winding dirt road to hot and dusty Kaunakakai, eleven kilometers away. The port superintendent asked the Japanese owner of a sampan, a small fishing boat, to take her out to the S. S. *Claudine* early in the afternoon, as that tiny interisland vessel came steaming along from Honolulu. Three or four hours later the *Claudine* delivered Sister Benedicta to Lahaina, about 35 kilometers across the channel. In a rented automobile, she dashed off to Wailuku, about twenty kilometers inland, gathered up Sister Magdalene, and returned with her to Lahaina in time to board a ship sailing for Honolulu at 9 o'clock that night. Off Kaunakakai the sisters were transferred to the waiting sampan, which brought them to shore "between one and two o'clock in the morning." The obliging chauffeur drove them to the brink of the cliffs above Kalaupapa "hours before daylight and as they did not dare to enter on the dangerous trail in the dark morning hours, they remained in the car. they were tired and chilly, so with joy they welcomed the first dawn of day, and started down the steep zigzag trail ... the thought of our dying Mother hurried them on." Surefooted Sister Benedicta came down the path without mishap. Sister Magdalene "slipped and falling on a sharp stone ... injured her knee but being a trained nurse she was used to suffering. ..."

Sister Benedicta achieved this feat of coordination and transportation, for a round-trip that covered about 160 kilometers, in less than twenty-four hours. To the surprise of everyone but herself, "they arrived in time for Mass, and both received Holy Communion."

"Mother was pleased to see Sr. Madelin, and said 'I have a nurse,'" wrote Sister Albina in her account of those last sad days. "She was very docile and said to Sr. Madelin I am in your hands. Do what you think is best." Sister Leopoldina explained that "Sr. Magdalina was Mother's night nurse, but during the day Mother was able to be dressed and remain in her chair most of the time, and when the bell would ring one of us would take her to the dining room, as it was her wish to be with us as much as possible trying to give us pleasure and banish all sad thoughts. . . ."

Sister Albina (who composed her narrative when she, too, was very old) mentioned two curious incidents that happened after Sister Magdalene's arrival. Reminiscences written by Sister Leopoldina, as well as statements dictated by Sister Benedicta and Sister Elizabeth, do not mention these incidents at all—either because they did not know about them, or else considered them not worth the notice.

Sister Albina, in her age, talked about these incidents, and many another memory, to younger sisters who served with her in Hawaii. Among those younger Franciscans was Sister Eymard Holmes, in 1981 a senior sister still on duty in Syracuse. Sister Eymard (who knew Sister Magdalene also, but not Mother Marianne), when asked about her impressions of the companions who attended Mother Marianne in her last illness, replied that Sister Albina "was sort of given a little to exaggeration and fancifulness . . . a rather vague sort of person." In other words, Sister Albina loved to create a stir of interest in her stories, even if she had to invent certain of their details or dramatize the delivery. In doing so, she managed to leave behind her at least two persistent puzzles. Sister Magdalene, on the other hand, says Sister Eymard, "was a very enthusiastic sort of person, and she was a nurse. I imagine she was very strict with patients." Sister Magdalene caused no mysteries, relied upon no exaggerations.

And yet Sister Albina loved Mother Marianne as wholeheartedly as did the other sisters—and had no reason to invent these incidents, unless possibly a bit of unconscious resentment of Sister Magdalene induced her to remember and to misinterpret Sister Benedicta's remarks.

Sister Albina taught herself to use the typewriter as well as the camera and other modern instruments. In typing her testimony, she wrote one phrase in shorthand according to the Pitman system. That squiggle presents readers with an enigma of the kind that would have delighted her. "After a few days," she wrote, Mother "was afraid of Sr. M., but she told only Sr. M. Benedicta and Sr. Madelin never knew it. [Mother] said to Sr. M. B. She is a _____. I am afraid of her. Sr. M. Ben. said are you afraid of us too. 'No, I am not afraid of my own sisters.'"

Several stenographers who know Pitman shorthand have concluded that the symbol purporting to represent Mother's term for Sister Magdalene means either "crazy woman" or "crazy religious." Sister Eymard, interviewed on February 22, 1978, rather doubted that Mother ever used the epithet: "[she] received every sort and kind of person in her home—people that were very wicked and wild, and she was never known to have called any of them, or her Sisters, any such name as that." But, continued Sister Eymard, if Mother did use the term, the intent behind it would not have been as critical as the words alone suggest: "When I was in the Islands, that was a very common expression among the Sisters. Actually, what it meant [is], 'She doesn't think the way I think.'" Furthermore, Sister Eymard thought, if Mother did employ the term, she called upon it either in jest or as a means of protesting Sister Magdalene's strict discipline: ". . . Sister Magdalene laid down certain rules to preserve her health, and Mother was afraid that she would be curtailed in what she really wanted to do. . . she wanted to be with the Sisters, and probably Sister Magdalene felt that she was too ill to move out of the bed. . . ."

Sister Magdalene's own account of Mother Marianne's last days, which appears in an undated clipping from a Utica newspaper of the 1940s, adds perspective. "She knew that the end was near," says the sister, "but on that day she insisted on joining the nuns at mealtimes. 'No tears' she said, 'Of course, I'm coming to the table. Why not?' That night she died, slept away, while we sat by her bedside." As a result of the interview with Sister Magdalene, the reporter concluded that Mother Marianne was a "valiant" woman to the end.

Now came the time of greatest anguish of the body. The torment was more than even Mother Marianne could endure in silence. ". . . [D]uring those sleepless nights," Sister Albina remembered, "she used to cry out loud, 'Sweet Heart of Jesus, pity me. Pity me.' She used to say it so pleadingly."

Mother Flaviana, having been warned that the end was near, came from Honolulu on August 8. She arrived just in time, for Friday, August 9, 1918, would be Mother Marianne's last day in this world.

On that last morning the sisters rose, as usual, at four o'clock. But soon they learned that this day would be different from all others.

"About half past four . . . she asked for all the Sisters," wrote Sister Leopoldina, "and as we all knew her end was near Sister M. Benedicta quickly called Rev. Father Maxim and she received the last Sacraments."

Sister Leopoldina called that early morning episode in Mother's condition "a weak spell." Considering what happened later in the day, her opinion seems to be closer to the truth than is Sister Albina's dramatic version: "Mother suffered an agony of about half an hour. She held Sr. Magdalen's hand till the other sisters came in the cell. Sister Magdalen gave Mother's hand to another sister and went to get the blessed candles. During this time the prayers for the dying were said."

The same comforts that she had given so often to dying lepers were given now to her. The same blessing of parting she had received from Father Gregory and from Father Damien she gave now to those beloved daughters, kneeling around her bed.

And, now, for her too, as St. Francis had promised his brothers, "when death draws near the storm will cease, and there will be a great peace."

"As soon as she was annointed all fear left her," wrote Sister Albina. " . . . knowing that they could do no more for Mother by their prayers the sisters left [her] with Sr. Madelin and went to Mass. On returning home from Mass great was their surprise to find Mother dressed and sitting in her wheel chair. . . . She desired to go to breakfast with the sisters, so Mary [Kiyoji] had the priveledge of again wheeling Mother into the refectory. . . ."

Sister Leopoldina's "only thought was of Mother, and how soon she must leave us, as I passed through the hall I know there was sadness in my face and how could it be otherways? Yet I would not have Mother see it, but I was surprised, there was Mother in her big chair they had placed in her favored corner in the parlor. Oh! Mother you here? For a minuet her dear eyes brightened with that old time smile, why I am waiting for you she said, in her soft sweet voice, in my heart I begged our Divine Lord to give me strength to be brave, than with new courage I asked her, are you able Mother dear to go out? Oh, I have been longing for the fresh morning air she said I know it will help me. and as soon as we reached the veranda She again said lovingly God bless you Sister. She only remained out a little while, when she told me, that will do sister take me in. She went to her room. . . ."

The second of Sister Albina's incidents occurred during the mid-day meal: "On reaching her place in the refectory Mother said, pointing to the back of her hand near her thumb. 'Did you see that light? It was the evil spirit. Do not leave me alone.'"

Did Sister Albina invent this statement, as a device for drawing attention to herself in her chosen role as historian? Or did Mother Marianne actually say that she saw "a light" upon the back of her hand? And if she did think that she saw it, what would it have meant to her? In sensible Sister Eymard's opinion, "It could have been that Mother was frightened for a moment. . . . And that's common among old people who are dying." A figment of a wandering mind, dazed with pain and sleeplessness, not really frightened, but awed perhaps by the imminence of the passage into eternity: this is the likeliest explanation for her mention of that troubling spot.

But, of course, to imaginations just as fanciful as Sister Albina's (and more attuned than hers to modern notions about psychoanalysis), other interpretations are possible. Did Mother Marianne, approaching the very portals of the realm of death, feel herself unworthy, still hampered by human frailties and therefore still too much the sinner ever to enter into the Kingdom of Heaven? Was she still regretting some ancient fault, committed against God or man, recalling some old offense still lodged in her memory? Or was she simply, in her great humility—and remembering that she was human, and therefore weak—taking this last chance to remind the sisters that she too needed their prayers, that no one who is still alive can be so presumptuous as to be confident of deserving a place in Heaven? A poem pasted in her scrapbook presents, in the words of an unknown author, similar thoughts about death—and about heaven:

> . . . So, I long, and yet fear to die,
> Not knowing what the future may be,
> But in God's great mercy I'll hope
> For a happy eternity,
> And strive while living in exile
> To be worthy of His promise given
> To those who love and serve Him,
> "To be happy forever in Heaven!"

Could these have been the thoughts behind her reply to Sister Magdalene, asking if she had any message for her nephew priest,

Father Alphonse Lehrscholl? "And she said," Sister Magdalene would write late that very night to Father Alphonse, "I might say something good about her if I could but to be sure and tell all the bad I know so you would perform some penance for her." Sister Magdalene's summary opinion about that statement should dismiss forever both the incident and any foolish interpretation of it: "If she still needs penance I do not know what will become of the rest of us. I feel privileged to have been with her even if I had to climb the pali to do it. To know her was to love her and she ruled with kindness for many years."

Sister Leopoldina's failure to mention this incident probably means that she never heard about it. In truth, the whole experience is completely incompatible with everything that is known about Mother Marianne—or with anything else that happened to her during this last day of life. She expressed no other wandering thoughts, no other fears, and, until the very end, experienced no lapse in consciousness. As Sister Leopoldina's account makes clear, Mother remained conscious until almost the last breath, asking for her companions' prayers as she drew near the passage through the valley of shadows into the light. She was aware that her time had come, but she said nothing. No last words passed those lips. No deathbed agony tormented the failing body. She was ready to go, prepared to face her God.

"Mother came to lunch," Sister Leopoldina wrote, "but could not eat. . . ." She was "happy to have Rev. Mother Flavianna with her in the evening she insisted on going to supper. Sister dressed her and placed her in her big chair, and it was her last time to answer the Convent bell. she remained with us, but could not eat, and seemed too weak to talk, when I was taking her from the dining room, where shall I take you Mother? She tried to smile, take me once more, she said, on veranda just for a little while, She was so feeble. I was in dread! When we reached the veranda, with an efferet she raised her hand as if in blessing and than it dropped heavily in her lap, a dear little girl happened to see Mother, and came quickly her little face deathly pale and tears filled her eyes, chocking with a sob she could not speak, it would have been nice had all the inmats been there to receive Mothers farewell blessing and they would have been there had they known. She again raised her hand waved to the little one and it dropped helplessly in her lap. Now Sister, she said! to my room She seemed to realize it was her last. The Sisters were waiting for her and she was soon resting peacefully on her pillow.

"About ten o'clock knowing Mother was about to leave us we were all kneeling in her room. . . . Mother loocked so peaceful her full red lips turned purple, her eyes and mouth were closed, and they never opened again, not a musle in her face moved and her breathing so easy one could scarcely know she was living only for the slight movement of her hand when we would stop praying. Mother Flavianna continued the prayers until a little after eleven when suddenly it seemed like a snap as if in her chest a slight movement of her shoulders and she was gone."

She left as quietly as she had lived.

After the sisters had recited the prayers for the dead, Mother Flaviana delegated tasks and responsibilities. Sisters Magdalene, Crescentia, and Elizabeth washed the body and clothed it for the last time in the holy habit of St. Francis. They arranged the empty husk in the iron cot in which the living Mother had slept for thirty years, lighted the blessed candles, blew out the lamps, and, softly closing the door, withdrew.

Sister Leopoldina, for the first time in thirty years, and Sister Benedicta ventured out beyond the Bishop Home's fence into dark Kalaupapa, going in search of Charlie, the coffin maker. They found him eventually, after searching about in the night, so "gray and cheerless . . . everything so bleak, the wind wailing mournfully as it swept through the long graceful limbs of the ironwood trees" that Mother Marianne had planted as barriers to Kalaupapa's storms. When they returned to the convent, after 1 o'clock, exhausted and saddened, Mother Flaviana sent them to bed at once. As she sank into her hard cot, Sister Leopoldina must have thought back to the other time she had knelt beside the bed of a dying Franciscan, in Syracuse, thirty-three years ago, during the night before she departed for Hawaii. Sister Magdalene, unable to sleep, sat down to begin a long and sympathetic letter to Father Alphonse, telling him that his aunt had just died "a holy death," and declaring that "we feel sure she has been welcomed in heaven by this time."

After Mass next morning, Sister Leopoldina's "first thought was to visit Mother's remains, but how I dreaded to look at her cold and lifeless and to know I can never again hear her consoling words, but I must. I opened the door softly, there was no one in the room and when I knelt by her bed it seemed to me Mother was still living there was no gloom or dark shadows of death there I took her hand in both of mine. She seemed to speak to me and it was such an unexpected consolation.

Sister she said, now I will help you more [than] I could before. It made such a lasting impression on my mind, that many times I have begged her help, and she has always kept her promice and since I left Mother's remains that morning I have never felt that she has left us, and we all feel the same, not one of us feel the sad vacancy that death is sure to leave. . . ."

Sister Benedicta, too, on September 10, in a letter to her Cousin Jessie in Schenectady, N.Y., telling about Mother Marianne's death, wrote: "I feel her presents more than in life, though she is not to be seen."

Later in the morning Charlie and his helpers brought the coffin they had been preparing for several weeks. Its beauty surprised the sisters—and touched them with this sign of the lepers' regard for Mother Marianne. ". . . in stead of a rough board box covered with cloth it was beautifully varnished with a nice silver cross, and silver handles, and it was made in the shape of a real casket with a round top. She looked a little tired but so peaceful, they placed her in the chapel, some of the lepers in deep mourning were kneeling around her, praying, when Sister Albina took the picture, the leper girls had made a beautiful large cross of flowers and firns with the word Mother made of small white flowers in the center of the cross, it was placed at the head of the coffin but it showes very little in the picture.

"They tried to bury Mother in the plot near the road where the King and his party had (according to Mothers wishes) erected the beautiful monument in memory of our Saintly Father Damine but it was impossible on account of the rocks which would have to be blasted and if they were to blast the rocks the monument would be distroyed, So they choised for Mother a beautiful plot not far from the monument at the foot of the little side hill on which is an orange grove and other trees which Mother had planted and tenderly caired for with her own dear hands, the lot is only a few steps from the roadside. Close in side the stone wall are great high ironwood trees. . . .

"On account of the intense heat Mother could not be kept, we were obliged to bury her four oclock Saterday evening, It seemed every body in the Settlement that could walk came to her funeral. It was very solemn as the long funeral wended its way slooly down the hill to the church, after the short servious was over, they brought her back to the home and lade her to rest while the lepers were kneeling around her grave praying and singing."

NOTES on Chapter XXI

1. Cause of Mother Marianne's death: Dr. Arthur Mouritz, who had served as physician to the Settlement before the Franciscans went to Kalaupapa, diagnosed her condition from afar, probably using information given him by Dr. Goodhue and Dr. Hollmann, two of the Leprosarium's physicians. Mouritz stated that "The immediate cause of her death was kidney and heart disease. (Tubular Nephritis and Mitral Valvular disease of several years standing.)" *A Brief World History of Leprosy,* 1943: p. 46.

2. Mutilation: Contrary to the general impression, among lepers who suffer this kind of mutilation, the tips of their fingers and toes do not simply "break off, all at once." Rather, the calcium and other minerals in the bones are resorbed gradually into the body and, as the supporting bones disappear, the nerves and tissues are destroyed. Ultimately, a patient such as Little Emma Kia may have no fingers or toes at all, not even stumps.

3. This must be our farewell, too, to the sisters who were most closely associated with Mother Marianne.

    Sister Renata Nash died at Malulani Hospital in Wailuku on July 27, 1921, at the age of 74.

    Sister Crescentia Eilers was 37 years old when she arrived in Honolulu. She served the lepers of Hawaii without interruption for 46 years, first at Kakaako and after 1889 in Kalaupapa. In 1929, when she was 83, younger sisters insisted that she "retire." They sent her to the novitiate adjoining the newly founded St. Francis Hospital in Honolulu, where she died on February 14, 1931. (At the time there was no special residence in Hawaii for retired sisters).

    Dear and wonderful Sister Leopoldina Burns, after serving as nurse to the lepers for forty-three years, retired to St. Francis Novitiate in August 1928. When the new Saint Francis Convent (a memorial to Mother Marianne) opened in 1931, in Manoa Valley, Honolulu, she was transferred there. She died in St. Francis Hospital on June 3, 1942, at the age of 87.

    Sister Benedicta Rodenmacher returned to Kapiolani Home in Honolulu as its superintendent in January 1929, retired to St. Francis Convent in August 1934, and died there July 26, 1942, at the age of 79.

    Sister Elizabeth Gomes spent nearly forty-one years at Kalaupapa, with intervals at other Franciscan missions in Hawaii. In April 1941, Sister Elizabeth observed her Golden Jubilee as a Sister of St. Francis. She died at St. Francis Hospital on Sunday, December 7, 1947, at the age of 80.

BIBLIOGRAPHY

Our biography is founded primarily upon manuscript sources. The list of these sources has been limited to the most important collections of documents. Less important records are acknowledged in the text or in relevant notes appended to each chapter.

Unless otherwise specified, original documents cited here (or authenticated copies of them) are kept in the Archives of the Sisters of St. Francis (AS), at their Generalate Offices, 100 Michaels Avenue, and at the Mother Marianne Office, 1024 Court Street, both located in Syracuse, New York 13208.

ARCHIVAL SOURCES AND PUBLIC RECORDS

I. *West Germany:* Heppenheim, SE Hesse: St. Peter's Parish: *Record of Births* (and baptisms), vol. 1831–1837 and vol. 1838–1842; *Marriage Records,* vol. 1810–1829 and vol. 1830–1836.
II. *United States.*
UTICA, New York: (a) St. Joseph-St. Patrick Parish: *Record of Baptisms,* 1842–1866; *Record of Marriages,* 1842–1901; *Record of Deaths,* 1842–1897; (b) Oneida County Office Building: *Record of Mortgages* 1842, 1845 and city maps; (c) Utica Public Library: *Population Census Records of Oneida County,* 1850, 1855, 1860, 1865, 1870, 1875; *Utica City Directories,* 1840–1900; (d) Oneida Historical Society, photos of early Utica and Barbara Kopp file; (e) St. Elizabeth Hospital, *Records of the Meetings and Acts of the Board of Trustees of the Incorporation of St. Elizabeth's Hospital and Home* (1870–1885).
RENSSELAER, New York; Archive of Friars Minor Conventual, Immaculate Conception Province: *Acta Prov. Imm. Con. BMV 1871–89: Ad Historiam Provinciae.*
SYRACUSE, New York: (a) Roman Catholic Chancery, *Sadlier's Catholic Directories* for 1860s and 1870s; (b) Onondaga County Public Library, *New York State Census of 1875 for Onondaga County;* microfilm collection of early Syracuse newspapers; *Syracuse City Directories* for 1870s and 1880s; (c) Onondaga Historical Association, reference file of newspaper clippings about St. Joseph Hospital in 1869, 1870s and 1880s; (d) St. Joseph Hospital Health Center, *Registers* 1869–1884; (e) Archives of the Sisters of the Third Franciscan Order Minor Conventual: (1¹) *Community Record Books: General Chapters.* Book 1, 1863–1876 and

entries have been copied into the second book and the
, *Record of Perpetual Vows* 1861–1883 and 1884–1915;
s 1861–1900s; *Record of Professed Sisters. Book I. English*
3; *Council Meetings. St. Anthony Motherhouse* 1891–1905;
s *III Franciscan Order* 1862–1893; *Investing and Profession*
21; *Record of Novitiate* 1872–1903; (2¹) Mission Record Books:
apters *at St. Clara Convent*, Utica, N.Y., 1860–1871; *St. Francis*
ony Convents, Syracuse, N.Y., 1862–1866; *St. Teresa Convent,*
teetings, Oswego, N.Y., monthly meetings, 1866–1898; *St. Joseph Hos-*
nute Book, Syracuse, N.Y., 1870–1922. (3¹) *Official Correspondence of*
iian Mission preserved by Mother Marianne: (a¹) Before Hawaiian Mission
33: copies of business letters at St. Joseph Hospital and St. Anthony Convent,
Syracuse, New York 1872–1883; letters of Father Fidelis Dehm, Minister Provincial, 1867–1872; letters of Sister M. Dominica Cumming, 1882–1883; (b¹)
Hawaiian Mission Correspondence 1883–1918: emissary: Father Leonor Fouesnel.
Government and Board of Health officials: Walter M. Gibson, Dr. George Trous-
seau, Samuel M. Damon, Dr. N. B. Emerson, W. O. Smith, Dr. Charles
Cooper, Lucius E. Pinkham, Lorrin A. Thurston. Vicars Apostolic: Bishop Her-
mann Koeckemann, Bishop Gulstan Ropert, Bishop Libert Boeynaems. Francis-
can ministers provincial: Father Joseph Lesen, Father Francis Neubauer, Father
Louis Miller. Provincial Superiors: Mother M. Delphine Mueller, Mother M.
Johanna Kaiser, Mother M. Margaret Haskin. Agents of Board of Health in
Hawaii: R. W. Meyer, John McVeigh. Letters of sister volunteers for Molokai in
1888. Circular Letters from religious superiors. Letters from others: H. P.
Baldwin, C. R. Bishop, Edward Clifford, "Brother" Joseph Dutton, Father
Wendelin Moellers, Father Joseph Julliotte. (4¹) *Records preserved by Mother*
Marianne: Branch Hospital Records; Bishop Home Records; The Origin and History of
St. Elizabeth Convent, Kalaupapa; *The Record of St. Elizabeth Convent*, Kalaupapa;
Journals of Mother Marianne 1900, 1901, and *Jottings* 1903–1905; notebook of
Mother Marianne containing copies of letters received by the sisters and by
Joseph Dutton relating to work at Molokai; copies of letters relating to important
mission business 1884–1917. (5¹) *Hawaiian Mission Correspondence collected by*
Sisters of Third Franciscan Order: (a¹) Letters preserved by sister authorities: Sister
M. Bonaventure Caraher to Mother M. Bernardina Dorn; Mother Marianne to
Mother M. Bernardina Dorn, Mother M. Delphine Mueller, Mother M. Johanna
Kaiser, and Mother M. Margaret Haskin. (b¹) Letters preserved by other sister
companions: Mother Marianne to Sister M. Cyrilla Erhard, Sister M. Ephrem
Schillinger, Sister M. Magdalene Miller, Sister M. Elizabeth Gomes, Sister M.
Helena Haas, and Sister M. Albina Sluder. (c¹) Letters of Mother Marianne to
Paul Cope and Mary Kiyoji. (6¹) Writings of Franciscan Sisters of the Hawaiian
Mission: (a¹) *Little History of the Lepers of Bishop Home, Kalaupapa, Molokai*
1896–1901, by Sister M. Leopoldina Burns. (b¹) *Franciscan Sisters in Hawaii*, by
Sister M. Columba O'Keeffe, 1923; *Sisters Coming to Hawaii*, by Sister M. An-
tonia Brown, 1929. (c¹) Notes of Sister M. Albina Sluder. (7¹) *Impressions of*
Mother Marianne by Contemporaries: in 1927, Mother Margaret Haskin encouraged each sister who had lived with Mother Marianne to write her impressions of
her, saying that "if at any time the canonization should be begun, the more letters
we have in that regard, the better for this worthy cause." Impressions were
written by Sister Crescentia Eilers, Sister M. Benedicta Rodenmacher, Sister M.
Antonia Brown, Sister M. Elizabeth Gomes, Sister M. Albina Sluder, and Sister
M. Columba O'Keeffe.

The Journals of Sister M. Leopoldina Burns are undated, although apparently they were begun in the 1920s at the direction of Sister Flaviana. Both an original set of notebooks and a rewriting of the same with more development of incidents are extant. In the latter set there are 56 chapters in 15 notebooks. Sister Leopoldina also wrote a *Little History of Mother Marianne's Work* which contains selections from the journals.

SOUTH BEND, Indiana: Archive of the University of Notre Dame: letters from "Brother" Joseph Dutton and Charles Warren Stoddard to Father Daniel Hudson; letters from Father L. L. Conrardy and Joseph Dutton.

HONOLULU, Hawaii: (a) Archive of Roman Catholic Chancery: Journal of Brother Bertrand 1882–1885; Diary of Father Wendelin Moellers 1895–1907; Bishop Koeckemann Correspondence, including letter from Mother Marianne dated September 15, 1888, defining spiritual needs to be met before she will accept mission to Molokai. (b) Archive of State of Hawaii: Hansen's Disease Records 1884–1919; Minute Books of the Board of Health 1881–1919; Board of Health Letterbooks 1884–1917. (c) University of Hawaii: microfilm collection of (selected) letters from Sacred Hearts priests and brothers of the Hawaiian Mission.

III. *Italy*, Rome: (a) surviving original letters from Sacred Hearts fathers and brothers of the Hawaiian Mission (of which a microfilm collection is available in Honolulu). (b) *Le Père Damien–Vie et Documents*, three-volume manuscript.

BOOKS

Adler, Jacob, and Gwynn Barrett, eds. *The Diaries of Walter Murray Gibson 1886, 1887*. Honolulu: University Press of Hawaii, 1973.

Beatificationis et Canonizationis Servi Dei Damiani De Veuster, Missionari, Sacerdotis Professi, Congregationis SS. Cordium Jesu et Mariae (Picpus), Positio Super Virtutibus. Rome: Guerra & Belli, 1966.

Bunson, Maggie. *Faith in Paradise*. Boston: Daughters of St. Paul, 1977.

Case, Howard D., ed. *Joseph Dutton, His Memoirs*. Honolulu: Honolulu Star-Bulletin, Ltd., 1931.

Chase, Franklin H. *Syracuse and Its Environs, A History*. Vol. 1, New York: Lewis Historical Publishing Co., Inc., 1924.

Clarke, T. Wood, M. D. *Utica for a Century and a Half*. Utica, N.Y.: The Widtman Press, 1952.

Colvin, Sir Sidney, ed. *The Letters of Robert Louis Stevenson*, vol. 3. New York: Charles Scribner's Sons, 1925.

Damon, E. M. *Siloama, The Church of the Healing Spring*. Honolulu: Hawaiian Board of Missions, 1948.

Daws, Gavan. *Holy Man: Father Damien of Molokai*. New York: Harper & Row, 1973.

Dehey, Elinor Tong, Compiler. *Religious Orders of Women in the United States*. New York: W. B. Conkey Co., 1913.

Deymann, Rev. Clementinus O.S.F. *Sister's Manual. Third Order Regular of St. Francis of Assisi*. Containing their Rule and a Practical Explanation Thereof. St. Louis, Missouri: B. Herder, 1884.

Durant, Samuel W. *History of Oneida County, New York, with Illustrations and Biographical Sketches of Some of Its Prominent Men and Pioneers*. Philadelphia: Everts and Fariss, 1878.

Dutton, Charles J. *The Samaritans of Molokai: The Lives of Father Damien and Brother Dutton Among the Lepers*. New York: Dodd, Mead, 1932.

Encyclopedia of Hawaiian Music. (George Kanahele, editor). [Entry for Henri Berger]. Honolulu: University Press of Hawaii, 1979.

Gerould, Katherine Fullerton. *Hawaii: Scenes and Impressions.* New York: Charles Scribner's Sons, 1916.

Gibson, Walter M. *Prisoner of Weltevreden and a Glance at the East Indian Archipelago.* New York: J. C. Riker, 1856.

Hewitt, William P., ed. *History of the Diocese of Syracuse. Story of the Parishes 1615–1909.* Syracuse: Catholic Sun Press. Wm. P. H. Hewitt, 1909.

Jacks, L. V. *Mother Marianne of Molokai.* New York: Macmillan Co., 1935.

Jörgensen, Johannes. *St. Francis of Assisi.* (Translated from the Danish by T. O'Conor Sloan). New York: Longmans, Green and Co., 1912.

Jourdan, Vital, SS. CC. *The Heart of Father Damien* (revised edition, translated from the French by Rev. Francis Larkin, SS. CC., and Charles Davenport). Milwaukee: The Bruce Publishing Co., 1955.

Manual of the Sisters of St. Francis. Rule, Spiritual Exercises, and Prayers. Compiled from the most approved sources, 1887.

Medcalf, Gordon, *Hawaiian Royal Orders.* Honolulu: Oceania Coin Co., 1962.

Mouritz, Arthur A. *A Brief World History of Leprosy: Hawaii: U. S. America: Philippines: Malaya: Fiji: China: India: Europe.* (rev. ed.). Honolulu: A. Mouritz, 1943.

_____. *The Path of the Destroyer: A History of Leprosy in the Hawaiian Islands and Thirty Years' Research into the Means by Which It Has Been Spread.* Honolulu: Honolulu Star-Bulletin Press, 1916.

Orchard, Dom Bernard (General Editor). *A Catholic Commentary on Holy Scripture.* New York: Thomas Nelson & Sons, 1953.

Prandoni, Mother M. Carmela, O.S.F. *Greater Love.* Syracuse: Sisters of the Third Franciscan Order Minor Conventual, 1960.

Rules and Regulations of the Institute of the Sisters of the Third Order of St. Francis of Syracuse, New York. U.S.A. Syracuse: Sisters of the Third Franciscan Order Minor Conventual, 1914.

Stevenson, Robert Louis. *The South Seas.* New York: P. F. Collier & Son Co., 1912.

Stoddard, Charles Warren. *The Lepers of Molokai.* Notre Dame, Indiana: "Ave Maria" Press, 1885.

Thomas of Celano. *Saint Francis of Assisi.* (Translated from the Latin by Placid Hermann, O.F.M.) Chicago: Franciscan Herald Press, 1962.

Winter, Heinrich. *Das schoene Heppenheim: Heppenheim an der Bergstrasse.* Heppenheim: Baumeister & Hilkert, 1969.

Yzendoorn, Reginald, SS.CC. *History of the Catholic Mission in the Hawaiian Islands.* Honolulu: Honolulu Star-Bulletin, 1927.

JOURNALS, REPORTS, ANNALS, RECORDS

Annual Announcement and Catalog of the College of Physicians and Surgeons of Syracuse University, Sessions of 1872–1873.

Biennial Report of the President of the Board of Health to the Legislative Assembly. Session of 1892. [Honolulu, Hawaiian Islands].

Bushnell, O. A. "Dr. Edward Arning: The First Microbiologist in Hawaii." *Hawaiian Journal of History,* 1 (1967), 3–30.

_____. "The United States Leprosy Investigation Station at Kalawao," *Hawaiian Journal of History,* 2 (1968), 76–94.

Creighton, Robert J. *The Honolulu Almanac and Directory* (1886).

Dedication of the Kapiolani Home for Girls, the Offspring of Leper Parents, at Kakaako, Oahu, by their Majesties King Kalakaua and Queen Kapiolani. Honolulu: Advertiser Steam Print, 1885.

Flintham, Lydia Stirling. *Franciscan Tertiaries First Established in the United States at Philadelphia, Pa., A. D. 1885.* (Reprinted from Records of American Catholic Historical Society, June 1904).

Fulmer, H. Clifford, M. D. "The Rise of the Medical College," *Syracusan,* vol. IX. no. 7, Jan. 9, 1917. Syracuse, N.Y.: Orange Publishing Co.

Historical Sketch of the Parish of the Assumption of the Blessed Virgin Mary 1845–1945. Syracuse: Franciscan Friars Minor Conventual of the Church of the Assumption, 1945.

Hummel, Rev. August. *Hundert Jahre katholische Ordensschwestern in Heppenheim a. d. Bergstrasse: 1861–1961.* Heppenheim: Otto Buchdruckerei, 1961.

Jeannette Clare, Sister M., O. S. F. *The Sisters of the Third Order of St. Francis, Glen Riddle, Pennsylvania, 1855–1955.* Philadelphia: William T. Cooke Publishing, Inc., 1955.

Larkin, Rev. Regis, (ed.). "The Coming of the Franciscans to Syracuse." *The Minorite,* December 1935. (Jubilee edition).

Leprosy in Hawaii. Extracts from Report of Presidents of the Board of Health, Government Physicians and others, and from Official Records. Honolulu, Hawaiian Islands, 1886.

The Molokai Settlement (Illustrated). Honolulu: Board of Health of Territory of Hawaii, 1907.

Onondaga County Medical Society 1906–1956. Sesquicentennial. Syracuse, New York: Sesquicentennial Celebration Committee of the Onondaga County Medical Society, 1956.

Report of the Special Committee to Visit the Kakaako Leper Settlement to the Legislature of 1888. Honolulu Gazette Publishing Co., 1888.

Reports of the President of the Board of Health for 1886–1918. Honolulu.

Sadlier's Catholic Directories, United States and British North America. New York: E. J. Sadlier & Co., 1868, 1869, 1871–1872, 1873–7.

St. Joseph's Parish Centennial 1841–1941. Utica, N.Y.: Franciscan Friars Minor Conventual of St. Joseph's Parish, 1941.

Speeches and Measures Proposed and Discussed by Hon. Walter Murray Gibson, Member for Lahaina in the Hawaiian Parliament of 1880, Honolulu 1881.

Statutes of the Royal Order of Kapiolani. Honolulu: Daily Bulletin Steam Print, 1883.

Syracuse City Directories for 1870s.

Thrum, Thomas G. "Retrospect for 1883." *Hawaiian Annual for 1884,* Honolulu.

Utica City Directories for 1840–1900.

NEWSPAPERS AND PERIODICALS

Syracuse, New York; *Catholic Sun, Evening Herald, Syracuse Morning Standard, Syracuse Daily Journal, Syracuse Daily Courier, Sunday Courier, Post Standard, Sunday Herald.*

Utica, New York: *Utica Observer Dispatch.*

Rome, New York: *Roman Citizen, Rome Sentinel.*

Hawaii: *Hawaii Catholic Herald, Hawaiian Gazette, Hawaiian Journal of History, Honolulu Advertiser, Honolulu Star-Bulletin, Ka Nuhou, Little Flowerland Bulletin* (St. Francis Novitiate, Honolulu), *Pacific Commercial Advertiser, Maui News, Daily Bulletin.*

Others: *Chicago Daily News, World Magazine, Feuilleton de L'Universe, Minorite, San Francisco Chronicle, Journal of American Medical Association.*

INDEX

ADDENDA 1983
(Continued Research or Developments)

Foreword. In December 1982 the Historical Report for the Cause of Mother Marianne was essentially completed by the Historical Commission set up on August 9, 1980 by the Most Rev. John J. Scanlan, then Bishop of Honolulu. The revised Report was completed in March 1983 and submitted to the Most Rev. Joseph A. Ferrario, present Bishop of Honolulu.

Bishop Ferrario, in response, wrote a letter of approval of the Report and support of the Cause to His Eminence Pietro Cardinal Palazzini, Prefect of the Sacred Congregation for the Causes of Saints in Rome. In May 1983 the Historical Report arrived at the Sacred Congregation and its acceptance was registered officially there.

Bishop Ferrario was authorized to set up an examining Tribunal to complete the first major stage of Mother Marianne's progress towards beatification and canonization. The Bishop's Tribunal will conclude the inquisitional, or research, stage. It will submit its findings to the Congregation for the Causes of Saints, upon which the Congregation in Rome will initiate the discussional stage of Mother Marianne's Cause.

Information about miracles attributed to the intercession of Mother Marianne is sought.

Possible beatification and canonization will rest on the Congregation's conclusions and the decision of the Holy Father.

Special mention is made here of the full and outstanding support also given the furtherance of the Cause of Mother Marianne from the Diocese of Syracuse, first from the Most Rev. David F. Cunningham, now deceased, and later from the Most Rev. Frank J. Harrison, present Bishop of Syracuse. The Motherhouse of the community to which Mother Marianne belonged and from which she proceeded to initiate great works of charity in New York State and Hawaii is in the Diocese of Syracuse.

p. 5. The house now standing on the property site at 706 Schuyler Street in Utica, New York is not the same original building owned and lived in by the Cope family.

p. 6. The younger brother of Mother Marianne, John Peter Cope, has been traced. He and his wife Rosalia with their two children born in Utica had moved to Newark, New Jersey in 1877 or soon afterwards. Six more children were born to them.

In 1983, there are nine great nieces and great nephews of Mother Marianne (and their children) descended from her younger brother who are now living in various cities in the United States of America.

John Peter also had adopted the Americanized version of the surname, namely Cope.

p. 21. Traditionally, Mother Marianne was said to have served at St. Peter's School in Rome, N.Y. The matter is unsettled whether she did or not. At one time the Franciscan Sisters taught in two schools in Rome, N.Y., in connection with St. Peter's Church and St. Mary's Church. They resided at Immaculate Conception Convent. The affiliation between St. Peter's School and the Franciscan Sisters ended shortly before the arrival of Mother Marianne. However, matters could have been in a transitional or cooperative state in some phase. It is apparent that she did serve at St. Mary's School for a short time.

p. 25. It is not claimed that the Franciscans who established the Third Order of St. Francis in America in 1855 in Philadelphia were the first congregation of Franciscan Sisters founded in the United States.

Photo section: Mary Zablan Sing died in 1983.

p. 244. More evidence has been found regarding Father James Tuohy and his later exemplary life. The spelling of his name is given both as Tuohy and Tuohey in these records, but records favor the spelling Tuohy.

p. 360. Rose Kiyoji died in May 1983.